Self, Symptoms
and Psychotherapy

WILEY SERIES ON
METHODS IN PSYCHOTHERAPY

Series Editors

Boris Semeonoff
Department of Psychology
University of Edinburgh

Franz Epting
Department of Psychology
University of Florida

Personal Construct Counseling and Psychotherapy
Franz R. Epting

Self, Symptoms and Psychotherapy
Edited by
Neil Cheshire and Helmut Thomae

Self, Symptoms and Psychotherapy

Edited by

NEIL CHESHIRE

AND

HELMUT THOMAE

JOHN WILEY & SONS

Chichester · New York · Brisbane · Toronto · Singapore

Library of Congress Cataloging-in-Publication Data:

Self, symptoms, and psychotherapy.
  (Wiley series on methods in psychotherapy)
  Includes index.
  1. Self (Psychology)   2. Psychology, Pathological.
3. Psychotherapy.   I. Cheshire, Neil M.   II. Thomae,
Helmut.   III. Series. [DNLM: 1. Mental Disorders—
etiology.   2. Psychotherapy—methods.   3. Self Concept.
WM 420 S465]
RC455.4.S42S45   1987   616.89'14   86–32565

ISBN 0 471 90548 8

British Library Cataloguing in Publication Data:

Self, symptoms and psychotherapy.—(Wiley series on methods in psychotherapy)
  1. Psychotherapy
  I. Cheshire, Neil   II. Thomae, Helmut
  616.89'14   RC480

ISBN 0 471 90548 8

Typeset by Bath Typesetting Ltd., Bath
Printed and bound in Great Britain by Anchor Brendon Ltd., Colchester, Essex

Contents

Contributors

CHESHIRE, Neil M. *Psychologist, Psychology Department, Ysbyty Gwynedd, Bangor, North Wales*

DAVIES, Robin H. *Consultant, Paediatrics Department, Ysbyty Gwynedd, Bangor, North Wales.*

EPSTEIN, Seymour *Professor, Psychology Department, University of Massachusetts, Amherst, USA*

GRUENZIG, Hans-Joachim *Psychologist, Psychotherapy Department, University of Ulm, West Germany*

KNASEL, Eddy G. *Occupational Psychologist, Careers Research Advisory Centre, Cambridge, England*

KORDY, Hans *Psychologist, Psychosomatic Clinic, University of Heidelberg, West Germany*

McREYNOLDS, Paul *Professor, Psychology Department, University of Nevada, Reno, Nevada, USA*

NEUDERT, Lisbet *Psychologist, Psychotherapy Department, University of Ulm, West Germany*

STRUPP, Hans H. *Professor, Psychology Department, Vanderbilt University, Nashville, Tennessee, USA*

THOMAE, Helmut *Professor, Psychotherapy Department, University of Ulm, West Germany*

VON ZEPPELIN, Ilka *Psychologist, Psychology Institute, University of Zurich, Switzerland*

ZITZELSBERGER, Angelika *Psychologist, Psychology Department G7, 17, Mannheim, West Germany*

Preface

This volume examines the ways in which disturbances in *Self* functions (such as identity-feelings, self-esteem, individuation and agency) may underlie the familiar neurotic disorders of depression, anxiety, obsessions, phobias and psychosomatic malfunctions (as well as certain personality traits and defects), the *symptoms* of which are presented every day to psychiatrists, clinical psychologists, psychoanalysts *et al.*, and at which various types of *psychotherapy* are directed.

In dividing the contents of the book into two parts—the first of which is concerned with broadly 'theoretical' issues while the second consists mainly of empirical research presentations—we reflect our two main objectives in assembling the volume. One is to show that modern psychoanalytic theories about the normal development of a sense of Self and personal identity (with its emotional aspects of self-regard, self-doubt and potential identity-problems) are no longer at odds, either psychologically or philosophically, with superficially contrasted approaches which explicitly employ concepts and hypotheses drawn not from psychodynamics but from social psychology, cognitive psychology, artificial intelligence or animal learning studies. The other main objective is to indicate some ways in which psychodynamic ideas about the origins of those personality disorders and neurotic symptoms which are associated with self-problems can be subjected to systematic empirical investigation as rigorously as other hypotheses in developmental, cognitive or clinical psychology; and the same goes for the associated hypotheses concerning the cognitive and emotional processes by which beneficial change takes place in psychoanalytically orientated psychotherapy.

By demonstrating thus, through a range of detailed theoretical and clinical studies, that psychodynamic approaches to the Self, and to the therapy of its symptomatic disorders, can attain a philosophical and scientific respectability which deserves to be acknowledged even in positivistic British and North American circles, we hope to add some momentum to the movement for the 'rehabilitation' of the Self and of psychodynamics which has got under way in the last few years. There is wide-ranging variety not only in the theoretical stances adopted by the different contributors, but also in the nature of the empirical observations which are taken as data-bases for the practical researches which some of them report in *Part II*. Far from wishing to emphasize differences, however, we are at pains throughout to argue that these diverse theoretical frameworks and empirical strategies can all be used to examine, illuminate, corroborate, refine or discredit certain basic psychodynamic notions which have a currency in this field.

The types of empirical data which our contributors invoke range over such varied observational material as the clinical description of presenting symptom-complexes (both in children and in adults), the findings of quasi-experimental investigations into aetiological and therapeutic factors, verbatim transcripts of patient–therapist exchanges in formal psychoanalysis, and psychometric tests of cognitive functioning, personality traits and self-perceptions. There is a pervasive interest in language, recognizing that psychoanalysis can be construed, at least in some respects, as a form of cognitive (and especially verbal) learning-theory, according to which an essential part of the Freudian Unconscious is populated (and mental and emotional life as a whole largely mediated) by the verbal images of linguistically construed experiences and apperceptions, which have taken place in the context of motivational processes governed by principles of drive-reduction. It follows from this construal that it should be possible to test, in respect of both philosophical coherence and empirical validity, a good many psychoanalytic hypotheses and assumptions, whether about the causes or the cure of neurosis, no less readily than comparable hypotheses and assumptions in general psychology.

Nor do we absolve psychodynamics from the need to meet such scrutiny by construing it as an 'hermeneutic', as apposed to a naturalistic or positivistic, discipline: for that proposal merely recommends *different* methods of assessing theoretical coherence and empirical validity (namely methods analogous to those used in translation and textual criticism) and does not imply *no* methods of assessment. In practice, however, the approach of our contributors is generally to take up the positivistic challenge, and to operate within that tradition to establish areas of *rapprochement* between psychodynamics and other branches of psychology, by presenting a variety of observations and theoretical arguments drawn from both clinical-therapeutic and experimental-psychometric situations.

It is a consequence of the interdisciplinary and intercultural character of this volume that a significant part of the material had to be translated, by the respective authors, from the original German. This necessity has served to bring into specific focus the general issue of the influence of language on ways of theorizing about the Self, and also the current controversy over the possible distortion suffered by Freud's original psychoanalytic notions when they themselves were translated into English in what we now know as the *Standard Edition* of his writings. Although the dispute itself is not discussed at any length, the issues involved do crop up here and there throughout *Part I*.

This note of Anglo-German collaboration is sounded again by the fact that Neil Cheshire's work on the book has been financially supported at different times by grants from the University of Ulm, the *Deutsche Forschungsgemeinschaft* and the Breuninger Research Foundation of Stuttgart. For this generous funding both Editors wish to record their grateful thanks. They warmly acknowledge also the editorial assistance of Helmut Thomae's clinical and academic colleague at the University of Ulm, Dr H.-J. Gruenzig; and the help of Neil Cheshire's research student from University College, Bangor, Frau S. Schlingensiepen, whose instant and infallible bilinguality was a facilitating asset on numerous occasions.*

But the main theme of the book, and the reason for its existence, is not such interlinguistic collaboration (which is of course commonplace enough) but the unusual degree of interdisciplinary receptiveness and understanding between psychoanalysts on the one hand and practitioners from other branches of psychology on the other. This theoretical interaction has enabled us to examine from various angles what relationship psychological and philosophical questions about the Self have to clinical questions about certain personality disorders and neurotic conditions, and to their treatment in psychotherapy. For, the image of psychoanalysts as doctrinaire and theoretically arrogant people who are dismissive of alternative accounts, and impervious to philosophical and empirical criticism (all of which they supposedly construe automatically as 'resistance'), is a stereotype which dies hard. To be sure, there was a time when suspicion and defensiveness on the part of psychonalysts and psychodynamic therapists was appropriate enough, since many of the relevant objective researches in general experimental psychology and in personality theory were represented as contradicting psychoanalytic hypotheses when the latter were 'operationally' defined out into simplistic behavioural terms. At the same time, the purveyors of laboratory psychology themselves were schooled in a positivistic scientism, which was equally blinkered in its way, and this disqualified them from tackling meaningfully the phenomena of interpersonal experience and of the development or disturbance of self-feelings.

Nowadays, however, the analysts and their sympathizers can appeal to objective researches which are supportive, as well as acknowledge those which are inconvenient. It may be this which has encouraged a growing number of them to have the confidence to 'go public' and compare their theories, methods and evidence with those of other branches of psychology and to see how each can clarify, correct and enrich the other. This volume, accordingly, is intended to exemplify that venture and to consolidate that spirit of *rapprochement*.

It will be evident that several of those helpers whose clerical and organization-

*Since many readers will already know the second Editor by the German form of his name (Thomä), we should point out here that, for ease of printing, we have throughout adopted the convention of substituting for the *Umlaut* in proper names an 'e' following the affected vowel.

al expertise the Editors have depended upon to produce the typescript must have been operating in a foreign language. In Ulm, therefore, we thank especially Frau A. Silberberger; while in Bangor we are particularly indebted to Mrs L. Ellis-Williams and Mrs A. Rees who were working, if not in their first language, yet in one somewhat nearer home.

NEIL CHESHIRE: *Bangor, Wales*
HELMUT THOMAE: *Ulm, West Germany*

Series Preface

This volume, the fourth* in the *Methods in Psychotherapy* series, breaks new ground in a number of ways. First, it is concerned not with a narrowly defined system or theoretical orientation, but with a broadly-based concept, here defined as the *Self*, which may be said to be central to the orientation shared by all the writers whose views are presented or whose research is reported in the text. Second, unlike its predecessors, the book is not the work of a single author, but—as already indicated—represents a symposium in the broadest sense: as *Chambers* puts it, 'a collection of views on a single topic'. Finally, and perhaps most significantly, the reader is given an opportunity of becoming acquainted with some aspects of contemporary continental European psychology, an area which has much to offer, but which tends to be neglected in English-speaking countries.

I do not propose to pre-empt what Neil Cheshire has said in his Introductions to *Parts I* and *II* by attempting to summarize the book's intention or its structure, except by calling attention to a phrase he uses repeatedly—*rapprochement* between what he calls the cognitive–empirical standpoint, on the one hand, and on the other the psychodynamic. Such *rapprochement* is seen to be made possible through recognition—or reinstatement?—of the Self as a valid psychological category. 'Self' is one of those concepts that are more easily understood than defined; William James perhaps came near enough when he defined the 'empirical self' as all that one is tempted to call by the name of *me* or *mine*. This does not, of course, imply adherence to a doctrine of egoism, in the sense of the primacy of self-interest, but rather a plea for the study of *experience*, understanding of which is essential to the process of psychotherapy.

Readers familiar with Neil Cheshire's earlier book *The Nature of Psychodynamic Interpretation* (Wiley, 1975), and with the first volume of Helmut Thomae's collaborative study *Psychoanalytic Practice* (Springer, 1987), will know that they can look forward to a stimulating discussion of a complex and fascinating topic.

BORIS SEMEONOFF

*Two early titles now out of print.

xiii

Learning to use the Self properly, when one
has been using it badly—what is that but
re-conditioning one's reflexes?

Aldous Huxley, *Eyeless in Gaza*, p. 60
(1936; reissued by Triad-Panther, 1977)

INTRODUCTION TO PART I

Theoretical Issues in Selfhood and Psychotherapy

Neil Cheshire

The historical and philosophical background to the re-admission of the Self to 'respectable' psychology, together with some critical discussion of the reasons both for the initial banishment and for the subsequent rehabilitation, provide the focus of Cheshire and Thomae's introductory first chapter. If that re-admission has been greeted not so much with the enthusiastic rejoicing appropriate to a prodigal son returned, but rather with that grudging accept-ance which attends the awkward fellow who can no longer reasonably be refused membership of the club, this is partly because the published expulsion itself was always something of an academic myth perpetuated for the sake of what the neighbours in other Departments might think.

For, those whose daily jobs required some systematic understanding of the formation, maintenance, disturbances and therapy of the Self (namely paed-iatricians, school-teachers, psychiatrists and developmental/clinical psycho-logists) had not been particularly keen on the edict of ostracism in the first place, and had consequently never really enforced it in their own territories. In recent years it has become inescapably clear that those who have a concern for mental and emotional development in general, and for the psychotherapy of its disorders in particular, can now approach the understanding of aspects of 'self and identity' from a number of different theoretical angles—cognitive, socio-logical, ethogenic, psychoexperimental, developmental, psychodynamic, etc.—and that many of the controversies and rivalries which had previously kept these approaches apart have now given place to a new spirit of construct-ive *rapprochement*.

In the next three chapters, Seymour Epstein (Chapter 2) and Cheshire and Thomae (Chapters 3 and 4) respectively tackle this *rapprochement* from different, but reciprocal, points of view. That is to say, Epstein discusses the development and maintenance of the self-system principally from the stand-point of a *cognitive* model which is powered by a consistency-seeking or dissonance-reducing motive, and shows that this contributes to the solution of a specific motivational problem which had bothered Freud and led him to revise his own psychoanalytic instinct theory (in a manner which many of his followers have found unconvincing).

Conversely, Cheshire and Thomae start by expounding a *psychoanalytic* theory of self-development and self-pathology which initially espoused Freud's revision (only to go beyond it eventually); but they make a point of showing that it is in many ways consistent with theories of cognition, perception and learning which derive from general psychology, even though the latter has come to be contrasted with psychoanalytic psychology. And yet their manifest differences in technical language should not distract us from seeing the latent similarities not only in the questions that they address but also, to a remarkable extent, in the answers that they suggest. In this way they exemplify one of the main purposes of this volume, which is to show that the theories and observations of clinical psychoanalysis on the one hand and of academic/experimental psychology on the other are not indeed necessarily at odds with each other, but have a great deal to say by way of mutual clarification and support.

All three chapters are concerned, for example, with what makes for a sense of dissonance, incongruity or imbalance within our self-systems, with the techniques which we normally use to deal with such states, and with the conditions in which those techniques break down and the system as a whole appears to disintegrate. These questions lead the three authors to ask what the basic motivating forces for psychological organization may be; and, while Epstein concludes (as George Kelly did back in the 1950s (Kelly 1955)) that the classic Freudian motive of the 'pleasure-principle' must give place, not so much to a parallel destructive drive as in Freud's own problematic revision, but rather to a still more fundamental drive towards cognitive security, Cheshire and Thomae discuss the alternative motivational principles propounded in 'object-relations' theory.

It had been a puzzle for Freud, as it must also be for any theory of personality based on the notion of 'cognitive balance', that in some situations people seem to need to perpetuate, or even to create, a state of mind which is in one way or another essentially unbalanced, unpleasurable or conflicted. Although we are familiar with Freud's solution in terms of the proposed 'death-instinct', we tend to overlook the fact that he toyed with an alternative hypothesis (which Thomae drew to Epstein's attention): *that* hypothesis can easily be construed in terms of people's attempts to restore the cognitive, or at least rational-emotive, balance within the self-system. If Freud had developed this alternative idea instead, Epstein argues, psychoanalysis would have been spared the embarrassing metapsychology of Eros and Thanatos, and would have realized that the fundamental motivating principle of psychic life is 'the need to maintain the integrity of a conceptual system ... for organising experience and anticipating events'.

If Freud had indeed done this, he would have anticipated by 35 years the well-known psychological theory of 'personal constructs' in which Kelly takes the successful anticipation of events and experiences to be the central motive for developing our individual cognitive and apperceptual apparatus, otherwise known as our 'personal construct system'. Much of what Epstein says about cognitive organization and balance could be translated quite readily into the terms of this theory, but he also makes it clear how his formulations are in some respects at odds with those of Kelly.

Specifically, he finds unsatisfactory Kelly's attempt to intellectualize away the problem of emotion, by regarding it as a special case of what Festinger called 'cognitive dissonance', and we may add that this limitation becomes especially evident in Kelly's overcognitive account of psychotherapy. For Kelly, having explicitly contrasted his own cognitive motivational principle with the psychoanalytic theory of instinctual drive-reduction which he saw as 'dyed with the deep tones of hedonism' (1963, p. 50), goes on to contrast his own view of the basic psychotherapeutic relationship (a supervisor advising his graduate student on a research project) with what he takes to be the psychoanalytic paradigm (parent helping child to deal with an anxiety).

Although this stereotypic contrast suggests that Kelly had not fully understood the concept of psychoanalytic 'transference', according to which the client will projectively cast his analyst in a variety of *different* roles at different times, it was in response to Epstein's challenge as to why some patients seem deliberately to create dissonance in the therapeutic relationship that Sandler (1985) has begun to talk in terms that might have been drawn straight from personal construct theory. He agrees that it is a puzzling phenomenon, and likens it to the well-attested situation in which a child who is being consistently ill-treated by his parents will nevertheless strenuously resist the efforts of welfare agencies to remove him from conditions of evident 'unpleasure'. It is as if the child prefers the predictability of what is familiar, even though unpleasant, to the unpredictability of what is unfamiliar but possibly more pleasant. This seems to suggest that childhood security derives not so much from 'good experiences' of a pleasure-giving sort, as Kleinian theory tends to imply (see Cheshire and Thomae's discussion in Chapter 4), but rather from reliable prediction and anticipation (even though what is predicted and anticipated is unpleasant), which is precisely in accordance with the basic axioms of Kelly's theory.

The idea that cognitive organization and structure are sought and maintained at almost any emotional cost, and that the fear of disorganization is worse than the fear of pain, is a theme of Epstein's chapter which underlines observations made in another field of stress-reaction, namely that of thought-reform and brain-washing. Such programmes are often explicitly aimed, to begin with, at making the victim question his beliefs about his friends, his work, his family and himself to such an extent that he begins to wonder *who* he is and what his place in the world may be; and, in this structureless limbo of what Laing has called 'ontological anxiety', he is prepared to take up any system of beliefs which will give some sense, organization and structure to his experience, even though this new 'self-theory' and 'world-theory' (in Epstein's terms) is seriously at odds with his previous self-system. In Lifton's (1964) well-known study, the doctor comes to believe that he must have been, after all, a spy, and that when he thought he was just seeing his patients, he was in fact passing on the messages of espionage. The need to validate a familiar belief-system, on the other hand, even at the expense of producing the experience of conflict, is used by Epstein to explain why some patients need to provoke conflict with their therapists in the transference.

Both Epstein and the object-relations theorists assume that the origins of security and self-esteem lie in early experience with a loving, accepting and valuing mother-figure. We do indeed expect, according to Freudian theory, that gratifying or frustrating experiences at the initial 'oral' stage of instinctual development will make certain personality characteristics more likely to emerge than others. The questions whether such 'oral traits' do in fact cluster together in the way that the theory requires (so that those supposedly reflecting *gratification* occur in the company of each other significantly more often than in the company of those supposedly representing *frustration*) has been the subject of a number of systematic empirical investigations (Kline, 1981, ch. 5). We know also from the specialized factorial studies of Kline and Storey (1977, 1980) that statistically valid dimensions of 'oral optimism' and 'oral pessimism' can be constructed on this theoretical basis, and can be measured independently of other established personality dimensions such as extraversion and neuroticism (Kline, 1979). The separate aetiological question of whether such trait-clusters develop as a result of different sorts of feeding-experience, rather than on some other causal basis, is, however, still open.

Some of the current psychoanalytic assumptions in this area have indeed been challenged, to some extent, by certain well-known researches in developmental psychology. It is many years now since John Bowlby drew the attention of his fellow analysts to the pioneering studies of emotional security in primates which had been carried out by Harlow and his associates. These classic experiments appeared to demonstrate, at least in the case of the macaque monkey, that the development of emotional security in the infant depended more upon the experience of 'contact-comfort' than upon oral gratification during feeding—a thesis which had been implicitly anticipated by, for instance, Margaret Ribble (1944) in her programmes of tactile 'stimulus-feeding' for neglected infants declining into marasmus. Much more recently, of course, Bowlby has produced a monumental *tour de force* of synthesis between such clinical and ethological investigations, on the one hand, and psychoanalytic theory on the other (Bowlby, 1973, 1980, 1984).

Another challenging finding from the experimental study of mother-infant bonding is that the perceptual modality which mediates and modulates this security-giving somatic interaction is not so much visual but rather auditory. The content of Epstein's paper invites, and the argument of Cheshire and Thomae's Chapter 4 explicitly introduces, reference to the psychoanalytic self-theory of Heinz Kohut, which makes much play with the contention that the origins of security and self-esteem lie in the infant catching and understanding the approving glint in its mother's eye. But two sets of observations suggest caution on this point. (1) It has been known for a long time that the infant's power of visual discrimination is limited by a fixed focus for about the first couple of months of life; and that, even when the so-called 'social smile' emerges after about three months, it is not based on the kind of interpersonal social perception which Kohut requires, but on a more-or-less mechanical response to a 'sign-stimulus' whose necessary components can be specified and replicated artifically (Spitz, 1946). (2) The range and subtlety of the infant's *auditory* discrimination, by contrast, and his ability to coordinate minute changes of posture and of muscle-tone with minute and transient features of the sound-pattern of his mother's voice, have been dramatically demonstrated by Condon (1979). Failing to develop the normal sensitivity and complexity in this sonic–somatic 'entrainment', as with the deprivation of contact-comfort in Harlow's experiments, seems to be correlated with impairment of security and emotional competence later in life.

It seems, therefore, that we cannot say that it is predictability *per se*, rather than some sort of pleasurable somatic experience, which underpins this sense of security. For the 'surrogate' mothers in Harlow's experiments who provided only food and not contact-comfort were just as predictable as those which provided the latter but not the former; and yet it was the availability of clinging which seemed to distinguish those infant monkeys who were secure enough to tolerate frustration and to explore and confront the unexpected in a way which, as we have already noted, is a mark of security. It is also relevant that for human neonates the sense of losing bodily support is a source of fear which does not have to be learned from experience, as even Watson (who was, of course, committed to attributing as much as possible to environmental learning) felt bound to concede (1919, pp. 199–200).

It is worth remembering also, in the light of what Cheshire and Thomae have to say in Chapter 1 about the relationship between self-image and body-schema, that another unlearned source of fear in primates is the perceived disorganization of body-image. For there is evidence that monkeys will react with horror and alarm when they come across what appear to be monkey-bodies in which an eye is out of place or an arm disconnected, even though they have never seen fellow animals injured in this or any other way (Hebb, 1946) (obviously the experiment quoted used model-bodies!).

Investigations into the reaction of human subjects to perceptual incongruity have taken a rather different form, but have served to illustrate the different ways in which people deal with the 'cognitive dissonance' which they experience when faced with a perceptual situation which contains some internal conflict or contradiction. Early experiments into the recognition of playing-cards that were exposed to view for only a fraction of a second showed that if the combination of colour and shape was made to conflict with the subjects' expectations (e.g. a black Ace of Hearts), then they would unwittingly use a form of 'perceptual defence'. This could take the form, for example, of being unable to recognize a card until it had been exposed for a much longer time than they needed for normal cards, or of 'correcting' their perception either to a normal Heart or to an Ace of Spades (Bruner and Postman, 1949). These perceptual reactions can readily be seen as analogous to the psychoanalytic defences of 'repression' and 'denial' respectively.

The array of hypotheses about the nature of these defence-mechanisms, and about the conditions in which they are deployed, is what most obviously marks off the psychoanalyst's way of discussing psychical conflict and dissonance, as illustrated by Cheshire and Thomae in Chapters 3 and 4, from that of the cognitive psychologists whom Epstein mentions; and McReynolds, as we shall see later in *Part II* (Chapter 8), explicitly tackles the task of showing how the two approaches may be combined. For it is the avoidance of these theoretical resources to do with defence-mechanisms which gives a particularly hollow ring to Festinger's (1957) well-known observations on cognitive dissonance. He is at a loss to explain why different people resolve their dissonances in different ways, and with different degrees of impairment to their general psychological functioning, so long as he ignores the rich assortment of hypotheses about the different forms of defence, the different purposes that they serve in the psychic economy, and the different degrees to which they are consistent with reason and reality (A. Freud, 1936; Laughlin, 1970; Madison 1961; Sandler and A. Freud, 1985).

There are many varieties of defensive technique with which to preserve one's cognitive system, lying between those that Epstein calls 'dissociation' and 'collapse'; and the problem is of course to explain why, and in what conditions, some people can manage successfully with hysterical tactics while others are driven to adopt more disruptive psychotic measures. This difference in egosyntonicity is clearly illustrated by Freud (1924) when he contrasts a patient's *neurotic* reaction to an emotional stress (repression and the formation of a conversion-symptom) with what would have been a *psychotic* one (delusional denial). He would have found more to applaud, one suspects, in the formulations of Fritz Heider about 'cognitive balance' than in those of Festinger, for the former was well aware that people (and indeed whole cultures) do need to construct belief-*elements* which may be untestable or counterfactual in order to preserve the balance of their belief-*systems*. Thus Heider (1958) quotes the case of the Ifaluk Indians who are peace-loving and non-violent people, and are also very positively disposed towards their children, whom they believe to be essentially innocent and good. But, since the children sometimes behave in violent and destructive ways, to which their parents are negatively disposed, the cognitive system of the adults is out of 'balance'. Balance is restored, however, by importing into the system the belief that the violence of the children is a product of evil spirits who have got into them, and is therefore not their own spontaneous behaviour. In this way, the Ifaluks can continue to be both positive about their children and negative towards violence in all forms.

This importation of a particular belief or hypothesis in order to preserve the integrity of a previously established system also occurs, according to some commentators, in the very different and much grander context (which Epstein also discusses) of the revision of the conceptual systems on which scientific explanations of events in the natural world are based. Epstein sees a parallel between the potentially constructive or reconstructive cognitive disorganization suffered by the schizophrenic, on the one hand, and the revolutionary collapse and replacement of conceptual paradigms which are said by Thomas Kuhn (1973) to characterize the progress of scientific understanding in general. But an essential part of Kuhn's account is the intermediate stage at which the hitherto accepted scheme, now threatened by conflicting new observations, is hedged about with qualifications, and special hypotheses are entertained *ad hoc* to explain away apparent anomalies.

Just such an *ad hoc* hypothesis was the suggestion (made in order to preserve Bishop Ussher's chronology against the heretical time-scale proposed by palaeontologists and geologists) that fossils were created, along with everything else, *as fossils* in 4004 BC. An *ad hoc* hypothesis is not necessarily false or untestable, as is sometimes supposed, but is defined by its system-preserving and dissonance-reducing function: it may also *happen* to be true. This technique of constructing a new belief, then, in order to preserve the balance of the existing system is used not only by the scientific community at large but also in the folk-beliefs of a particular culture and in individual psychopathology. It suggests that this is an area where cognitive psychologists, social psychologists and psychoanalysts should have much to share fruitfully with each other (cp. Oatley, 1984). Indeed, we can already find Sheehan (1985), in a recent study of the role of self-esteem in clinical depression, profitably applying Heider's triadic method of assessing balance/imbalance to *intra*-psychic construct-relationships (though without acknowledgement to Heider, curiously), and combining it with derivatives of Kelly's self-system technology.

Another area which these various specialisms evidently share with each other, and also with the developmentalists, is the way in which the attributes, attitudes and values of parents somehow become built-in to the mental apparatus of the child, and consequently profoundly influence his or her sense of identity, self-esteem and susceptibility to emotional conflict. This process, which is variously known as identification, internalization, incorporation or introjec-tion, and which becomes a focus both for Epstein and for Cheshire and

Thomae, is another area where cognitive psychologists have not always been aware of the richness and detail of psychoanalytic theorizing. They might reasonably complain, to be sure, that such theorizing is a great deal *too* rich and detailed for comfort. It is a topic in which the ubiquitous spatial metaphors, so easily ridiculed by the sceptic, reflect the need to have some way of talking about how the psychological properties of one self-system become transferred *into* (as it were) another self-system.

It has been the especial concern of that branch of psychoanalysis known as 'object-relations theory' which was devised originally by Melanie Klein and her associates (Segal, 1979), to envisage our emotional development and psychological organization in general in terms of an 'internal world' which from babyhood onwards gradually becomes populated by images, impressions and agencies derived from our experience of, and our feelings about, emotionally significant people and events in the external world of real life. This way of talking has boldly (some would say unashamedly) taken over a number of concepts which can be applied quite literally to the properties, processes, events and objects in the external physical world, and used them to describe the contents and functioning of this psychical world of 'internal objects' and mental 'representations'. Further complications ensue from the assumption that a great many of the properties and processes of this internal world are, of course, 'unconscious'.

Now, there is nothing *necessarily* amiss, either logically or scientifically, in taking the concepts and thought-forms in terms of which we account for some well-understood phenomena (say, the behaviour of solid balls in motion) and using them somehow by analogy to conceptualize some *other* phenomena that we are still trying to make sense of (say, the behaviour of gas molecules under pressure, or the relation between an electron and an atomic nucleus). There are those who assert, to be sure, that these tactics are *typical*, rather than exceptional, in real-life scientific theory-construction (Harré, 1970; Harré *et al.*, 1985, ch. 3). But they need to be used with due respect to their limitations, and to the need for observing certain logical constraints; and it has already been argued that an appreciation of these limitations and constraints has been conspicuously *absent* from most object-relations theorizing (Cheshire, 1966).

However, the attractions of this way of thinking about personality-development, psychopathology and the self-system are considerable, as Cheshire and Thomae point out in Chapter 1. Their claim is substantiated by the recurrent observation of what happens when perceptive theorists try to talk about the realities of personal action and interpersonal experience (rather than about 'human behaviour') *without* explicit recourse to psychodynamic concepts of an 'object-relations' type; they find themselves groping towards such ideas without apparently knowing it (Shotter, 1980; Farr and Moscovici, 1984; cp. Cheshire, 1980b), much as some experimentalists have indirectly validated controversial Kleinian theses without seeming to realize what they have done (see Chapter 4).

Alternatively, we can sometimes notice that a worker, who has initially emphasized a kind of behavioural constructionism, turns subsequently to an approach which 'shifts the locus of understanding ... to the relationships in which selves are made possible' (Gergen, 1984; but cp. Gergen, 1977), which is precisely what 'object-relations theory' is all about.

Chapters 3 and 4 accordingly indicate in some detail both what its attractions are, and how things can get out of hand logically speaking if the spatial metaphors which characterize it are not kept firmly in check. Sometimes, to be sure, it turns out that a philosophically alarming figure of speech about the properties of mental space is a useful sheep in clumsy wolf's clothing, which need not perturb the sensitive intellect after all. For example, with respect to the apparently unpromising psychodynamic metaphor of the 'gap' or 'distance' between certain self-representations (Sandler, 1985), Cheshire and Thomae show in Chapter 4 that it has become possible to give it a quite specific operational sense within the technology of Kelly's (1955) Personal Construct Theory.

For, in clinical depression seen from a psychodynamic point of view, the patient's self-representation of 'myself-as-I-am' is notoriously further away from that of 'myself-as-I-would-like-to-be' (ideal self) than it is in psychological health, but not as close as it is in manic states. By means of the self-identification form of Kelly's 'repertory grid' test, also used by Cheshire *et al.* in Chapter 7, psychologists have for some years now been able to measure systematically such distances (at least as consciously reported) in order not only to make diagnostic comparisons between different clinical groups, but also to record the changes in that distance within individuals over the course of psychotherapy or spontaneous remission (Hewstone *et al.*, 1981; Ashworth *et al.*, 1985). This illustrates the kind of cognitive–empirical–psychodynamic *rapprochement* which we are looking for throughout this volume.

Having been concerned, in the opening chapters of *Part I*, mainly with the issues involved in describing and investigating self-problems in their own right from various different theoretical standpoints, we now turn in the last two chapters of this *Part*, to the question of focussing psychodynamic theories on the treatment of such problems. This raises the questions whether the essential principles of psychodynamic therapy can be identified and abstracted from the 'full-dress' classical psychoanalytic situation, and whether in focussing upon specific and often conscious problems (such as McReynolds examines later in *Part II*, Chapter 8), the type of therapy which emerges has more in common with the 'cognitive' theories and methods of (say) George Kelly or Aaron Beck than with those of Freud and his followers.

The question whether the vital ingredients of a traditional long-term and intensive psychoanalysis—at least three times a week for at least two years, or some such—could be distilled and applied more 'actively' over a shorter period of treatment was of course addressed by Freud himself in a famous paper

(Freud, 1919), and again in the *New Introductory Lectures* (Freud, 1933, ch. 34). Although he regrets, in that discussion, any debasement of the *reine Gold*, 'pure gold', of psychoanalysis, yet he acknowledges that the realities of the psychiatric clinic and of the psychotherapeutic consulting-room make it inevitable that various psychodynamic alloys will be produced and put on the market. More recently Rycroft (1985) has returned to the question of what nuggets of psychoanalytic truth may be lost in the hasty panning necessitated by the briefer dynamic psychotherapies. And yet Freud was himself no stranger to shorter sequences of consultations which were not merely diagnostic but had an undoubted therapeutic impact, an extreme example of which is his ambulant (and apparently fairly successful) four-hour 'treatment' of the composer Gustav Mahler when on holiday in 1910. We are entitled to ask, then, What did Freud do with, and to, Mahler on that occasion to make him feel better; and can we not learn to do the same with our own patients and clients?

One sceptical answer with which we are nowadays familiar, and which is acknowledged both by Cheshire and Thomae in Chapter 5 and later on in this book by Strupp (Chapter 11), is that Freud did nothing more *specific* to make Mahler feel better than a parent would do with a child, a sympathetic teacher with a puzzled pupil, a priest with a penitent, or even just an insightful and supportive confidant with a troubled friend. Another view is that what he did was, in effect, a kind of covert Pavlovian 'desensitization' routine.

We may notice first, however, the growing interest in a conception of focal psychotherapy which emphasizes the processes of cognitive disentanglement and restructuring which inevitably go on during it (Beck, 1976; Ryle, 1982, 1984, 1985; Oatley, 1984; Wegman, 1985). From this way of talking, the novice may get the impression that what such 'cognitive therapy' offers is a procedure different in kind from psychodynamic therapy and based on separate, if not actually conflicting, theoretical principles.

But it had always been a tenet of classical Freudian theory that one of the aims and effects of psychoanalytic therapy was to investigate, reorganize and reinforce defective 'ego-processes', where such processes include, of course, the largely conscious cognitive functions of reality-testing, insight, adaptation, anxiety-management and learning from experience. Freud himself (1940, p. 34) was quite explicit that the early stages of this type of psychotherapy consisted of 'intellectual work' aimed at 'extending self-knowledge'; and ever since the 1930s (as Cheshire and Thomae show in Chapter 5) analysts as disparate as Hartmann and Stekel had been emphasizing the need to enlist in therapy the support of the patient's rational, cognitive resources in the therapeutic campaign against the neurosis. Whether one chooses to call them 'conflict-free spheres of the ego' (Hartmann), or 'logos' (Stekel), instead of talking about 'reconstruing', 'cognitive restructuring', 'strategies' or 'new perspectives', reflects a divergence in verbal style rather than in essential psychological theory.

It is important to be able to recognize when a so-called 'new approach' to this or that is no more than an old approach dressed up in new vocabulary. Thus the radical behaviourist, for example, may think to get rid of the 'dualistic' problem of the way thoughts can influence actions by deciding to call both thoughts and actions 'behaviour', and then rephrasing the question into the form (now apparently 'monistic') 'how does one behaviour influence another behaviour?' But nobody, apart from a radical behaviourist seemingly (such as Hayes, 1986), is deceived into believing that a significant *conceptual* distinction can be eliminated in this way by the trivial expedient of prescriptive definition. This is not to deny the value of such questions as whether, and how, the effect of a classical 'mutative' psychodynamic interpretation may involve what Kelly would call 'reconstruing' some aspect of one's experience, since the attempt to answer them may certainly lead to useful clarification (Cheshire 1975, ch. 3), even if Ryle's (1984) recent discussion of this point and associated issues fails to acknowledge that many of his contentions about 'restructuring personal systems' amount to a rephrasing of what others have said before. But to demonstrate a limited convertibility of this sort is by no means to show that the theoretical scheme associated with 'reconstruing' can be *substituted* for that associated with 'psychodynamic interpretation'. Thus if we 'go cognitive' and stay (exclusively) cognitive where psychotherapy is concerned, we intellectualize at our peril.

At all events, these are the sort of issues which Cheshire and Thomae address in Chapter 5, and one of the candidates for a defining characteristic of psychodynamic therapy which they necessarily discuss is, as we have just noted, the study of the 'transference-relationship'. Malan's well-known researches into the variables affecting the course and outcome of brief psychoanalytic therapies have been directed at the placebo hypothesis—that there are in fact *no* specific factors at work, but only certain rather general ones which operate by some kind of covert deconditioning (Malan, 1976, ch. 1). We are used to encountering this latter view among the behavioural therapists (cp. Eysenck, 1980), and we shall comment on it in more detail below, but it has been espoused also in moments of disillusion even by some psychodynamic therapists themselves, such as the author of Chapter 11 himself.

Something of a middle way in these matters has been pursued interestingly by both Koch (1983) and Ryle (1984), who argue that psychotherapeutic change may occur, not as the result of technically specific inputs from the therapists, but because certain generally beneficial attitudes and notions of the therapist are processed by the patient through his/her own individually structured 'personal construct system', into what are *in effect* personally 'specific' inputs for him or her (but different, necessarily, from the idiographically specific conversion that another patient would make from the same 'general' material). Specificity, in this view, is thus produced by multifarious determining factors *within* each patient. And yet there is really nothing new in this idea, for it is a familiar tactic of psychodynamic interpretation to leave an intervention deliberately vague or allusive, so that the patient may 'take' it at whatever level he/she is ready for (Cheshire, 1975, p. 202); and to insist that individual patients will take it, or anything else, in individually different ways is only to reiterate a commonplace of psychodynamics about 'transference', 'introjection' and the ubiquitous activity of 'phantasy' (cp. J. Segal, 1984). But we must now turn briefly to another aspect of the on-going debate about the respective places of 'general' and 'specific' factors in psychodynamic therapies.

When, in the 1950s, the behavioural therapies, which claimed to derive their special character and efficacy from experimentally validated learning theory, began to appear in some force on the psychiatric scene, and to challenge psychodynamic theories to a trial of strength, supporters of the older tradition argued that such beneficial effects as the behaviour therapies might have were due to the fact that they incidentally and inadvertently made use of therapeutic apparatus from the psychodynamic armoury, such as transference-interaction or guilt-reduction. It was noted, for instance, that a behavioural therapist who had eliminated a cat phobia, ostensibly by progressive desensitization, had also talked to the patient about her feelings towards her father. It then seemed necessary to show that, although such therapies *might* activate psychodynamic variables to a small and unsystematic extent, their efficacy (indeed their *greater* efficacy) could not be attributed to these incidentals but must be due to the close match between the basic psychological theory about how neurotic disorders could be unlearned in treatment and the actual causal processes by which they had been learned in the first place.

Indeed, the experimentalists launched a counter-attack which was designed to demonstrate that the concepts of their classical and operant conditioning theories could account not only for why their own therapies worked, but also for clinical phenomena that had hitherto seemed to require the colourful individuality of psychodynamic hypotheses to render them comprehensible. Thus we had the 'conditioned anxiety' reinterpretation of Freud's *Little Hans* case (Wolpe and Rachman, 1960), which in turn provoked return fire from Conway (1978) and Cheshire (1979; 1980a) who contended that the experimentalists' claim to plausibility was undermined by tendentious omission and culpable distortion of important elements in the story. But the doctrinal pretensions of those learning theorists who aspire to encompass all forms of therapeutic change under a single theoretical banner, regardless of which nominal brand of therapy has occasioned them, found a formidable champion in Hans Eysenck, who both played an active part in the early skirmishes and has also more recently set out a revised statement about how beneficial change in neurotic conditions (whether brought about by behaviour therapy, Rogerian counselling, the waiting-list, etc.) can be understood in terms of Pavlovian learning theory (Eysenck, 1980).

If a neurotic symptom, such as a phobic reaction, is to be thought of as a maladaptive conditioned response to a conditioned stimulus which has at some time in the past been associated with a naturally frightening stimulus, then we should expect, on the basis of the bell–salivation paradigm of Pavlovian conditioning, that the conditioned fear response would gradually fade away (extinguish) when the conditioned stimulus (say, an open space) does not continue to be associated with an *actually* frightening event, just as the dog's salivation to the bell extinguishes when the bell is no longer in fact associated with food (reinforcement). Why, then, do phobic reactions not remit spontaneously as a matter of course?; and why do several different kinds of psychotherapy, which use overtly different techniques for bringing about change, all have some measure of success?

Eysenck's answer is that neurotic reactions are learned not on the bell–salivation model (type A) of classical conditioning, but on the 'secondary-reinforcement' model of the morphine injection (type B) in which an animal which has been subjected to actual morphine injections eventually comes to produce the full morphine-reaction (including vomiting and other physiological changes) as a conditioned response to the conditioned stimulus of the touch of the experimenter's hands or the hypodermic needle. In this case, since the conditioned response carries with it in a sense its own aversive reinforcement, in the form of unpleasant physiological reactions, we do not expect it to extinguish *unless* the animal is given the chance to learn that no actual morphine will in fact be forthcoming. When the conditioned stimulus (CS) is presented only briefly, however, no such chance of unlearning is given, since the CS does not survive to be co-present with *reduced* CR anxiety, and the aversive conditioned reaction is if anything 'enchanced', according to Eysenck. This is held to be the typical situation in the case of the neurotic's everyday encounters with relevant conditioned stimuli.

On this view, the efficacy of any psychological therapy depends upon its striking a critical balance between the duration of the patient's exposure to the conditioned stimulus, on the one hand, and the strength of his conditioned response which is elicited, on the other. Almost any form of psychotherapy will *happen* to strike such a favourable balance *some* of the time—even though haphazardly, incidentally, and with a good deal of contamination from positively unhelpful balances—because even just talking to someone about one's troubles is a form of cognitive confrontation of relevant conditioned stimuli in a context which reduces the strength of the conditioned anxiety responses. That is why they all, including the waiting-list, work to some extent, assuming that the waiting-list patient also informally consults non-professionals or even just takes himself off to ruminate in the country. But the reason why the specific behavioural therapies work better, at least in the case of fairly circumscribed symptomatic neuroses (it is said), is that they concentrate characteristically and exclusively on this critical balance, and are careful to avoid sources of contamination.

The rationale for cultivating this therapeutically critical balance of forces is a moderately complex and sophisticated business, as Eysenck's lucid exposition of it indicates, and is quite *other* than what will generally be understood by the expression 'ordinary Pavlovian extinction'. On the contrary, Eysenck has to advance what he himself calls a *new* theory, involving the concept of 'enhancement', in order to make sense of it. Similarly, the corresponding causal story for neurotic phobias now has to be propped up with Seligman's (1971) notion of a built-in 'preparedness', on the part of at least some people, to react anxiously to certain things; a notion which manages to combine Tinbergen's classic ethological concept of 'sign-stimulus' with Jung's psychodynamic idea of an 'archetype', and still say nothing new. Nor, if the revised theory has really been consciously central to the behaviour therapies all along, so that it can qualify as '*non*-placebognic' in the terms of Gruenbaum's powerful discussion (1983), is it clear why it should be necessary for Eysenck to write a technical article, involving a novel theoretical modification, in order to explain to behaviour therapists, among others, why their various procedures have been working.

If, however, these first chapters of *Part I* to some extent exemplify contrasting procedures, one of the purposes served by the systems-theory paradigm of von Zeppelin's Chapter 6 is to override such contrasts by subsuming them under a more abstract level of conceptualization, insofar as the antithetical concepts of specificity and generalization (or replicability) are reconciled in the cyberneticist's axiom (or is it, rather, faith?) that to *define* a function minutely and coherently enough amounts in principle to specifying a programme for replicating it. The converse of this has more general implications for the radical operation of introducing conceptual rigour into the various ways of talking about the Self that we have encountered: it is that any such verbal formalization which can *not* be converted into that sort of specification must be intrinsically too vague or incoherent to play a logically reliable part in *any* theoretical network, in whatever terms it is presented.

Even if this converse assumption is tinged with grandiosity and therefore needs to be interpreted sceptically, it is, nevertheless, certainly the case that the epistemological technique of testing the coherence and rigour of psychological concepts by trying to transform propositions in which they figure into parallel propositions about the properties and processes of some fundamental information-processing, or control-system (whether that system be conceived in terms of a neurological model of the cerebral cortex, or of the hierarchically organized routines of artificial intelligence), represents a relevant challenge. For if the concepts in question pass the test, they can claim uniquely persuasive validation as a result. This exercise has seemed for several decades now to be a plausible way of pin-pointing limitations and muddles, of showing that superficially unfamiliar notions do not really imply unfamiliar processes, and generally of sorting wheat from chaff on the conceptual winnowing-floor.

It was applied pioneeringly by Hebb (1949) to the problem of perceptual learning in general psychology, and later and more broadly by Ashby (1960), by Young (1964) and by Miller, Galanter and Pribram (1960), under whose influence Cheshire (1966) subjected some specifically psychoanalytic concepts from Kleinian theory to the same sort of test. In so doing he followed the lead of Colby (1955) who had been one of the first to try to express some basic psychoanalytic concepts in cybernetic terms, and whose project has been further developed by Peterfreund (1971, with Schwartz; 1980). Concurrently, and on a much larger scale, a similar task was being undertaken on the concepts of unconscious 'defence-mechanisms' by the Zurich group of Moser *et al.* from the early 1960s onwards, with results that were to some critics surprisingly supportive of what had seemed problematical concepts (cp. Boden, 1974). It is this influential Zurich 'school' in which von Zeppelin collaborates, and whose conceptual outlook she presents in Chapter 6.

But the relevance of this kind of exercise had been intuited, of course, long ago by Freud himself in the neurological modelling sketch of the *Project* . . . which anticipated by several years some of Sherrington's classic discoveries in cortical neurohistology. And even those apparently quaint 'quantities of energy', inhibitory circuits and so on, which we find in Freud's draft turn out to be not entirely alien to modern neurology after all, as has been argued in recent times by Pribram and Gill (1976), whose well-known appraisal combines the viewpoints of neurologist and psychoanalytic theorist; and Freud's description there (1895, p. 366) of the way in which auditory verbal imagery functions as a 'secondary signalling system' in perceptual learning predates by some three decades Pavlov's account of this form of higher-order conditioning. The fact that Freud himself soon rejected the idea of a direct, as it were *digital*, transformation of his proposed psychological processes into neurological ones (because he realized that psychoneural isomorphism cannot be sustained) need not deter us from exploring, for the purposes of specific clarifications, the possibility of *analogical* transformation into the formal properties of an artificial intelligence system.

Chapter 6 thus represents a further step in the direction of the more general rehabilitation of psychodynamic self-theory, and its associated therapeutic methods, by showing that the problematic psychodynamic metaphor of a self-system, with which we began, can indeed be 'cashed' into conceptual currencies (such as those of cybernetics or artificial intelligence) which are acceptable in the theoretical dealings of general psychology today.

Unfortunately, however, it is as yet the exception for these inner-world metaphors to be 'cashable' so readily into *psychometric* currency, or into some other valid empirical coinage; and the point in drawing attention to these difficulties, with which much of *Part I* contends, is to encourage our theorists to contend yet more valiantly in the future, by persuading them to turn their efforts in this direction rather than that. For it would be the greatest mistake to let the sceptical critic draw us away from a potentially fruitful type of theory merely because there are still some evident bugs in its models and analogies.

What would have happened to the understanding and application of electro-magnetism in the middle of the last century if philosophers of science had turned up their noses at the mixture of images which Faraday used to conceptualize those mysterious 'fields of force', and had as a consequence dismissed the whole approach? For Faraday described these fields as being spanned by 'elastic cords of ether', which were responsible for drawing the iron filings this way and that.

Well, Faraday was incidentally wrong, of course, about those cords of ether, while being essentially right about electromagnetism! Maybe the same goes, to some extent, for our current models (whether cognitive or psychodynamic) of those very different, and even more obscure, forces which operate in the so-called 'inner world' to mediate both the development of self-concepts and the transactions of psychotherapy.

References

Ashby, W. R. (1960). *Design for a Brain*, second edition. Chapman and Hall, London.

Ashworth, C. M., Blackburn, I. M. and McPherson, F. M. (1985). The performance of depressed and manic patients . . . *Brit. J. Med. Psychol.* **58**, 337–342.

Beck, A. T. (1976). *Cognitive Therapy of the Emotional Disorders*. International Universities Press, New York.

Boden, M. A. (1974). Freudian mechanisms of defence: . . . Reprinted in *Minds and Mechanisms*, ch. 10, Harvester, Brighton, 1981.

Bowlby, J. (1973). *Separation: Anger and Anxiety*. Hogarth, London (Penguin, 1975).

Bowlby, J. (1980). *Loss: Sadness and Depression*. Hogarth, London.

Bowlby, J. (1984). *Attachment*, second edition. Penguin, Harmondsworth.

Bruner, J. S. and Postman, L. (1949). On the perception of incongruity: . . . *J. Personal.*, **18**, 206–223.

Cheshire, N. M. (1966). *Some Concepts of Object-relations Theory*. B. Litt. Thesis, Oxford University (Bodleian Library).

Cheshire, N. M. (1975). *The Nature of Psychodynamic Interpretation*. Wiley, London and New York.

Cheshire, N. M. (1979). A big hand for Little Hans. *Bull. Brit. Psychol. Soc.*, **32**, 320–323.

Cheshire, N. M. (1980a) 'Hands off Little Hans. *Bull. Brit. Psychol. Soc.*,**33**, 69–70.

Cheshire, N. M. (1980b). Project for a humane psychology: . . . In *Models of Man* (eds A. J. Chapman and D. M. Jones), pp. 356–358. British Psychological Society, Leicester.

Colby, K. M. (1955). *Energy and Structure in Psychoanalysis*. Ronald, New York.

Condon, W. S. (1979). Neonatal entrainment and enculturation. In *Before Speech* (ed. M. Bullowa), pp. 131–148. Cambridge University Press, Cambridge.

Conway, A. V. (1978). Little Hans: misrepresentation of the evidence? *Bull. Brit. Psychol. Soc.*, **31**, 285–287

Eysenck, H. J. (1980). A unified theory of psychotherapy: . . . *Z. Psychol.*, **188**, 43–56.

Farr, R. and Moscovici, S. (1984). On the nature and role of representations . . . In *Issues in Person Perception* (ed. M. Cook), pp. 1–27. Methuen, London and New York.

Festinger, L. J. (1957). *A Theory of Cognitive Dissonance*. Stanford University Press, Stanford.

Freud, A. (1936). *The Ego and the Mechanisms of Defence* (revised edition, 1966). Hogarth, London.

Freud, S. (1895). Project for a scientific psychology. *Standard Ed.,* **1**, (1966), 295–397.

Freud, S. (1919). Lines of advance . . . *Standard Ed.,* **17**, 157–168.

Freud, S. (1924). Neurosis and psychosis. *Standard Ed.,* **19**, 147–153.

Freud, S. (1933). *New introductory lectures, Standard Ed.,* **22**, 1–182.

Freud, S. (1940). *An outline of psychoanalysis. Standard Ed.,* **23**, 141–207.

Gergen, K. J. (1977). The social construction of self-knowledge. In *The Self* (ed. T. Mischel), pp. 139–169. Blackwell, Oxford.

Gergen, K. J. (1984). Toward self relationship. *Bull. Brit. Psychol. Soc.,* **37**, A102.

Gruenbaum, A. (1983). Explication and implications of the placebo concept. In *Placebo: Clinical Phenomena and New Insights* (eds L. White *et al.*) Guilford Press, New York.

Harré, R. (1970). *The Principles of Scientific Thinking.* Macmillan, London.

Harré, R., Clarke, D. and De Carlo, M. (1985). *Motives and Mechanisms.* Methuen, London and New York.

Hayes, S. C. (1986) A contextual approach to therapeutic change. In *Cognitive and Behavior Therapies in Clinical Practice* (ed. N. Jacobson). Guilford Press, New York (in press).

Hebb, D. O. (1946). On the nature of fear. *Psychol. Rev.,* **53**, 250–275.

Hebb, D. O. (1949). *The Organisation of Behaviour.* Wiley, New York.

Heider, P. (1958). *The Psychology of Interpersonal Relations.* Wiley, New York.

Hewstone, M., Hooper, D. and Miller, K. (1981). Psychological change in neurotic depression: . . . *Brit. J. Psychiatr.,* **139**, 47–51.

Kelly, G. A. (1955). *The Psychology of Personal Constructs,* 2 vols. Norton, New York.

Kelly, G. A. (1963). *Theory of Personality.* Norton, New York.

Kline, P. (1979). Psychosexual personality traits . . . *Brit. J. Med. Psychol.,* **52**, 393–395.

Kline, P. (1981). *Fact and Fantasy in Freudian Theory,* second edition. Methuen, London.

Kline, P. and Storey, R. (1977). A factor-analytic study of the oral character. *Brit. J. Soc. Clin. Psychol.,* **16**, 317–328.

Kline, P. and Storey, R. (1980). The aetiology of the oral character. *J. Genet. Psychol.,* **136**, 85–94.

Koch, H. C. H. (1983). Changes in personal construing . . . *Brit. J. Med. Psychol.,* **56**, 245–254.

Kuhn, T. S. (1973). *The Structure of Scientific Revolutions,* third edition. Chicago University Press, Chicago.

Laughlin, H. P. (1970). *The Ego and its Defences.* Appleton-Century-Crofts, New York.

Lifton, O. R. J. (1964). *Thought Reform and the Psychology of Totalism.* Penguin, Harmondsworth.

Madison, P. (1961). *Freud's Concept of Repression and Defence.* University of Minnesota Press, Minneapolis.

Malan, D. H. (1976). *Towards the Validation of Dynamic Psychotherapy.* Plenum, New York and London.

Miller, G. A., Galanter, E. and Pribram, K. H. (1960). *Plans and the Structure of Behavior.* Henry Holt, New York.

Oatley, K. (1984). *Selves in Relation:* . . . Methuen, London and New York.

Peterfreund, E. and Schwartz, J. T. (1971). *Information, Systems and Psychoanalysis* (Psychol. Issues 7, Monogr. 25/26). International Universities Press, New York.

Peterfreund, E. (1980). On information and systems models for psychoanalysis. *Int. Rev. Psychoanal.,* **7**, 327–345.

Pribram, K. H. and Gill, M. (1976). *Freud's Project Reassessed.* Hutchinson, London.

Ribble, M. (1944). Infantile experience. In *Personality and the Behaviour Disorders* (ed. I. McV. Hunt), vol. 2, ch. 20. Ronald, New York, cp. Endler, N. S. and Hunt, J. M. (1985). *Personality and the Behavioral Disorders*, 2 vols. Wiley, Chichester.

Rycroft, C. (1985). Where is psychoanalysis going? *J. Royal Soc. Med.*, **78**, 524–525.

Ryle, A. (1982). *Psychotherapy: A Cognitive Interpretation. . .* Academic Press, London.

Ryle, A. (1984). How can we compare different psychotherapies? *Brit. J. Med. Psychol.*, **57**, 261–264.

Ryle, A. (1985). Cognitive theory, object-relations and the self. *Brit. J. Med. Psychol.*, **58**, 1–7.

Sandler, J. (1985). Comments on the self and its objects. In *Self and Object-constancy: . . .* (ed. R. Lax *et al.*), ch. 4. Guilford, New York.

Sandler, J. and Freud, A. (1985). *The Analysis of Defence.* International Universities Press, New York.

Segal, H. (1979). *Klein.* Fontana/Collins, London.

Segal, J. (1984). *Phantasy in Everyday Life.* Harmondsworth, Penguin.

Seligman, M. E. P. (1971). Phobias and preparedness. *Behav. Ther.* **2**, 307–320.

Sheehan, M. J. (1985). A personal construct study of depression. *Brit. J. Med. Psychol.*, **58**, 119–128.

Shotter, J. (1980). 'Men the magicians: . . . In *Models of Man* (eds A. J. Chapman and D. M. Jones), ch. 2. British Psychological Society, Leicester.

Spitz, R. A. (1946). Anaclitic depression. *Psychoanal. Study Child,* **2**, 313–342.

Watson, J. B. (1919). *Psychology from the Standpoint of a Behaviorist.* Lippincott, Philadelphia and London.

Wegman, O. (1985). *Psychoanalysis and Cognitive Psychology.* Academic Press, London.

Wolpe, J. and Rachman, S. (1960). Psychoanalytic evidence: . . . Reprinted in *Critical Essays on Psychoanalysis* (ed. S. Rachman, 1963), pp. 198–231. Pergamon, Oxford.

Young, J. Z. (1964). *A Model of the Brain.* Oxford University Press, Oxford.

CHAPTER 1

The Rehabilitation of the Self

Neil Cheshire and Helmut Thomae

1.1   *A language for the Self*
1.2   *Anatomy of the Self*
1.3   *The self-system and its disturbances*

1.1   A Language for the Self

In case any doubts about the matter still lurk in perseverative minds, the studies reported in this volume, and the range and variety of work to which they refer, should be enough to persuade the sceptic that the Self is back. For three or four decades it had been virtually banished from many university Departments of Psychology, in the name of scientific respectability and behaviourism; so that, as Ralph Turner has put it (1977, p. 9), 'it nearly became a casualty of the healthy iconoclasm of early behaviourism'. But, in spite of this, the Self never really left child-development studies or personality theory (as is evident from Stern's (1985) recent empirical investigations into the infant's 'sense of self'), and certainly could not be ignored in the psychiatric clinic. Indeed, certain psychiatric and neurological *exotica*, to do with multiple personality and involuntary action, came to function as standard test-cases for philosophers wrestling with the concept of 'personal identity'. The ingenious science-fiction parable by Dennett (1981) hilariously epitomizes the point.

Quite apart from the two-edged influence of behaviourism upon general psychology (which helpfully cut away some misleading abstractions but also aroused needless and obstructive guilt about any attempt to accommodate sub-jective experience), the positivist philosophers in Europe and North America had been only too ready to expose conceptual confusion among the muddled language of those who still tried to talk about the Self. Ironically, however, although such philosophical techniques had themselves originated in German-speaking Europe, they left almost untouched a flourishing and obscure tradition of self-centred psychophilosophy in France and Germany. But they also left it very largely *in* France and Germany, to the disadvantage of the English-language student of philosophy and psychology whose intellectual upbringing tended as a consequence to be Spartan to the point of deprivation.

But it is now fully a quarter of a century since such diverse philosophical spirits as McMurray (1957) and Geach (1957), for example, struck back at these proscriptions and privations with *The Self as Agent* and Mental Acts respectively, and it is already more than a decade since Wylie (1968) could review the situation from a psychological standpoint under the title 'the present status of self-theory'. Still more recently, Rosenberg (1979) has surveyed a wide variety of ways of 'conceiving the Self', and Burns' (1979, 1982) reviews of the theories and researches have become well known to academic as well as to 'applied' psychologists; and in the 1980s the 'self-literature' has proliferated still further, as we shall see. The rapid development of psychiatry and psychotherapy, moreover, has made it still more urgent to find coherent and empirically usable ways of talking about all the varied developmental and clinical phenomena involving people's sense of self. We shall therefore press ahead, taking due notice on the one hand of the compendium of philosophical perils and signposts which the late Theodore Mischel has so valuably drawn up (1977), and concentrating as practically as possible, on the other hand, on making sense of the empirical material of pathological and therapeutic processes. We shall also take encouragement from the fact that, even in traditionally empirical and experimentalist Britain, an international conference on 'Self and Identity' could flourish in 1984 (see Boyle and Bull, 1984), while, across the Atlantic, Hamachek's (1987) multi-faceted 'encounters' with the Self are already into their third edition.

Since the material of this volume was originally bilingual, and therefore partly in need of translation, it was inevitable that we should come to reflect on the different ways of talking about the Self in different languages. This experience has sharpened our determination to distinguish what are merely linguistic features of such ways of talking, in particular languages, from deeper logical characteristics of the *ideas* behind the thought: to distinguish, in effect, *façons de parler* from Kantian categories. That is to say, we must not confuse the *linguistic* grammar of self-talk (whether in German or in English) with what Wittgenstein calls the '*logical* grammar' of the concepts involved.

After all, it came as a shock to some of the linguistic philosophers themselves to discover that their supposed philosophical insights did not always survive translation. Consequently, they were seen to be language-specific, and therefore to be more like psycholinguistic, as opposed to philosophical, demonstrations. This episode in the history of English-language philosophy has been memorably marked by the British dramatist Tom Stoppard (1978, pp. 60–63). In *Professional Foul*, one of the speakers at an international philosophy convention reduces the translators to confusion with a play on words that underpins his argument in English but makes nonsense in translation. This scene is taken to be an allusion to an historical visit to a French convention made in the late

1940s by Professor Ayer of Oxford, whose very influential book *Language, Truth and Logic* (Ayer, 1926) is often said to have brought positivism to Britain. So we must try to avoid making the same mistake ourselves.

Particularly for psychoanalysts, who may hold with Lacan that the unconscious is structured as a language, it is important not to assume that the world is structured in the same way as our own particular mother-tongue; and the risk of making this dangerously glib assumption has perhaps increased since some of Chomsky's work may have encouraged us to believe that different languages have certain 'deep structures' in common (e.g. Chomsky 1957, 1965). We have to ask '*Whose* language is the Unconscious structured as, and at what level?' It is salutary to bear in mind on these occasions the Trobriand Islanders and Hopi Indians, whose thought-forms have been contrasted so vividly with those of European 'literate' culture by Doris Lee and Benjamin Whorf respectively, because they give us the impression that the Trobriand or Hopi way of conceptualizing almost anything is guaranteed to be different from that prevalent in Western Europe and English-speaking countries (cp. Goody and Watt, 1972, p. 348). And yet, if languages have developed as vehicles for communicating experiences, will they not contain some psychologically valuable hints about how people over the ages have tried to make sense of their experience?

We hope that by drawing attention to one or two of these linguistic points which we have encountered in translation we may be able both to clarify them and to prevent ourselves from being misled by them. We have also another and rather more demanding goal as well: we hope to be able to show that there *are*, in fact, meaningful and coherent ways of conceptualizing the Self other than as a 'ghost in the machine' or as a mental homunculus who, just like 'psychic energy' in the past, has recently been threatening to take over the helm in areas such as perception and action-control, at any rate in psychoanalytic theory. Gordon Allport's warning on this point has been passed on by Mischel and Mischel (1977, p. 50).

We shall approach this second goal, in due course, by drawing attention to some of the ways in which both a general sense of self-identity and also particular self-perceptions may fail to develop adequately, may become disturbed, and may be experienced as improved or recovered after psychotherapeutic intervention. In the course of that approach, we shall find ourselves following the footsteps of one of the founding fathers of modern psychology, William James himself. But before we do that, we must complete our preliminary clarification of some problematical linguistic matters; and here again we shall find that we are standing on the shoulders of another eminent pioneer. For the sceptical position which we recommend was advocated not only by recent linguistic philosophers but also by an originator of psychoanalysis, none other than Freud's early collaborator Joseph Breuer.

From a linguistic point of view, it seems clear enough that the term 'Self' depends upon its ties with personal and reflexive pronouns. In many European languages, the word that is used to produce such semantic reinforcement, emphasis or intensification cannot take on by itself the grammatical role of subject in a sentence, whether as a name, noun or pronoun. Thus in the cases of colloquial or non-specialist English, German and French, the grammatically intensive parts of the language-forms 'myself', '*ich selbst*' and '*moi-même*' do not regularly stand by themselves. The fact that it is possible (at least in English and German) to separate them off, preface them with the definite article and thereby produce what looks like a reference to a substantive entity, may be no more than a limited and potentially misleading lexicographic phenomenon. Limited, because it is not a general characteristic of language *per se*, but a specific characteristic of some particular languages; misleading, because it seems to invite the unwary reader or hearer to try to identify and track down the mysterious object which this new noun apparently designates (cp. Toulmin, 1977, p. 297). When we speak ironically, therefore, of the rehabilitation and the anatomy of 'the Self', we are implicitly challenging the strength of these objections and not ignoring them.

Indeed, this invitation has proved so hard to resist that it has instigated in some cultures whole traditions of philosophical inquiry which have turned out (in the view of many commentators) to be fundamentally confused and, not surprisingly as a consequence, fruitless. We recall, for instance, David Hume's famous description of his introspective quest for the Self or the 'pure ego', in which he kept finding that he had, as it were, run up against a blank wall:

> "there are some philosophers, who imagine we are every moment intimately conscious of what we call our Self; that we feel its existence and its continuance in existence; and are certain, beyond the evidence of a demonstration, both of its perfect identity and simplicity ...
> But Self or person is not any one impression, but that to which our several impressions and ideas are supposed to have a reference ... for my part, when I enter most intimately into what I call my *Self* I always stumble on some particular perception or other, of heat or cold, light or shade, love or hatred, pain or pleasure. I never can catch *myself* at any time without a perception, and never can observe anything but the perception; when my perceptions are removed for any time, as by sound sleep, so long am I insensible of *myself* and may truly be said not to exist." (Hume, 1739, pp. 251–252)

In his later discussion of the same general question, Immanuel Kant expresses some surprisingly similar judgements (1787, pp. 394–401). Conversely, the modern linguistic philosopher John Austin used to argue that classical Greek philosophy, by contrast, was not distracted by this particular misguided quest precisely because the linguistic habits and usage of the language did not entice their thinkers in that particular direction. For, as generations of students have discovered to their dismay, classical Greek regularly expresses the self-reference or self-involvement of an action by using a separate form of the *verb* concerned (namely, the 'middle voice') instead of introducing reflexive or intensive pronouns. The implications for self-theory of this and other linguistic observations have been elaborated recently by Stephen Toulmin (1977, pp. 295–300).

In the context of empirical psychology, some of these problems of language have been illustrated in the work of Spiegel, who pointed out the difficulty of plausibly translating the original German term '*Ich-Gefühl*'. His English version was 'self-feeling', but this was translated back into German as '*Selbstgefühl*' (1959; 1961, p. 211). This term 'self-feeling' is related more or less closely to a number of other terms such as 'personal identity', 'I-feeling', 'I-identity (*Ich-Identität*)' and 'sense of identity'. Spiegel's discussion shows how the Self has only just come into flower, as it were, in the meta-language of psychoanalysis. In some of Freud's own writings, as Strachey has shown (1961, pp. 7–9), it was much the same thing as the colloquial 'I'; and, even after the clarifying structural formulations of *The Ego and the Id* (Freud, 1923), his usage is not entirely consistent. For, although he sometimes distinguishes different senses of '*Ich*' (namely, 'I' and 'the ego'), yet he elsewhere identifies '*das Selbst*' ('the Self') with '*das Ich*' ('the ego').

But his colleague Breuer was well aware, as we have noted above, that it is important to make sure, in the transfer from colloquial usage to the language of theory, that nouns are not necessarily assumed to be the names for substances. He gave the following warning, which has not always been heeded subsequently, to his fellow practitioners and theorists (Breuer and Freud, 1895, pp. 227–228):

> 'it is only too easy to fall into the habit of thought which assumes that every substantive (i.e. noun, Ed.) has a substance behind it—which gradually comes to regard consciousness as standing for some actual thing; and when we have become accustomed to make use of spatial relations, as in the term "sub-consciousness", we find as time goes on that we have actually formed an idea which has lost its metaphorical nature and which we can manipulate easily as though it was real. Our mythology is then complete.'

Breuer was also well aware, however, as realistic observers of human behaviour always have been, that in some circumstances and for some purposes people do need to find ways of talking about their own experience, which inevitably includes their experience of their own actions, wishes, dispositions, intentions, anxieties, reactions, hopes, fears and the rest of it. That is, they need to be able to describe the phenomena which seem to make them the person that they are

by defining their identity, especially when some disturbance in those phenomena gives rise to personal distress and even to physical impairment (cp.
Honess, 1982). In this way, it seems necessary to make what has hitherto been
the subject of thoughts and actions into the object of perception and contemplation. Even those philosophers who are well aware of the dangers of reifica-
tion and false hypostasis feel bound to concede that there are times when
people need to reflect upon and try to describe their own mental state (cp.
T. Mischel, 1977, p. 21; Hamlyn, 1977, *passim*). And we may take further philosophical reassurance, if it be required, from McGinn's recent argument (1982,
ch. 6) that the conceptual quest for the nature of that 'self' which is, does and
has mental-states is not inherently a pseudoproblem (as many of his Oxford
predecessors had contended).

During such processes of reflection, when people turn to themselves linguistically, as it were, they are likely to encounter themselves in many different selves
or roles. This discovery, that personality or personal identity does not consist in
some constant homogeneity but rather in the developing capacity to play a
range of different social and interpersonal roles, has been notably expounded in
recent years by the sociologist Erving Goffman (e.g. 1956, 1971). And psychoanalysts have been suggesting for a long time that, in the balanced personality,
this flexible but harmonious state coincides with an unconscious fusion with
what George Mead had called a 'significant other'. In this case, 'I-feeling'
(*Ich-Gefühl*) and 'self-feeling' are hardly distinguishable, which is why in German both terms may be used to describe the same phenomenal state of affairs.

For this reason, it may perhaps seem possible (and certainly philosophically
attractive) in everyday life to avoid thinking of a *categorical* self, and instead to
'translate out' any such references into dispositional terms, in the manner
which Gilbert Ryle (1949) repeatedly demonstrated. But certain clinical phenomena will always compel one to think again. Breuer's famous patient, Anna O.,
vividly illustrates the point. She found it necessary to describe some of her
pathological thoughts and feelings as being the products of her '*schlimmes Ich*';
and in so doing she became, as it were, the first *Ich-Psychologe* (ego-psycho-
logist) in the German language. In the *Standard Edition*, this 'bad I' of which
she spoke has been translated as her 'bad self' (1895, p. 46).

The fact that we tend to attribute functions to the Self, turn it into something
anthropomorphic and give it a substance, is surely tied up with the way in
which we slip into our theoretical constructions. It is as if we assume that such
constructions directly reflect the intrinsic form of our experience, rather than
being just one way, out of various possible ways, of actively 'construing' them.
Fortunately, the problems we have in connection with linguistic and theoretical
understanding are more easily solved, although some mistakes which occur in
translation do cause confusion.

'*Selbstbewusstsein*' and 'self-consciousness', for example, have different
meanings even though they are, in a sense, a 'straight' translation. In one usage,
'*Selbstbewusstsein*' is something of a technical or philosophical concept (which

we will not deal with at this point); in another usage, however, the same term expresses, informally or colloquially, the empirical state of a balanced person's self-feeling or self-esteem, whereas the words 'self-consciousness' and 'self-conscious', as we all know, mean something quite different. Someone who is self-conscious is insecure in himself: he is preoccupied with himself, is always observing himself, does not act spontaneously. Our pathologically self-conscious patients continually doubt themselves, ask themselves whether what they are doing is right and worry whether other people approve of the way they behave and how they look (cp. Thomae, 1980).

1.2   Anatomy of the Self

At the time when Breuer was still engaged with Freud in his therapeutic studies of hysterical patients, to which we have just referred, that other founding father of modern psychology whom we have also introduced, William James, published the first edition of his classic work, *The Principles of Psychology*. In the chapter which deals with 'the consciousness of Self', James distinguishes four aspects of the Self which can to some extent be considered separately. They are: the material self, the social self, the spiritual self and the pure Ego (1980, p. 291).

The term 'pure Ego' in this context has, of course, almost nothing to do with the 'Ego' of psychoanalytic structural theory. It is instead that same psycho-philosophical construct which we have already encountered eluding the intro-spective and logical grasp of both Hume and Kant; and James himself firmly recommended that psychologists should send it back to the philosophers as being an unmanageable abstraction suitable only for their contemplation.

The spiritual self, on the other hand, was very far from being an unusable abstraction in James's view, and his famous study of the varieties of religious experience (1902) is almost as well known as his *Principles*. A number of con-temporary psychologists have studied this topic in the light of modern psych-ology and philosophy, (e.g. Miles, 1959, 1971), and an eminent Oxford biolog-ist, Sir Alastair Hardie, has for some years now been directing systematic empirical research into the sociology, epidemiology and phenomenology of those accounts which large numbers of people will give of the religious, or quasi-religious, experiences which they have had in their everyday lives (cp. Beardsworth, 1977). But these phenomena lie outside the direct focus of this volume, and we shall in practice concentrate upon James's first two categories.

Under the general heading of 'the material self', James describes the 'bodily self' in a way which anticipates both Freud's 'body-ego' (1923, p. 19) and Schilder's 'body-schema' (1950; 1951. ch. 6). His phenomenological description of different states of 'self-feeling' may readily be accommodated in the psycho-analytic theory of disturbances in self-concept. James is well aware that observ-able variations in people's 'sense of personal identity' pose problems for any naive categorical conception of the identity of personality, and there has been continuous theoretical and clinical examination of the issues ever since. This has given rise in recent decades to a concern about the prevalance of 'ontological anxiety', which has had a revolutionary impact on some parts of Western psychiatry (cp. Laing, 1965, 1969; Cooper, 1978).

The assumption that such anxieties are closely connected, developmentally, with feelings about the 'bodily self' is encouraged by the fact that deep-seated disturbances in self-feeling seem to have their roots in insecurities relating to the body. (We use the term 'self-feeling', as William James did, instead of the more specific 'self-esteem' or 'self-valuation', in order to capture the stronger affective connotation of the corresponding German term *Selbst-gefühl*.) Consequently, it makes sense to look more closely at Freud's argument that the ego, that is the ego of psychoanalysis, originates in the body ego; and one of the interests which psychoanalysis has come to share in recent years with general developmental psychology is precisely this question of the relationship between somatic and psychological demarcation in the neonate and infant during the very first months of life.

Following the usage of Schilder and Brain, we would argue that what Freud is concerned with is the more general 'body-image' rather than 'body-schema'. This is because we understand by the latter term (*Körperschema*), which Schilder used in the early 1920s, the relatively set innate biological fact that the body serves as a model of three-dimensional space; whereas the individual body-*image* (*Körperbild*), Schilder's later term, has a less concrete reference and is connected with processes of primary socialization (Thomae, 1980, p. 244). As a result, it acquires emotional, evaluative and intentional properties, and necessarily provides the basis for the earliest attempts at communication and symbolization in the widest sense. These emotional and evaluative connotations of the way people perceive and identify with their bodies can now be investigated systematically with the techniques of 'personal construct' theory (cp. Feldman, 1975); and it is worth noticing also that the disruption of symbolic communication which is characteristic of psychotic identity-disorders has been interpreted by Freeman (1969, ch. 2) in terms of Hughlings Jackson's (1884) neglected theory of neurological organization and 'dissolution'. For that matter, the whole history of envisaging neurological models for the integration of personality goes back, *via* Fliess's (1961) reworking of some ideas of Federn, at least as far as Freud's own *Project* . . . (1895, pp. 360–371).

Indeed, the idea that the infant first comes to grasp fundamental causal and logical properties of his world by symbolizing them in bodily movements is central, of course, to Piaget's account of the 'sensorimotor' stage of cognitive development. This bodily representation is treated as a necessary precursor of the faculty of mental representation, which in turn underlies the natural acquisition of language; and the part that it plays in the formation of basic 'object-relations', in the Kleino-Freudian sense, is clearly recognized (Piaget and

Inhelder, 1966, ch. 1 and 3). We see also, incidentally, that a firm distinction between James's 'material self' and 'social self' has already broken down, because these internalizations to which we have just referred regularly take place during the process of socialization; that is in the context of interpersonal and emotionally loaded relationships with caretakers. But although the contents of self-feeling in connection with the body are consequently affected by these interactions, they are not totally accounted for in this way. This may be because of the part played by the biological functions of body-*schema* and motor autonomy as early means of expressing spontaneity and subjectivity.

Consider the fact that many developmental psychologists have recently been remarking how early in life infants show some grasp of what have been called 'shared understandings' and 'intersubjectivity', and have discussed how this fundamental component of becoming a person might be derived from the process of becoming a body (Newson, 1974; Shotter, 1974; Newson, 1979). A principal theme in that discussion has been the question of how 'personal powers', which define one's identity as a person, can develop from physical or bodily powers; that is, from such simple abilities as grasping, moving, reaching and placing concrete objects. Central among these personal powers are those to do with cognitive agency: the capacity to mean and to intend (cp. Shotter and Newson, 1982; Trevarthen, 1982). The infant needs to learn the fundamental difference between doing something by chance and doing it on purpose: he needs to distinguish between something happening and his making it happen; he needs to know what he *can* make happen before he can learn to intend to make it happen, and before he can *mean* something by what he does. It is fascinating to observe how the caretaker regularly draws the infant's attention to such differences without necessarily being aware of what she or he is doing (Gauld and Shotter, 1977, ch. 11). This fundamental sense of being able to make things happen, to have an intended effect upon one's world, is conspicuously impaired in pathological conditions where self-valuation is depleted, as in the depressions (cp. section 1.3 below).

This effectiveness as a person, or what Albert Bandural (1982) has called 'self-efficacy', is often assumed in the clinical field to be closely related to a personal sense of security, for which the body is of special importance. Efficient behaviour, whatever that may mean in a particular circumstance, is tied up with an ability of the body to function properly. The undisturbed, unproblematic, unobtrusive functioning of the body contributes significantly in its turn to a sense of security; that is, of security in one's own identity as well as in differentiation from others. The developmental origin of disturbances in such differentiation are, once again, a common concern of psychoanalysis and developmental psychology (cp. Cheshire *et al.*, Chapter 7).

The positive emotional repercussions of successful physical functioning have been underlined by George Klein (1976), who has given the name 'vital pleasures' to the elementary satisfaction which people derive from the movement and functioning of their own bodies. Everybody knows the delight which children show in demonstrating some newly acquired physical skill: 'Look, Mummy, no hands!'; and conversely the disappointment, and sometimes even anger, which they demonstrate when they are deprived, however inadvertently, of such an opportunity; 'Oh, Mummy, *I* could have done that!' In emphasizing the relatively unlearned and primordial quality of such 'vital pleasures', Klein is in effect supporting our suggestion that the body-schema (as opposed to the 'body-image') is relatively independent of social and cultural influences.

Further support may be invoked, rather surprisingly, from Berger and Luckman, who are well-known for emphasizing the power of social reality, but who argue on this particular point that the awareness of one's own body is independent of anything that society can teach one about it, and is a part at least of that subjective reality which cannot be attributed to external factors (1967, pp. 201–204). Be this as it may, if spontaneous and (later on) creative processes, in the widest sense of the term, did not exist side by side with primary internalization or identification, we should be without the 'magic of gesture' of the neurotic patient who can 'turn against' something with a self-asserting movement of the head; we should also be without the movement- and body-therapies, and even without the quest for self-actualization with its seductive prospect of discovering the 'true self'.

If successful physical functioning has such important consequences for the development of satisfactory self-feeling, it follows that any impairment or defect of such physical functioning must be capable of doing serious psychological damage to the sense of self. This is, of course what Alfred Adler maintained in his version of psychodynamic psychology, when he made 'organ inferiority' an especially potent source of those inferiority feelings against which, according to him, we are all campaigning all through our lives (Orgler, 1963, pp. 55–78). But one does not have to be an Adlerian to take this idea seriously. We may notice that the theme of specifically physical determinants in the development of the sense of identity has been taken up by Phyllis Greenacre (1958); that Margaret Mahler has described the 'demarcation of body-image' as the 'core' of this development-process (1963, p. 309); and that there is a recent study by Castelnuovo-Tedesco who writes (1981, p. 146):

'feelings of being different (which predominantly include sorrow, shame, envy and resentment, but also pride, uniqueness, special power, etc.) are commonplace in persons with physical defects; and inevitably play an important role in their adaptation. They may lead to an identity as "an exception".'

The physical determinants of the material self, however, are by no means confined to the physical body. The material, or empirical, self of each of us comprises all that he is tempted to refer to by the word 'me'. But it is clear that the line is difficult to draw between what someone calls *me* and what he simply calls *mine*; and since one and the same object or attribute may sometimes be treated as part of me, at other times as simply mine, and then again as if I had nothing to do with it at all, we see that we are dealing with fluctuating material. In its widest possible sense, therefore, a man's self is the sum total of all that he *can* call his: not only his body and his psychic powers, but his clothes and his house, his wife and children, his ancestors and friends, his reputation and works, his car, land and bank account. It may extend, in a paraphrase of the Tenth Commandment, to his ox, his ass and anything that is his.

For from all these things he may derive the same feelings. If they wax and prosper, he feels triumphant; if they dwindle and die away, he feels cast down. To use a chemical metaphor which Freud applied to the ego, this material self is the 'precipitate' of those object-cathexes which have become identifications. Evidently, its range will be different for different people. We all know those who suffer a scratch on their car as acutely as a gash on their own skin, whereas, for others, their car is just something to take them from A to B.

In this discussion of the 'social self', James introduces many issues which have subsequently been developed in social psychological theories of role-play, insight and social perception (compare Sarbin, 1954). But here again there are clear links with the 'material self' in studies of what has come to be known as 'social space', which is often investigated by means of simple and highly objective observations of the social effects of physical proximity (Argyle, 1975; Hall, 1968; Goffman, 1971, ch. 2). Less obviously concrete, but enormously influential, were the studies of the social self by James's associates Charles Cooley and George Mead, who conspicuously developed the Chicago School of sociology in the early years of this century. Their distinctive theories about the relation between self and society, which came to be known as 'social interactionism', were not without influence upon psychoanalysis, and they have been elaborated in recent decades by Erving Goffman. For an extensive exposition, see Hewitt (1984); and for an individualistic elaboration of some aspects of this approach, in the context of contemporary developmental psychology, see Shotter (1984).

Among the analysts themselves, Eric Erikson has clearly drawn to some extent upon their insights, while Donald Winnicott seems to be rediscovering 'social interactionism' for himself (and *malgré lui*) in parts of *Playing and Reality* (1971, ch. 9). By contrast, any such approach is conspicuously absent from the curiously isolated work of the Chicago-based analyst Heinz Kohut (1971), whose theories of 'primary narcissism' cast not so much as a glance in the direction of the Chicago School (cp. M. James, 1973).

These accounts of the development of self-feeling have typically emphasized the importance of interpersonal reflection, and of the way in which individuals come to perceive themselves very much through the mirror of interactions with others. Thus Cooley could sum up this orientation with the couplet 'each to each a looking-glass/reflects the other that doth pass' (1922, p. 184); and he might equally well have pointed to the fact that Henryk Ibsen, in the very last scene of *Peer Gynt*, had anticipated this view of where and how to find one's true self. For Ibsen has his hero return, from his world-wide wanderings in search of his true self, to confront the faithful Solveig who has been waiting for him. When he confesses that his quest has been unsuccessful, she gently chides him for having looked in the wrong places, and to his question 'Where was I myself, the entire, true man?' she answers 'In my faith, in my hope, and in my love' (1867, p. 421).

But, in practice, the quest for one's 'true' self or 'complete' self, seductive as it is for all of us (as it was for Peer Gynt himself), is arguably a misguided search for an unattainable idealized phantasy; a search energized by infantile anxieties, which are readily exploited by those who advertise do-it-yourself techniques for 'self-actualization' and for discovering one's true self. Certainly it will be important therapeutically to find out what a client's phantasy of his true self is; and certainly most of us do have from time to time what Maslow calls 'peak experiences', in which we catch a fleeting glimpse of a 'better', or more satisfying, self. But it is a far cry from that to allow the subcultural norms of an 'encounter group' to decide for us that our true self has at last emerged when we start to talk and react in a way that they approve. This is especially misleading, and potentially harmful, in the absence of a coherent theory of ego-integration, introjection of the group ego, transference and dependency-weaning, all of which are excluded from Carl Rogers' advocacy in *Encounter Groups* (1970; cp. Cheshire, 1973).

In a very different vein, Goffman can offer detailed analyses of the sorts of paraverbal cues which we regularly rely upon to determine what impression we are making upon other people (Goffman, 1955, especially pp. 31–33). These early ideas on what Cooley himself called the 'looking-glass self' have been instructively reviewed by McCall (1977) and commented on by Carveth (1984); and there exists today an experimental literature concerning not only how we learn about ourselves by attending to what characteristics other people see in us, but also how such self-discovery may derive from noticing our own reactions to particular events in the environment (Bem, 1972; Gergen, 1977, especially pp. 148–164). There has also been an extensive psychometric survey, based mainly on questionnaire methods, by Wylie (1974/1979); and a great deal of more recent work along these and other lines can be traced in Boyle and Bull (1984).

This ability to learn about ourselves from other people's reactions, however, is obviously vulnerable to distortion from two sources: a person may misinterpret the significance of the non-verbal signals which another person is giving out in response to him or her, or an agent may contaminate such an interaction from the start by himself giving out non-verbal signals which are inconsistent with the message or attitude which he wants to express. Both sorts of error will naturally lead to confusion, failure, anxiety and even withdrawal from social contact. They have become the characteristic focus of behavioural psychotherapy by means of social skills training (Trower *et al.*, 1978; but cp. Yardley, 1979), and we give a clinical example in Chapter 5 of the use of such methods in this context; but the problem is also encountered, of course, in the classic psychoanalytic dyad, and we illustrate this as well in that same chapter.

These interactive processes in general contribute toward self-differentiation and a stable self-feeling. From a psychoanalytic point of view they may be seen to fall into the context of internalization, externalization and object-constancy. A sense of unity, and of belonging inextricably to the external world, are combined in the healthy personality with a secure sense of self as differentiated from that external reality. Thus there is, so to speak, a sense of both participation and polarization, and along the continuum defined by this polarity we can locate a great part of psychopathology. It is to some of these disturbances of the sense of self that we now turn.

1.3 The Self-system and its Disturbances

A form which disturbances of the social self take especially frequently is that of a disorder of self-esteem. It would be enormously valuable if we could convert into usable and clinical therapeutic form James's own discussion of self-esteem and its vicissitudes. Indeed a great deal of therapeutic effort consists in practice in trying to devise some 'transformation rules', relevant to a particular patient's life-situation, for the law-like expression or 'equation' which James offers us. He is struck by the variety of strategies which people ordinarily use to meet challenges to their self-esteem, and writes (1890, p. 311):

'So we have the paradox of a man shamed to death because he is only the second pugilist or the second oarsman in the world. That he is able to beat the whole population of the globe minus one is nothing; he has "pitted" himself to beat that one; and as long as he doesn't do that nothing else counts. He is to his own regard as if he were not, indeed he *is* not. Yonder puny fellow, however, whom every one can beat, suffers no chagrin about it, for he has long abandoned the attempt to "carry that line", as the merchants say, of self at all. With no attempt there can be no failure; with no failure no humiliation. So our self-feeling in this world depends entirely on what we *back* ourselves to be and do. It is determined by the ratio of our actualities to our supposed potentialities; a fraction of which our pretensions are the denominator and the numerator our success: thus,

$$\text{Self-esteem} = \frac{\text{Success}}{\text{Pretensions}}$$

Such a fraction may be increased as well by diminishing the denominator as by increasing the numerator.'

It was a bold, if premature, gesture on James's part to try to summarize the relationship between people's self-esteem, success and aspirations in a simple three-term formula. We can indeed see immediate clinical applications of his last remark, that people often make the equation balance by giving up pretensions rather than by struggling to increase success, in David Malan's observation that untreated neurotics can produce spurious 'spontaneous recovery', and maintain symptom-freedom, by learning to *avoid* situations that produce anxiety for them rather than by overcoming such anxieties (1968). In the broader context of social psychology and personality theory there have been several important conceptual schemes which employ as a basic axiom some such notion of cognitive balance; among the best known are those of George Kelly (1955), Gregory Bateson (1956) and Leon Festinger (1957; 1964), but the impetus given by Fritz Heider in the 1940s was perhaps crucial (cp. Heider, 1958). It is this approach which Seymour Epstein and Paul McReynolds separately apply to problems of psychopathology and psychotherapy in this volume (see Chapters 2 and 8).

For our own part, in examining the alteration of anxiety in the process of treatment, we have been especially concerned with anxiety to do with humiliation, shame and disgrace (Thomae, 1981, *passim*; Mollon, 1984; Schwarzer, 1984). One important reason for dealing with this subject was the fact that nowadays more and more people with disorders of self-feeling are seeking psychotherapeutic treatment. The clinical relevance of this research subject, especially with regard to the technique of treatment, is therefore very great. Questions arise about the effectiveness of broadly different treatment methods, and about the techniques involved: both specifically in particular cases and conditions, and more generally with reference to overall strategies of therapy and their use in particular cases. Questions about the origin and removal of self-feeling disorders, and further questions about the answers given to these questions (which may be specific to particular schools of theory) are under theoretical scrutiny, and in a wider sense also under practical psychotherapeutic investigation (see Chapters 9 and 10).

It is presumably true also for this range of problems that what psychotherapists (or at least *successful* psychotherapists) of different schools actually *do* differs much less than what their textbooks on technique say they should or should not do; or, for that matter, than what they themselves claim to be doing (cp. Cheshire, 1982). For it emerges from outcome-studies of psychotherapy, such as are reviewed by Cheshire and Thomae (Chapter 5) and by Strupp

(Chapter 11), that effective therapists tend to be more alike in what they do, while less effective ones are more divisively doctrinaire.

Difficult as it may be to test the validity of theories in the therapeutic situation, at any rate therapy-comparisons made on the basis of verbatim records allow an insight into the verbal activity, and partly also into the thinking, of the therapist concerned. In our opinion, questions regarding the general and specific effectiveness of verbal treatment techniques can be answered, strictly speaking, only on the empirical basis of verbatim records; consequently we present throughout this volume several examples of the use of such data (cp. also Thomae, 1981, pp. 127–148).

Self-feeling disorders and ego-restrictions are the most general phenomena of psychological and psychosomatic illnesses. In some of them, such as depressive neuroses and psychoses, the experience of self-*dis*esteem is central; and this clinical phenomenon necessarily has a central place in the diverse theoretical accounts of depression, especially in Bibring's (1952) revision of Freud's classic statement (1917) and in Seligman's (1975) quite different experimentalist formulation or its revision by Abramson *et al.* (1978). Psychiatry and psychoanalysis have therefore always been faced with the task of bringing such changes in self-feeling, and ego-disturbances, into an explanatory scheme.

Neither in the field of psychopathology nor in the field of medicine in general can we imagine a subjectively perceptible development of symptoms that does not involve some impairment of self-feeling going along with it. We need to be able to deal with all those changes of self-feeling, self-concept and self-esteem that are severe in subjective experience, that persist for a long time without remitting 'spontaneously', and that could benefit from psychotherapeutic help because they are reversible in principle (cp. Axford and Jerrom, 1986). These qualifications bring all depressive disorders into the realm of psychopathology. In the centre of this range of cases stand the self-esteem disorders, for assessing which a number of psychometric techniques have been devised (Wells and Marwell, 1976; see also Chapter 2).

The depressive person has the feeling of being worthless and unable to do anything, and suffers from guilt-feelings which can take a delusional character. The affect includes despondency, inability to take any decisions, joylessness to the point of deep despair; in the physical area, lack of strength, lack of appetite to the point of refusing food, and insomnia. The state of despair can go so deep that suicide appears to be the only way out. In the case of less severe depression, the patient has, as a rule, the knowledge or hope that he would like to be or to become different; but he feels that he is unable to do so by himself, or with no more than such support as he has been receiving so far.

This tension, or cognitive dissonance, between 'wanting to be different' and 'feeling unable to be different' is characteristic of self-feeling disorders of this kind, and Paul McReynolds discusses a number of such examples in Chapter 8 of this volume. The conflict is epitomized in certain familiar terminological con-

trasts: the opposition or discrepancy between ideal self and real self becomes
for the psychoanalyst 'ideal ego *versus* real ego' (Thomae, 1980), and in the
technology of George Kelly's 'personal construct theory' it appears as
'myself-as-I-am *versus* myself-as-I-would-like-to-be' (Cheshire *et al.*, Chapter
7). It is to be found also in the so-called 'symptomatic neuroses', where we
encounter the well-known depletion of symptom-related self-feeling.

Symptom-related disorders of self-feeling include those which are circumscribed by, and related to, a particular situation, where they can be defined with
regard to time, by a perceptible beginning and by improvement after a change
in external circumstances. Examples of this would be impotence (with its
obvious effect on self-feeling), sudden headaches, and outbreaks of sweating,
blushing or stuttering.

From the foregoing discussion of different ways of conceptualizing the Self,
its development and its disorders, it seems that we need a rather general term
which emphasizes the functional and interactive properties of the Self without
prejudging the categorical nature of its components. We therefore introduce the
term 'self-system'. This we see as virtually synonymous with the term 'personality', in so far as that term is applicable to those psychological characteristics
and processes with which we are concerned. For present purposes, as we have
said, we are concentrating on dealing with psychopathological disturbances in
self-esteem, and on methods of alleviating them psychotherapeutically. Since
we have emphasized various sorts of *interaction* in trying to account for the
origin, development and amelioration of disturbances in self-esteem, it is appropriate to think in terms of a 'system'.

We envisage the self-system as a complex of psychic (part-)structures
involved in the regulation of affective, cognitive and behavioural functioning.
Since an essential characteristic of the self-system, as we know it in everyday
life, is by definition the capacity for self-reflection, this gives rise to apparently
awkward questions such as 'Who is the perceiver in self-perception?' or 'Who
does the controlling in self-control?' (cp. Secord, 1977; Mischel and Mischel,
1977; Harré, 1979, pp. 328–342). But if we see our self-system as a self-regulat-
ing system which deals with information, we can immediately invoke cybernetic
analogies to help us answer these questions.

For, in the context of systems-analysis, we certainly *can* ask realistically
which subsystem is controlling a certain output or which subroutine has been
activated to regulate a certain process, without either getting involved in the
infinite logical regresses which bothered Gilbert Ryle in the corresponding mental context (1949, Section (4) of ch. 9) or encountering David Hume's blank
wall to which we drew attention above. The contribution by von Zeppelin
(Chapter 6) indicates how cybernetic modelling can illuminate some of these
problems as they present themselves in the transactions of psychotherapy. At
this stage we simply want to point out that cybernetic models which have self-
feeling and the search for security 'at the helm' seem to be more comprehensive
and holistic than those that give that place to drives and their gratification.

Before such psychoanalysts as Sandler (1960), Argelander (1972) and Henseler (1974) introduced the search for security as 'helmsman' into the narcissistic regulatory system, McDougall had awarded this place to 'self-regard' (1919, ch. 7). But a theoretical problem had arisen, from the genetic point of view, as to how the early regulation of a drive determines the way in which self-feeling is controlled in later life. One solution has been to treat the quest for a stable identity as itself one of the primary drives, just as fundamental as survival and sexuality, and to construct a series of developmental stages, each with its attendant conflict to resolve (and corresponding risk of fixation if it were not resolved), by analogy with the established psychosexual stages of the Freud–Abraham theory. This is a thesis which Erikson, as is well known, has expounded in some detail (cp. 1963); but in a more general form it is central, of course, to many formulations of an existentialist character whether in general psychology or specifically in psychoanalysis (cp. Maslow, 1968; May, 1961; May *et al.*, 1969). Another answer has been to argue that genetic dependencies exist because drive-gratification involves the 'body-ego', whose importance in the development of a stable self-feeling is now widely recognized. Within the context of psychoanalysis, this line of reasoning has been expounded notably but controversially in recent years by Kohut (1971; cp. Thomae, 1980).

In depicting the structure of the self-system, we draw (as other contributors also do) both from the cognitive theories of general psychology and from that branch of psychoanalysis known as 'object-relations theory' which was developed out of Freudian theory principally by Melanie Klein and her followers. For present purposes, therefore, we follow Seymour Epstein and Paul McReynolds in designating the cognitive part-structure within an individual's self-system as his 'self-concept'; it was under this title that it was 'revisited' some years ago by Epstein (1973).

The self-concept encompasses all ideas and belief held by a person about himself, as well as those that relate to his interaction with the environment. From this it follows that it will be made up of self-representations on the one hand, and object-representations on the other. At the risk of explaining *obscurum per obscurius*, we may say that by 'representation' we mean part-models which the individual makes of himself (in the case of self-representations) and of his environment (in the case of object-representations). The various different ways in which these are connected and interrelated give them their own specific character, and it is these deployments and interactions which object-relations theorists try to capture in their precarious and philosophically problematic spatial metaphors. But when it comes to illuminating specific clinical phenomena that present themselves in psychotherapy, the sceptic may have to admit that these topographic and evaluative idioms (incorporation, projection, splitting, good object, persecutory object) do seem to have some significant uses. We discuss this further in Chapter 4.

Another major component of the self-system is, of course, its emotional aspect, which we call 'self-feeling'. For the moment we would just remark that inconsistencies and incompatibilities within the self-concept can bring about a decrease in self-feeling; and this point is elaborated, with reference to cognitive formulations of psychopathology and psychotherapy, by both McReynolds (Chapter 8) and Epstein (Chapter 2).

The extent to which the self-feeling is disturbed is a function of the relationships that obtain between incongruous representations. When, in terms of distance and evaluation, such incongruous representations are as it were both close and highly valued, then a severe and persistent detriment to self-feeling will result. The incongruity can be resolved, evidently, either by increasing the distance between the items involved or by reducing the evaluation of one of them. Such techniques for conflict-resolution have been described in a general way for a long time now within cognitive dissonance theory, and McReynolds discusses how they can be applied to psychotherapy. We also have quite a sophisticated psychometric technology, derived from personal construct theory, for locating such conflicts and monitoring their resolution (Bannister and Mair, 1968; Fransella and Bannister, 1977; Bannister, 1983).

The search for consistency within the self-concept may be seen as the basic principle of the self-system. We have seen above that there is a long line of cognitive theorists within general psychology who have propounded this sort of thesis; and it is one purpose of this volume to show how such theories and studies can enrich psychoanalysis, and how they can in turn be enriched by psychoanalytic insights and observations, as opposed to being construed as being at odds with each other. This search for consistency is also the search for a world free from inconsistencies, and this goal will never in practice be attained. The nearest we come to attaining it is perhaps in the limited sense of discovering a part-world consisting of a small number of well-known elements, characteristics and regulatory principles. The attractiveness of religious ceremonial and of games may perhaps derive, in their different ways, from the fact that they provide such part-worlds.

As these two examples indicate, however, we do not just *discover* our worlds; we *construct* them. To some extent, we all construct different phenomenal worlds, according to the different cognitive apparatus we have developed for construing our experience. One way in which we can reduce the risk of experiencing inconsistency or incongruity is to generate a construct system that is characterized either by 'looseness' (so that we do not expect any particular regularities in our experience), or by what is technically known as 'permeability' (such that almost any phenomenon can be subsumed under almost any construct). For example, if you want to avoid being bothered by the fact that the colour of my shirt clashes with that of my socks, you may either give up thinking in terms of one colour 'going with' another (that is, increase the 'looseness' of your construct system), or you may give up construing for hue and attend only to differences in lightness/darkness (that is, introduce more 'permeability').

There is now some experimental evidence that this is precisely what thought-disordered schizophrenics tend to have done; and that normal subjects will do the same kind of thing to protect themselves against the incongruity which arises from being given inconsistent feedback about their success on a cognitive task (Bannister, 1965; Bannister and Fransella, 1965; Lawlor and Cochran, 1981). What psychodynamics can add to this, in principle, is presumably hypotheses about why certain incongruities rather than others are most threatening; and why certain phantasies or defences, rather than others, are used to combat them.

We want to look in more detail, finallly, at a special case of inconsistency within the self-system. Here we suppose that there are a number of representations that make up the aspired ideal state of the self-system. That number, the configuration of these ideal-self representations we call the 'ideal self'; that complex of self-perceptions and self-functions that make up the actual state of the self-system, on the other hand, is called the 'real self'. We call the agreement between real self and ideal self on a *cognitive* level '*self-acceptance*'; *emotionally* it is experienced as an increase or decrease in *self-esteem*. If, following William James, this discrepancy is expressed in terms of a relationship between real-self and ideal-self, then the quantity of self-esteem is directly proportional to this quotient.

Any such lack of conformity between the real-self and the ideal-self becomes more important for the experiencing of self-esteem the more the relationship between the self-representations concerned is affected by evaluation. Now we can explain what seems at first paradoxical, taking up James's illustration. A man can be terribly ashamed because he is only the second best boxer or oarsman in the world. The fact that he is capable against the entire world population minus one is nothing to him, because of his extreme emphasis on the positive evaluation of that discrepancy. But another fellow who is easily defeated does not give a hoot, because for him the relation between the two self-representations involved is projected somewhere near the negative end of the evaluative dimension, either as a consequence of early personality development or by way of defence.

Slight inconsistencies within the self-system may lead to fruitful tensions, however, which will give rise to an expansion of the horizon of experiencing. This will contribute to an enrichment of personality and of the way in which it relates to the environment. The mechanisms involved in this sort of psychological enhancement, which is widely known as 'self-actualization', are by no means clear, but have been discussed extensively by Carl Rogers (1951) and Abraham Maslow (1968), for example.

Although we are not able to do more than merely touch on developmental factors in the formation of self-concept, we work on the general assumption that the self-concept is formed through the constant interactions with the caretaker (mother). At the same time, a concept of the environment is also formed.

These two concepts are further differentiated and generalized again through interactions and the way in which they are structured. In psychotherapy, as a consequence, when dealing with disturbances in self-concept, one has to decide on the extent to which interactions which stabilize the self-feeling and reduce inconsistencies are necessary to maintain or restore the consistency within the self-concept: that is, the extent to which sympathy, friendliness, acceptance and the like are necessary for self-'contentment', identity, security, etc.

A further essential constituent of the self-concept, whose developmental aspect we have encountered above, but which also plays a major part in some of the commonest psychopathologies as we saw there, is what Bandura has called 'self-efficacy'. We have seen that this refers to the way in which a person's actions affect the environment more or less systematically, thereby exercizing some degree of control over it and making predictable changes. So long as these environmental changes which are actively effected are in the individual's interest, this fundamental capacity or 'personal power' contributes to the stabilization and satisfaction of self-feeling. But some pathological conditions, most obviously the depressive disturbances, are characterized by an experienced loss of this capacity to be in effective control, to be a reinforcer for others and to be able to help oneself out of difficulty.

Depressive patients feel as if this self-determining capacity for significant action has been lost or diminished, and they typically experience what they do as being pointless. It is as if the possibility of controlling the course of events and of influencing people had escaped them. They have come to feel that their actions do not make any difference to their lot, and thus they demonstrate what Seligman (1975) has called 'learned helplessness', and what is known to psychodynamics as 'oral pessimism' (Kline and Storey, 1977).

The nature and origins of the self-concept disturbance which is a regular feature of reactive depression will be a recurrent subject of discussion to the chapters which follow. For the moment we would merely draw attention to Mollon and Parry's observation (1984, p. 137), in the context of examining the 'protective function of depression' for the 'fragile self', that:

> 'A simple unitary concept of lowered self-esteem or negative self-evaluation ... is not adequate to describe the radical alteration in the experience of the self which emerges in depression. Instead, a central characteristic of depression is what might be described as a collapse in the experience of the self and an uncertainty concerning its place in the world. Thus, rather than place the emphasis on self-evaluation, ... the prime disturbance is seen as relating to the *sense of self.*'

Other relevant aspects of this neurotically 'fragile' self have been described by Nekanda-Trepka (1983), Mollon (1984, 1986) and Schwarzer (1984).

At the other psychopathological extreme are the hypomanics, for example, who in a similarly unrealistic way presume that everything they do will automatically turn out well and make the world a happier place. Patients with this kind of disturbance often do not suffer at all themselves under these conditions; they do, however, make the world around them suffer a great deal, and they blame their environment for what may well be a bitter end.

References

Abramson, L. Y., Seligman, M. E. P. and Teasdale, J. D. (1978). Learned helplessness in humans: . . . *J. Abnorm. Psychol.*, **87**, 49–74.

Argelander, H. (1972) *Gruppenprozesse:* . . . Rowohlt, Hamburg.

Argyle, M. (1975). *Bodily Communication*. Methuen, London.

Axford, S. and Jerrom, D. W. A. (1986). Self-esteem in depression: . . . *Brit. J. Med. Psychol.* **59**, 61–68.

Ayer, A. J. (1926). *Language, Truth and Logic*. Reprinted text with new introduction, Penguin Books, Harmondsworth, 1946.

Bandura, A. (1982). Self-efficacy mechanisms in human agency. *Am. Psychol.* **37**, 122–147.

Bannister, D. (1965). The genesis of schizophrenic thought-disorder: . . . *Brit. J. Psychiatr.*, **111**, 377.

Bannister, D. (1983). Self in personal construct theory. In *Applications of Personal Construct Theory* (ed. J. Adams-Webber and J. Mancuso). Academic Press, Toronto.

Bannister, D. and Fransella, F. (1965). A repertory grid test of schizophrenic thought-disorder. *Brit. J. Soc. Clin. Psychol.*, **2**, 95–102.

Bannister, D. and Mair, J. M. (1968). *The Evaluation of Personal Constructs*. Academic Press, London and New York.

Bateson, G. *et al.* (1956). Towards a theory of schizophrenia. Reprinted in Bateson, G. (1973). *Steps to an Ecology of Mind*, pp. 173–198. Paladin, London.

Beardsworth, T. (1977). *A Sense of Presence;* . . . Religious Experience Research Unit, Oxford.

Bem, D. J. (1972). Self-perception theory. In *Advances in Experimental Social Psychology*, Vol. 6 (ed. L. Berkowitz). Academic Press, New York.

Berger, P. L. and Luckman, T. (1967). *The Social Structure of Reality*. Allen Lane, London.

Bibring, E. (1952). The mechanism of depression. In *Affective Disorders* (ed. P. Greenacre, 1953), pp. 13–48. International Universities Press, New York.

Boyle, M. and Bull, R. (eds) (1984). 'Abstracts' (Welsh BPS Conference on Self and Identity). *Bull. Brit. Psychol. Soc.*, **37**, A102–A128.

Breuer, J. and Freud, S. (1895). *Studies on Hysteria. Standard Ed. 2.*

Burns, R. B. (1979). *The Self Concept*. Longman, London and New York.

Burns, R. B. (1982). *Self-concept: Development and Education*. Holt, Rinehart and Winston, London.

Carveth, D. L. (1984). Psychoanalysis and social theory: . . . *Psychoanal. Contemp. Thought*, **7**, 43–98.

Castelnuovo-Tedesco, P. (1981). Physical defects. *Int. J. Psychoanal.*, **8**, 145–154.

Cheshire, N. M. (1973). Review of P. Kline, *Fact and Fantasy in Freudian Theory*. *Brit. J. Educ. Psychol.*, **43**, 97–98.

Cheshire, N. M. (1982). Doubtful it stood: . . . *Cambridge Quart.* **11**, 346–352.

Chomsky, N. (1957). *Syntactic Structures*. Mouton, The Hague.

40 *Self, Symptoms and Psychotherapy*

Chomsky, N. (1965). *Aspects of the Theory of Syntax.* MIT Press, Cambridge (Mass.).
Cooley, C. H. (1922). *Human Nature and the Social Order,* revised edition. Reprinted Schocken, New York, 1964.
Cooper, D. (1978). *The Language of Madness.* Penguin, Harmondsworth.
Dennett, D. C. (1981). Where am I? In *Brainstorms:* ..., ch. 17. Harvester, Brighton.
Epstein, S. (1973). The self-concept revisited, or a theory of a theory. *Am. Psychol.,* **28**, 404–416.
Erickson, E. H. (1963). *Childhood and Society,* second edition. Penguin, Harmondsworth.
Feldman, M. M. (1975). The body-image and object-relations: ... *Brit. J. Med. Psychol.,* **48**, 317–332.
Festinger, L. J. (1957). *A Theory of Cognitive Dissonance.* Stanford University Press, Stanford (Calif.).
Festinger, L. J. (1964) *Conflict, Decision and Dissonance.* Stanford University Press, Stanford (Calif.).
Fliess, (1961) *The Body Ego.*
Fransella, F. and Bannister, D. (1977). *Manual for Repertory Grid Techniques.* Academic Press, London and New York.
Freeman, T. (1969). *Psychopathology of the Psychoses.* Tavistock, London.
Freud, S. (1917) *Mourning and melancholia. Standard Ed.,* **14**, 237–258.
Freud, S. (1923). The Ego and the Id. *Standard Ed.,* **19**, (1961), 1–66.
Gauld, A. and Shotter, J. (1977). *Human Action and its Psychological Investigation.* Routledge and Kegan Paul, London.
Geach, P. T. (1957). *Mental Acts.* Routledge and Kegan Paul, London.
Gergen, K. J. (1977). The social construction of self-knowledge. In *The Self* (ed. T. Mischel), pp. 139–169. Blackwell, Oxford.
Goffman E. (1955). On face-work. Reprinted in *Interaction Ritual,* pp. 5–45, Penguin, Harmondsworth, 1972.
Goffman, E. (1959). *Presentation of Self in Everyday Life.* Penguin, Harmondsworth.
Goffman, E. (1971). *Relations in Public.* Penguin, Harmondsworth.
Goody, J. and Watt, I. (1972). The consequences of literacy. In *Language and Social Context* (ed. P. Giglioli), pp. 311–357. Penguin, Harmondsworth.
Greenacre, P. (1958). Early physical determinants in the development of the sense of identity. *J. Am. Psychoanal. Assoc.,* **6**, 612–617.
Hall, E. T. (1968). Proxemics. Reprinted in *Nonverbal Communication* (ed. S. Weitz), second edition pp. 293–312, Oxford University Press, New York, 1979.
Hamachek, D. E. (1987). *Encounters with the Self,* third edition. Holt, Rinehart and Winston, New York etc.
Hamlyn, D. W. (1977) Self-knowledge. In *The Self* (ed. T. Mischel), pp. 170–200. Blackwell, Oxford.
Harré, R. (1979). *Social Being.* Blackwell, Oxford.
Heider, F. (1958). *The Psychology of Interpersonal Relations.* Wiley, New York.
Henseler, H. (1974). *Narzisstische Krisen. Zur Psychodynamik des Selbstmords.* Rowohlt, Reinbek bei Hamburg.
Hewitt, J. P. (1984). *Self and Society:* ..., third edition. Allyn and Bacon, Newton (Mass.).
Honess, T. (1982). Accounting for oneself: meaning of self-descriptions, and inconsistencies in self-descriptions. *Brit. J. Med. Psychol.,* **44**, 41–52.
Hume, D. (1739). *A Treatise of Human Nature,* (ed. L. A. Selby-Biggs, and revised P. H. Nidditch, 1978). Oxford University Press, Oxford.
Ibsen, H. (1867). *Peer Gynt.* In *The Oxford Ibsen* (ed. J. W. McFarlane), vol. III (1972), pp. 351–421. Oxford University Press, London.

Jackson, J. Hughlings (1884). *The Croonian Lectures on ... the Nervous System.* London.

James, M. (1973). Review of H. Kohut, *The Analysis of the Self. Int. J. Psychoanal.,* **54**, 363–368.

James, W. (1890), *Principles of Psychology,* 2 vols. Holt, New York.

James, W. (1902). *Varieties of Religious Experience.* Longmans, New York.

Kant, I. (1787). *Critique of Pure Reason,* second edition (translated by J. M. D. Meiklejohn, 1934). Dent, London.

Kelly, G. A. (1955). *The Psychology of Personal Constructs,* 2 vols. Norton, New York.

Klein, G. S. (1976). *Psychoanalytic Theory: An Exploration of Essentials.* International University Press, New York.

Kline, P. and Storey, R. (1977). A factor-analytic study of the oral character. *Brit. J. Soc. Clin. Psychol.,* **16**, 317–328.

Kohut, H. (1971). *The Analysis of the Self.* International Universities Press, New York.

Laing, R. D. (1965). *The Divided Delf,* second edition. Penguin, Harmondsworth.

Laing, R. D. (1969). *The Self and Others,* second edition. Penguin, Harmondsworth.

Lawlor, M. and Cochran, L. (1981). Does invalidation produce loose construing? *Brit. J. Med. Psychol.,* **54**, 41–50.

Mahler, M. S. (1963). Thoughts about development and individuation. *Psychoanal. Study Child,* **18**, 307–324.

Malan, D. *et al.* (1968). A study of psychodynamic changes in untreated neurotic patients. *Brit. J. Psychiatr.,* **114**, 525–551.

Maslow, A. B. (1968). *Towards a Psychology of Being,* second edition. Van Nostrand, New York.

May, R. (ed.) (1961). *Existential Psychology.* Random House, New York.

May, R., Binswanger, L. and Ellenberger, H. F. (1969). Existential psychotherapy and *Dasein* analysis. In *Psychotherapy and Counselling* (ed. W. S. Sahakian), ch. 10. Rand McNally, Chicago.

McCall, G. J. (1977). The social looking-glass:... In *The Self.* (ed. T. Mischel), pp. 274–287. Blackwell, Oxford.

McDougall, W. (1919). *An Introduction to Social Psychology,* fourteenth edition. Methuen, London.

McGinn, C. (1982). *The Character of Mind.* Oxford University Press, Oxford and New York.

McMurray, J. (1957). *The Self as Agent.* Faber and Faber, London.

Miles, T. R. (1959). *Religion and the Scientific Outlook.* Allen and Unwin, London.

Miles, T. R. (1971). *Religious Experience.* Routledge and Kegan Paul, London.

Mischel, T. (ed.) (1977). *The Self.* Blackwell, Oxford.

Mischel, W. and Mischel, H. N. (1977). Self-control and the self. In *The Self* (ed. T. Mischel), pp. 31–64. Blackwell, Oxford.

Mollon, P. (1984). 'Shame in relation to narcissistic disturbance. *Brit. J. Med. Psychol.,* **57**, 207–214.

Mollon, P. (1986). Narcissistic vulnerability and the fragile self: ... *Brit. J. Med. Psychol.* **59**, 317–324.

Mollon, P. and Parry, G. (1984). The fragile self: narcissistic disturbance and the protective function of depression. *Brit. J. Med. Psychol.,* **57**, 137–145.

Nekanda-Trepka, C. J. S. (1983). Perfection and the threat to self-esteem ... In *The Self in Anxiety, ...* (ed. Schwarzer, 1984), pp. 125–132. North-Holland, Amsterdam.

Newson, J. (1979). The growth of shared understandings ... In *Before Speech* (ed. M. Bullowa), pp. 207–222. Cambridge University Press, Cambridge.

Newson, J. (1974). Towards a theory of infant understanding. *Bull. Brit. Psychol. Soc.,* **27**, 251–257.

Orgler, H. (1963). *Alfred Adler:* ... third edition. Sidgwick and Jackson, London.
Piaget, J. and Inhelder, B. (1966). *The Psychology of the Child* (translated by H. Weaver, 1969). Routledge and Kegan Paul, London.
Rogers, C. R. (1951). *Client-centered Therapy:* .... Houghton-Mifflin, Boston.
Rogers, C. R. (1970). *Encounter Groups.* Allen Lane/Penguin, London/Harmondsworth.
Rosenberg, M. (1979). *Conceiving the Self.* Harper and Row, New York.
Ryle, G. (1949). *The Concept of Mind* Penguin, Harmondsworth.
Sandler, J. (1960) The background of safety. *Int. J. Psychoanal.,* **41**, 352–356.
Sarbin, T. R. (1954). Role theory. In *Handbook of Social Psychology* (i) (ed. G. Lindzey). Addison-Wesley, Cambridge (Mass.).
Schilder, P. F. (1950). *The Image and Appearance of the Human Body.* International University Press, New York.
Schilder, P. F. (1951). *Brain and Personality.* International Universities Press, New York.
Schwarzer, R. (1984). *The Self in Anxiety, Stress and Depression.* North-Holland, Amsterdam.
Secord, P. F. (1977). Making oneself behave: ... In *The Self* (ed. T. Mischel), pp. 250–273. Blackwell, Oxford.
Seligman, M. E. P. (1975). *Helplessness:* ... Freeman, San Francisco.
Shotter, J. (1974). The development of personal powers. In *The Integration of a Child into a Social World* (ed. M. P. M. Richards), pp. 215–244. Cambridge University Press, Cambridge.
Shotter, J. (1984). *Social Accountability and Selfhood.* Blackwell, Oxford.
Shotter, J. and Newson, J. (1982) An ecological approach to cognitive development: ... In *Social Cognition* (eds. G. Butterworth and P. Light), ch. 3. Harvester, Brighton.
Spiegel, L. A. (1959). The self, the sense of self, and perception. *Psychoanal. Study Child,* **14**, 81–109.
Spiegel, L. A. (1961). Selbst, Selbstgefühl and Wahrnehmung. *Psyche,* **15**, 211–236.
Stern, D. N. (1985). *The Interpersonal World of the Infant:* ... Basic Books, New York.
Stoppard, T. (1978). *Professional Foul,* Faber and Faber, London and Boston.
Strachey, J. (1961). Editor's introduction to S. Freud, *The Ego and the Id. Standard Ed.,* **19**, 3–11.
Thomae, H. (1980). Auf dem Weg zum Selbst. *Psyche,* **34**, 221–245.
Thomae, H. (1981). *Schriften zur Praxis der Psychoanalyse: Vom spiegelnden zum aktiven Analytiker.* Suhrkamp, Frankfurt.
Toulmin, S. (1977). Self-knowledge .... In *The Self* (ed. T. Mischel) pp. 291–317. Blackwell, Oxford.
Trevarthen, C. (1982) 'The primary motives for cooperative understanding. In *Social Cognition* (eds. G. Butterworth and P. Light), ch. 5. Harvester, Brighton.
Trower, P., Bryant, B. and Argyle, M. (1978). *Social Skills and Mental Health.* Methuen, London.
Turner, R. H. (1977). Foreword to L. A. Zurcher, *The Mutable Self,* pp. 9–11. Sage, Beverley Hills and London.
Wells, L. E. and Marwell, G. (1976). *Self-esteem: Its Conceptualisation and Measurement.* Sage, Beverley Hills and London.
Winnicott, D. W. (1971). *Playing and Reality,* revised edition; Penguin, Harmondsworth (1974).
Wylie R. C. (1968). The present status of self-theory. In *Handbook of Personality Research and Theory* (eds. E. F. Borgatta and W. F. Lambert). Rand McNally, Chicago.
Wylie, R. C. (1974, 1979). *The Self Concept;* two vols., revised edition. University of Nebraska Press, Lincoln (Nebraska) and London.
Yardley, K. M. (1979). 'Social skills training: ...'. *Brit. J. Med. Psychol.* **52**, 55–62.

Self, Symptoms and Psychotherapy
Edited by N. Cheshire and H. Thomae
© 1987 John Wiley & Sons Ltd

CHAPTER 2

Implications of Cognitive Self-theory for Psychopathology and Psychotherapy

Seymour Epstein

2.1   The Repetition-compulsion

An important turning-point in the development of psychoanalytic theory occurred when Freud became aware that not all dreams could be attributed to unconscious wishes. He observed that a major symptom of soldiers who suffered from traumatic neurosis in World War I was repetitive dreams that were so frightening that the soldiers were often afraid to go to sleep. The dreams could not be explained by wish-fulfilment because they simply repeated the traumatic incident. Freud (1920) concluded that there was a principle more fundamental than the pleasure principle, which he named the 'repetition-compulsion'. He revised his general theory of personality by introducing the life and death instincts as the primary human motives. Freud then explained the repetitive dreams in the traumatic neurosis, as well as other forms of repetitive behaviour, including transference relationships in psychotherapy, by attributing them to the repetition-compulsion under the influence of the death instinct. This is hardly a satisfactory explanation, for it accomplishes little more than to attach a label to a phenomenon.

Few of Freud's followers accepted his theory of life and death instincts. There remains the problem of providing an adequate explanation of why repetition of distressing experiences occurs in dreams, in experiences in every-day life, and in transference relationships. The beginning of a solution lies in the further development of one of Freud's own observations. He noted (Freud, 1920, p. 28) that traumatic dreams 'are endeavouring to master the stimulus retrospectively, by developing the anxiety whose omission was the cause of the traumatic neurosis. They thus afford us a view of a function of the mental apparatus which, though it does not contradict the pleasure principle, is nevertheless independent of it and seems to be more primitive than the purpose of gaining pleasure and avoiding unpleasure.' Had he extended this idea further, it would have led him to the realization that the principle he sought was not the death instinct or the repetition compulsion, but the need to maintain the integrity of a conceptual system, or theory of reality, which is necessary for organizing experience and anticipating events. This principle has widespread implications for both normal and abnormal behaviour, and for psychotherapy.

In order to exist in a complex social world, it is necessary for human beings to have a theory of reality that includes subdivisions of a self-theory and a world-theory. Elsewhere (Epstein, 1973, 1976, 1979, 1980) I have presented a theory of personality, cognitive self-theory, that is based on this assumption. For present purposes, a brief summary will suffice. An individual's theory of reality is not a conscious theory that an individual can describe if asked to do so. It is a subconscious, or implicit, theory that the individual has unwittingly constructed during the course of a lifetime. Like any theory, it consists of a hierarchical arrangement of higher and lower order postulates. Some of the postulates are descriptive postulates, which are generalizations about the self and the world. Others are motivational postulates, which are generalizations about what one must do to achieve happiness and avoid pain. An example of a descriptive postulate is, 'Authority-figures are cruel and unjust.' An example of a motivational postulate is, 'You can avoid being injured by authority-figures by pleasing them.' Many of an individual's basic postulates consist of broad generalizations inductively derived from emotionally significant experiences. Thus, postulates such as the above could readily be derived from experiences with authoritarian father-figures. Postulates that are formed early in the development of a personal theory of reality play an important role in the further development of the theory, as all new experiences must be assimilated into the conceptual system that already exists. It is for this reason that experiences in childhood are particularly important.

A person's theory of reality, in effect, constitutes the person's personality. If a person thought differently about what he and the world were like and about what he must do to get by in the world, he would be a different person. He would perceive differently, feel differently, and behave differently. Thus, a person's identity depends upon preserving his theory of reality. It is no wonder, then, that a person will do all in his power to preserve his conceptual system, for the disorganization of the conceptual system is equivalent to the destruction of the personality. It is for this reason that psychotic disorganization is frequently symbolically represented in dreams by death.

A personal theory of reality does not develop as an intellectual exercise. It is a conceptual tool that fulfils certain basic functions, which are to maintain a favourable pleasure/pain balance, to maintain a favourable level of self-esteem, and to assimilate the data of reality. As these three functions can conflict with each other, behaviour is often a compromise among them. One of the principles may be sacrificed for another, as in the case of a delusion of grandeur, where assimilation of reality is sacrificed in order to maintain self-esteem.

Although there is a basic striving for unity, or coherence, in the self-system, it is never completely successful. Conflicts arise between different organizations within the self-system, and between the self-system and reality. Unity within the remainder of the system is sometimes achieved by dissociating those elements that cannot be assimilated into the main body of the system. When significant dissociations cannot be maintained, or the overall conceptual system is otherwise unable to fulfil its function, the system is placed under stress, which is experienced as anxiety. If the stress can not be defended against, the entire conceptual system is subject to collapse (Epstein, 1973, 1979; Goldstein, 1939; Rogers, 1959).

The theory proposed above has a long history. The view that people need personal theories of reality to organize their lives, much as a scientist needs a theory to organize his scientific pursuits, was introduced by Lecky many years ago (1945) and reiterated by Kelly (1955). The assumption that people have a basic need to maintain the stability and unity of their self-concepts has been emphasized by phenomenological psychologists such as Lecky (1945), Snygg and Combs (1949), and Rogers (1942, 1951, 1959), all of whom consider it to be the one most basic need of the organism. Earlier, Goldstein (1939) had proposed that humans have a basic need to comprehend and organize the data of their experience, and that when they can not accomplish this they experience anxiety. Goldstein noted that the brain-injured soldiers he studied attempted to reduce their anxiety by simplifying and restricting their environment. If they failed in this attempt, they were subjected to the 'catastrophic reaction', which involves helpless confusion combined with intense anxiety. Rogers (1951, 1959) and May (1950) have similar views on anxiety and disorganization. Social psychologists such as Festinger (1957), Brehm and Cohen (1962), Rokeach (1973), and Heider (1958) have presented theories and/or evidence in support of the view that individuals have a need to resolve cognitive dissonance or to establish cognitive congruity or balance in their conceptual systems.

Allport's (1937) concept of functional autonomy of motives assumes that there are self-maintaining integrative states that contribute to the coherence and stability of the personality. Despite considerable overlap with the above views, the theory I have proposed cannot be reduced to any of the other theories. Thus, Kelly's theory of personal constructs assumes that people function as scientists with the only aim of anticipating events. Kelly denies the importance of motives, and accords relatively little significance to emotions. His model of man is a robot with no heart and a computer in its head. Lecky and the other phenomenologists emphasize that the individual has but a single need, which is to maintain the unity of the self-concept. They ignore or attack the Freudian concept of a dynamic unconscious. Lecky explicitly states that the psychoanalytic view of unconscious conflict is incompatible with his own theory. All phenomenologists emphasize an individual's conscious constructs of the world, and de-emphasize unconscious processes. The social psychologists emphasize the need to maintain coherence at a conscious level between specific beliefs or values. None considers unconscious conflicts, or an overall integrative system that is analogous to a theory in science.

The theory that I have proposed is highly compatible with psychoanalytic theory as well as with many aspects of phenomenological theory. Unlike Kelly's theory of personal constructs, it accords a central role to emotion and motivation. Unlike the phenomenological theories, it recognizes three major sources of motivation, namely the motive to maintain a coherent conceptual system, the motive to maximize pleasure and minimize pain, and the motive to maintain positive self-esteem. Behaviour is viewed as a compromise among these three motives. Unlike the other theories, it emphasizes not merely a general conceptual system, but a unified personal theory of reality that includes a self-theory and a world-theory. By viewing a personal theory of reality as analogous to a scientific theory, it is able, in a scientifically respectable manner, to explain certain aspects of human behaviour that were previously viewed as embarrassments when proposed by phenomenological psychologists, such as the concept of a growth principle and of an executive self. The theory differs from traditional psychoanalytic theory in its greater emphasis on cognitive processes, on preconscious processing of information, and on an overall integrative system that has its own unique features and motivational properties. It has more in common with psychoanalytic ego-psychology and object-relations theory than with orthodox psychoanalytic theory.

With the above outline as a background, we are now in a position to examine the implications of the proposed theory for various forms of psychopathology.

2.2 Traumatic Neurosis

How can the frightening, repetitive dreams in the traumatic neurosis be explained without resorting to Freud's concept of a death instinct? The repetitive dreams can be viewed as an indication that the individual has had an experience that he can neither assimilate nor forget. The experience can not be assimilated because it is at variance with fundamental beliefs in an individual's conceptual system. It can not be forgotten because of the emotional intensity of the experience. As the memory of the experience can only be laid to rest by being assimilated, it keeps repeating itself. Ultimately the experience will either be assimilated or dissociated, in which case the memory will remain as a time-bomb awaiting some relevant event to trigger it. If it is assimilated, the person will recover, or will undergo a lasting neurotic change, depending on the nature of the assimilation. Let us examine the latter two possibilities.

To behave normally requires belief in a basic postulate that the world is a reasonably safe place in which to live, and that one's efforts make a difference. Most people believe, at a deep emotional level, that they are relatively invulnerable and that they are masters of their fate. This belief, false as it may be, allows them to feel secure and enjoy life. It is noteworthy, in this respect, that Horney (1945) describes the basic condition for neurosis as the establishment of exactly the opposite belief, namely that one is a helpless person in a hostile world. Horney did not have the traumatic neurosis in mind when she came to this conclusion, but was describing the conditions in childhood that foster the kind of insecurity that predisposes an individual to develop a neurosis in adulthood. Warfare is one of the few conditions in adult life that can reduce an adult to the status of a terrified child, thereby fostering the belief in an adult that he or she is a helpless person in a hostile world. The traumatic neurosis pits this new belief against the previous one in which the world was viewed as reasonably controllable and safe. If the old belief remains dominant it will nevertheless be modified by the traumatic experience, and the world will never again be perceived as entirely safe. The individual will become a sadder, but wiser, person, who knows there are some circumstances in life in which one is relatively safe and master of one's fate, and others in which one is not. If the new belief becomes dominant, the individual will become permanently anxious, and therefore neurotic.

2.3 The Demonic Fate Theme

A second kind of behaviour that Freud believed could not be explained by the pleasure-principle was the demonic fate theme, which has intrigued people ever since the ancient Greeks drew attention to it. Some people appear to be cursed by a relentless fate that causes them to experience the same unfortunate situation time and again, no matter what steps they take to prevent it. In his earlier theory, Freud explained such experiences by assuming they were instigated by the unconscious motives of the victim. In his later theory, he attributed the behaviour to the repetition-compulsion and the death instinct. Given the assumption that people need to maintain their theories of reality, a different explanation is suggested. Namely, people are motivated to validate their belief-systems, and they will go to great lengths, even destroying them- selves in the process, if necessary, to do so. The basic postulates in a person's theory of reality are derived largely from significant emotional experiences. Thus, people who have had an extremely unpleasant experience or series of experiences that has been incorporated as a basic postulate into their theory of reality must maintain the validity of that postulate in order to preserve the stability of their theory of reality. The earlier in life the unfortunate experience occurred, the more basic is the postulate derived from it, as early postulates influence the course of development of later postulates. Thus, a woman whose father was untrustworthy and beat her, and who, as a result, formed the view that men, in general, are untrustworthy and punishing might unconsciously seek out just such men in order to validate her belief-system. In the company of men who are trustworthy and kindly, she would tend to become anxious and disorganized, as such experiences would threaten her theory of reality. This is a further example of how basic beliefs in a theory of reality become self-fulfilling prophesies, and that even an unpleasant, but predictable, world is preferable to a chaotic one. It follows that there are some people who can only feel secure when they are miserable.

2.4 Transference

Freud observed that negative transference relationships in psychotherapy, like the demonic fate theme, involve a repetition of the past. He considered both phenomena to be examples of the operation of the repetition-compulsion and the death instinct. In what other way can one account for negative transference? Why should a patient try to influence a therapist to behave in the same negative way as a parent once behaved? The answer is the same as the one given to account for the demonic fate theme. Namely, the individual has a need to validate his theory of reality. Relationships with parent-figures are highly emotionally significant to a child. As a result, generalizations from such experiences become basic postulates in the child's theory of reality. The earlier the generalization is formed, the less differentiated it is apt to be, and the greater is its opportunity to influence the further development of an individual's theory of reality. Thus, based on early experiences with a deceitful father, an individual could develop a highly general belief that male authority-figures are not to be trusted. When the therapist behaves in a way that challenges this belief, the patient is highly threatened, because to give up the belief would disrupt the patient's theory of reality. Although the theory of reality is maladaptive from an external viewpoint, and is a source of misery and poor interpersonal relationships for the patient, it is at least a way of organizing the data of experience. The patient cannot give up the theory of reality because it is the only theory he or she has, and it is needed in order for the person to function. It is thus not surprising that the patient will do all in his or her power to provoke the therapist as well as any other male authority-figure to behave in exactly the way the patient believes, and fears, he will behave. It is because the generalization which gives rise to the negative transference reaction occupies such a central position in the patient's theory of reality that changing it in psychotherapy can have profound effects. We shall return to the issue of transference when we discuss the maintenance of self-esteem.

2.5 Fear of Success

Psychologists have recently become aware that many people fear success almost as much as they fear failure. Originally it was thought that this phenomenon was characteristic only of women. More recent research has indicated that the fear of success is equally prevalent in men (Canavan-Gumpert, *et al.*, 1978). Many people, of both sexes, unconsciously set up hurdles to their own progress. Such people, should they succeed despite themselves, do not enjoy their success. At the same time, they are highly threatened by failure, and failure increases their motivation to succeed. Thus, they are caught in a conflict from which there is no escape. They have a view of themselves as desperately wanting to succeed, but as not being able to achieve it, either because of their own limitations or because of unfavourable circumstances. The explanation that has been offered to account for this phenomenon is that some individuals learned as children to feel guilty about their aggression or competitive strivings. Their past experiences have led them to believe that their success means someone else's failure, and invites rejection (cp. Canavan-Gumpert *et al.*, 1978).

An alternative, not contradictory, explanation follows from the consideration that a person's overall self-evaluation is one of the most central postulates in an individual's theory of reality. A profound change in self-evaluation would thus be unsettling, as it would destabilize the individual's theory of reality. Accordingly, individuals will not only resist information that can significantly lower their self-esteem, they will resist information that can significantly raise their self-esteem. Of course, since people prefer high to low self-esteem, they will tend to resist downward more than upward changes in self-esteem. Most acceptable of all will be relatively small upward changes in self-esteem, as this represents a compromise between their desire for high self-regard and the need to maintain the stability of their theory of reality. It is thus not surprising that many people who fear success can allow themselves a moderate degree of success, but will sabotage their own efforts when an opportunity for greater success becomes available. Such behaviour is often witnessed in athletic events, where an athlete repeatedly makes it to the semi-finals but never to the finals. To be a winner one must think of oneself as a winner. People have a way of forcing the world to conform to their image of it.

2.6 Schizophrenic Disorganization

The perspective provided by cognitive self-theory can elucidate some aspects of schizophrenia. Thomas Kuhn (1973), the philosopher of science, has noted that when a scientific theory is invalidated or can not fulfil its functions, the theory is abandoned. A state of disorganization then follows until it is replaced with another theory. If personal theories of reality are similar to theories in science, it follows that there should be a condition in human behaviour in which the disorganization of an individual's personal theory of reality occurs and is associated with intense anxiety and desperate attempts to replace it with a new theory. Just such a condition is observed in acute schizophrenic reactions. The disorganization may vary from a state of confusion about who the person is and his place in the world to a complete loss of all conceptual functioning, to the extent that the person reports experiencing nothing but a void. It will be recalled that the basic functions of a personal theory of reality are to assimilate the data of experience, to maintain a favourable pleasure/pain balance, and to maintain a favourable level of self-esteem. It is threats to these functions that often precipitate acute schizophrenic reactions. More specifically, acute schizophrenic reactions may be precipitated by an upsurge of unassimilable impulses, such as unacceptable homosexual feelings, by experiences that produce high levels of misery and remove hope of future happiness, and, most often, by blows to self-esteem, such as rejection by a loved one or failure.

Why does disorganization occur when it is not the result of organic impairment? Does it have any function? According to Kuhn (1973), scientific revolutions are one of the routes by which science advances. Sometimes a scientific theory can not be improved by modification. Bandaids can no longer patch it up. For progress to occur, the theory must be dismantled and its contents rearranged in a new organization. If this analogy is applied to personal theories of reality, it leads to the interesting speculation that schizophrenic disorganization can be a route to recovery. A number of people who have recovered from schizophrenia report that such, in fact, is the case. One, for example, stated the following:

'Remember, when a soul sails out on that unmarked sea called Madness they have gained release much greater than your loss —and more important. Though the need which brought it cannot well be known by those who have not felt it. For what the sane call "ruin"—because they do not know—those who have experienced what I am speaking of, know the wild hysteria of Madness means salvation.' (Jefferson, 1974)

A few psychologists and psychiatrists have come to the same conclusion. Menninger, for example, observed, 'Some patients have a mental illness and then get well and then get weller! I mean they get better than they ever were.... This is an extraordinary and little-realized truth.' (Silverman, 1970, p. 63)

Given observations such as the above, one is tempted to frame a hypothesis on how schizophrenia arose in the human condition. Such a hypothesis is that schizophrenic disorganization arose in the course of evolution as an emergency reaction to correct maladaptive conceptual systems. If this is true, then nature, like science, provides two routes to the improvement of personal theories of reality. One is through incremental learning, which corresponds to Kuhn's concept of normal science. The other is through disorganization, which corresponds to Kuhn's concept of scientific revolutions. I do not mean to imply that disorganization is necessarily a constructive process, for the reorganization can result in a poorer adjustment than the original one. It is to note that, as a desperate emergency reaction, disorganization at least provides an opportunity for a new, and perhaps better, organization. (For a more extended discussion of this view, see Epstein, 1979.)

2.7 Paranoia

The major symptoms of paranoid psychosis are delusions of grandeur and delusions of persecution. Freud explained delusions of persecution by assuming they are a reaction to unconscious homosexual attraction. He argued that the paranoid says to himself, 'I don't love him, I hate him.' To justify his own hatred, he then assumes the other person hates him. The final outcome is represented by the thought, 'Of course I hate him. He's persecuting me.' Although Freud may have been right for some cases of paranoia, the disorder is too broad in scope for it to be associated only with unconscious homosexuality.

Paranoid delusions have been induced by loss of sleep, by mind-altering drugs, and by senility. How is one to explain how a disorder with such specific content can be produced by such varied conditions? Sleep deprivation, drugs, and senility are all conditions that can induce states of disorganization. Unacceptable homosexual impulses that cannot be assimilated also provide an impetus to disorganization. Such observations suggest that paranoid symptoms are a defence against disorganization. That is, the basic threat that the paranoid is defended against is not a specific impulse, but disorganization of his overall theory of reality. In order to combat the threat, the paranoid develops delusions of grandeur or delusions of persecution. The delusions correspond to untestable hypotheses. As the entire defence system rests upon these hypotheses, it is understandable why there is a need to retain them no matter what the evidence.

In his book *The Three Christs of Ypsilanti*, Rokeach (1964) described how he brought three paranoid patients, who all claimed to be Jesus Christ, to the same hospital, Ypsilanti. He was interested in how they would react to each other's presence. After all, the logic was irrefutable that they could not all be Jesus. They agreed with this argument. Each noted, however, that he was the true Jesus, and the others were simply crazy. Delusions of grandeur serve a special function of bolstering self-esteem. Delusions of persecution, on the other hand, externalize threat so it can be recognized and dealt with. There are few experiences in nature that can induce greater coherence in personality than when an individual mobilizes his resources to confront a known danger. It is for this reason that people sometimes undertake dangerous activities, such as sky diving and big game hunting. Although the world of the paranoid with delusions of persecution is a frightening one, the threat at least can be combatted, which is far less distressing than the chaos of disorganization.

2.8 Self-esteem

One of the most basic postulates in an individual's self-theory is the individual's overall self-assessment, or self-esteem. As a fundamental postulate, self-esteem is resistant to change, and, when it does change, it produces widespread changes throughout an individual's self-theory, or personality. It is therefore not surprising that many psychotherapists consider a change in self-esteem to be a basic factor in improvement in psychotherapy (cp. Chapters 5, 9 and 10). Of course, the changes that I am referring to here are relatively enduring changes, i.e. changes in the baseline of self-esteem. It is obvious that temporary fluctuations around a person's baseline of self-esteem occur daily without significant consequences.

Where does self-esteem come from, and why is it such a central postulate that it resists enduring change despite repeated disconfirmatory evidence? Particularly interesting is the observation that people resist not only evidence that can lower their self-esteem, but also evidence that can raise their self-esteem. There are many prize-winning scientists, highly successful business men and internationally acclaimed actresses who feel insecure and personally inadequate. Such feelings often drive them to further effort, yet, no matter what they accomplish, the feeling of inadequacy persists. Marilyn Monroe reported that whenever she received applause, she felt it was happening to someone else (Luce, 1964). While still a highly successful actress, she took her life.

The failure of self-esteem to correspond realistically to accomplishments can be explained in two ways, not necessarily incompatible with each other. William James (1910) observed that self-esteem varies directly with the ratio of accomplishments to aspirations, as we have seen in Chapter 1. It follows that no matter how much individuals accomplish, so long as they aspire to greater achievement they will be dissatisfied with themselves. By the same token, no matter how little people accomplish, so long as they do not aspire to accomplish more they will be satisfied with themselves. Yet this tells only part of the story. Some people, such as Marilyn Monroe, accomplish more than they ever dreamed they would, and yet are dissatisfied with themselves. The other factor that is involved is that any postulate that is as basic as self-esteem and as irrational and resistant to modification by experiences in adulthood has its roots in childhood. High self-esteem can be viewed as the equivalent of self-love, that is, as a feeling of unconditional acceptance and warmth that the individual experiences toward himself or herself. A person with high self-esteem provides himself/herself with a feeling of love and acceptance that is similar to the unconditional love conveyed by a parent to a child.

Herein lies a clue to the origin of self-esteem, namely it is an outgrowth of the parent–child relationship. Self-esteem is acquired through the introjection of a love relationship with a parent in the following manner. Because the young child desires to receive love from a parent and to avoid rejection, the child internalizes the parent's values, and thereafter judges itself by the same standards with which it was judged by the parent (Epstein, 1980; Sullivan, 1953). Such a reaction is extremely useful to the child, for, by reacting to itself in the same manner as the parents once treated it, it behaves in a manner that maximizes the likelihood that the parent will approve of its behaviour. Having internalized the parent's tendencies to bestow and withdraw affection, the individual continues to evaluate himself/herself as others once did, which may bear little relationship to accomplishments in adulthood.

Elsewhere (Epstein, 1980. p. 106) I have described the self-evaluative reactions of people with high and low self-esteem as follows:

'People with high self-esteem, in effect, carry within them a loving parent who is proud of their successes and tolerant of their failures. Such people tend to have an optimistic view about life, and to be able to tolerate external stress without becoming excessively anxious. Although capable of being disappointed and depressed by specific experiences, people with high self-esteem recover quickly, as do children who are secure in their mother's love. In contrast, people with low self-esteem carry within them a disapproving parent who is harshly critical of their failures, and registers only short-lived pleasure when they succeed. Such people are apt to be unduly sensitive to failure and to rejection, to have low tolerance for frustration, to take a long time to recover following disappointments, and to have a pessimistic view of life. The picture is not unlike that of children who are insecure in their parent's love.'

Once a general level of self-esteem is established, it is resistant to change for two reasons. One is that, as a fundamental postulate in the self-system, self-esteem is anchored in place by a broad network of beliefs. Should self-esteem change, it would therefore destabilize the entire self-system and provoke high levels of anxiety. In order to avoid such anxiety, the individual has to avoid major changes in self-esteem. Accordingly, individuals will not only resist decreases in self-esteem, they will resist large increases in self-esteem. Normally a compromise will be affected between a desire to have high self-esteem and a desire to maintain stability in the self-system, so that small upward changes in self-esteem are the most acceptable changes of all.

The second reason that self-esteem tends to be stable is that sudden decreases in self-esteem are particularly distressing. Given that a base-level of high self-esteem is more pleasant than a base level of low self-esteem, individuals will be motivated to maintain the highest level of self-esteem they can that will not expose them to excessively frequent decreases in self-esteem. Thus, a balance is reached between maximizing the base-level of self-esteem and minimizing sudden decreases in self-esteem. The more insecure the individual, the lower the level of self-esteem that he or she will settle for, as decreases in self-esteem are particularly aversive for such individuals. To draw an analogy in economic terms, the less money a person has in the bank, the less the person dares invest, and, as a consequence, the greater the likelihood the person will remain in poverty.

If self-esteem is acquired largely through the internalization of appraisals by significant others, then it is reasonable to suspect that the internalization of assessments by significant others could provide a powerful means for influencing self-esteem. Such a hypothesis has important implications for psychotherapy and particularly for understanding the value of transference reactions. The following case illustrates this phenomenon in a particularly interesting manner, as the patient provides herself with her own self-esteem-enhancing therapy in the form of a delusion. Unable to change her low self-regard by the direct application of logic, the patient resorts to an imaginary relationship with William Shakespeare. Sometimes she views herself as Shakespeare and sometimes she regards him as a trusted friend. In the following passage she uses the relationship to keep from being swept up in a mania of screaming in a mental hospital:

'I do not have the power to resist the hysteria and bedlam which has broken loose this morning... My own brain is quivering on the verge of dissolution... I cannot stand it! Shakespeare! For God's sake where are you! Sit here and help me hang on to this pencil! I tell you I cannot stand it. I feel the roots of my hair drawing together so I know it is standing on end and the flesh of my arms is all goose-bumps... But no matter—you just hang on to this pencil and write something; write it fast for we cannot afford to lift our voices even one little peep. You hang on to this pencil and put something on paper. Anything—anything! I am not going to lift my voice in this howling... I know I am as insane as the wildest one here. I'm going—I feel that crazy "light" feeling in the temples and my eyes are not seeing things rightly. Write, damn it. Write something. Anything, it does not matter... I need you now if I ever needed you... Well—that was that, William. We made it! Thank you!... I am most grateful to you. The doctor ... can think what he likes of delusions of grandeur—but what you did for me, I could not do for myself. We made it! Whether the world ever knows it or not—the writing you have been doing for the last half hour is an indication of greater genious than all your previous works put together.' (Jefferson, 1974, pp. 191–195)

With the aid of her relationship to Shakespeare, the patient improved until she was assigned to a better ward, where there was no place for delusions. In the following passage, she bids Shakespeare farewell:

'So goodbye William. You were one grand delusion! If you had not come to me, perchance this transfer would have been to a place still lower in this limbo—instead of this step upward. I shall hate to lose you—but I cannot take you with me because delusions of grandeur are not allowed upstairs. Goodbye William. I am most grateful to you for coming to me. Goodbye. And may long years of peace and rest attend you in your quiet English grave.' (p. 238)

Let us examine more closely the reason why self-esteem is powerfully influenced by the reflected appraisal of a significant other. The implicit logic in such a relationship is as follows: 'If I admire you, and I know that you like and respect me, then I must be a worthwhile person, for I respect your judgement.' It is thus not surprising that cures by love occur in everyday life. More often, unfortunately, such cures are sabotaged by the behaviour of the person with low self-esteem, who, unable to accept that he or she is loveworthy will tend to create situations that will cause the significant other to behave in a way that will destroy the relationship. This will temporarily relieve anxiety in the person with low self-esteem, as there will be no need to reorganize the self-system. As the patient, despite conscious wishes to the contrary, is motivated to maintain a familiar level of self-esteem, the patient will do all in his or her power to provoke the therapist to behave in a manner such as to allow the patient to retain his or her self-assessment. A further strategy to which the patient may unconsciously resort is to reduce his or her respect for the therapist through the intrinsic logic that if the patient is not worthy of respect, and the therapist respects the patient, then the therapist's judgement is faulty. It is for such reasons that management of the transference relationship is often one of the most important tasks in psychotherapy.

It would be interesting to test the hypothesis that a major source of improvement in psychotherapy is through an increase in self-esteem via the reflected appraisal of the therapist. To conduct such research, it is necessary to assess the following three beliefs during the course of psychotherapy: (1) the patient's level of self-acceptance, or self-esteem, (2) the degree to which the patient likes, respects, and admires the therapist, and (3) the degree to which the patient believes the therapist likes, respects, and accepts the patient. If the hypothesis is correct, the above three variables should be positively correlated with each other and with improvement over sessions. Possibly such information could be unobtrusively obtained from a content-analysis of therapy sessions. However, it is likely that much of the information would not be available, as the patient might not talk about certain feelings, such as feelings toward the therapist. Thus, a more fruitful approach may be to have the patient rate his or her feelings immediately following a therapy session. In that case, it would be important to assure the patient that the therapist would not see the ratings, for, unless this is done, the patient will not honestly rate the therapist, either out of concern for his feelings, or in an attempt to influence the therapist through the ratings. Moreover, if the therapist were aware of the ratings, the therapist could behave in a manner that could influence further ratings.

The rating scales could be made as simple or as elaborate as desired. At the minimum, three ratings would be required, which would consist of global ratings by the patient of self-acceptance, of the patient's admiration of the therapist, and of the patient's view of the therapist's acceptance of the patient. It would, of course, be more revealing if the ratings were more differentiated. Thus, with respect to self-acceptance, the following components of self-esteem could be assessed: general self-acceptance; competence; likeability, or popularity; lovability, or belief in one's ability to elicit love from someone who matters; moral self-acceptance versus guilt; will-power; ability to influence others; body appearance; and body functioning (cp. Epstein, 1976, 1979; O'Brien, 1980). It is likely that reflected positive appraisals by a therapist would influence some of the above components, such as lovability and moral self-acceptance, more than others, and that some are more importantly associated with overall self-acceptance than others. Of course, there may be marked individual differences in the relationships of the different components of self-esteem to overall self-acceptance, which poses an interesting question for future research. With respect to assessments of the patient's feelings toward the therapist, it would be interesting to evaluate separately the degree to which the patient likes, respects, admires, and identifies with the therapist, as they may not play an equal role in influencing self-esteem. Similarly, it would be interesting to evaluate separately the degree to which the patient believes the therapist likes, non-judgementally accepts, and respects the patient.

The question should be considered as to whether having the patient make the kinds of ratings described above could interfere with psychotherapy. In studies to date that have used far more extensive rating scales, no untoward effects were observed (e.g. Orlinsky and Howard, 1975). Yet the possibility must be considered that the research could have different effects in different settings and with different psychotherapeutic procedures. Of course, before any procedure is extensively employed, it should be used in an exploratory manner, and modified or abandoned, depending on the preliminary findings.

2.9 Summary

One of the most basic motives in human behaviour is the need to maintain the stability and coherence of a person's theory of reality. Such motivation can account for behaviour that is not readily explained otherwise, such as the symptoms of the traumatic neurosis, the demonic fate theme, and the transference neurosis. Any personal theory, even one that produces misery, is preferable to none, as in the absence of a theory of reality an individual would be helpless in a chaotic world. Thus, it is not surprising that maintaining a personal theory of reality is often more important than maintaining life itself. Accordingly, individuals are motivated to validate their personal theories of reality, even if it means recreating over and over again certain unpleasant experiences that substantiate their worst fears. Other instances of repetition represent attempts to assimilate emotionally significant experiences that are inconsistent with an individual's theory of reality.

A summary of a personality theory was presented in which it was assumed that all individuals have personal theories of reality that are composed of self-theories, world-theories, and beliefs about the relationship between the two. It was demonstrated that, in addition to explaining the symptoms that Freud attributed to the repetition-compulsion in the traumatic neurosis, the demonic fate theme, and the transference neurosis, the theory that was presented can elucidate a number of other conditions, such as fear of success, acute schizophrenic disorganization, paranoid delusions, and the regulation of self-esteem. Self-acceptance, or self-esteem, is one of the most basic postulates in an individual's self-theory, and, accordingly, changes in self-esteem have widespread effects on the entire personality. A hypothesis with important implications for psychotherapy is that reflected appraisals from significant others represent an important means for changing self-esteem. More specifically, it was hypothesized that to the extent that an individual with low self-esteem admires and respects a significant other who is perceived as liking and respecting the individual, the individual will experience an increase in self-esteem. A study was outlined for testing this hypothesis.

References

Allport, G. W. (1937). *Personality: A Psychological Interpretation*. Holt, New York.
Brehm, J. W. and Cohen, A. R. (1962). *Explorations in Cognitive Dissonance*. Wiley, New York.
Canavan-Gumpert, D., Garner, K. and Gumpert, P. (1978). *The Success-fearing Personality*. Lexington Books, Lexington (Mass.).
Epstein, S. (1973). The self-concept revisited, or a theory of a theory. *Am. Psychol.*, **28**, 404–416.
Epstein, S. (1976). Anxiety, arousal and the self-concept. In *Stress and Anxiety*, vol. 3 (eds I. G. Sarason and C. D. Spielberger), pp. 183–224. Hemisphere, Washington (DC).

Epstein, S. (1979). Natural healing processes of the mind: (i) Acute schizophrenic disorganisation. *Schizophr. Bull.*, **5**, 313–321.

Epstein, S. (1980). The self-concept: a review and the proposal of an integrated theory of personality. In *Personality: Basic Issues and Current Research* (ed. E. Staub). Prentice Hall, Englewood Cliffs (NJ).

Festinger, L. (1957). *A Theory of Cognitive Dissonance*. Stanford University Press, Stanford (Calif.).

Freud, S. (1920). *Beyond the pleasure principle. Standard Ed.*, **18**, 3–64.

Goldstein, K. (1939). *The Organism*. American Book Co., New York.

Heider, F. (1958). *The Psychology of Interpersonal Relations*. Wiley, New York.

Horney, K. (1945). *Our Inner Conflicts*. Norton, New York.

James, W. (1910). *Psychology: The Briefer Course*. Holt, New York.

Jefferson, L. (1974). *These are My Sisters*. Anchor Press/Doubleday, New York.

Kelly, G. A. (1955). *The Psychology of Personal Constructs*, 2 vols. Norton, New York.

Kuhn, T. S. (1973). *The Structure of Scientific Revolutions*, third edition. University of Chicago Press, Chicago (Ill.).

Lecky, P. (1945). *Self-consistency: A Theory of Personality*. Island Press, Long Island (NY).

Luce, C. B. (1964). What really killed Marilyn. *Life Magazine*, August.

May, R. (1950). *The Meaning of Anxiety*. Ronald Press, New York.

O'Brien, E. J. (1980). The Self-report Inventory: Construction and Validation of a Multidimensional Measure of the Self-concept and Sources of Self-esteem. Unpublished doctoral dissertation, University of Massachusetts at Amherst.

Orlinsky, D. E. and Howard, K. L. (1975). *Varieties of Psychotherapeutic Experience: Multivariate Analyses of Patients' and Therapists' Reports*. Teachers College Press, Columbia University, New York.

Rogers, C. (1942). *Counseling and Psychotherapy: Newer Concepts in Practice*. Houghton Mifflin, Boston.

Rogers, C. (1951). *Client-centered Thearpy: Its Current Practice, Implications and Theory*. Houghton Mifflin, Boston.

Rogers, C. R. (1959). A theory of therapy, personality and interpersonal relationships as developed in the client-centered framework. In *Psychology: A Study of a Science*, vol. 3: *Formulations of the person and the social context* (ed. S. Koch), pp. 184–256. McGraw-Hill, New York.

Rokeach, M. (1964). *The Three Christs of Ypsilanti*. Knopf, New York.

Rokeach, M. (1973). *The Nature of Human Values*. Free Press, New York.

Silverman, J. (1970). When schizophrenia helps. *Psychol. Today*, **4**, 63–65.

Snygg, D. and Combs, W. (1949). *Individual Behaviour*. Harper and Row, New York.

Sullivan, H. S. (1953). *The Interpersonal Theory of Psychiatry*. Norton, New York.

Self, Symptoms and Psychotherapy
Edited by N. Cheshire and H. Thomae
© 1987 John Wiley & Sons Ltd

CHAPTER 3

The Self and its Objects in Freudian and Kleinian Theory

Neil Cheshire

3.1 *Introduction: topography of the Self in psychoanalysis*
3.2 *Ferenczi: transference, displacement and introjection*
3.3 *Freud: depression, identification and the superego*
3.4 *The Kleinians: the inner world expands*

3.1 Introduction: Topography of the Self in Psychoanalysis

Just as the school-room fame of Julius Caesar rested in days gone by upon his having divided Gaul into three parts, so Freud's popular reputation among a more modern generation of students derives from his having divided the human mind into *id, ego* and *superego*. The only similarity between these two schematic trisections is that they were ·among the least important and least original innovations which the respective campaigners made. For, in both instances, it may fairly be said that the divisions in question already existed, and therefore needed not to be made *de novo* but only to be given a name; while in Freud's case the picturesque (and at times almost flippant) 'structural' formulations of *The Ego and the Id* (1923, esp. ch. 2) can be seen to have raised at least as many questions for psychoanalytic theory as they have answered.

Psychoanalytic theory about the relations between the technical concept of ego, on the one hand, and established non-analytic conceptions of self-functions and personal identity, on the other, were authoritatively reviewed in the 1950s by the important Freudian theoretician Heinz Hartmann (1950, 1956), and they have been productively appraised and related to normal development-al psychology over many years by Erik Erikson (esp. 1963, ch. 7; 1968, ch. 5). Both these writers have, of course, made their own original contributions to the development and refinement of psychoanalytic self-theory; some of Hart-mann's seminal suggestions, for example, have been followed up influentially by Jacobson (1954, 1964) and by Sandler and Rosenblatt (1962), while Erikson's creative application of Freudian ideas to identity-development throughout everyday life has brought psychodynamic insight and liberation to therapists, educationists and child-care workers who would never be likely to consult the psychoanalytic journals. In recent years, considerable interest has been shown in Britain and North America in trying to align the attitudes and arguments of 'continental' phenomenology with psychoanalytic ego-theory (e.g. Laing, 1965, 1969; Wilden, 1968; Ricoeur, 1970, esp. pp. 344–418); and the same may be said of the social-constructivist viewpoints which we have touched upon in Chapter 1 (Carveth, 1984; cp. Gauld and Shotter, 1977, ch. 11; Wilshire, 1982; Shotter, 1984; Marsella *et al.*, 1985).

As Hartmann indicates (1950), Freud's original formulations to do with the nature of the psychoanalytic ego, its psychological functions and its relation to other components of personality and of the 'mental apparatus' did not always relate them consistently to such self-functions as are denoted in the informal language of 'self-esteem', 'self-control', 'self-deception', 'self-knowledge', 'self-punishment', 'self-interest', etc. Indeed, we may take note of Bettelheim's more recent contention (1983, ch. 8) that this gap has been misleadingly widened for readers of English by the editors of the *Standard Edition* having adopted pseudoscientific Latin terms to translate the original German words (*das Es, das Ich* and *das Überich*) which have altogether more immediate and commonplace connotations.

At all events, Freud repeatedly defines the ego, at various stages of his thinking, in terms of its 'functions'. We can follow him from the early emphasis on 'consciousness and voluntary movement' toward the realization that important parts of the ego must be unconscious; through the recognition of its roles in mobilizing defences against anxiety (much elaborated by Anna Freud (1937)), and in mediating the rational and reality-orientated 'secondary process'; up to the systematization in the 1920s which stresses the importance of anticipation and introduces the 'danger signal' account of anxiety; to the continued refinements in later papers which, in Hartmann's view, had not been adequately appreciated even by psychoanalysts themselves. As Hartmann puts it (1956, pp. 290–292), the ego is eventually 'defined as a system of functions' which serve integrative, modulatory and homeostatic purposes, and thereby invite, on the one hand, comparison with certain biological balance mechanisms which were expounded famously by Cannon and, on the other, clarificatory reformulation in terms of basic cybernetic principles, such as von Zeppelin presents in Chapter 6 of this volume. The context and details of Freud's fluctuating formulations have been charted scrupulously by Laplanche and Pontalis (1973, pp. 130–143); and the conceptual status of the ego in current psychoanalytic thinking has been reviewed more recently by Padel (1986), who also discusses in some detail the important American symposium of 1982.

Since some of the main clinical considerations which led Freud to elaborate a theory of ego-processes were the phenomena of narcissism, of masochism and of depression, and the role of insight in bringing about therapeutic change, we may reasonably expect his discussions of these topics to indicate how far we can translate technical ego-talk into everyday statements about our 'self-knowledge', 'self-criticism' and so on. To some extent, indeed, our expectation is fulfilled. For, in his classic account of depression (1917), Freud offers an explanation of the associated symptoms of self-denigration and potential self-destruction in terms of changes taking place in the ego as a result of object-loss; and it is worth noticing that the difficulty of depicting theoretically the elusive psychical processes involved elicits some memorably piquant metaphor from Freud, of which a firm favourite is the evasive image 'the shadow of the object has fallen upon the ego' (p. 250). Elsewhere, in the posthumous *Outline...* (1940, p. 177), Freud tells us that, in psychoanalytic therapy, 'the method by which we strengthen the weakened ego has as a starting-point an extending of its self-knowledge', and this observation immediately confirms our assumption that accurate cognitive appraisal of our own personal powers is a necessary condition of that intrapsychic regulation and environmental adaptation which characterizes a healthy ego.

The reassurance, however, is short-lived when we notice that the relation which obtains in this formulation between ego and 'Self', according to which the former can take the latter as an object of knowledge, is not consistent with what Freud has said elsewhere in analysing narcissistic self-love and masochistic self-injury. For, in those discussions, 'the term ego became interchangeable with "one's own person" or with "the Self"' (Hartmann, 1956, p. 287). Hartmann also points out that the ego which becomes the object of an emotional drive or 'libidinal-cathexis' in self-love or self-destruction sometimes seems to correspond, in Freud's formulation, to 'one's own person' (as opposed to other people), and sometimes to one particular component system of the personality as opposed to other (internal, component) systems of the personality. On the other hand, when Freud writes (1923, p. 40) that the 'self-preservative instinct . . . must be assigned to the ego', the scope of the 'Self' here must clearly be greater than the ego and include it. To put it crudely, then, Freud sometimes writes as if the Self were more than the ego, and sometimes as if it were less. His followers have expressed a variety of views about the relation between 'ego' and 'Self', at one extreme of which is Eissler's contention that the Self is to be regarded as 'an independent structure, comparable to the ego but developing only in adolescence' (see Jacobson, 1964, p. 24). The unclarity of the situation has been summarized disarmingly by Meissner (1979, p. 347): 'The status of the self in . . . psychoanalytic theory is as yet undefined.'

This talk of structures and agencies within the personality, which is already problematic enough for those who have philosophical scruples about applying the concepts of spatial relationships metaphorically to psychological powers and processes, seems to run into further difficulty when one is trying to accommodate such concepts to pathologies of self-function. For if it is the Self which is the *object* of the self-love in narcissism, of the destructiveness in masochism and self-defeat, and of the obsessive anxiety in hypochondria, it is tempting to ask what other agency or subsystem is the *subject* which is actively doing the loving, the destroying and the worrying in these cases. For if you make the subject of the verb some other part of the ego, as Freud does in the account of depression (1917, p. 247), you run the risk of making the 'Self' merely a *part* of the ego, which seems to put things the wrong way round. It may be objected that this is a grammar-generated quibble which some languages can avoid by using an inflected form of the verb for its middle and passive voices, along the lines discussed in Chapter 1. This is borne out by the fact that there does not seem to be a similar problem in the case of inanimate devices which are said to have a 'self-destruct' capability, for it is easy enough to understand that one part of a physical system may be able to initiate a process which has the effect of destroying the whole system.

At all events, Freud's other answer was to construe this object-self as a part of the total personality-system which was developed as the result of somehow building into that system certain modes of functioning which have been perceived as characterizing significant others (that is, 'psychological objects') in the outside world. This has opened the door to that whole branch of psychoanalysis which is known as 'object-relations theory', which is a theory both of normal personality-development and of psychopathology (cp. Eagle, 1983b, 1984; Rothstein, 1985). Its chief protagonist was, of course, Melanie Klein, who advanced it as a natural development of ideas implicit, or even explicit, in Freudian theory. To orthodox Freudians, however, it seemed to have more than a whiff of heresy about it, and it did, historically, occasion fierce controversy within the British Psychoanalytical Society in the early 1940s (cp. Segal, 1979, ch. 8; Kohon, 1986, pp. 38–45; Grosskurth, 1986, pp. 279–362). We are not concerned with this controversy in itself, but only with the question of how such an approach can help us to understand the development of the self-system and the origin of disturbances in self-functions.

It will be evident at the outset that the basic conception that the self-system is constructed, in some measure and in some sense, out of components brought in from outside will have to face searching questions about the conceptual status of such components. For example, What can these entities *be* which are thus brought in?; and, with reference to the nature of the psychological processes *by which* they are brought in, *How* can something which started out as a property or individual in the external world become part of the child's mental apparatus? (cp. Schafer, 1976, ch. 8). We have already noticed Freud cannily cloaking these issues in evasive figures of speech; and we shall find that some of his followers are less successful in keeping the metaphors of mental space coherent (see Chapter 4), and that they consequently run the risk of bringing this whole way of talking into disrepute. But even if these crucial hypotheses have not always been formulated coherently in the past, what matters is whether they *can* ever be formulated (or reformulated, if necessary) in ways that make empirical and epistemological sense. Some attempt has already been made to show that many of them can indeed be rescued from incoherence by being converted, on the one hand, into the philosophical language of 'dispositional' concepts and, on the other, into specifications for elementary neurophysiological modelling (Cheshire, 1966, ch. 7 and 9). The associated general principle of using the theoretical constructs of cybernetics and systems-theory to build clarificatory models which should sort wheat from chaff in psychodynamics has been hinted at by Colby (1955), and has been expounded rigorously by Boden (1974); and related to the on-going process of analytic therapy by Peterfreund (1983). In Chapter 6, von Zeppelin applies this principle specifically to the question of describing change in self-concept during psychotherapy.

3.2 Ferenczi: Transference, Displacement and Introjection

In order to understand how the concept of 'internal object' is used by different writers, it will be necessary to sketch something of its history and to be on the lookout for changes in meaning as its usage is extended. We shall need also to consider the logical status of certain closely associated concepts (such as introjection, incorporation, identification and projection) because the notion of 'internal object' is bound up with them, and its meaning is often conveyed by reference to them.

For many of these terms have suffered a largely unarticulated extension of meaning, such that an idea introduced by Freud on the level of illustrative simile has been taken up more literally by others and been given a more central role in their accounts of mental life. The course of the development of the idea of 'internal objects' had not been well mapped, until the reviews of Kernberg (1977, ch. 1–4), Tuttman (1981), Grotstein (1982) and Eagle (1983)—unless we include Jacobson (1964); and it is still necessary for us to trace how the idea of 'internal', 'incorporated' or 'introjected' objects arose out of the earlier idea of object-cathexis (cp. Eagle, 1984). The general view on this point, among writers on object relations theory, is that Freud's exposition of reactive depression and of the 'superego' are *loci classici* for his (at least implicit) adoption of the notion of internal object. Even earlier traces are to be found, as we shall see, in Ferenczi.

We have said above that it will not be possible to treat 'internal objects' in isolation, but that certain allied mechanisms will have to be considered. This is because the idea of internal objects *per se* gained ground only after some currency had been given in psychoanalytic writings to the general notion of a process by which objects (in the original sense of some emotionally important person or thing) were somehow transformed into, or treated as, part of a person's mind or Self, as opposed to part of the 'external word'. Thus the protagonists of an 'internal objects' approach to behaviour typically claim to be following up and elaborating ideas implied or adumbrated by Freud and

Ferenczi. They tend to point to Freud's discussions of identification (1921) and of the superego (1923); but since the emphasis there is more on the fact of the process than on the status of the 'object' involved, we are at once thrown back on trying to understand the nature of the *process* he was postulating, namely 'introjection'. In introducing this term to his writings, Freud explicitly acknowledges (1915, p. 135) that he is borrowing it from Ferenczi. An attempt to understand the concept of internal objects has therefore to start with Ferenczi and Freud.

The essay which historically introduced 'introjection' to the psychoanalytic world (Ferenczi, 1909) starts by drawing attention to Freud's discovery of the important part played by 'transference' relations in the analysis of hysterical patients. It continues with the further claim that this same process of transference is responsible also for a much wider range of behaviour than that of the hysterical patients towards the analyst. Thus he says he has become convinced that the whole 'apparently motiveless extravagance of affect' of the neurotic is due to transference by means of which 'long forgotten psychical experiences are (in the unconscious phantasy) brought into connection with the current occasion'.

The next move is to establish the hysteric's capacity for *displacement*, by which he means such behaviour as the substitution of oral for (repressed) sexual gratification, and the sublimation of destructive impulses into, for example, campaigning for teetotalism. Ferenczi then argues that 'transference' should be regarded as one specific form of 'displacement': for what has been displaced in the psychoanalytic transference situation is the childish need for parent-figures, so that 'the physician is always one of the "revenants"... in whom the neurotic hopes to find again the vanished figure of childhood'. The parallel here with such later developments as the lost objects in Freud's discussion of melancholia (1917, p. 245) and the parental image of the superego (Freud, 1923, p. 47) is clear enough.

But this general 'passion for transference', which 'we may regard as the most fundamental peculiarity of the neuroses', is connected, in Ferenczi's view, with neurotics' 'flight from their complexes' and can be seen to involve, or to lead to, the process of introjection. To show how this is the case he contrasts neurosis with paranoia, thus:

> 'Whereas the paranoiac expels from his ego the impulses that have become unpleasant, the neurotic helps himself by taking into the ego as large as possible a part of the outer world, making it the object of unconscious phantasies. This is a kind of diluting process, by means of which he tries to mitigate the poignancy of free-floating, unsatisfied and unsatisfiable, unconscious wish-impulses. One might give to this process, in contrast to projection, the name of *introjection*.' (1909, p. 47)

Now these 'free-floating...unconscious wish impulses' are released or created when the 'psychosexual hunger' has been 'detached' from certain (forbidden, guilty, etc) 'ideational complexes' and 'seeks satisfaction from external objects'. The result of this is, as Ferenczi says later when pointing up the connection between transference and introjection, that the 'stimulus-hungry affects' of repressed impulses are

> 'constantly ready to transfer on to the persons and objects of the outside world, to bring these unconsciously into connection with the ego, to introject' (1909, p. 60).

From this presentation it emerges, firstly, that introjection is conceived of as a defensive technique which is resorted to as a means of coping with libido that is at a loose end, as it were (Ferenczi's translator calls it 'diluting', but the appropriate metaphor would surely be 'blotting' or 'soaking up'); secondly, that introjection occurs after an original cathexis has been renounced and broken (under repression); thirdly, that the connection between introjection and identification, so important for Freud and for self-theory, is already alluded to; fourthly, that what is taken *into* the ego in introjection is part of the *outer* world and *external* objects—there being no mention of *internal* objects as such, although there is of 'unconscious phantasies'; and fifthly, that introjection is explicitly linked and contrasted with *projection*. This last feature recurs later where Ferenczi says:

> 'the paranoiac projection and the neurotic introjection are merely extreme cases of physical processes the primary forms of which are to be demonstrated in every normal being' (p. 50);

and it no doubt accounts for Fuchs' (1937) observation that the Kleinians take up the notion of introjection in its original form.

About the relation between introjection and 'internal objects' more will have to be said later. For although Ferenczi explicitly puts the concept of unconscious phantasy into the picture, the *things* concerned (the things taken 'into the ego') are *real* things ('outer', 'external'); and this raises the question whether there is a sense in which something may be unconsciously 'taken into the ego', or 'associated with the ego-complex' *without* becoming what the Kleinians call an 'internal object'. It may be that rescuing the notion of unconscious phantasy from incoherence will involve dispensing with phantasy-objects, in the same sort of way that a Rylean reductionist account of memory tries to do without 'memory-images'. As Ryle put it (1949, p. 234):

> 'a person picturing his nursery is, in a certain way, like that person seeing his nursery; but the similarity does not consist in his really

> looking at a real likeness of his nursery, but in his really seeming to
> see his nursery itself. ... He is not being a spectator of a resemb-
> lance of his nursery, but he is resembling a spectator of his nursery.'

Again, Ferenczi is not irrevocably committed in this essay to the spatial
formulation that in introjection something is established *inside* the ego, or
whatever; mere unconscious 'connection' with the ego, for instance, can count
as introjection. But, even more loosely, the neurotic is said to be introjecting
when he has found someone 'with whom he can identify himself, to whom he
can transfer feelings, whom he can thus draw into his circle of interest...' We
shall see below that Freud too used a variety of metaphors to describe the
process he envisaged when speaking of introjection, but the danger of being too
unspecific (perhaps in order to avoid dimly foreseen problems) is that almost
any perceptual or relational activity becomes subsumable under the wider
definition, so that one may be left with a special term that has no very special
meaning. But before moving on to Freud's treatment of the concept, we should
note an illuminating, and in some ways puzzling, example of introjection which
Ferenczi gives. He refers to Jung's word-association procedure, according to
which the analyst, in order to get a lead into the patient's troublesome
'complexes', offers a stimulus-word and invites the patient's first association to
it. Ferenczi continues, in his own italics:

> '... *it is not that the stimulus-words evoke the complicated reaction,
> but that the stimulus-hungry affects of neurotics come to meet
> them;* ... *the neurotic introjects the stimulus-word of the experiment.*'
> (1909, p. 51)

This is remarkable for the fact that Jung's method has obvious resemblances
to procedures in current clinical use which are known as *pro*jection, not
*intro*jection, techniques! Now the assumption behind this standard nomencla-
ture is, of course, that, in introducing associations and structurings for this sort
of essentially ambiguous or ill-defined stimulus-material, the subject is attributing to that material properties, characteristics, etc. which in reality derive from
his own mental make-up, and is thereby 'projecting' them, throwing them
forth, from himself. But Ferenczi wants to say, on the contrary, that the
association or connection between stimulus-material and phantasy-content
comes about as a result of the former having been taken into the realm of the
latter. And yet there is also an element of movement *from* the person
concerned: for the 'stimulus-hungry affects ... come to meet' the stimulus-
words. This same question, of Ferenczi wanting to substitute *intro-* for
*pro-*jection, arose explicitly in his correspondence with Freud. After reading the
manuscript of *Mourning and Melancholia* in February 1915, Ferenczi wrote: 'A
*pro*jection of the shadow of the object on the narcissistic ego is your description

of what I prefer to describe as *intro*jection' (1949, p. 247). Clearly the topographical metaphors are already giving trouble, as Cheshire has pointed out before (1966, p. 41); and Laplanche and Pontalis have subsequently confirmed that when Ferenczi speaks of introjection, 'he ends up by using the word to designate a type of behaviour ... that might equally well be described as projection' (1973, p. 230). We shall have to consider later how such difficulties may be avoided.

Freud: Depression, Identification and the Superego

It seems to be in *Instincts and their Vicissitudes* (1915) that Freud first uses the word 'introjection', with due acknowledgment to its originator. It appears in the context of the pleasure-principle and the process seems to be regarded as virtually coextensive with positive cathexis. He writes (pp. 135–136):

> 'Under the dominance of the pleasure-principle a further development now takes place in the ego. Insofar as the objects which are presented to it are sources of pleasure, it takes them into itself, 'introjects' them (to use Ferenczi's term); and, on the other hand, it expels whatever within itself becomes a cause of unpleasure.'

The point at issue is repeated and elaborated several times in the course of the paper, with the word 'incorporation' sometimes being used for the purpose. For example:

> 'For the pleasure-ego the external world is divided into a part that is pleasurable, which it has incorporated into itself, and a remainder that is extraneous to itself. It has separated off a part of its own self, which it projects into the external world and feels as hostile. .... If ... an object turns out to be a source of pleasure, it is loved, but it is also incorporated into the ego.'

This can be seen to reflect a somewhat unspecific view of the introjective/incorporative mechanism, and appears at times almost to amount to such a reformulation of the idea of libidinal cathexis as is to be found explicit in Fairbairn. It seems that at this stage Freud thought that any positive attitude towards a person or thing should be regarded as a wish, or attempt, to bring that 'object' into some sort of proximity with the ego; and he even goes so far as to introduce the notion of physical movement directed to that end. But the concept of physical distance could easily become logically embarrassing where a mental construct such as the 'ego' is concerned. For there seems to be no doubt that the 'objects' involved are tangible, physical things: they are not yet designated 'internal', and Freud has previously made it clear what (at this stage) he means by an object by saying that it is 'the thing in regard to which, or through which, the instinct is able to achieve its aim', and that this aim is 'in every instance satisfaction, which can only be obtained by removing the state of stimulation at the source of the instinct' (p. 122).

It will be noted that Freud here follows Ferenczi in linking introjection with projection, but departs from him in not treating it as a defence against the anxiety left over from an abandoned or thwarted cathexis. He seems to regard it rather as a primary means of libidinal satisfaction. However, Freud *did* emphasize and elaborate these other aspects in later writings, and the main discussions in which the introjection of objects is involved are those concerning depression (1917), identification (1921) and the superego (1923).

The first draft of the famous essay on depression was finished a matter of weeks *before* Freud began writing the one in which, as we have seen, he adopted Ferenczi's term 'introjection' (see *Standard Ed.*, **14**, 239). The fact that it carries a publication date two years *later* than that of the other may therefore perhaps mislead us by making it look as though he acknowledged the term 'introjection' in 1915 and then failed to use it in 1917 when theorizing about mourning and melancholia. We can say, however, that the published version ignores Ferenczi's specific suggestion that 'introjection' *should* be used in that context.

But he does make use there of phrases very similar to those which occur in his treatment of introjection, and does refer to oral incorporation. It is also clear, from a remark he makes later when discussing the superego, that he thought his analysis of melancholia very relevant to the questions of introjection and of the formation of 'internal objects' (the superego being, in Kleinian eyes, a major Freudian precedent for internal objects). For he observes (1923, p. 36) that he has already had occasion to argue that in depression 'an object which was lost has been reinstated within the ego'; and, when discussing identification in *Group Psychology. . .* (1921, p. 68), he indicates that he *then* viewed melancholia in terms of 'internal objects', by writing that in that condition 'the introjection of the objects is . . . unmistakably clear'. Part of the interest of the melancholia paper, for present purposes, is that Freud does attempt there to forestall the question of *how* an 'object' can be thus 'reinstated', and thereby to cope (implicitly) with the question of what *sort* of thing an internal object is.

Thus at various points in the essay he eschews the spatial metaphor of taking something 'into the ego' and tries to express in more or less literal terms what he supposes to be going on in the mind of the mourner and of the melancholic. For he writes that normally, when reality-testing has shown that the loved object no longer exists, '. . . the existence of the lost object is psychically prolonged. Each single one of the memories and expectations in which the libido is bound to the object is brought up and hypercathected' (1917, pp. 244–245).

A change of metaphor shows that Freud was not entirely committed to the picture of importing or setting up inside the ego something which was, in effect, not there before. It is enough for his purpose to indicate that part of the ego-system appears as it were in a different light as a result of something that has happened to its object, and he can therefore speak of the 'shadow of the object' having fallen upon the ego. It is not so much that an *object* is taken *into the ego* but rather that part of the *ego* is taken as an *object*. Freud accordingly writes that, in the well-known self-denigration and self-blame characteristic of the depressive, '. . . part of the ego sets itself over against the other, judges it critically, and, as it were, takes it as its object' (p. 247). Here we appear to have internal objects in all but name, and we certainly seem to see the germ of the superego and of the notion of 'splitting the ego' which is given such importance by Klein and Fairbairn. In this way the ego is *made* the object of attitudes, impulses, accusations etc. which were originally directed against the lost object (p. 248); and so thorough is this transference or displacement that it may result even in the destruction of the substitute object, which means, of course, suicidal self-destruction:

'. . . the ego can kill itself only if, owing to the return of the object-cathexis, it can treat itself as an object—if it is able to direct against itself the hostility which relates to objects in the external world' (p. 252).

Another echo of Ferenczi is the specific introduction of *identification*, so that the stage is now set for chronic controversy over the relation between object-cathexis, object-relation, introjection and identification—a controversy which has exercised many subsequent commentators (e.g. Schafer, 1968; McDevitt, 1979; Meissner, 1979). But how does Freud reconcile his claim that the modification of the ego in melancholia, which he describes in terms of identification, occurs as a *consequence* of the break-up of a cathexis, with the view that identification *antedates* cathexis in the course of psychic development? His answer to this involves appeal to 'regression'. For he argues that a 'precondition' of the shadow of the object thus falling upon the ego is a strong but brittle attachment to the original object, in fact a 'narcissistic' object-choice. When this happens,

'the object-cathexis . . . can regress to . . . narcissistic identification with the object: . . . the love-relation need not be given up . . . It represents of course, a regression from one type of object-choice to original narcissism' (p. 251).

This in turn raises the whole question of the existence and nature of a primary narcissistic phase characterized by a relative or complete absence of object-relations and more or less dominated by introjective identifications. This topic has proved to be one of the growth-points for psychoanalytic self-theory in recent years, notably in the work of Mahler *et al.* (1975) and of Kohut (1971, 1977).

Any theory of the self and its objects, whether overtly psychodynamic or not, needs some account of *identification*. The seventh chapter of *Group Psychology* ... accordingly begins with the affirmation that 'identification is known to psychoanalysis as the earliest expression of an emotional tie with another person'; and this is repeated later in the words '... identification is the original form of emotional tie with an object' (Freud, 1921, pp. 60, 65). Then comes an echo of the apparent indecision noted above, in that an explicitly oral portrayal of the subject is followed by a more guarded one. Thus the claim that

> 'Identification ... is ambivalent from the very first; ... It behaves like a derivative of the first *oral* phase of the organisation of the libido, in which the object that we long for and prize is assimilated by eating and is in that way annihilated as such.' (p. 61)

is succeeded by the admission that 'We can only see that identification endeavours to mould a person's own ego after the fashion of the one that has been taken as a "model".' This relatively conservative clay-modelling imagery is reverted to later, and there is also another use of the 'shadow' metaphor which we have met above.

Freud goes on to apply the former picture to the phenomenon of symptom-imitation, saying that

> '... the symptom may be the same as that of the person who is loved, ... in that case we can only describe the state of things by saying that *identification has appeared instead of object-choice, and that object-choice has regressed to identification*' (p. 64).

This is the position that was reached at the end of the essay on melancholia; but whereas there was no explicit mention there of introjection, Freud goes on here to link regression and introjection, saying that, in a 'regressive' way, identification 'becomes a substitute for a libidinal object-tie, as it were by means of the introjection of the object into the ego' (p. 65). And although it is clear from quotations presented above that it is not merely *regressive*, postcathectic, identification that is seen in introjective terms, yet it does seem to be in the context of reaction to lost or rejected relationships that Freud is most confident in attributing introjection. For he writes (p. 67) that

> 'Identification with an object that is renounced or lost ..., introjection of this object into the ego, is indeed no longer a novelty to us'.

and he gives as an example of this process the situation when an child loses a kitten and then declares itself to *be* the kitten and imitates it.

It has become a commonplace clinical observation, of course, that in depressive bereavement-reactions the bereaved person will temporarily take over some quite specific attribute (voice, gait, attitude, habit) of the relative who has died. Freud also specifically reformulates the melancholic's reaction in terms of object-introjection, and in doing so makes it clear that he now regards the struggle or division within the ego, which he had previously described with some caution and apology, as being between an internal object 'contained' by part of the ego and that other substructure of the ego which we have come to know eventually as the 'superego', the 'ego-ideal'. Freud writes that melancholia also shows us the ego

'divided, fallen into two pieces, one of which rages against the second. This second piece is the one that has been altered by introjection and which contains the lost object. But the piece which behaves so cruelly is not unknown to us either . . . We have called it the "ego-ideal", and . . . have said that . . . it gradually gathers up from the influences of the environment the demands which that environment makes upon the ego . . .' (p. 68).

We see from this that the vague 'critical agency' which featured in the essay on melancholia has now been identified as the 'ego-ideal'; and we also see that he is looking for the origins of this agent in environmental demands and influences which have been 'gathered up' in the course of development. Some two years later, Freud (1923) specifies the source of these demands and influences as parental taboos, threats, constraints and so on, and treats their 'gathering' in terms of introjection as well.

In *The Ego and the Id* (1923, ch. 3), Freud refers back to both the principal works we have considered above (1917, 1921) as containing ideas relevant and germinal to the theory of superego-formation that he is now proposing. After reiterating that in melancholia 'an object-cathexis has been replaced by an identification', he goes on to say that he has 'come to understand' that this mechanism is more common than he had supposed and plays a major role in determining the 'character' of the ego. He illustrates the idea that this 'replacement' reflects a regression to a primitively oral form of object-relation by alluding, in a footnote, to the belief among some savages that 'the attributes of animals which are assimilated as nourishment survive as part of the character of the persons who eat them' (p. 36). And he continues:

'When . . . a person has to give up a sexual object, there quite often ensues a modification in his ego which can only be described as a

reinstatement of the object within the ego, as it occurs in melancholia; the exact nature of this substitution is as yet unknown to us.
It may be that by undertaking this introjection, which is a kind of
regression to the mechanism of the oral phase, the ego makes it
easier for an object to be given up or renders that process possible'
(p. 36).

This may even be the 'sole condition' on which the id can 'give up its objects'
or, presumably, survive the loss of an object. At any rate, 'the ego is a
precipitate of abandoned object-cathexes and ... contains a record of past
object-choices'.

This last passage provides a cogent *locus classicus* for theorists of Kleinian
persuasion who pretend to the mantle of Freud, and their case is strengthened
by the mention, a little later, of 'conflicts between the different identifications
into which the ego is split up'. It is becoming apparent too that Freud no longer
regards introjective identification as a merely defensive, postcathartic manoeuvre; and he specifically acknowledges (p. 37) the situation where identification (and therefore presumably introjection) is 'simultaneous' with cathexis and
antedates the loss of the object, in this way conserving 'in a certain sense' the
'object-relation'. We have noted above that the notion of preserving an
object-relation 'in the ego' differs importantly from that of setting up the object
itself therein: for it may well be that the former avoids the logical difficulties
inherent in the latter.

In the case of the infantile object-relations of the male child, Freud specifies
that the identification with the father is 'direct and immediate' and is not 'in the
first instance, ... the consequence of an object-cathexis': it takes place 'earlier
than any object-cathexis' (p. 39). The boy does, however, make an 'object-
cathexis' of his *mother* from the start. But after the dissolution of the 'Oedipus
complex' this latter object-cathexis has to be given up, and this leads normally
to an 'intensified identification with the father'. However, this post-oedipal
identification does *not* involve 'the absorption of the abandoned object into the
ego'—contrary, says Freud, to what 'our previous statements would have led us
to expect'.

Now, the assertion that identification can occur on a non-incorporative
model obviously raises the questions of *when* does it so occur, and of how can
one *tell* whether a given identification is incorporative or not. And why should
an intensified identification with *father* in this situation be based on an
introjection of the lost object, when what is *lost* is the *mother*? Freud seems to
be aware that a muddle is developing, and, after referring to infantile bisexuality, he pleads:

'It is this complicating element introduced by bisexuality that makes
it so difficult to obtain a clear view of the facts in connection with

the earliest object-choices and identifications, and still more difficult to describe them intelligibly. . . . It may even be that the ambivalence displayed in the relations to the parents should be attributed entirely to bisexuality and that it is not, as I stated just now, developed out of an identification in consequence of rivalry' (p. 43).

Freud thus admits that he is not clear just how identifications are created during, and as a result of, the oedipal phase, but he insists that the result is that the child emerges partly identified with both parents. The 'precipitate', consisting of 'these two identifications . . . combined together', which is formed 'in the ego' turns out to be the superego (p. 44). But this superego is not just a 'deposit' left by the earliest object-choices: it also represents 'an energetic reaction-formation against such choices'. That is to say, since it was formed in the first instance as a repressive agency, it mediates prohibitions as well as ideals. Freud says in fact that it 'owes its existence' to having repressed the Oedipus complex. We are already familiar with the idea of introjection as a palliative against anxiety, as a preservation technique in depression, and as a regression to identification; but Freud now presents it as also having repressive and progressive possibilities (the latter, insofar as it conduces to maturity and independence). It has also turned out that the 'critical agency' of melancholia, previously set over against that part of the ego modified by introjection, is itself the product of introjection.

This clearly opens the way to the view that *all* ego-structures, and consequently the greater part of the whole self-system, take rise from that mechanism. Just such a radical and comprehensive 'object-relations theory' of identity-development and psychopathology was propounded, of course, by Melanie Klein and her associates, but, before turning to them, let us take stock of how Freud's innovations in this area promote understanding both of normal self-differentiation and of disturbances in self-functioning.

Conspicuous disturbances of the self-concept, taking the very different forms of homosexuality and grandiose psychotic delusions, seemed to Freud to challenge his original instinct-theory, because in those cases libido has taken, in some sense, some part of the ego itself (instead of part of external reality) as its object. The grandiose psychotic has cathected his own power-fantasies in preference to a realistic assessment of his personal powers, and grossly exaggerates the efficacy of his own thoughts and words in 'magical thinking'. But this over-valuation of the Self and its powers was, Freud thought, not solely a pathological phenomenon but also characteristic of a normal developmental stage of infancy when the child has not yet learned, from accumulated contacts with the world 'out there', to distinguish what she *can* do from what she would *like* to do: the stage of 'infantile omnipotence'. From the primitive narcissistic state in which she gets emotional gratification from her own wishes and fantasies, the child gradually acquires the perceptual and adaptive powers to differentiate herself from the rest of the world and to choose external objects to serve her libidinal purposes (Jacobson, 1964, ch. 1; Laplanche and Pontalis, 1973, pp. 255–257). This transition, of course, may be less than complete and less than fully secure; and Freud saw evidence of its precariousness in the disturbed self-concepts, infantile emotions and regressive defences of his neurotic and schizoid patients. It is the Kleinians, however, who have theorized most extensively about early self-differentiation and its relation to the schizoid phenomena of 'borderline personalities', while Freud's clearest statements about self-concept and object-relations were to be found in his explanations of self-denigration in reactive depression, and of how self-confident or self-effacing traits are associated with patterns of superego-formation.

Explicit reference to self-esteem as a fundamental ingredient of personality which is impaired in depression is introduced by Bibring (1953) in his revision of Freud's account of depression, a revision which also includes detailed discussion of the part played by 'learned helplessness' long before the much-quoted work of Seligman (1975). Thus Bibring writes (1953, p. 27): '... basic depression represents a state of the ego whose main characteristics are a decrease of self-esteem, a more or less intense state of helplessness, ... inhibition of functions, and a ... particular emotion'.

By specifying 'introjection' as the medium of identification in the setting up of the superego, initially as a defence against oedipal anxieties, Freud proposed to explain why some people develop more rigid self-control than others do, or demand more of themselves, or are more resilient in adversity, or are more prone to defeat themselves, etc. And this mechanism becomes a central concept, along with its corollary 'projection', in all subsequent object-relations theory about personality-development and psychopathology.

3.4 The Kleinians: The Inner World Expands

We turn now to the views of Melanie Klein and her followers about the role of 'internal objects' in self-theory. Those theses that are not derived from Klein herself either can be traced back to Freud or Ferenczi, or have been put forward by an authoritative associate of hers (cp. Segal, 1964, p. vii; 1979, ch. 7). The first item that we consider is Heimann's (1952) discussion of introjection and projection which Riviere describes (1952, p. 23) as the 'first account of these processes specifically devoted to examining them' from the Kleinian point of view. But it is perhaps an intimation of squalls ahead that Riviere tries to forestall objections that are likely to be made to certain sorts of proposition involved in theorizing about internal objects (pp. 20–22). Heimann herself touches on the same point in the course of her essay, namely the general question, which inevitably arises in connection with the concept of infantile phantasy, of how to put into words what is supposed to be going on in the neonate's mind. It is easy enough to complain about what sorts of thing can *not* coherently be said about neonate mental processes, and we shall return below to consider what *can* perhaps be said instead; but for the moment we are concerned merely with what the Kleinians *want* to say on the subject, with special reference to the particular postulates of introjection and internal objects.

After outlining the ideas of Ferenczi and Freud about the relation between libidinal cathexis and introjection of the object, Heimann discusses perception in general and appears almost to redefine introjection in the very general terms of stimulus-reception.

> 'When the ego receives stimuli from outside, it absorbs them and makes them part of itself, it introjects them. When it bars them off it projects them, because the decision of their harmfulness is subsequent to a trial introjection. Selection, discrimination, etc. are based on introjection and projection' (1952, p. 125).

Now, what can it be to 'bar off' a stimulus? We may think, perhaps, of the reticular formation of the brain-stem blocking or switching off neural impulses coming in from peripheral receptors so that they do not reach the cortex; or, which may amount to the same thing, of an experimental subject 'failing to see' a red ace of spades presented tachistoscopically. When this happens, however, the 'stimuli' presumably do not reach the ego at all, and in any case it would be misleading to call *this* 'projection' because nothing is in any sense 'thrown forth'. But if there has been a 'trial introjection' preceding the projection, then the stimulus has not been 'barred off' in the required sense to begin with.

However, it is well known that some 'perceptual defence' experiments, which have involved recording concomitant autonomic reactions, do suggest that *some* information can be taken in from the stimulus-word even when it is not consciously 'seen'; and this can be regarded as support for the idea that some such preconscious filtering does occur (cp. Kline, 1972/1981, pp. 210–238). Heimann's distinction seems to be more like that between attending to a stimulus, or source of stimulation, and ignoring it. But if *that* is what is meant, then it is not very interesting to claim that introjection and projection are the 'instruments' for the 'very formation' of the ego (p. 126). Because clearly the great majority of learning and adaptation depends upon these mechanisms if they are defined so broadly, and from this it follows *a fortiori* that a *part* of such general adaptation (namely, ego-formation) is likely to be due to them. Although Heimann claims to be in the tradition of Ferenczi more closely than Freud was (p. 131), a clear discrepancy may be noted in her assertion that when the ego 'thrusts forth libidinal impulses' to make an object-cathexis, 'this represents a projection of what is good and useful'. For this appears to conflict with Ferenczi's own view that, when 'stimulus-hungry affects . . . come out to meet' stimuli, this is, or leads to, an instance of *intro*jection, as we have seen above. It also touches on the question, raised above by Freud's diverse expressions, of *what* is introjected. Heimann's explanation (p. 127) that the 'objects' introjected are 'psychological entities' does not help: the question at issue is *what* psychological entities, and what is the point of saying that they are *introjected*.

Heimann goes on to elaborate the Kleinian view that introjection, etc. of objects starts with the neonate's very first perceptions and experiences, and that as a result of such processes the ego itself (and not just the superego as Freud tends to suggest) is produced.

> 'Beginning with the introjection of the breast, the infant proceeds to introject all his objects. Since these are psychological entities . . . introjection and projection lead to . . . the development of the ego and the superego, the formation of character . . . . The view that introjection leads to the formation of the superego is fully accepted in psychoanalytic thought, whereas it is not generally recognised that introjection plays an identical part in the building up of the ego' (pp. 127, 130).

Part of the evidence for this is that the infant comes to imitate his objects and 'represents by his own body what he has noticed about the person he is concerned with, thus showing that he has absorbed, "introjected", him (or her)' (p. 128). But how do such observations 'show' anything of the sort? The infant has 'thrown' something from (or of) the other person 'into' itself in only a highly figurative sense: the question is whether it is a theoretically *useful* sense. Unless 'introjection' has become just another name for imitation, we still need independent evidence that a *separate* process has occurred upon which imitation somehow depends. (What would be the point, for example, of explaining to a child how a camera works by saying, 'Well, you see, it *introjects* things'?)

At any rate it seems that the ego is being regarded no longer as *containing* certain introjected objects (as a pod contains peas) but rather as *consisting of* such objects (as a molecule consists of atoms). This general Kleinian view is contrasted by Heimann with that of Freud, who 'explicitly acknowledged the influence of introjection on the formation of character (i.e. the ego) only after the decline of the Oedipus complex'. And yet Heimann insists that 'Melanie Klein's findings concerning ego-formation are fully in line with Freud's work': this is because they demonstrate 'certain conclusions which follow from Freud's exposition' but have generally been left undrawn (p. 130).

One such conclusion is that projection, as well as introjection, is an important factor in superego-development. For the element of 'energetic reaction-formation' by reason of which the superego consists not just of idealization but also of taboos, such as 'you *must not be* such and such (like your father)', indicates, according to Heimann, that 'the introjection of the parents is a selective process' such that the ego 'introjects certain of their aspects and projects others'. But once it is allowed (p. 137) that *aspects* of objects, or even objects in certain roles, are what is introjected, then the parent-figures could be supposed to have been introjected in their (phantasied) tabooing, prohibiting roles as well as in idealized aspect, thus obviating the need to appeal to projection.

The Kleinian view is then that the superego (and ego) can be said to start with the very first part-objects (mother's breast, father's penis) 'introjected' by the infant under pressure of extravagant phantasies about them; and that, as intelligence, experience and reality-testing develop, these 'objects' are converted 'more and more to the likeness of the real parents until they appear in the way described by Freud as the superego' (p. 136). Heimann recognizes, though, that this theory invites the question, 'When does an act of introjection contribute to ego-formation, and when to the formation of the superego?' The answer is that it depends upon which aspects of the parent (object) the child is mainly concerned with at the time: 'The emotional situation in which the child performs the act of introjection decides its results' (p. 137).

This dictum, and Heimann's remarkable example of a child who introjects his mother while she is washing him, shows that introjection is capable of being regarded as an action occurring more or less at points in time, apparently very much like taking a photograph. Once again, if it is the *function*, etc. of the object, and the emotional context, that are the effective variables in the operation, then it is a gratuitous complication to introduce the *object* in itself at all, since, as Bergson put it (1911, p. 199): 'In order to follow the indications of instinct, there is no need to perceive *objects*: it is enough to distinguish *properties*.' Furthermore, motivation or 'perceptual set' are also important determinants of what stimulus-properties of a situation are responded *to*, and thereby of the character of the resultant 'internal object': thus 'the aspect selected corresponds with the infant's predominant urge' (p. 143). We are perfectly familiar with the idea of a child attending to/ being impressed by/ learning from different features of a perceived situation (mother as feeder, mother as comforter, father as lifter-up-to-the-ceiling, etc.); and those situations which involve parents no doubt provide a unique combination of evaluative (superego) and informative (ego) content. But we have to ask what is gained by hanging such learning on the peg of 'introjected *objects*', and we shall see that other theorists have preferred to think in terms of 'imagos' (Fuchs, 1937) or 'representations' (Jacobson, 1964, ch. 5).

One advantage of the Kleinian system is, according to Heimann (p. 138), that it 'covers better those aspects of the superego system in which protection and encouragement, rather than fear and inhibition, prevail'. It does so by asserting that when a child's parents encourage him to do something new, such 'experiences . . . are internalised and form a pattern for the superego. Moreover on the first of any such occasions, an introjection occurs resulting in the child's greater courage at the time.' This courage apparently results from 'an expansion of the ego' due to the 'assimilation' of its good objects. On the face of it, this account looks as though it is providing a theoretical explanation or analysis of the origins of self-esteem in infancy, and it seems furthermore as if this account can claim powerful support from the later and completely independent empirical investigations of Coopersmith (1967). For did not that study show (pp. 208–215) that boys who displayed high self-esteem had parents who had respected the boys' points of view even as young children (whereas the parents of low self-esteem boys had tended to ignore theirs), so that the former children could be said to have developed esteem for themselves as a result of having introjected those agents by whom they were already esteemed?

And yet this situation is significantly different from Heimann's example of 'courage', for there the *connection* between the assimilation of merely 'good' objects and the generation of *courage* specifically (or what we might better call 'morale') is left unexplained; and it must also be conceded that the 'higher natures', which according to Freud (1923, p. 47) we knew in our parents and took into ourselves as the superego, were regarded by him as having kind and supportive features as well as the threatening and restrictive ones which are emphasized traditionally. In any case, it is not 'experiences', rather than objects, which are said there to be 'internalized'; and, again, unless there are independent criteria for the ego-expansion that is said to take place (so that we can tell both that the ego really *has* expanded, and also that the courage is a *result* of that expansion), the explanation of how the child develops courage is logically parallel to that bogus explanation of how a camera takes photographs which we introduced above.

Furthermore, the introjective process which is postulated to explain courage and self-esteem is· significantly different from that invoked by Freud to account for self-*dis*esteem and self-blame in depression. For, whereas the brave or self-esteeming child has introjected, and identified with, the *agent* who is not afraid of some psychological 'object' or who actively esteems the child as 'object', the self-critical depressive is said to have introjected the (part-)*object* towards which his own active hostility and resentment was directed. Thus the proposed mechanisms for explaining good self-feeling (introjection of esteeming *subject*) and bad self-feeling (introjection of criticized *object*) are by no means as parallel as they need to be for the purposes of a general theory. This is partly because in this context the term 'object' gets uses in at least three different senses, as Laplanche and Pontalis point out (1973, pp. 273–276), and the theorists are not always careful enough to avoid sliding from one sense to another; and partly because the Kleinians are opting to generalize the paradigm of introjection which they find in Freud's account of superego-formation rather than that by which he originally explained depression. From this point of view, chronic low self-esteem (the so-called 'depressive personality', or the factor isolated by Kline and Storey (1977) as 'oral pessimism') would result from having introjected depriving, rejecting or fault-finding parent-figures. And here again psychoanalytic theory, about the connection between 'oral frustration' and depressive personality traits, can look for support to the well-known researches of Coopersmith, who found that mothers who had weaned early, experienced feeding-problems or vacillated between breast and bottle belonged significantly more often to low-esteem boys than to their classmates with higher self-esteem (1967, p. 154).

However, if the Kleinians have in some way turned their backs on the Freudian account of clinical depression, it is not for any lack of interest in the phenomena of depressive affect and negative self-concept: on the contrary, they give them a central place in the course of normal (and not just pathological) emotional development.

According to Kleinian theory, the infant regularly goes through a depressive phase as early as the second half of the first year of life. This is because, at about the age of six months, the baby begins to realize that the bad object towards which he had previously been directing hateful and destructive phantasies, and the good object which had been receiving loving and preserving phantasies, are in fact one and the same person, namely the mother. It is supposed that the infant has previously conceptualized the source of all its pleasant, comfortable and satisfying experiences as a benevolent good object, while the source of its unpleasant experiences of discomfort, hunger or loneliness is attributed to a hostile bad object who is attacking the infant. These two objects are felt to be quite separate agencies, and this stage of psychological development is consequently known as paranoid-schizoid. When the baby comes to realize that good object and bad object are one and the same person, namely mother, it follows that the target of all the infant's hateful and destructive wishes had really been the loved mother. This realization precipitates a state of guilt-ridden depression, from which the infant recovers only by coming to understand that it can make reparation for the damage which it has, in phantasy, inflicted upon the loved good object (Segal, 1979, ch. 7 and 9).

About the paranoid-schizoid position, Klein herself says (1952, p. 200):

> 'The recurrent experiences of gratification and frustration are powerful stimuli ... for love and hatred. As a result, the breast, in as much as it is gratifying, is ... felt to be good; in so far as it is a source of frustration, it is ... felt to be bad. ... the infant projects his love impulses and attributes them to the gratifying (good) breast, just as he projects his destructive impulses outwards and attributes them to the frustrating (bad) breast. Simultaneously, by introjection, a good breast and a bad breast are established inside. ... the good breast becomes the prototype of all helpful and gratifying objects, the bad breast the prototype of all ... persecutory objects.'

This last sentence indicates how it might be held that these first introjected objects form the core of the superego, as Klein asserts. The source of feelings of support or threat postulated here is different from (and of course much earlier than) those of Freud's theory, the frustrating breast being substituted for the punishing father-figure.

But the quotation also illustrates two kinds of problem which commentators have encountered in Kleinian theory: the first is to do with the use of metaphor and the possibility that the concept of internal object may be redundant, and the second concerns the cognitive powers which Klein apparently attributes to the very young infant. The use of the drawing-board metaphor of 'prototype' suggests that the infant designs, as it were, the concept of gratifying objects (internal and external) on the basis of its representation of the good breast; and yet the concept of mediating objects may well be unnecessary, since all that matters is how *attitudes* and *expectations* about further encounters with the world are determined by previous experiences of actual objects (and by phantasies about them) before such negative attitudes come to colour the child's perceptions of actual objects and events as being, or likely to be, good or bad. Learned dispositions subsequently directed towards actual objects, rather than the construction of mental object-models, are all that the theory seems to require at this point. In which case we can rewrite Heimann's dictum (1952, p. 148) that the external object 'provides the experience from which the internal object is constructed' to read that it 'provides the experience from which perceptual and emotional dispositions are acquired'.

Secondly, the assumption, in the second sentence of the above quotation, that the baby in the first half of its first year can somehow already conceptualize a separate object as the causal source of a 'good experience', may attribute to infants a degree of cognitive sophistication which they do not yet possess. In Piaget's well-known experiments to do with moving physical objects from one place to another in full view of the child and then letting it look for them, it seemed that infants cannot, until about the beginning of the second year, reliably abstract a displaced *object* (as such) from the *action* of displacing it; and this makes it doubtful that the infantile intellect is equal to the task which Klein proposes (Piaget, 1950, pp. 109–110). Since this issue is crucially relevant, it is remarkable that Solnit (1982) should have been able to publish his recent psychoanalytic discussion of 'object-constancy' in infancy without making any reference to Piaget's classic studies of this topic. This question of the relation between the Kleinian and Piagetian conceptions of the 'permanence' or 'constancy' of psychological objects had already been addressed quite specifically by Bowlby (1980, ch. 25), and has been elaborated subsequently by Leon (1984) and by some contributors to Lax (1985).

On the other hand, a good deal of work in developmental psychology has shown that at least some of Piaget's methods, by using experimental situations that were not personally meaningful to young children, have underestimated their cognitive competence (Bryant, 1974; Donaldson, 1978). So much so, that the Kleinians are now able to mount a counter-attack against this sort of objection when it is raised in the context of the 'depressive position', and can plausibly appeal to an ingenious experiment by Bower (1977) as confirming that they were right all along in asserting that infants *do* make a significant perceptual *Gestalt*-synthesis at about this time. They can also invoke the findings of another developmental study (Ainsworth *et al.*, 1974) which may be seen as fitting in with their notions about persecutory phantasy in infants.

The hypotheses in question, on which these empirical studies impinge, concern the so-called 'paranoid-schizoid position' of the first half-year of infancy during which the baby is supposed to construct the phantasy of a benevolent 'good object' out of its experiences of comfort and need-gratification, but also to attribute its experiences of frustration and distress to the persecutory activity of a 'bad object'. This situation is said to be changed radically at the middle of the first year, when the baby, according to Klein, comes to perceive its mother as 'a whole person' (who must therefore combine in herself both the loved and hated attributes of the hitherto separate good and bad objects).

From the first part of the account it would follow that a mother can minimize the likelihood that her baby will develop a sense of 'persecuted' insecurity, corresponding to Erikson's 'basic mistrust', by ensuring that its experiences of frustrated distress (inevitable as they no doubt sometimes are) are kept as few and as short as possible. One practical way of doing this would be to respond to its crying with comfort regularly and promptly (e.g. at night-time waking). On this view, mothers who comfort promptly should produce secure infants who have 'basic trust' in their world and can therefore begin to tolerate frustration. According to Skinnerian learning theory, however, the opposite should occur: because to respond with comfort to the crying is to 'reinforce' that crying, so that mothers who comfort readily will (it is alleged) train up crying in their babies *more* than will mothers who ignore crying. Well, which of these conflicting predictions is nearer the mark: the psychodynamic Kleinian or the 'scientific' Skinnerian?

The results of an empirical investigation by Ainsworth *et al.* (1974) tend firmly in favour of Klein rather than Skinner. Those babies whose cries were attended to relatively promptly during their first six months cried *less* readily at the start of their second year than did other babies whose crying had been ignored. So that, so far from having 'learned' to cry because their 'crying-behaviour' had been 'reinforced', it seemed that what the comforted babies had learned was 'basic trust' in a 'good object', as a result of which they became better able to tolerate frustration *without* crying. Studies such as this, and others into the minutiae of infant–mother communication and 'intersubjectivity' (e.g. Trevarthen, 1979; Condon, 1979; Lock, 1978, *passim*), have compelled laboratory-oriented developmentalists to take psychodynamic notions about the mental capacities of infants a great deal more seriously than they had been inclined to do.

Klein's other hypothesis about the 'paranoid-schizoid position' is another case in point. Her claim that infants are already perceiving their mothers as 'a whole person' by the middle of the first year was so wildly at odds with what the academics thought they knew about the cognitive limitations of infants, on the strength of the accepted demonstrations of Piaget, that it could safely be treated with scorn (cp. Cheshire, 1966, ch. 4). After all, had not Piaget shown that the infant does not have a clear and firm concept even of an 'object' until the beginning of the second year, and that he can still make radical mistakes about the concept of a 'person' when already into his third year? Nevertheless, the results of an ingenious experiment by Bower (1977, p. 202) again come down in favour of Klein and against the academic orthodoxy.

Bower arranged for mothers to watch their infants play in an experimental play-room, and set up an optical apparatus to project mother's image on a screen which the babies could see and react to without being in direct contact with her. These images could be quite literally 'split', so that, instead of seeing just one figure, the babies sometimes saw three separate images of their mother, side-by-side in somewhat different conditions of illumination and definition. The split-image condition did not bother the babies who were less than about six months old, and they would happily interact with the different images separately; but slightly older infants, in the second half of their first year, were quite definitely disturbed by the 'multiple-mother' situation and reacted with various forms of distress as if they felt that something was wrong. Bower concludes, without mentioning Klein and evidently without having the least idea that he is quite specifically corroborating a controversial Kleinian thesis: 'I would contend that this in fact shows the young infant (less than five months) thinks he has a multiplicity of mothers, whereas the older child knows he has but one.'

Two modest cheers, perhaps, for Melanie Klein. Although her ideas about a 'paranoid-schizoid' stage and its implications have remained central to much of object-relations theory, it has nevertheless branched out in new directions from her pioneering formulations. Some of the subsequent theorists and commentators have added to the metaphors for the inner world in a bewildering way, but others have seen the need to clarify them and to render them both psychologically and neurologically realistic, as Sutherland has remarked in his useful review of the 'British School' of object-relations theory (1980, pp. 851–853). These issues are taken up by Cheshire and Thomae in Chapter 4.

References

Ainsworth, M. D. S., Bell, S. M. and Stayton, D. J. (1974) Infant–mother attachment. . . In *The Integration of a Child into a Social World* (ed. M. P. M. Richards), ch. 6. Cambridge University Press, Cambridge.

Bergson, H. (1911). *Matter and Memory* (translated by N. M. Paul and W. S. Palmer). Swan Sonnenschein, London.

Bettelheim, B. (1983). *Freud and Man's Soul*. Chatto and Windus, London.

Bibring, E. (1953). The mechanism of depression. In *Affective Disorders* (ed. P. Greenacre), pp. 13–48. International Universities Press, New York.

Boden, M. A. (1974). Freudian mechanisms of defence: . . . Reprinted in *Minds and Mechanisms*, ch. 10, Harvester, Brighton (1981).

Bower, T. G. R. (1977). *A Primer of Infant Development*. Freeman, Oxford.

Bowlby, J. (1980). *Loss: Sadness and Depression*. Hogarth, London.

Bryant, P. E. (1974). *Perception and Understanding in Young Children*. Methuen, London.

Carveth, D. L. (1984). Psychoanalysis and social theory: . . . *Psychoanal. Contemp. Thought*, 7, 43–98.

Cheshire, N. M. (1966) *Some Concepts of Object-relations Theory*. B. Litt. Thesis, Oxford University (Bodleian Library).

Colby, K. M. (1955). *Energy and Structure in Psychoanalysis*. Ronald, New York.

Condon, W. S. (1979). Neonatal entrainment and enculturation. In *Before Speech* (ed. M. Bullowa), pp. 131–148. Cambridge University Press, Cambridge.

Coopersmith, S. (1967). *The Antecedents of Self-esteem*. Freeman, San Francisco.

Donaldson, M. (1978). *Children's Minds*. Fontana/Collins, London.

Eagle, M. N. (1983). The epistemological status of recent developments. . . In *Physics, Philosophy and Psychoanalysis* (eds R. S. Cohen and L. Landan), pp. 31–55. Reidel, Dordrecht.

Eagle, M. N. (1984). *Recent Developments in Psychoanalysis: A Critical Evaluation*. McGraw-Hill, New York.

Erikson, E. H. (1963). *Childhood and Society*, second edition. Penguin, Harmondsworth.

Erikson, E. H. (1968). *Identity: Youth and Crisis*. Norton, New York.

Ferenczi, S. (1909). Introjection and transference. In *First Contributions to Psychoanalysis* (translated by E. Jones, 1952) pp. 35–93. Hogarth, London.

Ferenczi, S. (1949). Correspondence with Freud. *Int. J. Psychoanal*, 30.

Freud, A. (1937). *The Ego and the Mechanisms of Defence* (translated by C. Baines). Hogarth, London.

Freud, S. (1915). Instincts and their vicissitudes. *Standard Ed.*, 14, 109–140.

Freud, S. (1917). *Mourning and melancholia. Standard Ed.*, 14, 237–258.

Freud, S. (1921). Group psychology. . . *Standard Ed.*, 18, 65–143.

Freud, S. (1923). The ego and the id. *Standard Ed.*, 19, (1961), pp. 1–66.

Freud, S. (1940). An outline of psychoanalysis. *Standard Ed.*, 23, 141–207.

Fuchs, S. H. (1937). Introjection. *Int. J. Psychoanal.*, 18, 269–293.

Gauld, A. and Shotter, J. (1977). *Human Action and its Psychological Investigation*. Routledge and Kegan Paul, London.

Grotstein, J. S. (1982). Newer perspectives in object and relations theory. *Contemp. Psychoanal.*, 18, 43–91.

Hartmann, H. (1950). Comments on the. . . theory of the ego. Reprinted in *Essays on Ego Psychology* (1964), pp. 113–141. Hogarth, London.

Hartmann, H. (1956). The development of the ego concept in Freud's work. Reprinted in *Essays on Ego Psychology* (1964), pp. 268–296. Hogarth, London.

Heimann, P. (1952). Certain functions of introjection and projection. . . In *Developments in Psychoanalysis* (ed. J. Riviere), pp. 122–168. Hogarth, London.

Jacobson, E. (1954). The Self and the Object-world. *Psychoanal. Study Child*, 9, 75–127.

Jacobson, E. (1964). *The Self and the Object-world.* International Universities Press, New York.

Kernberg, O. F. (1977). *Object Relations Theory and Classical Psychoanalysis.* Aronson, New York.

Kline, P. (1972/1981). *Fact and Fantasy in Freudian Theory,* first and second editions. Methuen, London.

Kline, P. and Storey, R. (1977). A factor-analytic study of the oral character. *Brit. J. Soc. Clin. Psychol.,* **16**, 317–328.

Kohon, G. (1986). Notes on the history of the psychoanalytic movement.... In *The British School of Psychoanalysis* (ed. G. Kohon), pp. 24–50. Free Association Books., London.

Kohut, H. (1971). *The Analysis of the Self.* International Universities Press, New York.

Kohut, H. (1977). *The Restoration of the Self.* International Universities Press, New York.

Laing, R. D. (1965). *The Divided Self,* second edition. Penguin, Harmondsworth.

Laing, R. D. (1969). *The Self and Others,* second edition. Penguin, Harmondsworth.

Laplanche, J. and Pontalis, J. B. (1973). *The Language of Psychoanalysis* (translated by D. Nicholson-Smith). Hogarth, London.

Lax, R. *et al.* (eds) (1985). *Self and Object-constancy: Clinical and Theoretical Perspectives.* Guilford, New York.

Leon, I. G. (1984). Psychoanalysis, Piaget and attachment... *Int. Rev. Psychoanal.,* **11**, 255–278.

Lock, A. (ed.) (1978). *Action, Gesture and Symbol.* Academic Press, London.

Mahler, M. S., Pine, F. and Bergman, A. (1975). *The Psychological Birth of the Human Infant.* Hutchinson. London.

Marsella, A. J. *et al.* (eds) (1985) *Culture and Self:* ... Tavistock, New York and London.

McDevitt, J. B. (1979). The role of internalisation in the development of object-relations... *J. Am. Psychoanal. Assoc.,* **27**, 327–343.

Meissner, N. W. (1979). Internalisation and object-relations. *J. Am. Psychoanal. Assoc.,* **27**, 345–360.

Padel, J. (1986). Ego in current thinking. In *The British School of Psychoanalysis* (ed. G. Kohon), pp. 154–172. Free Association Books. London.

Peterfreund, E. (1983). *The Process of Psychoanalytic Therapy:* ... Analytic Press, Hillsdale (NJ).

Piaget, J. (1950). *The Psychology of Intelligence* (translated by M. Piercy and D. E. Berlyne). Routledge and Kegan Paul, London.

Ricoeur, P. (1970). *Freud and Philosophy:* ... (translated by D. Savage). Yale University Press, New Haven and London.

Riviere, J., (ed.) (1952). *Developments in Psychoanalysis.* Hogarth Press, London.

Rothstein, A. (ed.) (1985). *Models of the Mind.* International Universities Press, New York.

Ryle, G. (1949). *The Concept of Mind.* Penguin, Harmondsworth.

Sandler, J. and Rosenblatt, B. (1962). The concept of the representational world. *Psychoanal. Study Child,* **17**, 128–145.

Schafer, R. (1968). *Aspects of Internalisation.* International Universities Press, New York.

Schafer, R. (1976). *A New Language for Psychoanalysis.* Yale University Press, New Haven.

Segal, H. (1964). *Introduction to the Work of Melanie Klein.* Tavistock, London.

Segal, H. (1979). *Klein.* Fontana/Collins, London.

Seligman, M. E. P. (1975). *Helplessness:* . . . Freeman, San Francisco.

Shotter, J. (1984). *Social Accountability and Selfhood.* Blackwell, Oxford.

Shotter, J. and Newson, J. (1982). An ecological approach to cognitive development: . . . In *Social Cognition* (eds G. Butterworth and P. Light), ch. 3. Harvester, Brighton.

Solnit, A. J. (1982). Developmental perspectives on self and object constancy. *Psychoanal. Study Child,* **37,** 201–218.

Sutherland, J. D. (1980). The British object-relations theorists: . . . *J. Am. Psychoanal. Assoc.,* **28,** 829–860.

Trevarthen, C. (1979). Communication and cooperation in early infancy: . . . In *Before Speech* (ed. M. Bullowa), pp. 321–347. Cambridge University Press, Cambridge.

Trevarthen, C. (1982). The primary motives for cooperative understanding. In *Social Cognition* (eds. G. Butterworth and P. Light), ch. 5. Harvester, Brighton.

Tuttman, S. (1981). *Object and Self.* International Universities Press, New York.

Wilden, A. (1968). *The Language of the Self.* Johns Hopkins, Baltimore.

Wilshire, B. (1982). *Role-Playing and Identity.* Indiana University Press, Bloomington (Ind.).

Self, Symptoms and Psychotherapy
Edited by N. Cheshire and H. Thomae
© 1987 John Wiley & Sons Ltd

CHAPTER 4

New Ways in the Object-relations of the Self

Neil Cheshire and Helmut Thomae

4.1 *Introduction*
4.2 *Theoretical descendants of Melanie Klein*
4.3 *Problems and resolutions*
4.4 *Applications to research in psychotherapy*

4.1 Introduction

Against the general background of Klein's ideas, though by no means necessarily in agreement with them, both Balint (e.g. 1956, 1968) and Winnicott (e.g. 1964, 1971) had notably explored the relation between the quality of an infant's earliest maternal bonding and his or her subsequent psychopathology and sense of identity. Balint's emphasis on what he called 'primary love', and his description of the part played in schizoid self-problems by an early 'basic fault' in mother–infant interaction, are well known; and so are Winnicott's clinical investigations of the separation-individuation stage of infancy, which introduced the seminal concept of 'transitional objects' (1971, ch. 1). But, in so far as this emphasis on early object-relations was placed within the theoretical context of the gratification of more fundamental libidinal drives, because forming object-relations is seen as a *means* of satisfying basic instinctual needs, this concentration upon infantile object-relations does not in itself challenge or supplant (any more than Klein's own focus did) traditional psychoanalytic drive-theory in its later form. These, and other associated, theoretical developments have been critically reviewed in some detail by Eagle (1984) and by Rothstein (1985), and are exemplified *passim* in Kohon (1986) and Grosskurth (1986).

4.2 Theoretical Descendants of Melanie Klein

This challenge was, however, eventually made by Fairbairn, who explicitly rejected Freudian instinct theory and substituted object-seeking in place of the pleasure-principle as the primary emotional drive in psychological functioning. The fact that Fairbairn has only recently become well known outside British psychoanalytic circles is due no doubt partly to the fact that his views were too radical and heretical to be promoted by British analysts in general, and partly to the fact of his geographical and academic distance from the psychoanalytic mainstream. Nevertheless, perhaps precisely because of this difference in intellectual background, his theoretical formulations (1941, 1963), complex and challenging as they are, do have an apparent logical rigour and internal consistency which appeals to those who are alienated by the philosophical indiscipline of the Kleinians (even though a detailed examination of his writings may show them to have their own looseness and inconsistency beneath the surface: cp. Cheshire, 1966, ch. 5). Fairbairn's work found an energetic champion in Guntrip (1952, 1961), and to some extent more recently in Kernberg (1972, 1977, 1979), without whom his radical extension of object-relations theory would be even less familiar to us than it is.

But, although Fairbairn's revision is radical in the sense that it puts object-seeking at the root of psychological and emotional development, and attributes to wish-satisfaction only a secondary role, yet he insists (as the Kleinians had done in their turn) that this theoretical move is not a contradiction of Freud but an exposition and articulation of a shift of emphasis which is to be found latent in Freud's own thinking, and he was 'very strongly against people attributing a new school to himself' (Sutherland, 1980, p. 843). Fairbairn expresses his theoretical reorientation in this way (1952, p. 137):

> 'The ultimate principle from which the whole of my special views are derived may be formulated in the general proposition that libido is not primarily pleasure-seeking, but object-seeking. The clinical material on which this proposition is based may be summarized in the protesting cry of a patient to this effect—"You are always talking about my wanting this and that desire satisfied; but what I really want is a father." '

Fairbairn revises the picture of the inner world by depicting it in terms of relationships among a multiplicity of what he calls 'endopsychic structures' instead of conflicts between emotional forces: the whole story is about structures rather than impulses and energy. And yet, as we shall see, these structures (which themselves are not without a place in the Freudian scheme of things) have to be energized from somewhere, and do indeed turn out to be charged with what look remarkably like positive and negative forms of libidinal energy. As Fairbairn himself put it (1952, pp. 84–85):

> 'I had already become very much impressed by the limitations of "impulse psychology" in general. . . . Impulses cannot be considered

apart from the endopsychic structures which they energise and the object-relationships which they enable these structures to establish; and, equally, instincts cannot profitably be considered as anything more than forms of energy which constitute the dynamic of such endopsychic structures.'

These considerations lead Fairbairn to a theory about the normal development of the self-system which is by far the most complex picture drawn by any of the object-relations theorists; and to a new account of the development of personality traits and characteristics, which is to take the place of the traditional psychosexual stages which Freud had taken over from Abraham. They lead him also to a theory of defences and psychopathology in which the chief dynamics are internalization, externalization, acceptance, rejection and excitation; and where the influence of Fairbairn's clinical preoccupation with schizoid problems to do with the differentiation and integration of the self-system is apparent.

He seems to be concerned to say, in the above quotation, that instincts, etc. are abstractions derived from the behaviour of what he calls structures, and this would be readily agreed by many instinct theorists themselves. And, although he is content to call such instincts 'forms of energy', what he apparently wants to resist is the tendency, which he attributes to Freud (and to some extent also to Klein), to hypostatize them and treat them as separable, independently existing, forces which act upon passive structures. From what he says elsewhere (e.g. 1952, p. 150), however, it seems that he cannot decide whether he thinks that instincts *consist in* the activity of psychical structures or whether they are forms of energy of which such structures somehow *partake* as if by some process like Platonic *methexis*. Guntrip attempts to specify the difference less rhetorically by saying (1961, p. 274):

'Internal tensions are always the tensions of object-seeking drives, which does away with the difference between appetitive and reactive tendencies. Innate needs and reaction to libidinal objects are parts of one whole, but aggression can now take a secondary place as simply a reaction to the frustration of libidinal needs, and not a permanent drive or mental entity *per se*.'

The last phrase here is directed against Klein whom he has earlier accused of unnecessarily calling in the idea of aggression as an innate drive. But it is arguable that she has merely grafted the Thanatos story on to her accounts of infant behaviour without its being logically necessary to them. It is also debatable that Kleinians would want, much less that they *need*, to say specifically that aggression is a 'mental entity in itself' (whatever that may mean). Again, one still needs an explanation of *why* aggression should occur as a reaction to frustration: to say that it simply does so is to beg this whole question. Klein at least recognizes the need to consider the point, and it may be objected that Fairbairn himself has to smuggle in an implied answer to it in his own concept of an 'antilibidinal ego', which we shall encounter later (cp. Greenberg and Mitchell, 1983).

Another line of argument which Fairbairn uses relates to his interest in schizoid phenomena; an interest which was shared by Bion, whose obscure (and some would say obscurantist) formulations have been related to this context by Grotstein (1982, *passim*) and also by Hamilton (1982). For Fairbairn, the schizoid personality is to be understood as arising not so much from a problem of impulse-control as from a struggle to achieve good object-relationships in face of the deep-seated fear that love, and seeking-for-love, are destructive. This results in a splitting of the ego, a concentration on internalized objects, and a reluctance to make cathecting advances to the external world. It is held to derive from difficulties in the early part of the oral phase (which is characterized by sucking), whereas the depressive person's fear of destroying its good object by hate is attributable to a disturbance occurring at the later (biting) stage of the same phase.

Fairbairn claims that analysis reveals that such schizoid anxieties are more widespread than is generally supposed, and sees this as providing further support for his contention that the search for object-relations is the basic human motivation. He has to concede, of course, that superficially pleasure-seeking or need-satisfying behaviour does occur; but he regards it as a 'deteriorated' form of response, in which a 'safety-valve process' takes over to relieve the tension that has built up as a result of failure to achieve some object-relationship. Students of Kohut will find this idea turning up again in his writings, more than two decades later, without reference to Fairbairn: for example, 'I have come to see ... destructiveness ... not as the manifestation of a primary drive ..., but as a disintegration product which .../.../... arises originally as a result of the failure of the self-object environment to meet the child's need for ... empathic responses' (Kohut, 1977, pp. 114–116).

From such clinical observations as these, it followed inevitably, says Fairbairn, that he should also question the validity of Abraham's phase-theory of ego-development and the aetiological theory based upon it. The traditional zones are to be understood merely as 'channels mediating the primary object-seeking aims of the ego'; and Abraham's phases, apart from the two oral ones, as false abstractions from various 'techniques employed by the ego for regulating relationships with objects'. The idea of phase-fixation producing certain psychopathological states needs to be reconstructed, except in the case of schizophrenia and depression, in terms of such specific techniques (Fairbairn, 1952, pp. 162–179).

What Fairbairn wants to substitute is the idea of a transition from immature object-dependency, characterized by primary identification with the object and by an (oral) attitude of 'taking', towards mature dependence based on different-iation of the object and on a predominantly 'giving' (second genital) attitude. This transition starts when, after the late oral phase, the differentiated object is replaced by accepted and rejected objects which 'tend to be treated largely as internalized objects'. At this point, excretory processes acquire emotional and developmental significance because (and only because) the child has to draw upon his own experience for models of rejecting and object-controlling tech-niques. Paranoid, obsessional and oedipal conflicts can be reconstructed in these terms (1952, pp. 36–37), with the nature of the object-relation determining the quality of the libidinal adjustment at any particular stage, and not *vice versa*. This systematic internal dependence is epitomized in Fairbairn's revision-ary dictum (1952, p. 32):

> 'It is not in virtue of the fact that the genital level has been reached that object-relationships are satisfactory. On the contrary, it is in virtue of the fact that satisfactory object-relationships have been established that true genital sexuality is obtained.'

Since the ego's earliest relation to its object is that of identification, followed or accompanied by incorporation, the transition to a mature 'anaclitic' re-lationship with a differentiated object must involve some process of externaliz-ation or mental expulsion; hence the subjective significance of excretory func-tions, as we have just seen. It also conduces to various sorts of conflict between wishes and fears relating to the internal and external world. The enormous complexities which are generated in the internal world by the splitting of those objects and ego are expounded in the account of 'endopsychic structure'; but, for the purpose of the revised psychopathology of 1941, Fairbairn codifies the relevant possibilities in terms of the acceptance or rejection of the internalized or externalized object. There (1952, pp. 28–58) he refers hysterical, paranoid, obsessional and phobic reactions severally to one of the four possible combi-nations. According to this scheme, the hysteric, for instance, accepts the externalized object (as illustrated by the hypercathexis of people and causes) and rejects the internalized one (as can be seen in 'the characteristic hysterical dissociation' and in conversion disabilities). The paranoid position, however, is precisely the reverse of this. The phobic is said to externalize both objects, and the obsessional to treat both as internal.

This makes neat taxonomy and allows for some plausible analogies with clinical observations. But we may entertain the suspicion that this convenience has been achieved at the expense of a remarkably elastic concept of the 'object', which can cover both a desired state of independence (for the phobic) and also the phantasied contents of the breast (for the obsessional). The examples given are to be regarded as extreme stereotypes: the average person will draw on all four possibilities in different situations, and the selection which he makes will depend, according to Fairbairn, on the nature of the object-relationships which he established at the oral level.

These then are the possible vicissitudes of the transition process. Two consequences which follow from Fairbairn's views on internalization, object-seeking and splitting are that there is a plurality of ego-structures and that repression acts not on impulses but on objects. Fairbairn disarmingly admits (1952, p. 133) that in expounding these complexities he becomes tangled in the web he is weaving, and the uninitiated might be well advised to approach the topic by way of Sutherland's summary (1980, pp. 843–848). But, from the point of view of the Self and psychotherapy, we must at least notice one important implication of his scheme, which is the development of a tripartite ego. For, in order to cope with the ambivalence which it has towards the internalized object, the 'original ego' (which he later agreed to call the 'self', following Guntrip) is split into separate 'exciting' and 'rejecting' objects; but *ex hypothesi* this cannot be done without also splitting off those parts of the ego that are attached or closely bound to both objects (1952, p. 170). There are formed, as a result, a 'libidinal' ego (corresponding to the 'exciting object'), an 'antilibidinal' ego and a 'central' ego. It is tempting to complain that Fairbairn has merely been carried away by the implications of the spatial metaphors in which he describes his observations. He does try to argue, however, that this way of talking has advantages over others, and his claim has been supported for a couple of decades now by the British philosopher of science J. O. Wisdom. He has offered his own formulation (couched in terms of endoatomic structure) in order to clarify, and even to render testable, differences between Freud, Klein and Fairbairn (Wisdom, 1962; Cheshire, 1966, pp. 139–143); and he also revives both Freud's own neuroanatomical imagery and his later instinct theory in preferring to attribute to the ego a 'libidinal lobe' and a 'destructive lobe' as well as a 'control system' (Wisdom, 1963, 1984). Nor does he disregard the relation between these endopsychic models and the properties of the phenomenal self, since, as Cheshire has put it (1966, p. 139):

> 'According to the usage which he (i.e. Wisdom) introduces, "orbital" introjection occurs when an object comes to "form part of the inner world of the self and be viewed by the self as an internal object": in this case the internal object so created is of the type to be called "orbital introject". On the other hand, an introjected object may "form part and parcel of the outlook of the self; the self may look at the world, including its inner world, through the eyes of this introject"... When this happens, it is a "nuclear introject".'

With regard to the rewriting of psychoanalysis with object-seeking instead of pleasure-seeking as the basic motivational postulate, but without any essential contradiction of Freud himself, Wisdom comments that Fairbairn made 'a nice job . . . of it' (1984, p. 314), and a curious kind of silent approval can be discerned even in Gedo's (1979) 'metapsychological assessment'. Having explained that there are several different, but coherent, ways in which the drives of object-seeking and pleasure-seeking might be related in a theoretical system, he draws attention to Kohut's attempt, eventually abandoned, to entertain them side-by-side, and comments on Loewald's paradoxical idea that the traditional drives develop out of earlier object-relational experiences with the mother. He then concedes (p. 365) that among the possible relationships is that of elevating object-relations 'to a position of decisive significance as one of the sources of human motivation, perhaps even the exclusive one'. But he does not even mention Fairbairn. May we take it that 'silence gives consent' in this instance? If so, we have to set against it Balint's (1956) attempt to show that Fairbairn's proposition about libido being object-seeking rather than pleasure-seeking is a conceptual solecism which becomes linguistically acceptable in English only because of the substitution in translation of the anglo-latin term 'libido' for the German '*Lust*' (pleasure, desire). We have touched in Chapter 1 on such problems to do with forms of language and forms of thought, and can only comment here that Balint's argument would be more plausible if Freud had not often used the term *libido* himself as an apparent alternative to *Trieb* (instinct).

There is no doubt that the basis for later trustful relationships, self-confidence, self-regard and altogether a basic feeling of self-esteem, is laid by the affective exchange with significant others in infancy. But psychoanalysis has not refrained from also trying to probe further back beyond these earliest object-relations, into an original undifferentiated state of being which Freud (1914) called 'primary narcissism'; and it is necessary to take account, if only briefly, of the influential development in this area of theory which is associated with the work of Kohut (1971, 1977). Kohut attributes to the primitive self all kinds of qualities which are traditionally given to the state of primary narcissism. The 'ideal', which is one pole of Kohut's 'self', contains a kind of sense of completeness and wholeness, whereas the other pole is defined by ambition. The goal or aim of this ambition is the restoration of the lost ideal, that is to say the restoration of completeness. Psychological objects (in practice, people) play a major role in this primary state of affairs in so far as they provide, if everything goes well, a 'mirror' which reflects this ideal. The various kinds of transference described by Kohut are stages in this mirroring, and they are described in various ways to which we come later. Certainly this general metaphor of the mirror, which had been used previously in this developmental context by Winnicott and by Mahler, has exerted a powerful fascination over many writers approaching from different angles; see, for example, the sensitive *vignette* by Pines (1984) and the ambitious thesis of Romanyshyn (1982).

The basis of Kohut's self-psychology lies clearly in Freud's hypothesis of primary narcissism, although some of the latter's speculations in terms of energy and the psychic economy are given up or not mentioned in the later work of Kohut. We must therefore introduce at least the contrast between *Allmacht* (omnipotence) and *Ohnmacht* (powerlessness) which Kohut elaborates, pausing only to regret that the obvious polar term 'impotence' is too heavily laden nowadays with sexual connotations to be useful in this context.

Although the assumption of primary narcissism has been convincingly rejected by Balint (1968), we must still notice some passages from Freud which indicate his own ambiguity towards the assumption. For example: 'A small living organism is a truly miserable, powerless thing, is it not? Compared with the immensely powerful external world, full as it is of destructive influences. A primitive organism, which has not developed any adequate ego-organization, is at the mercy of all these "traumas". . . . The differentiation of an ego is above all a step towards self-preservation' (1926, p. 203). We take it then that human wishful thinking, even to the extent of the omnipotence of thoughts, is a reaction-formation in the sense of creative phantasy-activity to overcome, and in some way become independent from, external powers and influences. Are those creative possibilities and those unconscious phantasies nothing more than, or mainly, correlates of instinctual wishes? This line of thought is to be found in Freud's theories about narcissism, but there is also another theme which is neglected in the literature and certainly not considered in the recent psychoanalytic theories of the Self. This neglected tradition is as follows:

'The "omnipotence of thoughts" was, we suppose, an expression of the pride of mankind in the development of speech, which resulted in such an extraordinary advancement of intellectual activities. The new realm of intellectuality was opened up, in which ideas, memories and inferences became decisive in contrast to the lower psychical activity which had direct perception by the sense-organs as its content.' (1937, p. 113)

Thus magical thinking does not re-establish a primary state of lost narcissistic grandiosity, but creates a new world. Day-dreaming in connection with frustrations is, after all, an everyday experience. But, as we know, there never was a Paradise, and we therefore project it either into the personal or historical past beyond our knowledge, or into the future (literally *ad infinitum*). It is remarkable that Freud tried to provide somehow a realistic basis for the Utopias of mankind: namely Paradise conceived as the repressed and completely forgotten state of primary narcissism. The whole question of the part played by narcissism in the reciprocal relation between the self-centred construction of society and what some have called the 'social construction of the

Self' has been discussed elaborately by Fine (1986) and indirectly by Shotter (1984).

We are aware that it is not possible to decide on an empirical basis whether the satisfaction or frustration of a baby is accompanied by a blissful state of mind or its contrary: that is, whether in frustration it experiences fear of annihilation, starvation or death. But we have many means of discovering which theory is more consistent with findings in other disciplines. Another point which is important for the evaluation is how many presuppositions are built into one or the other theory. For instance, assessment of the degree to which self-feelings are grandiose depends on the assumption that there is a grandiose self to start with, be it narcissistically cathected or not; while the other hypothesis is built upon the assumption (in Kleinian theory) that the danger coming from the 'bad object' is enhanced by destructive impulses projected into it. From a practical and therapeutic point of view, it has very decisive consequences whether we give omnipotence or powerlessness the primary place in psychological development. The controversy between Kernberg and Kohut illustrates this: for whereas Kohut (1971) pleads for the archaic primacy of the grandiose self, Kernberg (1975) regards feelings of grandiosity in narcissistic or borderline cases as reaction-formation. There is no need to comment further here on these divergencies, since they have been reviewed by Ornstein (1974), by Saperstein and Gaines (1978) and by Russell (1985). But it is worth saying a word about the implications for therapy.

If we consider feelings of grandeur as reaction-formation, we remain within the psychoanalytic frame of reference; that is, between the person and his/her environment. Oscillations in the experience of self-regard and self-esteem, whether mild or strong, go back to interpersonal conflicts and defence processes (because every intrapsychic conflict in the psychoanalytic sense has its forerunner in conflictual relationships). Conflictual tensions start at the beginning of human interaction between the baby and the mothering person, due to differences in rhythms and perceptions (Condon, 1979; Emde, 1983). The typical resolution of such conflicts may lead to 'splitting-off' as an intrapsychic process, which is often the basis of an extreme oscillation in self-feelings or ego-states. We then find a patient full of self-condemnation, self-reproaches, guilt-feelings, and with very low self-esteem; and at the beginning of treatment we shall perhaps find, in the split-off part of his personality (and then only *via* latent dream-thoughts) some grandiose self-representations.

Why should we imagine that split-off processes started independently of interpersonal interactions? For it is a feature of Kohut's approach, as Wachtel has commented (1982, p. 268), that he 'treats the evolution of the Self and the evolution of conflict as rather independent processes'. Even if the drama of human tragedy started with Paradise lost, there is no need to suppose that, since then, human life begins with primary narcissism, and its reflection in exhibitionistic grandiosity, rather than with states of tension, both pleasurable and unpleasurable, and altogether with an intense interplay of all our senses. The question of when interpersonal conflicts are internalized, and become intrapsychic conflicts, is quite another matter.

In spite of this. Kohut's therapeutic contribution has been considerable. Not only did he give a positive valuation to all kinds of feelings named with the prefix 'self' and formerly qualified as narcissistic in the bad sense; but more importantly, his emphasis on empathy fulfilled two needs in the psychoanalytic community. Classical psychoanalytic technique had reached a state of rigidity with doubtful therapeutic results and applicable only to a small percentage of people in need of psychotherapy; these were the so-called 'suitable cases' who were possibly confined to representatives of the 'YAVIS syndrome' (young, attractive, verbal, intelligent and successful). Although we doubt whether Freud himself would approve of the classical technique, since, as far as we know, he never practised psychoanalysis in the manner described as classical by, for example, Menninger and Holzman (1973), nevertheless Eissler's (1963) basic model technique became the exemplar for many analysts. Kohut himself (1977) has given, in his report about the first analysis of Mr Z., a remarkable description of his understanding of the difference between such classical technique and the new lines seemingly derived from his discoveries about the early development of narcissistic personalities.

Psychoanalysts who for various reasons have a different understanding of classical technique, such as Cremerius (1979) or Aaron Green (the pseudonymous classical analyst whom Janet Malcolm (1980) makes the spokesman of the traditional New York Psychoanalytic Institute), may dispute that Kohut's description gives a true picture of classical technique. But it is not a mere fiction: on the contrary, we only have to look at a prototypical description of the psychoanalytic process and the stages of regression in the influential textbook of Menninger and Holzman (1973) just mentioned. Their fictitious typical analyst mainly remains silent, and frustrates the patient almost to the point of complete demoralization.

Against this bleak picture Kohut set the empathic understanding of the analyst, his acceptance and his attempt to make up for the defects of the Self by mirroring the supposed grandiose exhibitionistic wishes of the patient. If wishes and needs, whether of a primary or secondary nature in Lewin's sense, are frustrated almost to the point of total demoralization, then a loss of security and safety (Laing's 'ontological security') can be predicted. For silence in itself can be terribly destructive, and it is a very unusual deprivation not to be found in man's natural environment; hence the particularly callous English punishment of 'sending somebody to Coventry' (i.e. forbidding the group to speak to him or her). On an unconscious level, such extreme deprivation may be experienced as annihilation or extinction, or at least as a severe threat to the feeling of personal identity as described by James or Erikson (see Chapter 1). The need to preserve the integrity of the ego is a primitive motive for defence

(Freud, 1910; A. Freud, 1937), and the whole theory of defence mechanisms implies a regulatory, or even cybernetic, system of some kind (not necessarily based on a pleasure/unpleasure principle) which monitors, on the psychological level of relationships with objects, one's developmentally primitive self-feelings of well-being or threat.

Kohut introduces a narcissistic regulatory system which appears to be independent of the pleasure/unpleasure principle; but his construction is full of metaphors taken from the theory of instinctual drives, and assumptions derived from the so-called classical psychoanalytic situation with all its frustrations and inherent threats as described above. We can therefore understand Kohut's enthusiasm for what he calls narcissistic equilibrium, and for its restoration in self-psychology, as an attempt to make up for the damage he had unwittingly produced in the first analysis of Mr Z., and in other therapies where the importance of establishing basic trust in an appropriate therapeutic situation was neglected.

Nobody will doubt the overall importance of helping patients to develop basic trust in the analytic situation, so that they feel safe enough to give up some of the attitudes which they themselves, as well as the analyst and even the social environment, consider to belong to their false selves. But it is an open question whether the more specific technical recommendations which Kohut makes, both as regards therapeutic practice and in respect of his theory of the various forms of narcissistic transferences or self-transferences from which the former are derived, are well based or particularly useful. These recommend-ations include the much-used concept of 'self-object' (Kohut, 1977, ch. 4), which appears to be an internalization of those aspects of other people which are experienced as reflecting back to the primitive Self its own grandiosity. As such, it can surely be conceptualized as a special case of a Kleinian 'internal object', which has also some affinity with Jacobson's 'self-representation', and the gratuitous proliferation of dubious neologisms could usefully be checked (cp. Kernberg, 1977, pp. 115–116). However, there are those who take the concept seriously, and it has been discussed in the wider context of general object-relations theory by, for example, Grotstein (1982, pp. 57–69).

4.3 Problems and Resolutions

At various points in the course of this survey, we have pointed out that this way of talking about the 'inner world' of feelings and mental processes is on the face of it beset with fairly familiar philosophical difficulties. These difficulties spring largely from the use of terminology, which has a clear and practical meaning when applied to physical space, positions and objects, to refer metaphorically to psychological states and processes which are 'in' the mind in a vastly different sense from that in which a toy is 'in' a shop window. At one time, under the influence of G. Ryle (1949), it was thought, at least in some British philosophical circles, that if a theorist had used spatial metaphors in talking about mental processes this was sufficient to convict him or her of systematically muddled talk. Since then, however, it has had to be admitted that some 'mental acts' (cp. Geach, 1957) clearly do take place in (physical) space and time: for example, Sir Mortimer Wheeler's 'decision' to become an archaeologist just did take place on a particular Friday morning in London at the corner of the Strand and Trafalgar Square, and at no other time or place. And, more importantly, we have become familiar with the contention that the drawing of metaphors and analogies from well-understood systems in order to help in conceptualizing the functioning of one that is ill-understood, is a regular feature of scientific theorizing, and not necessarily a sign of ignorance and confusion (Hesse, 1966; Harré, 1970).

Nevertheless, a great deal hangs, of course, on just *how* such quasi-metaphorical models are constructed and used. When there are clear and systematic procedures for converting talk about 'projection', 'introjects', 'persecutory objects', 'ego-splitting' and intrapsychic 'distances' into talk about specific dispositions, thoughts, feelings, habitual reactions, traits, etc., then there may indeed be no problem. Nobody supposes, for instance, that talk in other contexts about the 'dominance' of a gene or the 'charm' of a quark implies, respectively, the intention to get the better of another gene or to seduce a fellow-quark. So much so, that it has become an established game in information-technology to give deliberately mentalistic and personalized names to the minutely specified objective processes which the computer-machinery carries out. We have noticed above how Wisdom (1962, 1963, 1984) has maintained just such a philosophical surveillance over some parts of object-relations theory, and we would draw attention to a recent review by Eagle (1983b) of the 'epistemological status' of object-relations theory. Our own comments here will be confined to a few remarks about the concepts of 'internal objects' and the process of 'internalization', and about the misuse of spatial metaphors, to all of which we have referred in the course of this chapter.

We noticed that the Kleinian account of early emotional development seems at various points not to need an *introjection* theory, about how aspects of physical objects 'out there' are converted into non-physical 'internalized objects' in the mind, but only a *learning* theory about how (or even just about the *fact that*) the dispositions to feel, think, react or expect-certain-things develop out of certain critical perceptual experiences very early in life. Klein's reason for insisting on something more categorical seems to have been connected with the belief that you cannot build egos out of dispositional processes but you need something more like 'structures' for a psychic edifice of any substance. But an answer to that would be to construe 'ego-structures' themselves as complexes of rather well-established dispositions (which can, of course, be *dis*-established as a result of brain-washing, psychotic illness or frontal-lobe degeneration).

Jacobson's (1964) recommendation that we should speak unequivocally of 'representations', within the psyche, of emotionally significant objects in the outside world, seemed a commonsensical way of getting round some of the difficulties (without, incidentally, doing anything to appease the Ryleans), partly perhaps because these representations seemed to have a respectable ancestry in the cognitive 'maps' and 'plans' of some academic psychologies of perceptual learning (Tolman, 1948; Miller *et al.*, 1960; Neisser, 1976, ch. 6). Her extension of the concept to 'self-representations' alongside 'object-representations' has been hailed by Sandler (1985) as making it a great deal easier to conceptualize the phenomenology of personal change as experienced by patients in therapy or by people in general in an intense formative relationship (dependent child, introspective adolescent, young person in love, mourning widow). This enthusiasm has led, however, to a good deal of unbridled talk about 'the representational world' (Sandler and Rosenblatt, 1962) as we shall see shortly.

We are still left, however, with the perennial problem of what to say about the 'observing' self which seemingly contemplates these representations like a person in a picture-gallery (a conceptualization which Ryle roundly condemned!), and of what to say about how they are formed. We shall see below that, while some of the prevalent talk about how these representations relate to the Self and to themselves are patently confused, nevertheless others can be empirically fruitful. As far as the process of internalization or representation-formation goes, it has been reviewed at length by Schafer (1968) and discussed more briefly and more recently by Meissner (1979) and McDevitt (1979). The latter laments the fact that as yet 'there is no satisfactory conceptualization of the processes by which external objects come to influence and affect the internal psychic organization' (p. 346), since even Schafer's definition is unsatisfactory. For it is too broad, in that it takes in even ordinary cognitive processes of perception, thinking and concept-formation, and thus becomes merely the name for a whole range of psychological functions without explicating any of them.

However, Schafer's extensive review of the various usages which are in the field, so to speak, can hardly be encapsulated into a single 'definition'; and elsewhere (1976, ch. 8) he conspicuously avoids any such prescription, but concentrates instead on mapping the 'logical grammar' of this and cognate terms according to the ways they are actually used by theorists. Nor is there anything intrinsically amiss, in any case, in arguing that the mechanism is best conceptualized as a more general one than had initially been supposed, so that both certain cognitive activity and also the more familiar emotional cathexes and identifications are best thought of, for the purposes of a coherent and realistic theory, as being special cases of that general process. Indeed, this is often the logical form of a theoretical advance in the natural sciences; and in the present context we may call to mind Freud's uncertainty about the relation between repression and the other apparently more specific mechanisms of 'defence' (Madison, 1961), and Eagle's (1983a) recent theoretical treatment of intellectual interests as a form of 'object-relations'. If we go still further, and accept Erdelyi's (1985) contention that Freud's psychoanalytic theory as a whole is essentially a comprehensive cognitive psychology which has been systematically misconstrued by literal-minded clinicians, then it will be necessary (and not merely convenient) that its basic postulates should be able to comprise what McDevitt calls 'ordinary cognitive processes of perception',

McDevitt's illustrations of how introjection can be seen at work, as it were, in the behaviour of young children passing through Mahler's stages of 'separation-individuation' and Piaget's levels of cognitive development at the same time is in its way more fruitful, with its implicit ostensive definitions. Thus, when a one-year-old gets separation-comfort from a doll or teddy-bear as 'transitional object' in Winnicott's term, this is evidence of 'introjection'; and a two-year-old's 'delayed imitation' play with a doll, which Piaget regards as marking the transition from 'sensorimotor intelligence' to preoperational thought (because it implies the existence of 'mental representations'), is seen as evidence of 'identification' with the absent mother.

We may compare Leon's (1984) perceptive attempt to integrate the conceptualizations of Piaget, Klein and Mahler; and draw attention also to the argument of Main *et al.* (1985) that these Mahlerian stages in the attainment of emotional security and identity-differentiation can be related closely to the sequence of cognitive steps which the Piagetian infant takes from the earliest levels of sensorimotor intelligence to the critical intellectual breakthrough of 'representational' (i.e. preoperational, in this context) thought. In the light of these integrative efforts, we would ask why the special psychodynamic 'representations' of Jacobson *et al.* could not have been grafted on to the existing notions of Piaget, in the manner of Schneider's (1981) substantial contribution to a synthesis, rather than added to the proliferation of doubtfully different formulations (cp. also Blatt and Lerner, 1983, pp. 191–195).

Unfortunately, the difficulty of sustaining this metaphor of an internal world composed of mental representations is illustrated by Kanzer's (1979, p. 328) comments on Meissner's ideas. He says that Meissner and Rapaport want to make a distinction between 'a structured internal world and a more diffuse inner world which is an intrapsychic map of external reality', and he goes on to suggest making a similar distinction between 'the external world carved out in the psychic apparatus and the outer world of "real objects" '. But this 'outer world of real objects' is simply a part of what Meissner and Rapaport call 'external reality', and what is 'carved out' in the psyche cannot be the external world itself but only some representation of it corresponding exactly to that 'intrapsychic map' attributed to Meissner and Rapaport. So it seems either that Kanzer is making heavy weather of a very elementary distinction between a mental representation and the real thing which it represents; or else that he has become confused by this equation of 'mental' with 'inside' and 'physical' with 'outside', and has lost sight of the fact that the distinction he recommends is already there (by implication) in what Meissner and Rapaport have said.

The early attempt by Heimann (1952) to clarify the theoretical status of 'internal object', and the mechanisms by which it is set up, also ran into difficulties with its spatial metaphors. Thus she writes (pp. 142–143) that for the infant an 'object' is:

> '...what either tastes or feels pleasant in his mouth and during swallowing, and is therefore good, or something that tastes nasty, hurts the mouth and throat, cannot be swallowed or cannot be got into the mouth (i.e. frustrates) and is therefore bad. If it is good it is swallowed; if it is bad it is spat out. ... The oral object is not only held in the mouth, but either swallowed and incorporated, or spat out and expelled, and the mechanisms of introjection and projection are bound up with the sensations and phantasies experienced in the contact with the object.'

But consider two different 'objects': a feed of milk, and the teat of the feeding-bottle. They both presumably may meet the criteria for a good object, but whereas the milk is swallowed the teat is not. So only one of them suffers the alleged fate of the good (literal) object. It will be said, of course, that the teat is incorporated and perhaps even swallowed 'in phantasy'. But this is not the point: if what is important is *phantasy*-incorporation, whether or not accompanied by reality-swallowing, then leave swallowing out of it altogether. To bring it in only gives the impression that good objects are incorporated in phantasy by virtue of being swallowed in reality, which apparently is not what is meant.

Secondly, what are we to make of the metaphor that introjection and projection are 'bound up with' sensations and phantasies? Perhaps what is meant is that what is introjected are sensations, etc. *derived* from (literal) objects, as opposed to objects (of any sort) themselves. However, in view of the wish to say that people-in-certain-roles and aspects-of-situations are also material for introjection, 'sensations' would have to be replaced in the formulation by 'perceptions' (in a wide sense). But this would destroy part of the internal-world/external-world dichotomy, because the *perceptions* as such are not external to the perceiver in the way that the perceived *objects* themselves may be. Heimann does in fact say later (p. 148) that 'the external object provides the experience from which the internal object is constructed'; and this is a much more sober formulation, reminiscent of Freud's cautious metaphors and dispensing with the misleading picture of taking something into the mind.

But the important question, of course, is *what* is constructed and *how*: we need not another impressionist picture, but something more like a working diagram.

It would be easy but pointless to multiply examples of how this insistence on a two-worlds dichotomy is necessary to the perpetuation of introjection/projection metaphors, and yet too easily degenerates into muddle. One favourite quotation from Guntrip (1961, p. 31), however, cannot be resisted: '...it emerges that we live in two worlds, an outer environment and an inner environment'. There is something Chaplinesque about the idea of being surrounded from the inside; for it is reminiscent of that scene in *The Great Dictator* where Chaplin returns from the battle leading a group of prisoners, and, when asked how he managed to capture them single-handed, replies 'I surrounded them.' But we have also seen, in the course of our travels through object-relations theory, that it may well be possible to rescue many of these metaphorical formulations from incoherence by translating them either into propositions involving precise dispositional concepts or into some kind of conceptual model which might even be neurologically based (in the manner of Freud's own *Project* . . .). One commentator who sets out along this path with commendable intentions is Sandler.

The difficulty in applying the metaphors of introjection, internalization, etc. consistently to actual observed behaviour was remarked more than 20 years ago by Sandler (1962) when he tried to give them some 'operational' sense for the purpose of constructing the *Hampstead Index*. The logic of his solution was essentially to provide a dispositional reduction of the meaning of such terms as denote the various processes of internalization; and this he aimed to do through the medium of the concept of a 'self-schema', which was to be strictly analogous with Head's (1926) much-respected neurological concept of 'body-schema' to which we have referred in Chapter 1. From the functioning of a person's self-schema, the neurologist can infer which normal formative processes (such as the myelination of the cerebellum) have either not occurred or become damaged, and Sandler's idea was analogously to infer from the functioning of a person's self-schema the nature and quality of the introjective processes which must have occurred in order to produce it. Sandler interprets Head's idea as amounting to a system of sensorimotor 'sets' which have been built up, often 'outside central consciousness', as a result of previous experience and feedback, so that 'such schemata modify the impressions produced by incoming sensory impulses in such a way that the final sensations of position or locality rise into consciousness charged with a relation to something that has gone before'.

This has obvious links with the argument sketched above to the effect that all the Kleinians need is a theory about learned dispositions, which any theory of perceptual learning needs anyway, and not a theory about the introduction of problematic 'objects' into a problematic 'internal world'. Head was quite clear, says Sandler, that 'the processes which go into the formation of the body-schema . . . are predominantly . . . unconscious'; and he proposes that it provides a precedent for the notion of a self-schema arising from the cumulative unconscious effect of those early emotional contacts with people and the world which some call object-relations. In so far as part of the function of such a self-schema would be to predispose a person to produce certain sorts of response-pattern, emotional attitude, apperception, association of ideas, etc. to particular incoming stimuli, it can be seen to correspond in general terms to the Kleinian 'background of phantasy' against which all mental and behavioural activity is alleged to go on. It also has affinities with some aspects of Kelly's 'personal construct system' as we shall see.

Thus having established what appears to be a respectable precedent, Sandler extends the central notion to 'representations of others, in particular of important love and hate objects'; and he claims to elucidate, in the light of these formulations, the problematical psychic mechanisms with which he began. But he does not explain *how* the concept of representation or of 'schema' is to be transferred, in the same Headian sense, to such *objects*. It is important that he should do so: for, since the set-complex which comprises the self-schema is defined by its dispositions as a subject *towards objects*, the term 'object-schema', in order to be analogous, would have to denote sets, reaction-potentials, etc. *of* the object *towards* something else. What we are trying to explain, however, by means of the mechanisms in question, is the dispositions *of* the Self (self-schema) *to* the objects concerned, or rather to the world *via* the alleged internal objects.

So the concept of 'schema' has not in fact been transferred in the same sense in which it has been vindicated by analogy with Head. Instead, Sandler has reverted to a colloquial notion of mental representation which invites the very objections about unseen internal cinema-shows that Head's dispositional reduction had avoided in the case of neuromotor functioning. His attempts to clarify individually, in the context of this scheme, the notions of 'internalization', 'identification', and 'introjection' illustrate this reversion; and, when 'incorporation' is discussed, even the original self-schema seems to have regressed from the sophistication afforded it by association with Head's paradigm, to the primitive conception of some sort of internal picture or manikin. For Sandler writes that the activity of this mechanism would amount to 'a change in the shape of the self-representation so that the taking in of an object . . . is represented'.

Sandler acknowledges these risks in a later discussion (1985) where he disarmingly concedes at one point that his formulations raise 'all sorts of philosophical problems'. Nevertheless, for him these hazards are outweighed by the advantages of conceptualizing certain clinical problems, and he prepares the ground for introducing the notion of 'self-representation' by arguing the need to clarify the relationship between the 'self' and the Freudian 'ego'. This is a relationship which we have already seen being described as 'undefined' in psychoanalytic theory, but which Weidenhammer (1985) also has attempted to clarify. Sandler's initial discussion of the way in which the concepts in a scientific theory are gradually made more precise will remind analysts of the similar passage with which Isaacs begins her classic article on the contentious concept of 'unconscious phantasy' (1952). She is concerned to defend the concept against the charge of imprecision, but she does not realize that it is not imprecision of itself, but only certain *sorts* of imprecision, that threaten the usefulness and logical coherence of a concept, as Waismann's (1951) discussion of the 'open texture' of scientific concepts has shown. The particular sort of imprecision which characterizes, and (some would say) vitiates, the spatial metaphors of object-relations theory is the failure to specify what the philosophers of science call 'the area of negative analogy', and there has already been some discussion elsewhere of how this applies to the specific formulations of both Isaacs and Sandler (Cheshire, 1966, ch. 1 and 8).

As we have noted above, there is no problem about the 'dominance' of genes and the 'charm' of quarks because those who use the metaphors are sufficiently clear about how the behaviour of dominant genes *differs* from that of one person dominating another, and about how that of a quark with left-handed charm is *unlike* a left-handed person charming someone else. To be more specific, when physicists use the analogy of a solid ball bouncing about or spinning round in an orbit, in the cases of the gas molecule and the electron respectively, they need to be able to specify not only how the molecule and electron *are* behaving like balls, but also how they are *not* doing so: for example, by being infinitely elastic in the case of the gas molecules, and by taking zero time to jump from one orbit to another in the case of the electrons.

As soon as you begin to think of the mind as like a region of space in which events, processes and objects can be located, it becomes hard to know what further concepts to do with the properties of *physical* space may meaningfully be transferred to this metaphorical *mental* space. If the same sorts of thing can happen in another part of the town as happen in this part, it is tempting to suppose that the same would be true for different parts of the mind, so that the sort of thing that goes on in this part may also go on in that part. But what happens when that part has been designated an 'unconscious part', or as what Sandler calls a 'non-experiential realm of the mind'? Does it make sense to suppose that *all* psychological processes that can occur consciously can also go on unconsciously?

On the face of it, it seems nonsense to assume that even those processes of which consciousness is a necessary attribute could also occur unconsciously; and yet we know that Freud himself tried to face up to the problem of 'unconscious emotion' (1915a, pp. 177–179), while both Isaacs (1952) and Sandler regularly employ the notion of 'unconscious experience'. Various attempts have been made to persuade analysts that all they really need for their theoretical purposes is some much less problematic conception of unconscious *reaction* or *disposition*-formation, which can readily be accommodated both to the logical demands of the philosophers and to the empirical constraints of the neurologists (MacIntyre, 1958; Wisdom, 1984; cp. Schafer, 1976; Anscombe, 1981; Bowers and Meichenbaum, 1985). And we have indeed seen Sandler apparently taking off in this direction.

The spatial metaphors still get out of hand, however, even in the later discussion. The idea that 'representations', whether of the self or of its objects, have a shape which can change as a result of 'defensive activity on the part of the ego' is used to reformulate certain questions about identity, conflict and motivation. But the sceptical philosopher will complain that we are not told what alterations in ideation, feeling or behaviour are the consequence of a particular representation becoming (say) narrower, rounder, more symmetrical or whatever. That is to say, there are no correspondence-rules linking theoretical statements about the shape of a representation with observation-statements about a person's actions and experience.

Nor is it clear, why, when a person's self-image changes from being a 'dirty' one to being 'clean and tidy', that should reflect a change in *shape*, as Sandler (1985) puts it, rather than a change in colour, brightness, texture or structure. Suppose Mr Smith takes a course of assertion-training and comes out of it thinking of himself as positive, decisive and potentially successful, whereas he did not do so before. We may be tempted to say, with Sandler, that the shape of Smith's self-representation is now different from what it was. But, unless we can say in what *way* the shape has changed (e.g. that it is now rounder, narrower, less concave, etc.) then we are not using the concept of *shape* systematically at all, but only the concept of being *different*. It becomes a case where, in Wittgenstein's phrase 'the beetle has dropped out of the box'.

The same goes for Sandler's example of the child who begins to identify with her mother by adopting the same style of walking. If we say that Mary's self-representation is now shaped more like her mother-representation, but cannot also say *how* the shape itself is different, then we are in effect using only the notion of *similarity* and not the specific notion of *shape*. The difference between this and Freud's picture of 'the shadow of the object' falling upon the ego is that for Freud the specific metaphor of 'casting a shadow' stays (as we saw above) at just that, namely, an affecting figure of speech, and is not given any systematic theoretical significance *qua* shadow.

When it comes to discussing the difference between the representations of one's 'ideal self' and one's 'actual self', the difficulty in applying the shape-metaphor systematically is again apparent. For the discrepancy or coincidence between these two representations should be conceptualized, according to the new formulation, in terms of a difference or similarity in their *shape*; but Sandler chooses to change the spatial metaphor and to speak of a *gap* between them. Ironically, we shall see below that this metaphor of a 'gap' *can* be given some systematic operational sense, within the psychometrics of personal construct theory, which cannot be given to that of 'shape'.

It is worth noting, as a postscript to this insistence upon the importance of negative analogy, that, by contrast with the difficulty of attributing a coherent meaning to the idea of 'shape' in the context of *self*-schema, it is easy to give a clear empirical significance to statements about someone's *body*-schema having a certain shape. For we can literally draw on paper the outline of the distorted body-schema in many cases: that of the surgical patient suffering the 'phantom limb' illusion; that of the anorexic girl who thinks she is much fatter than she is; that of the psychotic child who treats the adult's hand as part of his own body but disowns his own foot; or that of the normal three-year-old whose cerebellum is not yet fully myelinated and who consequently still mistakenly thinks that he can reach some object without taking a step nearer, or that he can stand upright under a low table. We can even extend to the body-schema the psychoanalyst's joke about some parts of the ego-system being 'soluble in alcohol', because it has been shown that the extended body-image of bus-drivers who are slightly drunk becomes significantly *narrower*, in the operational sense that they will confidently expect to be able to drive their bus through a gap which is in fact too narrow, and which they had rightly judged to be so when sober (Cohen and Clark, 1979, pp. 167–168).

4.4 Applications to Research in Psychotherapy

In what ways, then, can the tenets and hypotheses of object-relations theory be applied to the understanding of self-problems in clinical diagnosis, in the context of psychotherapy and in the course of normal psychological development? In the clinical field, it has perhaps led to a focus in psychotherapy on relations with 'significant others', especially in the earliest months and years of life, and as these are reflected in the on-going relationships of therapy itself and the patient's everyday life. This has meant a change from the therapist being concerned mainly to devine hidden impulses, gratifications and defences; but the two approaches are necessarily interrelated, because personal relations are the context within which such emotional needs are either fulfilled or frustrated. In so far as such a change may have taken place in specifically psychoanalytic treatment, it has probably made the therapeutic situation less artificial and less threatening for the patient, but it would be a mistake to suppose that such changes in practice are entailed by the acceptance of object-relations hypotheses, if only because, on the one hand, the Kleinians (as opposed to the Fairbairnians, say) typically see no need to make such a change, and remain comparatively distant and silent, while, on the other hand, the same sort of change in therapeutic practice would equally well have followed from an acceptance of much vaguer notions about the importance of interpersonal processes in general (such notions as Sullivan (1953), for example, had been canvassing for some time).

In the hope of devising a method for identifying particular object-relational conflicts and resources in the personality, and with a view to allowing the therapist to focus on them fairly soon rather than having to wait for evidence of them to turn up in the therapy, Phillipson (1955, 1973) developed some 30 years ago a structured projective technique which he named specifically the *Object Relations Technique*. Although the basic principle was the same as that of Murray's *Thematic Apperception Test* (1938), the material was designed more systematically in terms of its content and affective impact.

With respect to content, the ambiguous visual stimuli on the cards are designed to evoke object-relations situations involving a person alone, a dyad, a triangular situation (with the possibility of oedipal implications), and a person in relation to a group. The affective impact of each situation is varied in the course of the test by having each one depicted in different visual styles: (A) a diffuse, cloudy manner reminiscent of the 'texture' effects on the Rorschach and intended to arouse 'dependency-feelings'; (B) a stark, sharp-edged chiaroscuro of uncompromising silhouettes; and (C) a style in which some touches of colour and definite line are combined with a somewhat heavier version of style A, with the intention of introducing an emotionally provocative effect parallel to that of the Rorschach colour cards.

A number of studies (cp. Phillipson, 1973) have shown that this technique, in the hands of competent clinicians, can indeed pinpoint areas of object-relations conflict, and associated defensive reactions and resources of the self-system, in a way that illuminates them for subsequent psychotherapy. It is very remarkable, therefore, and a lamentable reflection upon the parochiality of much psychoanalytic research, that, in their recent survey of clinical research concerned specifically with the application of object-relations theory, much of which makes extensive use of projective methods, Blatt and Lerner (1983) make *no mention at all* of this acutely relevant instrument.

Their study concerns itself instead with a number of clinical and psychometric researches into various aspects of self-concept, psychopathology and psychodynamics which are certainly germane to object-relations theory, but which are by no means all *specific* to it in the sense of reflecting hypotheses which are derived exclusively from that particular theory and no other. They report, for example, investigations by Mayman, who has tried to find ways of gaining psychometric access to the self-concept by attending to certain features of peoples' responses to the much-maligned Rorschach cards (p. 202). Little attention, however, seems to be paid to the questionable validity of some of the traditional Rorschach indices, such as the assumption that people who have achieved a mature level of object-relations will find a fair sprinkling of lively human percepts ('M-responses') in the blots. Thus they write (p. 217) that 'the human response provides a vehicle for assessing the content and the level of cognitive organisation in the concepts of self and of the object-world'. But Eysenck (1959) has complained, needless to say, that normative data from non-clinical samples suggest that the underproduction of '*M*' is a psychological limitation which afflicts the human race as a whole. Mayman's further demonstration that inexperienced judges were scarcely less accurate than 'more experienced' Rorschach workers at predicting pathology, on the basis of unscored content of Rorschach protocols, is uncomfortably reminiscent of Strupp's well-publicized finding (from the Vanderbilt study) that amateur therapists were scarcely less effective at some forms of counselling or psychotherapy than were well-trained ones (see Chapter 11).

While we would support Blatt's own plea (p. 211) for the more systematic and rigorous use of projective techniques, it is unfortunate that he does not point out an important step which has already been taken in this direction by applying to such material the statistical method which Holley has called 'G-analysis' (cp. Kline, 1983, pp. 56–59). This procedure, which resembles a poor man's discriminant function analysis, has been used to demonstrate that it is indeed possible, when comparing the Rorschach protocols of clinical criterion-groups (say depressives or schizophrenics) with those of controls, to identify specific features of those protocols which, when considered as a cluster, reliably discriminate sheep from goats.

Another source from which some quasi-experimental rigour could be introduced into the projective study of object-relations theory is suggested by Blatt and Lerner's reference to Mayman's work with the *Early Memories Test*. Mayman analysed the material elicited by this test in terms of the classical psychosexual stages and defence-mechanisms, and by reference to 'self-feelings' of various sorts, none of which are specific to object-relations theory. However, Kragh and Smith (1970) have developed over the last decade or so a perceptual technique which combines tachistoscopic and projective methods of stimulus-presentation in such a way that the stages by which people build up, monitor and organize their apperception of emotionally significant scenarios can be analysed in just such a manner. The subject is presented with an emotionally significant scene (depicting dependency, rivalry, object-loss, etc.) at an exposure too short to allow recognition at once; and then exposure-time is gradually increased until the picture is completely grasped. At each successive exposure, subjects are asked for their provisional interpretation of the content of the picture, and the emerging sequence of perceptual hypotheses and revisions can be construed as reflecting the developmental sequence of anxieties, projections and defences which have contributed to that person's present apperceptions of such emotionally significant situations. The method is called 'percept-genetics' (cp. Kline, 1972/1981, pp. 229–237; Cooper and Kline, 1986); and clearly there is enormous scope for applying this objective and quantifiable technique to projective material (such as Phillipson's) which focusses on the specific concepts and assumptions of object-relations theory. Its immediate relevance to the psychodynamics of perception has been argued by Westerlundh and Smith (1983).

By contrast with some of the rather non-specific studies of which we have complained, the work of Urist appears to have had some success in detecting patterns of self-object differentiation, clarity of object-boundaries and quality of object-relations; and all these phenomena are construed in theory-specific terms (p. 208). But, although there are clear implications here for the assessment of those 'border-line personalities' beloved of object-relations theorists, there is no attempt to connect all this with the well-known psychotic phenomena of 'over-inclusive thinking' and of 'loose construing', which non-psychodynamic clinicians have been describing systematically for the last couple of decades (Payne, 1960; Bannister, 1965; Lawlor and Cochran, 1981). An opportunity to show that object-relations theory can be integrated into general psychology, rather than being quaintly at odds with it, has therefore been lost. But there have been other commentators who have tried their hands at this exercise in integration. For example, Ogden's (1983) recent attempt to clarify Fairbairn's account of the early splitting of the ego and of part-objects, by insisting that the process necessarily produces two 'suborganizations', one of which is associated with the Self and the other with the object, has itself been critically reviewed and elaborated by Ryle (1985). But it is another unhappy example of the narrow parochiality of object-relations studies that precisely this same clarification had already been made 20 years previously by Wisdom (1963; cp. 1984) in his distinction between 'orbital' and 'nuclear' introjects, as we have seen in Section 4.2. Neither Ogden nor Ryle, however, mentions his contribution.

Ryle is concerned to show that the central concepts of object-relations theory can be purged of that anthropomorphic mentalism which has bothered so many critics, and he proposes that this can be done by recasting them in terms of the 'schemata', 'plans', 'routines' or 'procedural sequences' of currently respectable cognitive psychology. This is in much the same spirit as that in which Cheshire (1966) had invoked neurological models and philosophical dispostionism, and had previously argued the relevance of Miller *et al.*'s (1960) TOTE theory with its constituent cognitive 'plans'. Ryle pays particular attention to the rehabilitation of the concepts of splitting, projection, resistance and transference; and he reminds us in the course of his discussion that the psychometric technology of personal construct theory has been brought to bear upon traditional hypotheses about the workings of the transference in therapy.

For not only can the patient be presented with individual 'significant others' from the therapeutic situation, to be construed on a range of elicited constructs, with a view to reflecting such transference phenomena as the 'idealization' of the therapist (Ben-Tovim and Greenup, 1983), but also relationships *between* significant others (e.g. mother-with-me-as-a-child, father-with-my-brother-as-a-child, therapist-with-me-now, etc.) can be treated as elements to be construed for similarities and differences in the traditional way (A. Ryle, 1982). There are obvious possibilities here for checking whether certain types of patient do indeed project certain object-relations rather than others, and for seeing whether recovery goes along with any particular pattern of change in such transference-projections. For instance, to return to a question raised above, we already know that this technique can make quantifiable sense out of the spatial metaphor of the apperceived 'distance' between a patient's 'ideal self' and 'actual self', for we can observe this distance getting shorter (in terms of accumulated scale-points on construct-ratings) in the case of people recovering from depression (Hewstone, *et al.*, 1981; Sheehan, 1985; Ashworth *et al.*, 1985).

All this encourages us to think that some coherent theses, to do with normal psychological development and with the psychopathology and psychotherapy of self-problems, can indeed be rescued from the often muddled metaphors in which object-relations theory has been formulated in the past. And certainly a variety of indirectly supportive observations have been forthcoming from a number of unexpected sources. We have seen, for example, how the revival of social constructivist and/or symbolic interactionist accounts of the ontogenesis of the self-concept has led some of its exponents to invoke internal object-relations in all but name. Again, as experimental developmental psychology becomes more humane and more personally meaningful to the infants concerned, we find evidence of intersubjectivity, shared understandings and attribution-of-agency appearing not only in the play-therapy clinic but now also in the laboratory as well. If Ainsworth *et al.* (1974) can corroborate a Kleinian thesis about the development of persecutory phantasies in infancy, without knowing that they have done so, and if Bower (1977) can confirm a crucial Kleinian tenet about the 'depressive position' in equal ignorance of what he has done, what will such workers and their colleagues not discover when they *have* learned what to look for?

Finally, it is often said that an important test of the strength and usefulness of a theoretical system is whether it can be applied fruitfully to areas of observation other than those from which it was itself derived. Well, whatever its other limitations may be, this is a test which object-relations theory can convincingly pass. For we may notice two recent demonstrations of how its concepts may be used to enhance the understanding of different aspects of normal intellectual functioning. Eagle's (1983a) argument to the effect that people's intellectual 'interests' can illuminatingly be construed as a form of object-relations contains echoes of Brentano's influential thesis about mental processes being necessarily object-directed; and it is worth remembering that Freud himself had attended many of Brentano's philosophy lectures as a university student, and had come to hold him in high personal regard (Clark, 1980, p. 34). Secondly, and on a grander scale, another philosophical ally of object-relations theory, Richard Wollheim, has found it appropriate to construe not only certain central issues in aesthetics, but also many familiar questions about identity, autobiography and self-development in terms of this psychodynamic system (Wollheim, 1985, ch 8, 4 and 7).

References

Ainsworth, M. D. S., Bell, S. M. and Stayton, D. J. (1974) Infant–mother attachment ... In *The Integration of a Child* ... (ed. M. P. M. Richards), ch. 6. Cambridge University Press, Cambridge.

Anscombe, R. (1981). Referring to the unconscious: ... *Int. J. Psychoanal.*, **62**, 225–241.

Ashworth, C. M., Blackburn, I. M. and McPherson, F. M. (1985). The performance of depressed and manic patients. ... *Brit. J. Med. Psychol.* **58**, 337–342.

Balint, M. (1956). Pleasure, object and libido. Reprinted in *Problems of Human Pleasure and Behaviour*, pp. 281–291, Hogarth, London, 1957.

Balint, M. (1968). *The Basic Fault:* ... Tavistock, London.

Bannister, D. (1965). The genesis of schizophrenic thought-disorder. ... *Brit. J. Psychiatry*, **111**, 377.

Ben-Tovim, D. I. and Greenup, J. (1983). The representation of transference through serial grids: ... *Brit. J. Med. Psychol.*, **56**, 255–261.

Blatt, S. J. and Lerner, H. (1983). Investigations in the psychoanalytic theory of object relations... In *Empirical Studies of Psychoanalytic Theories* (ed. J. Masling), ch. 6. Analytic Press, Hillsdale (NJ).

Bower, T. G. R. (1977). *A Primer of Infant Development*. Freeman, Oxford.

Bowers, K. S. and Meichenbaum, D. (1985). *The Unconscious Reconsidered*. Wiley, Chichester.

Cheshire, N. M. (1966). *Some Concepts of Object-relations Theory*. B. Litt. Thesis, Oxford University (Bodleian Library).

Clark, R. W. (1980). *Freud: The Man and the Cause*. Cape/Weidenfeld and Nicolson, London.

Cohen, J. and Clark, J. H. (1979). *Medicine, Mind and Man*. Freeman, Reading and San Francisco.

Condon, W. S. (1979). Neonatal entrainment and enculturation. In *Before Speech* (ed. M. Bullowa), pp. 131–148. Cambridge University Press, Cambridge.

Cooper, C. and Kline, P. (1986). An evaluation of the Defence Mechanism Test. *Brit. J. Psychol.*, **77**, 19–31.

Cremerius, J. (1979). Gibt es zwei psychoanalytische Technike? *Psyche*, **33**, 577–599.

Eagle, M. N. (1983a). Interests as object relations. In *Empirical Studies of Psychoanalytic Theories* (ed. J. Masling), ch. 5. Analytic Press, Hillsdale, NJ.

Eagle, M. N. (1983b). The epistemological status of recent developments... In *Physics, Philosophy and Psychoanalysis* (eds R. S. Cohen and L. Landan), pp. 31–55. Reidel, Dordrecht.

Eagle, M. N. (1984). *Recent Developments in Psychoanalysis: A Critical Evaluation*. McGraw-Hill, New York.

Eissler, K. R. (1963). Notes on the psychoanalytic concept of cure. *Psychoanal. Study Child*, **18**, 424–463.

Emde, R. N. (1983). The prerepresentational self and its affective core. *Psychoanal. Study Child*, **38**, 165–192.

Erdelyi, M. (1985). *Psychoanalysis: Freud's Cognitive Psychology*. Freeman, Oxford.

Eysenck, H. J. (1959). The Rorschach test. In *The Fifth Mental Measurement Year Book* (ed. O. K. Buros). Gryphon Press, New Jersey.

Fairbairn, W. R. D. (1941). A revised psychopathology of the psychoses and neuroses. Reprinted in *Psychoanalytic Studies of the Personality*, pp. 28–58; Tavistock, London (1952).

Fairbairn, W. R. D. (1963). Synopsis of an object-relations theory of the Personality. *Int. J. Psychoanal.*, **44**, 224–225.

Fine, R. (1986). *Narcissism, Self and Society*. Columbia University Press, New York.

Freud, A. (1937). *The Ego and the Mechanisms of Defence* (translated by C. Barnes). Hogarth, London.

Freud, S. (1910). The antithetical meaning of primal words. *Standard Ed.*, **11**, 154–161.

Freud, S. (1914). On narcissism. . . *Standard Ed.*, **14**, 67–102.

Freud, S. (1915a). The unconscious. *Standard Ed.*, **14**, 159–215.

Freud, S. (1926). Inhibition, symptoms and anxiety. *Standard Ed.*, **20**, 77–174.

Geach, P. (1957). *Mental Acts*. Routledge and Kegan Paul, London.

Gedo, J. E. (1979). Theories of object-relations: a metaphysiological assessment. *J. Am. Psychoanal. Assoc.*, **27**, 367–373.

Greenberg, J. R. and Mitchell, A. (1983). *Object relations in Psychoanalytic Theory*. Harvard University Press, Cambridge (Mass.).

Grosskurth, P. (1986). *Melanie Klein: Her World and Her Work*. Hodder and Stoughton, London.

Grotstein, J. S. (1982). Newer perspectives in object–relations theory. *Contemp. Psychoanal.*, **18**, 43–91.

Guntrip, H. (1952). A study of Fairbairn's theories of schizoid reactions. *Brit. J. Med. Psychol.*, **25**, 86–103.

Guntrip, H. (1961). *Personality, Structures and Human Interaction*. Hogarth, London.

Hamilton, V. (1982). *Narcissus and Oedipus:* . . . Routledge and Kegan Paul, London.

Harré, R. (1970). *The Principles of Scientific Thinking*. Macmillan, London.

Head, H. (1926). *Aphasia and Kindred Disorders of Speech*, 2 vols. Cambridge University Press, Cambridge.

Heimann, P. (1952). Certain functions of introjection and projection. . . In *Developments in Psychoanalysis* (ed. J. Riviere), pp. 122–168. Hogarth, London.

Hesse, M. B. (1966). *Models and Analogies in Science*. University of Notre Dame Press, Notre Dame (IN).

Hewstone, M., Hooper, D. and Miller, K. (1981). Psychological change in neurotic depression: . . . *Brit. J. Psychiatry*, **139**, 47–51.

Isaacs, S. (1952). The nature and function of phantasy. In *Developments in Psychoanalysis* (ed. J. Riviere), pp. 67–121. Hogarth, London.

Jacobson, E. (1964). *The Self and the Object-world*. International Universities Press, New York.

Kanzer, M. (1979). Object-relations theory: and introduction. *J. Am. Psychoanal. Assoc.*, **27**, 313–325.

Kernberg, O. F. (1972). Critique of the Kleinian School. In *Tactics and Techniques*. . . (ed. P. L. Giovacchini), pp. 62–93. Hogarth, London.

Kernberg, O. F. (1975). *Borderline Conditions*. . . Aronson, New York.

Kernberg, O. F. (1977). *Object-Relations Theory and Classical Psychoanalysis*. Aronson, New York.

Kernberg, O. F. (1979). Some implications of object-relations theory . . . *J. Am. Psychoanal. Assoc.*, **27** (suppl.), 207–239.

Kline, P. (1972/1981). *Fact and Fantasy in Freudian Theory*, first and second editions. Methuen, London.

Kline, P. (1983). *Personality: Measurement and Theory*. Hutchinson, London.

Kohon, G. (ed.) 1986). *The British School of Psychoanalysis*. Free Association Books, London.

Kohut, H. (1971). *The Analysis of the Self*. International University Press, New York.

Kohut, H. (1977). *The Restoration of the Self*. International University Press, New York.

Kragh, U. and Smith, G. (1970). *Percept-Genetic Analysis*. Gleerups, Lund.

Lawlor, M. and Cochran, L. (1981). Does invalidation produce loose construing? *Brit. J. Med. Psychol.*, **54**, 41–50.

Leon, I. G. (1984). Psychoanalysis, Piaget and attachment. . . *Int. Rev. Psychoanal.*, **11**, 255–278.

Madison, P. (1961). *Freud's Concept of Repression and Defence*. University of Minnesota Press, Minneapolis.

Main M. *et al*. (1985). Security in infancy, . . . In *Growing Points of Attachment Theory*. . . (eds I. Bretherton and F. Waters), pp. 66–104. Chicago University Press, Chicago.

Malcolm, J. (1980). *The Impossible Profession*. Knopf, New York.

MacIntyre, A. C. (1958). *The Unconscious*. Routledge and Kegan Paul, London.

McDevitt, J. B. (1979). The role of internalisation in the development of object-relations. . . *J. Am. Psychoanal. Assoc.*, **27**, 327–343.

Meissner, N. W. (1979). Internalisation and object-relations. *J. Am. Psychoanal. Assoc.*, **27**, 345–360.

Menninger, K. A. and Holzman, P. S. (1973). *Theory of Psychoanalytic Technique*, second edition. Basic Books, New York.

Miller, G. A., Galanter, E. and Pribram, K. H. (1960). *Plans and the Structure of Behavior*. Henry Holt, New York.

Murray, H. A. *et al*. (1938). *Explorations in Personality*. Oxford University Press, New York.

Neisser, U. (1976). *Cognition and Reality*. Freeman, San Francisco.

Ogden, T. H. (1983). The concept of internal object relations. *Int. J. Psychoanal.*, **64**, 227–241.

Ornstein, A. (1974). A dread to repeat. . . *Annu. Psychoanal.*, **2**, 231–248.

Payne, R. W. (1960). Disorders of thinking. In *Symptoms of Psychopathology* (ed. C. G. Costello), ch. 3. Wiley, New York.

Phillipson, H. (1955). *The Object Relations Technique*. Tavistock, London.

Phillipson, H. (1973). *A Short Introduction to the Object Relations Technique*. NFER–Nelson, Windsor.

Pines, M. (1984). Reflections on mirroring. *Int. Rev. Psychoanal.*, **11**, 27–42.

Romanyshyn, R. (1982). *Psychological Life from Science to Metaphor*. Open University Press, Milton Keynes.

Rothstein, A. (ed.) (1985). *Models of the Mind*. International Universities Press, New York.

Russell, G. A. (1985). Narcissism and the narcissistic personality disorder: . . . *Brit. J. Med. Psychol.*, **58**, 137–148.

Ryle, A. (1982). *Psychotherapy: A Cognitive Interpretation*. Academic Press, London.

Ryle, A. (1985). Cognitive theory, object-relations and the Self. *Brit. J. Med. Psychol.*, **58**, 1–7.

Ryle, G. (1949). *The Concept of Mind*. Penguin, Harmondsworth.

Sandler, J. (1962). Psychology and psychoanalysis. *Brit. J. Med. Psychol.*, **35**, 91–99.

Sandler, J. (1985). Comments on the self and its objects. In *Self and Object-constancy:* . . . (eds R. Lax *et al*.), ch. 4. Guilford, New York.

Sandler, J. and Rosenblatt, B. (1962). The concept of the representational world. *Psychoanal. Study Child,* **17**, 128–145.

Saperstein, J. and Gaines, J. (1978). A commentary on the divergent views between Kernberg and Kohut . . .*Int. Rev. Psychoanal.*, **5**, 413–423.

Schafer, R. (1968). *Aspects of Internalisation*. International Universities Press, New York.

Schafer, R. (1976). *A New Language for Psychoanalysis*. Yale University Press, New York and London.

Schneider, H. (1981). *Die Theorie Piagets*. Huber, Berne.

Sheehan, M. J. (1985). A personal construct study of depression. *Brit. J. Med. Psychol.*, **58**, 119–128.

Shotter, J. (1984). *Social Accountability and Selfhood*. Blackwell, Oxford.

Sullivan, E. S. (1953). *The Interpersonal Theory of Psychiatry*. Norton, New York.

Sutherland, J. D. (1980). The British object-relations theorists: . . . *J. Am. Psychoanal. Assoc.* **28**, 829–860.

Tolman, E. C. (1948). Cognitive maps in rats and men. *Psychol. Rev.*, **55**, 189–208.

Wachtel, P. L. (1982). *Resistance: Psychodynamic and Behavioural Approaches*. Plenum Press, New York and London.

Waismann, F. (1951, reprint). Verifiability. In *Logic and Language*, vol. 1 (ed. A. G. N. Flew), pp. 117–144. Blackwell, Oxford.

Weidenhammer, B. (1985). Ammerkungen zur Theorie des Selbst. . . *Anal. Kritik*, **7**, 162–179.

Westerlundh, B. and Smith, G. (1983). Perceptgenesis and the psychodynamics of perception. *Psychoanal. Contemp. Thought*, **6**, 597–640.

Winnicott, D. W. (1964). *The Child, the Family and the Outside World*, second edition. Penguin, Harmondsworth.

Winnicott, D. W. (1971). *Playing and Reality*. Reissued 1974 by Penguin Books, Harmondsworth.

Wisdom, J. O. (1962). Comparison and development of the psychoanalytic theories of melancholia. *Int. J. Psychoanal.*, **43**, 113–132.

Wisdom, J. O. (1963). Fairbairn's contribution on object-relations, splitting and ego-structure. *Brit. J. Med. Psychol.*, **36**, 145–159.

Wisdom, J. O. (1984). What is left of psychoanalytic theory? *Int. Rev. Psychoanal.*, **11**, 313–326.

Wollheim, R. (1985). *Thread of Life*. Cambridge University Press, Cambridge.

CHAPTER 5

General Factors and Specific Techniques in Self-concept Therapy

Neil Cheshire and Helmut Thomae

5.1 Introduction

We have already observed in Chapter 1 that practising psychotherapists are being required even more frequently nowadays to deal with disturbances of self-feeling in their patients, and we commented that these disturbances not only present themselves in a variety of more or less specific forms, but also are treated by a variety of more or less symptom-specific methods. The forms in which they appear range from the personality trait of 'low self-esteem' (known to Adlerians as chronic 'inferiority feelings', and to students of Cattell as low loadings on those dynamic factors which go to make up 'self-sentiment'), through a generalized lowering of morale in clinical depression, to various sorts of quite narrowly circumscribed social anxieties such as interview-phobia or stage-fright. They are most conspicuous, of course, in those schizoid identity-disturbances which characterize 'borderline personalities' and in the 'threatened identities' who are the subject of the range of studies collated recently by Breakwell (1983). But we confine ourselves here mainly to less severe neurotic phenomena.

5.2 Psychodynamics and Behaviouralism

When symptomatology is relatively specific, it is tempting to suppose that it will be most appropriate to use so-called 'behavioural' techniques, which are ostensibly derived from theories of psychological conditioning, and which concentrate upon the particular stimulus–response–reinforcement contingencies which precipitate or serve to maintain the unwanted behaviour; and we may include in this group the associated spin-offs of modelling, role-play, assertion-training and cognitive behaviour-modification. On the other hand, when the disturbance is more diffuse and pervasive, we tend to think in terms of more cognitive and/or experiential methods involving self-understanding, problem-solving, insight, interpretation, the dynamics of relationships and the mysteries of self-actualization.

In practice, however, we know that such methodological contrasts, which fuelled theoretical controversies in the 1950s and 1960s, can rarely be sustained, if only because even psychoanalysis has some of the characteristics of a 'learning theory', and because there are no such things as 'stimuli' and 'contingencies' *in vitro* but only as apperceived and negotiated by intentional and culture-sharing agents. Hence the current interest in the integration of different psychotherapeutic methods at a technological level (Reisman, 1971; Murray and Jacobson, 1971; Marmor, 1966; Marmor and Woods, 1980; Wachtel, 1977, 1982; Fensterheim and Glazer, 1983; Goldfried, 1982; Yates, 1983; Arkowitz and Messer, 1984), as well as from the point of view of a unified theory of psychotherapeutic change (Eysenck, 1980; and see below). Indeed, it is over 20 years now since Marmor canvassed the idea that the two approaches, 'behavioural' and psychoanalytic, 'have certain basic factors in common which ... are more significant than their theoretical differences' (1962, pp. 287–288).

Another consideration leading to the same conclusion is the fact that we are often confronted by cases where the patient's immediate complaint concerns a specific behavioural limitation which, when it is explored, turns out to be associated with some much more general problem of identification, self-concept or object-relations. One of Thomae's patients, for example, developed a writer's cramp when writing his name (i.e. declaring his *identity*) at a post-office counter, in the presence of a woman whom he unconsciously associated with his father; since that time the patient had been unable to write at the post-office, because the cramp always reappeared there. Or again, Bannister and Fransella (1986, p. 161) have described the case of a young man who presented with a quite specific telephone-phobia but who, when that had been symptomatically cured, went on to complain of several progressively more general social, interpersonal and existential anxieties which required successive 'layers' of therapy.

Now, it is just such cases which used to divide psychological therapists into 'behavioural' and 'psychodynamic' camps. Members of the former would claim typically to address the specific symptom as a maladaptive perceptuomotor habit which needed to be deconditioned from the particular stimuli which had come to control it, while the latter school would supposedly tackle the more general issue of the patient's identification-anxieties as 'represented' by the symptom. Furthermore, the methods of the former approach would be specific, concrete and symptom-directed (desensitization, relaxation, competing responses, habituation, etc.), while those of the latter would involve the whole interpersonal relationship between patient and therapist. These crude and misleading half-truths were based not only upon the false premise, noted above, that an account of 'learning' plays no part in psychoanalysis as a general theory of psychological functioning nor in its specific hypotheses about symptom-formation, but also upon a neglect of the fact that even the earliest pioneers of psychoanalysis used a range of very specific, symptom-directed tactics when they realized that some relatively idiopathic conditioned-anxiety had become established.

Thus, in the very first exposition of clinical psychoanalysis, Freud gives two examples of throat-constriction as an hysterical 'conversion' symptom, both of which he cured symptomatically: one by massage under light hypnosis, the other by what would nowadays be called 'assertion training' (Breuer and Freud, 1895, pp. 169–171). Again, in his own exposition of psychoanalytic method, Stekel lists a variety of means for bringing about therapeutic change in a patient. One of them, which today's 'cognitive therapies' have rediscovered and cloaked in different jargon, was that of deliberately marshalling the patient's reason or intellectual understanding in his struggle against the symptom: 'I activate his *logos*' (Stekel, 1938, p. 315).

The theoretical principle concerning what balance the analyst should strike between such specific and 'active' interventions as these, on the one hand, and the more general methods of exploring unconscious anxieties and defences, on the other, was in fact the subject of Freud's (1919) paper on the 'new ways' in psychoanalysis. And conversely, if psychoanalysis has always been more specific and behavioural than some of its critics realize, it is instructive to notice that many advocates of behaviour-specific techniques are now acknowledging the importance of general, interpersonal factors more readily than some of them used to. For example, recent studies of the therapy of agoraphobia, a condition which closely involves the self-concept, suggest that 'behavioural' techniques are most effective when carried out with the continuous and reliable emotional support of a 'significant other' (Thorpe and Burns, 1983); that is, as the analysts would want to say, when they are conducted in the context of a 'transference relationship'.

Disturbances of self-feeling, then, are treated nowadays by a great number of psychotherapeutic methods, which can be traced back, on the one hand, as far as the origins of psychoanalysis and, on the other, to the application of techniques which are deduced from behavioural learning theory. We propose to illustrate this range and variety of psychotherapeutic methods here by presenting a number of clinical vignettes, each of which depicts a different kind of therapeutic transaction (carried out either by H.T. or by one of his colleagues), and to set them in the context of a contentious theoretical debate which has rumbled on in this field: namely, the question whether it is possible to identify the variables which bring about psychotherapeutic change, and to distinguish those that have a 'general' facilitating effect upon all such activity from those that play a specific part in overcoming specific difficulties (whether such difficulties are intrinsic to the psychological disturbance being treated or are a by-product of the way in which therapy is being conducted).

Our clinical examples are taken first from a self-assertion group, then from an individual therapy conducted by a psychodynamically orientated social worker, and thirdly from two formal psychoanalyses; but such distinctions do not, of course, imply (after the cognitive turn which behavioural therapy has taken) that psychodynamic elements are necessarily absent from assertion-training in a wider sense (and we have seen above that Freud himself used assertion-training in the case of Rosalia H.). Thus in the case of psychotherapeutic treatments of different origins, the question arises which items from the entire stock, or which parts of a particular procedure, are especially effective, and which others have a more general character. The distinction is analogous, of course, to that in physical medicine where the effect of medicaments related to, and aimed at, curing a particular disease (as opposed to more generally suppressing pain or reducing fever) is traditionally designated 'specific'.

There is some evidence, as we have noted above, that successful therapists who are operating out of different theoretical schools, so to speak, are approaching each other in their practice; that is to say, that what they actually *do* with their patients is not quite so different as their theoretical descriptions and reasoning might lead one to expect. This is sometimes combined, however, with a certain monopolistic outlook according to which the adherents of one kind of theory (A) claim that those who subscribe to a rival theory (B) achieve therapeutic success only in so far as they are in effect putting into practice (unwittingly and in spite of themselves) certain therapeutic principles (typical of school A) which they consciously disclaim.

Thus we can find psychoanalysts insisting that behaviour therapy inadvertently manipulates the 'transference relationship', and behaviour therapists arguing that psychoanalysis works (insofar as it works at all) by a clumsy version of Pavlovian deconditioning. And somewhere in the middle we may note Jerome Frank's (1974) contention that all psychotherapeutic treatments become effective by means of an unspecific placebo factor in the form of 'suggestion'. But not even this apparently neutralist thesis can escape the distinction between generality and specificity, because Frank still has to explain why suggestion sometimes has a general, facilitating effect on the therapeutic interaction while at others its effect seems to be symptom-specific.

The problem for psychotherapy research, which applies especially to the field of disturbances of self-feeling and their psychological treatment, is to distinguish between such general and specific variables, and to understand the part they play in the complexity of the interactions between patient and therapist; and to do this so far as possible (at least in terms of a positivistic paradigm) by means of empirical control and quantitative measurement. We discuss below some of the research of this kind which has been done on Carl Rogers' suggestions for general factors in therapeutic effectiveness; and, in the *Introduction to Part II*, N.C. examines a very different investigation of broadly the same topic by Gelder *et al.* (1973).

On the assumption that psychotherapeutic techniques reflect the complexity of self-concept theories, it becomes evident that the self-system can be therapeutically influenced at many points and in many ways. In practice, this is apparent from the fact that self-assertion training, for example, is applied in the first instance to quite specific and isolated sectors of overt behaviour, whereas psychodynamically orientated interpretations may be aimed at much more general attitudes, anxieties or dispositions, and be intended to alter the balance of James's self-esteem equation (which we introduced in Chapter 1) either by reducing the power of the phantasies which have been inflating the lower term on the right-hand side, or by enabling the patient to raise his valuation of the upper term.

The classical psychoanalytic theory that neuroses are 'overdetermined' illustrates some of the complexity within the system (cp. Litowitz, 1978); and, although this conception has already abandoned a simple linear model of cause-and-effect, it has not yet been coherently mapped on to a substitute process-modelling system, such as von Zeppelin outlines in Chapter 6 (but cp. Peterfreund and Schwartz, 1971; Peterfreund, 1983; A. Ryle, 1982; Erdelyi, 1985). Such cybernetic models do, however, allow us to clarify and formalize the processes whereby therapeutic interventions which are orientated towards one point may, or even must, have effects on other sectors as well. Thus the experience of 'behavioural' techniques, which are based on the unlearning of maladaptive responses and the relearning of adaptive ones (and which reject the assumption that unconscious motivating conflicts must still be operating to maintain psychological malfunctioning), may still have quite far-reaching phenomenological effects upon the way the patient perceives himself as a person, most notably by changing the sense of 'locus of control' (Rotter, 1966) from external to internal. Our first vignette illustrates this point.

5.3   Taking Behavioural Steps

5.3.1   'One small step for me . . .'

This short sequence from a behaviourally orientated therapy-group, which was treating pathologically insecure patients, is intended to illustrate one of our central contentions regarding the effect of therapeutic techniques: namely, that therapeutic techniques that are derived from different theories of therapy start operating from different conceptions of self-esteem, and consequently can be expected to have a certain kind of general effect on the entire system as well as their immediate specific impact upon symptomatic behaviour.

Mr B., the patient whom this illustration concerns, sought treatment because of his insecurity, which he experienced over a wide range of social encounters and work-situations, and which was very painful for him. Particularly when dealing with his colleagues and his superiors, he frequently stammered, blushed and had outbreaks of sweating. In about the sixth session he takes part in the following scene, which is acted out by the group in the form of role-playing. Mr B.'s boss (acted by a member of the group) comes to see him at his work-place to get some information. When Mr B. finds that he does not know the answer immediately, he begins to step from one foot to the other, blushes, grins embarrassedly, and finally starts giving a rather confused answer.

In the subsequent discussion, Mr B. says that he felt his 'boss' close to him physically, and that he had been unable to defend himself against this pressure. It is therefore suggested to him that, when the role-play is repeated, he should see whether it would perhaps help him if he made a step backward to get some distance, at least from the physical pressure.

In the repeat-performance of the scene, Mr B. is seen acting quite differently. Mr B. manages to take that step backward; and this time he does not blush, his embarrassed grin is much slighter, and after a concentrated short pause he is able to start answering coherently. Following this performance, Mr B. is amazed at the striking effect of the small step (and so are the rest of the group!). He felt much more at ease and secure in this second scene, and was able to allow himself the short pause in which he could think about his answer.*

We understand the step backward as getting some distance from an oppressing situation; a distance which, on the one hand, is very direct and concrete, but, on the other, is also symbolic. For it is not only for the poet Thomas Campbell (1799) that 'distance lends enchantment to the view', but also for the many psychologists, from the early *Gestalt* theorists through Kurt Lewin and up to Hermann Witkin, who have laid emphasis upon figure-ground differentiation and upon the value of field-independence when the forces of the 'life-space' or *Umwelt* are crowding in. This sort of psychological distance not only affords a better view, but also saves us from becoming the victim of a situation which is difficult to survey clear-headedly, and provides us with the

*The Editors are grateful to the therapist involved, Dr. H.-J. Gruenzig, co-author of Chapter 10 below, for providing this material.

space necessary to become 'self-efficacious' in Bandura's phrase. Thus it was physical distance that symbolized for Mr B. a necessary psychological detachment, and enabled him to maintain the equanimity which had previously deserted him, thereby allowing him to follow Horace's famous advice: *aequam memento rebus in arduis servare mentem.* From this beneficial experience he was able to achieve a changed view of himself and a more positive self-concept, as the result of a simple practical training which had its starting-point exclusively in the overt non-verbal behaviour of physical movement.

Our second clinical *vignette* is also an example of a therapeutic intervention which consists of taking literal behavioural steps, but in this case the psychodynamic resonances and reverberations of the immediate physical activity, in its particular interpersonal context, were at once more fundamental and more wide-ranging than in the episode with Mr B. Furthermore, the patient not only provides her own psychodynamic interpretation of the significance for her of the overt behaviour, but also behaves subsequently in such a way as to validate her own interpretive construction.

5.3.2 Further Behavioural Steps*

This patient, Miss F., was a 17-year-old girl who had been inflicting injuries on herself for two years and who engaged in other acts of self-destruction. Sessions with her proved difficult in so far as there were long periods of silence, which often could not be broken at all. The material pointed towards a disturbance in the preverbal phase of communication and identification with her mother.

Various features of Miss F.'s behaviour in the course of treatment encouraged the therapist to take unconventional steps in handling this state of tension, and on one occasion she suggested *a walk* to the patient. Miss F. agreed to this proposal, on condition that the therapist did not expect that she (Miss F.) would talk more than usual as a result. The patient was silent during the walk, and took her leave with a short remark, saying: 'that was like mother and daughter.' This concrete offer of an everyday behavioural interaction represented the gratification of a wish the patient had had with regard to her mother. At the same time she was able to recall a family scene which had been experienced at the age of four and was remembered as harmonious.

The following sessions showed how this walk had brought the decisive turning point in the therapy. The patient began to talk about her body, especially those aspects which were bothering her in connection with her femininity. Her appearance began to change, and it was obvious that she was identifying with the therapist (for example, by choosing a similar hairstyle). So it could be said that from this point of departure has come about a positive and favourable change in the patient's image of being a woman, insofar as those

*The Editors are grateful to the therapist involved, Frau G. Martin (Department of Psychotherapy, Ulm University), for permission to use this material.

respects in which the mother had failed her were greatly reduced in importance during the remainder of the sessions. The 'behavioural' intervention, therefore, appears to have had phenomenological-psychodynamic repercussions in at least three directions: (1) by being apperceived *as* a 'mother–child' situation; (2) by releasing her from being preoccupied with negative feelings towards her mother, and reviving some 'good objects' from childhood; and (3) by occasioning a positive and adaptive identification with the therapist as a female figure. It is by no means clear how this could have been accomplished by verbal means.

5.4 Conditions for Self-orientated Therapy

The most general objective of psychotherapeutic methods applied to disturbances of self-feeling is the restoration of the unity of the person in his/her experience and his/her activity. This objective can be maintained also in so-called symptomatic neuroses, where the symptom is understood as an expression of a maladaptive solution of conflict, and where the goal of therapy becomes the resolution of 'affectocognitive dissonances' (to anticipate McReynolds' usage in Chapter 8). The notion of 'unity of the person' includes the idea that the most disparate spheres of life and problems, with all their ramifications, valuations, cognitions and emotions, are experienced as belonging to the person, as part of oneself, and that they are integrated in a stable ego-identity.

On this view, the mental contents which participated in such intrapsychic dissonances are to be integrated with other contents; but in order to transform the existing incompatibility into consistency, the consistency already established necessarily has to be temporarily dissolved or loosened. Since such dissolution of existing consistencies and organization understandably evokes some degree of anxiety and insecurity in the patient, analysts try to avoid, or at least to minimize, it. Sceptical critics, however, have argued that anlysts can get the patient to accept their interpretive constructions largely because they have initially made him or her vulnerable and suggestible in this way; and there is no doubt that this means of 'softening-up' a victim is regularly exploited by 'brain-washers' and 'thought-reformers' of various sorts (Lifton, 1964; but cp. Cheshire, 1975, pp. 43–46). Freud, however, had anticipated this objection, and argued quite explicitly at various points that his methods did not entail imposing one particular belief-system on the patient. He wrote, for example (1940, p. 175):

> 'However much the analyst may be tempted to become a teacher, model and ideal for other people and to create man in his own image, he should not forget that that is not his task in the analytic relationship. . . In all his attempts at improving and educating the patient, the analyst should respect his individuality'.

For these reasons, it is, of course, a fundamental principle of dynamic psychotherapy that the background conditions against which its transactions take place should be such as to enable the patient to tolerate the anxiety, insecurity, vulnerability and sense of threat which accompany the dissolution of existing consistencies and the challenge to established defences. The relationship with the therapist, therefore, must be such as to generate a sense of security, freedom from anxiety, acceptance, reliability, confidence and help. A number of terms have been coined to designate such benign conditions, namely 'working alliance' (Greenson), 'mild positive transference' (Freud), 'holding function' (Winnicott) and 'helping alliance' (Luborsky); and their usage has been reviewed in some detail by Hartley and Strupp (1983). They are all attempts to describe the central features of what Freud himself (1940, p. 173) also called our 'pact' or 'bargain' (*Vertrag*) with the patient, long before the term 'contract' became popular in the context of psychotherapy. From the point of view of behaviour therapy, these benign conditions, under whatever name, have the common property in a neo-Pavlovian learning-theory conceptualization of the psychotherapeutic process such as Eysenck (1980) expounds, of providing environmental stimuli which serve to reduce the intensity of conditioned anxiety-responses. We comment on this view more extensively in the *Introduction to Part II*.

Techniques for establishing such conditions assume especial importance at the beginning stage of any therapy, but they are of particular consequence in treating disturbances of self-feeling where this 'beginning' represents the main stage, because they already start to operate directly on a principal aspect of the disturbance, namely the lack of self-confidence. But a benign relationship of this sort between patient and therapist does not appear automatically: it has to be created by the therapist, and even sometimes to be defended by him against the patient's attempt to disrupt it (to which Epstein refers in Chapter 2). Consequently, the entire technical repertoire which serves to produce this *general* background of a supportive, helpful, trustworthy relationship is referred to as 'general psychotherapeutic techniques'. Insofar as they produce or increase confidence in the relationship between patient and therapist, diminish anxiety, and contribute towards security and similar feelings on the part of the patient (and possibly also on the part of the therapist), they may be said to enhance self-esteem—and even to do so quite unrealistically at times.

This unrealistic enhancement, however, can be considered as a basic condition for the effectiveness of *special* therapeutic techniques which are aimed at integrating elements in the disturbance which have already been identified. This is because the unsettling of the self-concept, which is brought about as a rule by certain special techniques (such as the interpretation of defences, dependency or negative transference), can be accepted only on the basis of the trustful relationship with the therapist, or indeed on the basis of a (relatively artificial) enhancement or confirmation of self-esteem within that relationship. If the enhancement of self-esteem is the only therapeutic measure used, it has at best a momentary effect which is not sustained over a longer period nor outside the therapeutic setting. It is precisely this defect which undermines Rogers' account of how participants in 'encounter groups' transfer their group-facilitated and group-accepted disinhibition to the world at large; for, without a theory of selective introjection or ego-elaboration, there is no reason why such people should function any better *outside* the group than they did before (Cheshire, 1972).

How, then, is this esteem, acceptance, confidence, reliability, etc. conveyed? Evidently not just through the therapist's well-chosen words. The little child does not trust in his mother just because she gives him verbal assurances of her credibility, but because her behaviour is consistently experienced as trustworthy over and over again. Indeed, we know from the classic work of Bateson *et al.* (1956), which has been extended and popularized by Laing (1965, 1969) as noted in Chapter 1, that there can be devastating effects on identity-formation and the self-concept when a mother's verbal signals about her emotional reliability are combined with non-verbal signals conveying a conflicting message (cp. Brown *et al.*, 1972; Leff *et al.*, 1982). We are prompted to ask, therefore, with a glance in the direction of Kohut, if the patient misses such signs because the analyst is sitting behind her? Freud's move from the foot of the couch to the head, for respectable 'scientific' reasons of reducing potentially contaminating visual feedback to the patient, had the effect of depriving her of just those cues which social-skills theorists regard as especially rich in information for modulating one's self-concept. Indeed, we present below a clinical *vignette* in which the patient conspicuously turns her head specifically in order to seek, as it seems, such reassuring non-verbal feedback. But the one which we present next illustrates an analytical therapist (H.T.) working on setting up those conditions of trust, acceptance and security which we have been discussing.

5.4.1 *The Internalization of Confidence*

The theme of the sessions is characterized, with respect to symptomatology, by anxiety about damage as a reaction to a harmless cystitis. The patient suffers from continuous micturition which she attributes to the possibility of having injured herself during masturbation. Mrs E. tries to get an idea of her genital area by means of anatomy books. She localizes her complaints in her entire abdomen, and imagines that by pressing and rubbing she has destroyed a muscle, as with the possibility of damaging the vesical sphincter during a difficult birth. The patient is severely affected by this anxiety and suffers from disturbances of sleep and work.

Despite an increase in her complaints, Mrs E. expects from the analyst a clear answer as to whether it is possible, from a medical point of view, that she has injured herself during masturbation. His reassurance reduces her anxiety, but also makes her feel that she has somehow coerced or seduced the analyst. New dangers would arise from this; coercion, confession and seduction get mixed. She is afraid that the analyst would lead her to some place where everything is allowed, as if in his view of life no guilt existed. The patient vacillates between two ideas: she sees in the analyst on the one hand the seducer, and on the other hand the moralizer. Her resort to pietistical devoutness seems to be a way out of the threatening loss of boundaries within herself which would disturb and destroy everything. But this devoutness no longer means very much to her, particularly since she had already loosened her relations to the Church before the analysis, because she had not experienced any alleviation of her troubles, but only renewed worries in connection with the moral prohibitions of the Commandments.

In this phase, a decisive turn in the transference-relationship was brought about by the experience of the analyst giving an explanation for his technique. She experiences this as evidence that he can take her into his confidence. His readiness to let her participate in his thinking as a special 'treasure' provides a new level in the relationship and in the transference. The fact that she is allowed to get an insight and is thereby less excluded, makes the aggressive penetration in the analyst's 'head' (the drilling of a hole) unnecessary and provides a friendly-joyful, playful level for approach and participation. She begins to feel something like: 'If *he* can risk trusting *me* (with his trade-secrets), then *I* can risk trusting *him* with my own secret wishes, fears and hopes.' For H.T. as therapist, however, this allowing an insight into his psychoanalytic thinking was nothing extraordinary, and what offered a new experience to the patient was a quite common situation from his point of view.

In a secondary transference to her superior, she had placed a 'tremendous respect' in him; and this referred particularly to the boss's lack of time, which did not allow a little dispute to be clarified by further conversation. The patient also expressed a 'terrible fear of being thrown out', and H.T. had said quite incidentally that this would disappear by itself without any encouragement from him. But she had for a long time transferred this anxiety to the therapy-situation by way of a mini-symptom, in the form of leaving the consulting-room regularly some minutes before the end of the session.

H.T. did not deal particularly with the manifold determination of this behaviour, and it gradually changed by itself. Among other things, the patient wanted to avoid the whole meeting being 'annulled' by her being sent away by the analyst (as she was by her boss). The patient obviously experienced the confidence communicated by H.T. as an expression of great freedom, as if he had got rid of some kind of restriction. They then worked on the fact that the patient had known for a long time what H.T. thought about important themes in her experience, and that she was 'allowed to penetrate and to know'. Here is a detailed account (by H.T. in the first person) of the relevant episode in the psychoanalysis, with some *verbatim* material translated from the German.

5.4.2 The Therapist's Treasure

The patient put forward a problem with her superior and made it clear that she feels more at ease with him. She attributes her success in a somewhat exaggerated way to psychoanalysis and to me. Then we talk about the question of encouragement, and I say that by encouragement, which she wants, she would be deprived of fully enjoying her own success. We also talk about the exaggerated respect she still has. To my surprise, the patient then asks me: 'Did you notice that you have just given an explanation for your technique, which you do very seldom?' In answer to my question, the patient tells me that she was impressed by my remark that something disappeared by itself. (Looking at it afterwards: I *have* given an encouragement, after all, by saying that a great deal happens by itself and not everything has to be fought for.)

Then the patient talks for a long time about how extremely positive my statement had seemed to her, and she sees it as an expression of my freedom.

Mrs E.: Don't you like the freedom which I attribute to you in this connection?

H.T.: (I tell her that I am surprised that she thought she was not allowed to penetrate into my thoughts and to learn the reason for statements and considerations, although she had really known this for a long time.)

Mrs E.: But that *I* could express it, that was tremendously new to me.

H.T.: It almost seems that, only after I have expressed it, are you allowed to know something which is quite obvious and which you have known for a long time.

Mrs E.: There was still more connected with it, namely the image I always had that you are guarding your treasure. (She laughs.) I always had the feeling ... head, book, and all those things—and if you yourself open your head I needn't drill into it, and that is something quite different. It is a frankness or freedom which comes from you (it may be something different, but it's that sort of thing). I think it is somehow evidence of confidence if you say, 'I do it for such and such a reason' ... I'd find it out somehow, but it seems to be different when you say it than it is when I say it.

With regard to the open book, it should be mentioned that the patient had in the meantime read an article of mine and also one I had published together with my wife. Somehow she had attributed to the 'Freud Bible' (that is, to some notional Freudian scriptures enshrining commandments about how to conduct oneself in analysis) a prohibition against acquiring knowledge about psycho-analysis; and she was therefore astonished to find that I considered her curiosity to be something quite natural, and that the 'Freud' books were just as open to her as the anatomy books which she had consulted. I gave her the same impression with regard to some inquiries she made about my family back-ground about which she had had a vague idea before the analysis, insofar as my connections with the 'Christian' Bible are concerned. From this increase of confidence, and this identification with the analyst's insight-conveying func-tion, new and more intensive transference phantasies developed, and a steady working relationship was guaranteed.

5.5 The General and the Specific

It will be apparent that the school of psychotherapy which has most conspic-uously combined, on the one hand, a practical concern with the client's self-perception, and the influence of the therapist on that self-perception, with, on the other hand, a theoretical insistence on the *generality* and non-directive-ness of its techniques for occasioning a beneficial psychological change, is that of Carl Rogers. He has identified the main ingredients of a productive therapeutic atmosphere as being the 'triad' of empathy, genuineness and warmth on the part of the therapist. For him, however, it is a matter of positive policy to refrain from making specific interpretations, whether of content or of transference-dynamics, and he has consequently antagonized the more psycho-dynamic therapists by his arguably ill-conceived criticism of such interpret-ations (cp. Cheshire, 1975, pp. 62–68).

Nevertheless, all students of psychotherapy owe him a considerable debt for having been the first to publish significant transcripts of episodes from therapeutic sessions, combined with clients' 'before' and 'after' self-reports, so that the nature of his evidence could be scrutinized by others. Thus, from a scientific point of view, he acknowledged that a valid theory and method of psychotherapy should in principle be susceptible of systematic empirical inves-tigation.

It is accepted, then, that a gain in self-esteem, self-regard and self-security is a principal object in client-centred therapy; and the assumption is that this gain is facilitated by the therapeutic triad of non-specific empathy, warmth and genuineness to which we have just referred. Against this background, empirical studies involving the Q-sort method to reflect the psychological 'distance' between a client's ideal self and actual self were able to show that a narrowing of the gap had indeed occurred during therapy; and we now have a more sophisticated psychometric technology, derived from Kelly's Personal Con-struct Theory, for these and similar purposes, some of which are described by Cheshire and Thomae in Chapter 4, and by Cheshire *et al.* in Chapter 7.

Clearly such a reduction of phenomenological distance can be brought about in practice either by reducing the aspirations of the ideal self *vis-à-vis* the actual self, or by strengthening and increasing the more realistic capacities and enterprises (real self) of the client in proportion to his phantasies. In terms of James's self-esteem equation (which we introduced in Chapter 1), this change of balance corresponds to increasing the value of the left side of the equation by either increasing that of the numerator while holding the denominator constant, or by reducing the value of the denominator while the numerator is held constant.

Rogers's assumption seems to have been that his 'non-directive' technique brings about this sort of change by reflecting back to a client, within the supportive atmosphere of the triad, those comments of the client which were relevant to assessing discrepancies and potential adjustments between the realities of his resources and situation, on the one hand, and the aspirations of what others have called 'the wishful self', on the other. Although questions have been raised about the possibility, and even the desirability, of maintaining the elements in the triad for therapeutic purposes, and even more about the alleged non-directiveness of the method, what mainly concerns us here is the possibility of assessing the potency and generalizability of these background components of the therapeutic relationship.

This issue has been reviewed by Mitchell *et al.*, who comment that 'the recent evidence, although equivocal, does seem to suggest that empathy, warmth and genuineness are related in some way to client change but that their potency and generalizability are not as great as was once thought' (1977, p. 483). Two further characteristic general components of the Rogerian method which have been questioned are the notion of facilitative skills and the idea of confrontation: partly because it is not at all clear that these facilitative skills have been adequately identified or that they are in themselves as effective as Rogers implied, and partly because the assumptions surrounding the use of confront-ation as a tactic are not well elucidated. Several studies related to these topics have been summarized by Berenson and Mitchell (1974) who report that the number, strength and direction of the correlations among empathy, warmth, genuineness and concreteness, immediacy and reference to significant others, were 'vastly different for high as opposed to low facilitators'; and that 'therapists rated high and low on empathy, warmth and genuineness provided very different encounters for their clients'. This means that the capacity for therapeutic facilitation is very far from being a virtually unitary general trait, loading equally highly on each of three contributory factors; and it indicates that you can be a 'high facilitator' without rating highly on all the supposed components of facilitation. Elsewhere, Mitchell *et al.* (1977, p. 490) draw the conclusion that

'casting the therapists into two groups based on empathy, warmth and genuineness led to two different matrices which we believe more accurately characterized the integration of skills and behaviours which are unique to these two distinct groups of therapists.'

For our purposes it is significant that these studies are already drawing a distinction between rather general attributes of the therapist and the therapeutic situation, on the one hand, and the deployment at different phases in the therapy of specific tactics and skills, on the other. So that, although the ingredients of the triad may well be necessary and perhaps even sufficient to establish a favourable therapeutic atmosphere early on, nevertheless, once this has been established, different interpersonal skills may continue to be necessary at subsequent stages even though none is likely to be sufficient in itself.

This raises the whole question of the extent to which a particular therapist's actions and tactics need to be adapted not only to the general type of disturbance (in terms of diagnostic category) from which the patient suffers, but also to the specific problems and anxieties of the therapeutic 'here and now'. Mitchell *et al.* (1977) consequently suggest that

'high levels of empathy might overwhelm a schizophrenic client early in therapy and that, instead, empathy might best be increased slowly over time within the context of uniformly high levels of warmth. On the other hand, with a neurotic, initially high levels of warmth might best be lowered somewhat in the middle phase of therapy in order to heighten negative aspects of the 'transference' and increase anxiety sufficiently so it becomes an excellent stimulus for change.'

From these comments it follows, for the purpose of relating this technique to the handling of self-feeling disturbances, that the specific technique deployed to help a client whose disturbance arises from one sort of intrapsychic conflict may well be quite different from those which are appropriate to the treatment of another client whose self-feeling disturbance has a different specific source. Indeed, Curtis (1985) has drawn attention to the fact that Kohut, in his recommendations about the treatment of 'narcissistic' disturbances of self-functioning (cp. Chapter 4) lays primary stress on the role of empathy, and relegates the classical manoeuvres of interpreting transference and resistance to a secondary place. Consequently, Kohut's approach to those cases leads to a form of 'interactional reparative therapy' whose methods sometimes clash with the traditional tactics of psychoanalytically based therapy.

From another point of view, the therapeutic inadequacy of the Rogerian triad, when it is not supplemented by a repertoire of specific techniques adapted to specific purposes, is firmly asserted by Strupp (1977, p. 4):

'The patient does not abandon a neurotic pattern of behaviour ...
because he is exposed to the therapist's warmth, genuineness and
empathy, or because his expectations of help and succour are
aroused by the therapist. To some extent, this is the case, but by and
large it does not go very far; indeed, this is where many forms of
'supportive therapy' stop.'

In an attempt to go beyond this and say positively what is required to make
empathy work, Gurman introduces his 'empathic specificity hypothesis',
according to which empathy, in order to be effective, needs to be directed at a
particular target in the psychodynamics of the patient, and to be combined with
an appropriate use of confrontation. He even goes on to suggest that, when
such empathy is combined with too little confrontation (and confrontation can,
of course, be set up by many different sorts of intervention), it may actually be
'anti-therapeutic' (Gurman, 1977, p. 503). Conversely, there is always the
chance that a confrontation or intervention directed at a particular issue may
trigger off, to an unexpected extent, an anxiety which is fundamental to the
client's self-perceptions. Thus Mitchell *et al.* go on to say:

'although all confrontations run the risk of aborting the therapeutic
alliance, those pose a greater threat which force a client to doubt
certain 'myths' about himself, his family, etc., which he considers
central to his functioning, no matter how precarious.'

It is worth noticing that here we find Mitchell *et al.* making the same sort of
distinction between the background climate of a therapeutic alliance and the
specific techniques which need to be deployed at particular times. But since
confrontation is only one type within the whole range of interpretations (or,
more generally, interventions), they seem to be ignoring the positive mutual
interaction between interpretations and the therapeutic alliance, which thereby
brings about an improvement in the patient's self-feelings.

It will have become clear, from the reviews and discussions which we have
presented so far, that any attempt to investigate systematically the particular
factors which are responsible for therapeutic change finds itself forced to make
a distinction, at least for theoretical purposes, between those rather general
background features which are thought to be helpful in creating the sort of
psychological atmosphere in which therapeutic change is likely to take place,
and those specific tactics and types of intervention which are relatively specific
to particular schools of thought to do with psychopathology and with the
nature of psychotherapy as applied to disturbances in self-feelings. We have
already found this distinction being conceptualized in terms of sufficient and
necessary causal conditions, a formulation which goes back to the philosophical analysis of causal relationships; and the other main formulation in terms of

specific and non-specific factors has its origin in the medical classification of the agents involved in the aetiology of diseases and in their treatment.

Thomae (1980, p. 152) has illustrated the latter point by reminding us that although physical diseases used to be thought of as being produced by a specific agent which produced a specific morphological change against which a specific remedy was directed, this idea has had to give place to the notion of multicausal determination, and to the idea that many diseases come about only as the result of a combination between a pre-existing disposition and a potentially pathogenic agent) as in the familiar case of tuberculosis). From this it follows that we should be cautious about transferring a too rigid distinction between specific and non-specific agents to the corresponding analysis of the factors involved in psychotherapeutic change, especially in a context where the malfunction, against which therapy is directed, is thought of as multicausally produced on the theoretically problematic principle of 'overdetermination'. Nevertheless, these are in fact the terms in which the main debate about the agencies of therapeutic change has often been conducted.

But we would draw attention first to another way of conceptualizing the distinction which has appealed independently to Strupp (1974) and Thomae (1981, p. 74), and which Strupp and Binder (1984, p. 108) have taken up again recently: namely the phenomenon known in Gestalt-perceptual theory as 'figure-ground reversal'. This is exemplified by the well-known picture which can be seen either as a white vase against a black background or as two black profiles facing each other against a white ground (cp. Gregory, 1972, pp. 10–12). The idea is that, for some therapeutic purposes (such as a change in the conflict or anxiety which a patient presents), the therapist may need to bring into the foreground, and use in a specific and characteristic way, an item of his therapeutic repertoire which had previously been in the non-specific background. Indeed, we have seen an example of this in Gurman's insistence that empathy should not always be left in the Rogerian background but sometimes has to be used as a very specific tool focussed on a specific psychological target. Not surprisingly, this particular perceptual analogy had been used extensively in that school of theory and practice known as 'Gestalt therapy', which also emphasizes the psychological correspondences between the early organization of *body*-perception and that of *self*-perception, and which consequently advocates that patients be trained in somatic sensitivity as a means of defining and clarifying their sense of personal identity (Perls *et al.*, 1951, pp. 25–29 and 411–413).

5.6 Reason and Interpretation

We have seen that this initial enhancement of self-esteem, which is brought about by *general* factors in the therapeutic relationship, needs to be accompanied and underpinned eventually by such changes in the balance of intrapsychic forces (Freud's 'psychic economy') as will enable the patient to function more adaptively in the world at large, in order that his heightened estimation of himself (that is to say, of his own feeling, actions, values and intentions) will be confirmed, rather than rejected, by the significant others in his extratherapeutic environment. The nature of such necessary individual changes will depend, of course, on the psychopathology involved in the particular disturbance of self-feeling which is being treated.

We can usefully contrast the techniques which are used to bring about such modifications as are *specific* to particular patients, situations or forms of disturbance, with those that serve to produce and maintain a *generally* favourable interpersonal context for the treatment. In short, we may say that specific techniques are applied when general factors alone are not sufficient to bring about the necessary individual changes. For example, a self-esteem problem cannot be removed by strengthening self-confidence if the presenting lack of self-esteem is due to an irrational, unconsciously determined phantasy of greatness (as in one of James's illustrations) or to some neurotically determined fear of success (such as Epstein discusses in Chapter 2.) But, although cognitive behavioural therapists may be right in arguing that traditional psychodynamic approaches have underestimated what can be achieved through the agency of reasoning, problem-solving and conscious control, there is no point in expecting an intellectual 'discussion with the patient', such as Epstein recommends in Chapter 2, to be effective unless the determining phantasy or conflict is already preconscious; and this is unlikely to be the case when the processes involved are operating in what Freud described as the dynamic unconscious.

5.6.1 Cognitivism

Some of the special techniques that are most characteristic of psychodynamic therapy are concerned with the business of gaining access to such processes and bringing them under ego-control; they involve eliciting 'manifest' material by such methods as free association, dream-recall and projective testing, and interpreting the 'latent' content and dynamics of such material. It may be thought that, despite superficial differences in terminology, a *rapprochement* with so-called cognitive therapies is not far to seek here, because the cognitivist's 'problem-solving' and the reality-testing entailed by psychodynamic 'ego-control' are not far apart: after all, both are forms of cognitive monitoring, and some concept of 'insight' seems to be common to both. Various attempts have been made, of course, to describe the particular kind of affecto-cognitive restructuring which psychodynamic interpretations are meant to achieve (Cheshire, 1975, ch. 3 and 10; Edelson, 1975, 1984, *passim*; Erdelyi, 1985; Wegman, 1985); and, since all of them involve some element of cognitive reorganization, either implicitly or explicitly, it is tempting to ask what is the difference between the specific technique of psychodynamic interpretation and some of the interventions typically practised by those therapists who call themselves cognitive (cp. A. Ryle, 1982).

If we look, for example, at techniques derived from Kelly's Personal Construct Theory, which specifically sets its face against any idea of emotional motivation (let alone unconscious emotional processes), we may pick out first 'fixed-role therapy', and then that kind of remedial construct-teaching which has been demonstrated by Fransella (1972, pp. 159–226). In the former, the client is given directed practice in acting towards other people in the manner to be expected of someone whose affectocognitive system for processing perceptual experience is organized *differently* from that of the client. For example, if a client is dominated by the anxiety that people in authority are hostile and rejecting (which means that the constructs in which these terms figure are too tightly and rigidly linked within the construct system), then he/she is trained to act the part of someone whose construct system is structured differently, and who can consequently act towards someone in authority as if that person were quite likely *not* to be hostile and rejecting.

Insofar as such actions and dispositions are validated by experience, those links within the construct system which had previously been too rigid and exclusive are loosened and supplemented by others. In the case of Fransella's therapeutic procedure, a pathogenic *lacuna* in the client's personal construct system was filled by quite specifically training him to attend to and construe certain features of his experience which he had not previously conceptualized. Thus the stammerers who turned out to be unable to 'construe for smoothness' were given concentrated practice in noticing, introspecting, describing and comparing various experiences of smoothness, regularity, roughness, etc. in different perceptual modalities, so that their affectocognitive repertoire was effectively elaborated and enriched. For a substantial review of this whole field of 'personal construct' counselling and psychotherapy, see Epting (1984).

This method has obvious affinities with the purely educational technique of getting students to discriminate and conceptualize relevant perceptual properties within their field of study, to which they are at the outset relatively insensitive: the music student has to be trained to construe minutiae of pitch, tone and rhythm which seem scarcely distinguishable at first, just as the intending botanist has to practise construing the minutely different textures of leaves and bark. We have noticed above that this similarity of method has misled Kelly himself into construing psychotherapy too exclusively as an educational procedure instead of being content with asserting merely, as Freud himself did, that psychotherapy has educational *aspects* (cp. Marmor, 1962; Freud, 1940, p. 175).

The cognitive techniques of Beck's therapy for depression, and more recently for anxiety-reactions also (Beck and Emery, 1985), are even more conspicuously intellectual and instructional. So much so, that many of them would not seem out of place in a philosophy seminar, consisting as they do in lessons on how to identify and avoid the false inferences and overgeneralizations which lead to logically invalid conclusions about the hopeless state of one's self and one's situation. But it would be simple-minded in the extreme to suppose that what makes a person prone to drawing false inferences in respect of self-valuation is a lack of skill in deductive reasoning, just as we do not suppose that someone who is in the grip of a hand-washing compulsion is merely ill-informed about the cleansing properties of soap and water.

In the case of Beck's techniques (Beck, 1976; Beck *et al.*, 1980; Beck and Emery, 1985), we have to ask which comes first, the impoverished self-esteem or the disposition to certain types of errors of reasoning: for it is just as likely that the latter is a manifestation of the former as that the former is a consequence of the latter. Indeed we know enough about the emotional and interpersonal conditions which predispose people to the depressive and self-denigratory characteristic of 'oral pessimism', whether we attribute them to libidinal frustration at the oral stage (cp. Kline, 1972/1981, pp. 41–44) or to infantile separation-loss experiences as described by Bowlby (1980, ch. 12–14), or to parental child-rearing attitudes later in life (Coopersmith, 1967).

This kind of irrational and unrealistic debasement of self-valuation and of perceived self-efficacy is similarly seen by Seligman (1975) as being the product of a faulty process of learning. In this case the basic error is identified as inappropriate stimulus-generalization, which leads to a sense of helplessness being evoked, as a conditioned response to situations *other* than that in which the person has actually been, or *seemed* to be, helpless (but see later work on this topic by Abramson *et al.* (1978) and by Hargreaves (1985)). When such depressive distortions of self-feeling are construed in this way, the appropriate treatment is naturally seen as cognitive-educational: you teach people how to decide which of their existing 'repertoire of responses' will have some effect upon the situation, or else you train up relevant new responses (failing that, you teach them how to run).

But the whole question of the relation between helplessness, impaired self-esteem and precipitating experiences of loss or failure had been discussed with rather more sophistication, and more than 20 years previously, by Bibring (1953) in his influential revision of Freud's object-loss theory of depression. The same sorts of comment apply to the techniques of what has come to be known as 'cognitive behaviour modification' (Meichenbaum, 1977), in which patients are taught to think about their disturbed action-patterns and thought-habits in a certain way, to impose certain structures and avoid others, and even to issue instructions to themselves. These, however, are all instances of what Stekel, as we have already noted, called 'activating the patient's *logos*', and of what Hartmann (1939) meant by mobilizing 'conflict-free spheres of the ego'. For if *logos* and ego-sphere will not obey their own instructions, there is no point in their giving them.

One obvious way in which psychodynamic interpretations differ from these various other more or less exclusively cognitive transactions is that they are concerned to depict and communicate the (typically indirect and symbolic) connection between something the patient does, or does not do, and the hypothesized affectocognitive processes (anxiety, wishes, conflicts, defences, etc.) of which it is a manifestation; these processes are often, but not necessarily, presumed to be unconscious. Typical subject-matter for such interpretations are, of course, the pattern and content of free association, all manner of selective perceptions and memories, misperceptions, lapses, false assumptions (as in the episode about Mrs E. above), etc. It also covers personal interactions with the therapist, which include much non-verbal behaviour such as deviations from routine, changes in dress or manner, coming late, missing appointments, going early (Mrs E. again) and changes of posture on the chair or couch. But the material which is most characteristic of all for classical psychoanalysis must presumably be that of dream-reports (cp. Thomae and Kaechele, 1987, ch. 5). For this reason, our last three clinical *vignettes* will illustrate the use of symbolic interpretation directed at the latter two types of data: postural change (the case of Miss T.) and dream material (Miss T. again and Mr S.).

5.6.2   *Interpretation of Movement: Looking for a 'Good Self'*

The episode from Miss T.'s analysis (which was conducted by H.T.) takes up in practical terms the question which we raised from a theoretical point of view above, concerning the deprivation of visual feedback in classical psychoanalysis, and the need to prevent this deprivation from threatening the patient's security which 'general factors' are fostering. It also vividly exemplifies two other themes that recur throughout this volume: the use of that defence which consists in reducing the value of the term 'aspirations' in James's equation in order to prevent the value of the left-hand side of the equation from dropping too far; and the verbal formalization of an affectocognitive discrepancy, such as McReynolds discusses in Chapter 8. It will be noticed, however, that the latter is not treated as a specific dissonance to be tackled in its own right and to be resolved by balancing the cognitive books, but rather as a particular expression of a more general and fundamental anxiety whose ramifications need to be explored in depth before the patient can expect to bring it under ego-control.

Miss T., a school teacher, was in her late thirties when she presented with a distressing and incapacitating disturbance of self-feeling, which was connected with the objective physical condition of virile hair growth (hirsutism), and the whole course of her psychoanalysis is the subject of the content-analysis study presented by Neudert *et al.* as Chapter 10. The patient's insecurities referred to almost all spheres of life, and derived in a special way (both objectively and *via* a vicious circle) from the hirsutism, in the sense that the patient is at a disadvantage compared with other women. Miss T. feels that she cannot command any influence psychosexually, and her ability to assert herself in her profession is also limited. At work, she sees herself as a pupil rather than as teacher, and when there are examinations she becomes as it were an examinee herself, since she ascribes any inadequacy in her pupils' performance to herself.

During puberty, Miss T.'s existing sexual anxiety had increased because of the hirsutism, so that she was unable to assert her strong sensuality in heterosexual relations but had vainly sought consolation in scrupulous religious confessions. She lapsed into a despair which for many years did not allow any hope, except perhaps from further retreat and devoted self-sacrifice. There was also a limitation of simple social relations in everyday life or in professional activities.

Early in therapy, the unconscious determinants of her debased self-feeling and yearning self-representation found expression in a dream which, when contrasted with a second dream at this stage, can be taken as representing the ideal self and the real self. It showed her on the one hand as a most beautiful and attractive Raphael madonna (ideal self), but also, on the other, as a disgusting woman all covered with hair (apperceived real self). The second dream reflects deep hopelessness and scepticism toward the analyst who seemed not to be attaching enough importance to the reality of her physical limitation, and to be proceeding on the assumption that it would be possible to alter reality, as it were, by a change of attitude. As we are dealing with the initial phase of the treatment, one of the analyst's tasks should be to create a basis of confidence, and we have to contend at the outset in this case with the patient's sense of resignation and of the impossibility of changing things.

In the first session, the patient's shortness of breath (which, although not unconnected with the weather and with vestiges of infantile bronchitis, nevertheless disappeared completely and imperceptibly in the course of treatment) served to symbolize an intense feeling of general psychological constriction and lack of elbow-room. Ambivalences and dissonances were evident everywhere. They have to do with nearness and distance; and with the longing for reassurance which, however, would obstruct an active and aggressive assertion of herself in her profession. She finds recognition indirectly by offering herself as a 'rubbish-bin' (*Abfalleimer*). Thus her conflicts are essentially resolved by imposing on herself a self-limitation which has become her second nature; that is, by reducing the 'aspirations' term in James's self-esteem equation, as mentioned above. In taking us through the following *vignette*, H.T. assumes the grammatical first person.

The fact that the patient has now sought treatment is, on the whole, a sign that she is looking for a change. I encourage her to protest against her fate: 'I understand you to mean now that because of your looks, i.e. because of your hair growth, you wrote off a lot of things, and then came the day when you didn't want to be committing the depreciation and self-limitation any more.' In a subsequent observation, which is also intended as an encouragement, I formulate the problem which she has with regulating nearness and distance, and with attempting to gain more elbow-room while still maintaining reassuring bonds with her parents (and while still having the chance of going home again and again with the same old hopes), in this way: 'You would like to become freer, to gain more elbow-room; but then there is the obligation of going on holiday together.' This is an example of precisely that sort of conflict-formulation which McReynolds discusses in Chapter 8, and which is also analogous to A. Ryle's (1982) 'dilemmas'.

While the patient indirectly satisfied her strong desire for recognition and acceptance by letting herself be used as a rubbish-bin, she also expresses her concern that it might be too much for me if she started giving freer rein to her longing. I therefore try to make it clear to her that being a rubbish-bin has become too much for *her*, and that this is why she is worrying about *me*. She replied to this: 'Yes, I thought about that before, how it is really, it comes automatically, doesn't it, such a reflection.' The following session was characterized by a wide fluctuation in her self-feeling. After the visit to her parents she described her inability to have any influence on people and situations, or to assert herself. She traces this inability back to her weak position in the family hierarchy, which is between two apparently more successful brothers. It becomes obvious how closely successful actions are connected with self-confidence, but also how strong is her dependence on recognition by 'significant others'.

The subject of security versus insecurity is raised at the beginning of treatment. The special form of the psychoanalytic dialogue, and of the physical arrangements, become the subject of an exchange. The patient experiences the arrangement as indicating that she is not allowed to see any of my reactions, and that I want to hide myself. On the other hand, I describe her turning on the couch as a very natural attempt to overcome the deprivation which undoubtedly exists, and to obtain, by means of eye-contact, both confirmation of the other person's presence and also a basis for judging his reactions. I explain that, on the one hand, these are consequences of the fact that reassurance is missing because of the arrangement (since this can aggravate existing insecurities), but that, on the other hand, it indicates that she is inclined to expect negative reactions.

It is essential to make the patient understand the purpose of the arrangement and of the unusual form of the dialogue, because otherwise her security will be undermined in a therapeutically unfavourable way. Thus it was important here to be able to correct Miss T.'s mistaken idea that the arrangement involving interruption of eye-contact is chosen in order to eliminate mutual influence, and to underline the fact that the apparent deprivation might be overcome at any time by a turn of the head.

5.6.3   Dream-interpretation: Body-image and Images of Damage

Our penultimate clinical illustration is taken from another case in which the
disturbance of self-image is connected with a disturbed sense of body-image,
with the important difference that here the corresponding 'organ inferiority', as
Adler would have called it, is almost entirely imaginary (by contrast with the
objective physical symptom of Miss T.). In the episode which we feature here,
the analyst (again H.T.) uses the classical specific technique of symbolic
interpretation of dream-material to identify some significant anxieties and
defences in the patient, and to imply ways in which a more adaptive way of
organizing the processes involved might be achieved. The extract also includes
a characteristic example of the specific technique of 'interpreting the transference', when the analyst indicates that Mr S. has cast him (H.T.) in the role of
Mr S's superego.

Mr S. is a 40-year-old married engineer who had had many neurotic
symptoms before the torticollis with which he presented. He is a compulsive
personality, prone to severe guilt-feelings, and for years he had been suffering
from hypochondriacal symptoms which centred around his supposedly
deformed head, nose and chin. He had had a body-image disturbance for some
time, in that he always held his head a little to the side in order to be able to
hide his nose and chin which he imagined to be too small. This imagined
smallness signals a castration anxiety, which first appeared in the course of
treatment in the symptomatic form of imagining that his penis was too small.

He was immediately convinced that his torticollis was at least partly
psychogenic, because he had himself observed variations in the symptom in
different situations: whenever people looked at him, he became embarrassed
and his head turned involuntarily to the right. His life-long insecurity centred
around his deformed body-image. This sudden spasmodic turning of the head
to the right, which lasts several minutes and occurs more frequently in public,
had been distressing Mr S. for about a year. It had resisted treatment by general
practitioners, neuropsychiatrists and other less orthodox 'healers', as well as
in-patient medication in a neurological hospital.

During psychoanalytic therapy, the latent aggressive impulses which were the
the force behind his distorted conception of his body-image, became evident in
the transference. Firstly there were dreams about machinery that had been
smashed or damaged in various ways. Then, after a session in which I had
asked him to make a small contribution to the treatment-fee, he brought a
dramatic dream: I, the analyst, who had previously had one leg amputated, had
now lost my other leg and was therefore doubly amputated. On the manifest
level also, a vicious fight took place between some other men, head-hunters so
to speak, who decapitated each other and played ball with their heads. These
two types of dream reflect some progress from static, impersonal images to
damaged machines towards ideas of cruel and violent interpersonal actions.

The extracts from a single analytic session which follow are *verbatim* translations unless enclosed in parentheses.

Mr S.: I have the feeling I see things a little clearer this morning.

(Mr S. tells last night's dream, here summarized. He is spending his holiday at someone else's house, where a pipe bursts spurting out a lot of water. He has it turned off, since he does not know where the fault is. He discovers that the pipe has been sawn off, for a length of 20 cm. It could only function like that because it was all cemented in.)

H.T.: (During this dream-report, I recall similar earlier dreams which all showed damage to the body-image. I see progress in that the patient has better access to his unconscious aggressions now, and I immediately have the phantasy that the damage to the water pipe refers to the urinary tract.)

Damage is terrible when it concerns you, because it is always a matter of all-or-nothing, and any slights and injuries take on incredible dimensions. It is always about your whole body, about all of you: crooked nose, small penis, attacks and so on, damage, injury.

Mr S.: In the past I was far too preoccupied with things emotionally ... (long omission). ... About this seeing clearer now: that is because I am satisfied with things at home and at work. I get on with the main people in my life, I notice my own feelings more clearly.

This morning, for instance, when I drove into the car park down there, I didn't manage to swing the car round in time and I went into the bumper of a car that was parked. I got out to look at it. The dust had been knocked off the bumper in one place; it wasn't a hard knock, but I got out wondering if you had seen me—as if I might go away without seeing to it. It is a little bit of a bad conscience, as if I ought to do more. I ought to point it out, make people aware of it. It is what I said earlier, ... making the small big. Of course, I thought about it briefly out there and I arrived at the conclusion really, I was thinking of it, what would it have been if I had told you that I had driven into it, and asked you 'Can you see anything?—That isn't a big deal (is it)?'

(Although we cannot be dealing with the residue of the dream, because the dream preceded this morning's events, the incident in the car-park is very important for the transference. I begin by approaching this on the superego level.)

H.T.:   But you can tell for yourself, you don't really need that; but it is like being given the blessing, it is OK, don't you think? You haven't done anything terrible.

Mr S.:   Yes, someone else getting in and telling me it is all right: it isn't enough for me to tell myself. I often need this reasurrance which I repeatedly seek from others. Is it OK or not? I can't reassure myself whatever it is about.

5.6.4   *Transference-interpretation: Therapist Seen as Superego*

Our last *vignette* contains a number of examples of the therapist interpreting material which the patient brings (whether from dreams, free association, childhood memories or report of recent behaviour) as having a special reference to the therapist himself; and as thereby reflecting, on the assumption that there is a 'projective' aspect to the 'transference-relationship', important features of the patient's own attitude to himself and to 'significant others' in his emotional life, past and present (that is, to his 'object-relations'; see Chapters 3 and 4).

This technique of 'interpreting the transference' is one of the most characteristic tools of psychodynamic therapy, deriving of course directly from classical psychoanalysis (e.g. Strachey, 1934; Thomae and Kaechele, 1987, ch. 2), but it is also one which may seem to cut across the distinction between 'general factors' and 'specific techniques' with which we began. For the assumption is that the benign general background conditions discussed above will more or less inevitably lead to the therapist being used as a screen for the projection of such anxieties, wishes, conflicts, etc. as are important to the patient from time to time; and yet the therapist has to decide in specific instances which material, *if any*, should be interpreted as having this function.

We say 'if any' because it is of course possible to conduct psychotherapy *without* interpreting the transference, even though such a transference has been established. Indeed it used to be orthodox doctrine that, in relatively brief psychotherapies, which are the subject of Strupp's Chapter 11, such interpretations positively ought *not* to be made, in case they lead to involvements and dependencies too intense to be resolved before the end of treatment. But the pioneering empirical work of David Malan has apparently provided powerful evidence to the contrary.

From the results of two elaborate investigations into the factors which affect the outcome of brief psychodynamic therapy, Malan concluded that those patients who improved most during such therapy were those to whom the therapist had most systematically given 'transference interpretations', linking that patient's attitudes towards the therapist with his or her childhood attitudes towards parent-figures. Thus, in reviewing the first of the two studies, Malan writes (1976b, p. 229): 'The clinical evidence pointed unequivocally to the hypothesis that the transference/parent-link was the most important single factor in the technique of this type of therapy'. He claims further that this conclusion is sustained by the evidence from the even more methodical second study, so that the efficacy of a classic 'specific technique' of psychoanalytic treatment has been demonstrated unequivocally.

'Since the central therapeutic mechanism in psychoanalytic therapy ... is the working through of the transference-relationship in terms of the relation to people in the patient's past, the fact that the transference/parent-link has been shown to have an important relevance to outcome in both series constitutes a *scientific validation in a clinical setting of a fundamental psychoanalytic principle.*' (Malan 1976a, p. 55; see also Malan, 1979, ch. 9).

This claim about the therapeutic centrality of transference and its interpretation has received further support from a recent study by Luborsky *et al.* (1985), who call it, in response to a remark by Gruenbaum, 'Freud's grandest hypothesis'. Their empirical investigation, using Luborsky's (1984) techniques for identifying 'core conflictual relationship themes', was able to provide some validation for nine specific theses, derived from Freud's writings, about the nature, development and susceptibility to modification of transference-interactions.

One way in which such interpretations have regularly been supposed to work is by showing the patient that, if she looks at certain elements of her mental life in a different way (attributes a different 'meaning' to them), then coherent patterns of motivation and reaction will emerge, such that what had seemed confused, pointless and out of control has now fallen into place (Cheshire, 1975, ch. 3). This resolution of dissonance helps to improve the quality of integration in the patient's self-system, and leaves him or her with the feeling that 'it all makes sense to me now'. Or, as Mr S. puts it, in the illustration which follows, 'It is all explicable to me.'

Mr S. went on to talk about the repairs and alterations which he was carrying out on his house. In this context he shows quite a strong will, and puts his ideas into practice without consulting others. The therapist tries to cover a good deal of ground in his next interpretation. It is particularly important to him to interpret the transference in the here-and-now, and to bring in the processes of 'reparation' which can be seen in the patient's tendency towards compulsive perfectionism. He therefore connects the event preceding this session with an earlier episode.

In order to explain this part of the interpretation, it should be added that the greater part of the patient's fee is paid by a health insurance, while he himself pays only the balance. When his own contribution slightly increased, because the insurance payments were reduced, he unconsciously experienced the analyst's demand as a dangerous attack. After this he had a number of dreams about serious fights between two men, during which he clearly saw the analyst as doubly amputated.

H.T.: This is still connected with the damage, with damaging, breaking things, something could break. When you can't do something perfectly it is as if the damage was done to your body—a scratch on your body which you received ... The greater the damage experienced, the greater is your anger about what is happening to you ... like that time you received a scratch from me when I told you you had to pay part of the fee yourself, even though it wasn't much. And then you dreamt about this fight between two men and my leg was off or my head was off. In your dream you could get back at me, so to say, injure me in revenge. And then it all has to be undone, like your idea this morning of calling me to witness that you hadn't done anything to the car ... As if your own senses didn't provide sufficient information.

Mr S.: This perfection is something I thought about this morning. But why these accompanying events, this external damage? When something happens it is immediately related to my body, which is affected in such a strong way, without me noticing it or sensing it at first.

H.T.: Look at the pipe-damage in your dream: the water-pipe is the urination 'water-works'. Jumping to the physical, this is where one is vulnerable. Your sensitivity and vulnerability are still very great. It is all connected with the water-pipe and the house that one is. Someone has maliciously taken a saw to it; in the dream it had been sawn through, hadn't it?

(Because of earlier experiences with the patient, I was sure I could give a direct interpretation. When he reacted by saying that the pipe had been damaged from the start, I had the immediate phantasy that he might be thinking of very early damage.)

Mr S.. It was damaged from the start, when it was put in.
H.T.: Put in already damaged, I see.

Mr S.:	The cause was the fault which occurred when it was installed. It lies much deeper, and some comparison with birth goes along with it. I remember my mother telling me that she had a very difficult birth with me: they had to use forceps, and that was the reason why my head was deformed.
H.T.:	Deformed in the production?
Mr S.:	It is strange, as if I was back in my mother's womb in this case, but everything there is so clean, so pure, so regular. And now there is a big jump stretching a couple of years to kindergarten; we had to sleep there, too.

(The patient goes on to tell of his first injury. He and his brother were playing in a field sloping down from the farmhouse where they lived, when he loosened the brakes on a cart which rolled downhill and ran over his brother who was sitting in a depression hollowed out by the scratching of the hens. His brother was not hurt.)

H.T.:	Or did he just have scratches?
Mr S.:	(The cart continued to roll down the hill towards the road, but came to a halt in a shed where it caused considerable damage.)

All hell was let loose.

H.T.:	Because you had nearly killed your brother. You would have become a brother-murderer, Cain and Abel.
Mr S.:	Yes. (long pause) When I think back it is like that, on the one hand; on the other hand I was something of a little hero. I was three or four years old or so. 'The things he can do . . .' (they said).
H.T.:	All this putting things in motion, loosening the brakes, getting that cart to go. But one is happy to be reassured that things weren't so bad, that all is well. Look at this morning when you would have liked to consult me about the car,—no damage was done, nothing has happened to the car, your brother, the cart. Reassurance and quickly making up for it . . . for the damage one has caused; also for damage one has not caused, because one always thinks one did do it, one is the culprit, so to speak.
Mr S.:	(after a long pause) Funny, I remember another incident also concerned with damage, also with a car. (He goes on to tell of a minor traffic accident.) ... On one of the ships, an engineer once questioned me about diesel engines and I didn't know any of the answers. I told myself I would have to learn it. I felt I wasn't able to sail as an assistant

under those circumstances. I didn't feel I had the ability. I sat down and tried to learn the things one ought to know ... so that I wouldn't give the impression of not knowing things ... It affects me very deeply, just as it did then, being put on the spot like that. I certainly made something small into something big then, just as I did this morning. It was a test of the ability to survive.

H.T.:   But not knowing things almost becomes an evil deed, too. Not just not knowing things, but also doing something bad by not knowing things.

(It seems important to show his ambition and his striving for knowledge as an instance of reaction form- ation, because he repeatedly complains about all his intellectual shortcomings. He is never happy with any achievement. Nothing will overcome his unconscious wishes to damage and control the object except insight into his own unconscious intentions, I think.)

Mr S.:   Hmh, yes.
H.T.:   That makes it not just a deficiency which can be made up, but something evil, almost an evil deed.
Mr S.:   Well, yes, I began to think, 'You are there wanting to do a job you shouldn't be doing, because he has said you lack something. You don't belong there.'
H.T.:   Yes, yes.
Mr S.:   I wasn't being accused of this really, but I made myself into this person who was no good. 'Why do you let this happen to you when you did well during the apprenticeship and in exams? Why behave as if you were nothing?' This is where the defensive bit comes in, this weighing up. I can't afford to be bad ... without knowledge. When someone asks a question in the office about something I don't know much about, I actually manage to create these situa- tions myself.
It is all explicable to me.

References

Abramson, L. Y., Seligman, M. R. P. and Teasdale, J. D. (1978). Learned helplessness in humans: ... *J. Abnorm. Psychol.*, **87**, 49–74.
Arkowitz, H. and Messer, S. B. (1984). *Psychoanalytic Theory and Behaviour Therapy: Is Integration Possible?* Plenum Books, New York.
Bannister, D. and Fransella, F. (1986). *Inquiring Man*, third edition. Croom Helm, London.

Bateson, G. *et al.* (1956). Towards a theory of schizophrenia. Reprinted in *Steps to an Ecology of Mind* (Bateson, 1973), pp. 173–198. Paladin, London.

Beck, A. T. (1976). *Cognitive Therapy of the Emotional Disorders.* International University Press, New York.

Beck, A. T. and Emery, G. (1985). *Cognitive Therapy of Anxiety and Phobic Disorders.* Basic Books, New York.

Beck, A. T. *et al.* (1980). *Cognitive Therapy of Depression.* Wiley, Chichester.

Berenson, B. and Mitchell, K. (1974). *Confrontation for Better or for Worse.* Human Resource Development Press, Amherst (Mass.).

Bibring, E. (1953). The mechanism of depression. In *Affective Disorders* (ed. P. Greenacre), pp. 13–48. International Universities Press, New York.

Bowlby, J. (1980). *Loss: Sadness and Depression,* Hogarth, London.

Breakwell, G. M. (ed.) (1983). *Threatened Identities.* Wiley, Chichester.

Breuer, J. and Freud, S. (1985). Studies on hysteria. *Standard Ed., 2.*

Brown, G. W., Birley, J. L. T. and Wing, J. K. (1972). Influence of family life on schizophrenic disorders: . . . *Brit J. Psychiatry,* **121,** 241–258.

Campbell, T. (1799). The pleasures of hope. In *Complete Poetical Works* (ed. J. L. Robertson, 1907). Oxford University Press.

Cheshire, N. M. (1975). *The Nature of Psychodynamic Interpretation.* Wiley, London and New York.

Coopersmith, S. (1967). *The Antecedents of Self-esteem.* Freeman, San Francisco.

Curtis, H. C. (1985). Clinical perspectives on self-theory. *Psychoanal. Quart.,* **54,** 339–378.

Edelson, M. (1975). *Language and Interpretation in Psychoanalysis.* Yale University Press, New York.

Edelson, M. (1984). *Hypothesis and Evidence in Psychoanalysis.* Chicago University Press, Chicago.

Epting, F. R. (1984). *Personal Construct Counseling and Psychotherapy.* Wiley, Chichester.

Erdelyi, M. (1985). *Psychoanalysis: Freud's Cognitive Psychology.* Freeman, Oxford.

Eysenck, H. J. (1980). A unified theory of psychotherapy: . . . *Z. Psychol.* **188,** 43–56.

Fensterheim, H. and Glazer, H. I. (eds) (1983). *Behavioural Psychotherapy:* . . . Bruner/ Mazel, New York.

Frank, J. D. (1974). Therapeutic components of psychotherapy. *J. Nerv. Ment. Dis.* **159,** 325–343.

Fransella, F. (1972). *Personal Change and Reconstruction.* Academic Press, London and New York.

Freud, S. (1919). Lines of advance in psychoanalytic therapy. *Standard Ed.,* **17,** 157–168.

Freud, S. (1940). An outline of psychoanalysis. *Standard ed.,* **23,** 141–207.

Gelder, M. G. *et al.* (1973). Specific and non-specific factors in behaviour therapy. *Brit. J. Psychiatry,* **123,** 445–462.

Goldfried, M. R. (1982). *Converging Themes in Psychotherapy.* Springer, New York.

Gregory, R. L. (1972). *Eye and Brain,* second edition. Weidenfeld and Nicolson, London.

Gurman, A. S. (1977). The patient's perception of the therapeutic relationship. In *Effective Psychotherapy* (eds A. S. Gurman and A. M. Razin), pp. 503–543. Pergamon, Oxford.

Hargreaves, I. R. (1985). Attributional style and depression. *Brit. J. Clin. Psychol.,* **24,** 65–66.

Hartley, D. E. and Strupp, H. H. (1983). The therapeutic alliance: ... In *Empirical Studies of Psychoanalytic Theories* (ed. J. Masling), pp. 2–12. Analytic Press, Hillsdale (NJ).

Hartman, H. (1939). Ich-Psychologie und Anpassungsproblem. Translated as *Ego Psychology and the Problem of Adaptation*. International Universities Press, New York (1958).

Kline, P. (1972/1981). *Fact and Fantasy in Freudian Theory*, first and second editions. Methuen, London.

Laing, R. D. (1965). *The Divided Self*, second edition. Penguin, Harmondsworth.

Laing, R. D. (1969). *The Self and Others*, second edition. Penguin, Harmondsworth.

Leff, J. *et al.* (1982). A controlled trial of social intervention ... *Brit. J. Psychiatry*, **141**, 121–134.

Lifton, R. J. (1964). *Thought Reform and the Psychology of Totalism*. Penguin, Harmondsworth.

Litowitz, B. E. (1978). On overdetermination. In *Psychoanalysis and Language* (ed J. H. Smith), ch. 10. Yale University Press, New York.

Luborsky, L. (1984). *Principles of Psychoanalytic Therapy:* ... Basic Books, New York.

Luborsky, L. *et al.* (1985). A verification of Freud's grandest clinical hypothesis: ... *Clin. Psychol. Rev.*, **5**, 231–246.

Malan, D. H. (1976a). *The Frontier of Brief Psychotherapy*. Plenum Press, New York.

Malan, D. H. (1976b). *Toward the Validation of Dynamic Psychotherapy*. Plenum, New York and London.

Malan, D. H. (1979). *Individual Psychotherapy and the Science of Psychodynamics*. Butterworths, London.

Marmor, J. (1962). Psychoanalytic therapy as an educational process. In *Science and Psychoanalysis* (ed. J. H. Masserman), vol. v, pp. 286–299. Grune and Stratton, New York.

Marmor, J. (1966). Theories of learning and the psychotherapeutic process. *Brit. J. Psychiatry* **112**, 363–366.

Marmor, J. and Woods, S. M. (1980). *The Interface between the Psychodynamic and Behavioural Therapies*. Plenum Press, New York and London.

Meichenbaum, D. H. (1977). *Cognitive Behaviour Modification*. Plenum Press, New York.

Mitchell, K. M. *et al.* (1977) A reappraisal: ... In *Effective Psychotherapy* (eds A. S. Gurman and A. M. Razin), ch. 18. Pergamon, Oxford.

Murray, E. J. and Jacobson, L. I. (1971). The nature of learning in ... psychotherapy. In *Handbook of Psychotherapy and Behaviour Change* (eds A. E. Bergin and S. L. Garfield), pp. 709–747. Wiley, New York.

Perls, F., Hefferline, R. F. and Goodman, P. (1951). *Gestalt Psychotherapy*. Souvenir Press, London.

Peterfreund, E. (1983). *The Process of Psychoanalytic Therapy:* ... Analytic Press, Hillsdale (NJ).

Peterfreund, E. and Schwartz, J. T. (1971). *Information, Systems and Psychoanalysis* (Psychol. Issues 7, monogr. 25/26). International Universities Press, New York.

Reisman, J. (1971). *Toward the Integration of Psychotherapy*. Wiley, London.

Rotter, J. B. (1966). Generalised expectancies for ... control of reinforcement. *Psychol. Monogr.* **80** (whole no. 609).

Ryle, A. (1982). *Psychotherapy: A Cognitive Interpretation:* ... Academic Press, London.

Seligman, M. E. P. (1975). *Helplessness:* ... Freeman, San Francisco.

Stekel, W. (1938). *The Technique of Analytical Psychotherapy* (translated by E. and C. Paul, 1950). Bodley Head, London.

Strachey, J. (1934). The nature of the therapeutic action of psychoanalysis. *Int. J. Psychoanal.*, **15**, 127–159. Reprinted (1969) in **50**, 275–292.

Strupp, H. H. (1974). On the basic ingredients of psychotherapy. *Psychother. Psychosom.*, **24**, 249–260.

Strupp, H. H. (1977). A reformulation of the dynamics of the therapist's contribution. In *Effective Psychotherapy* (eds S. A. Gurman and A. M. Razin), pp. 3–22. Pergamon, Oxford.

Strupp, H. H. and Binder, J. L. (1984). *Psychotherapy in a New Key*. Basic Books, New York.

Thomae, H. (1980). Auf dem Weg. zum Selbst. *Psyche*, **34**, 221–245.

Thomae, H. (1981). *Schriften zur Praxis der Psychoanalyse: Vom spiegelnden zum aktiven Analytiker*. Suhrkamp, Frankfurt.

Thomae H. and Kaechele, H. (1987). *Psychoanalytic Practice: (i) Principles*. Springer-Verlag, Berlin and Heidelberg.

Thorpe, G. and Burns, L. E. (1983). *The Agoraphobic Syndrome:* . . . Wiley, New York.

Wachtel, P. L. (1977). *Psychoanalysis and Behaviour Therapy*. Basic Books, New York.

Wachtel, P. L. (1982). *Resistance:* . . . Plenum, New York and London.

Wegman, C. (1985). *Psychoanalysis and Cognitive Psychology*, Academic Press, London.

Yates, A. J. (1983). Behaviour therapy and psychodynamic therapy: . . . *Brit. J. Clin. Psychol.*, **22**, 107–125.

Self, Symptoms and Psychotherapy
Edited by N. Cheshire and H. Thomae
© 1987 John Wiley & Sons Ltd

CHAPTER 6

Outline of a Process Model of Psychoanalytic Therapy

Ilka von Zeppelin*

6.1   The Therapeutic Relationship Considered in Terms of a Cognitive Model

This chapter attempts to explain the therapeutic relationship and the therapeutic process by means of a cognitive regulation model, which treats the analyst–patient relationship as the interaction of two 'process-systems' (cp. Moser *et al.*, 1981). This interaction follows explicit or implicit relation-rules; and each of these process-systems, which can be broken down into regulation-*contexts* (with their own specific functions) linked in a multiprocessing system, has its own cognitive regulation-system (Figure 1). Reference will be made to this model, which is based on Clippinger's (1977) model of the psychoanalytic dialogue, and on Schneider and Sandblad's (1979) modelling approach, only where this is necessary to the understanding of the therapeutic relationship.

One principal assumption of this model is that, in both analyst and patient, models of the therapeutic situation are being developed continuously, with reference to (1) the regulation system of the analyst, (2) that of the patient, and (3) the interaction as a process. A special context (CXT relation) is set up for the generation and regulation of relationships. Here both persons concerned form their

---

*In collaboration with Neil Cheshire, who helped to prepare this revision of an earlier version.

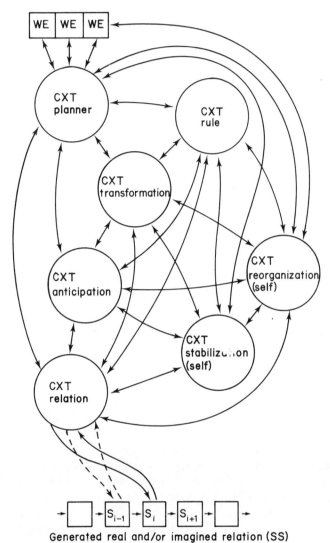

Generated real and/or imagined relation (SS)

Figure 1   Diagram of a process model of the way situation-
sequences (SS), real or imagined, are generated

own (cognitive) model of the relationship into which may be entered those *wishes* that have passed through an internal simulation and transformation process. Wishes have a complex structure: in general, they comprise two processors, namely a representation of the subject and one of the object, and a series of linking interaction-process units (cp. Sandler and Sandler, 1978).

Relation-rules are prepared, and an emotional involvement is formulated, for every step of the relation generated. The relation-rules comprise (1) those that are attributed to the communicative 'hardware' of the interaction regulation. These are of interest only when significantly disturbed, and manifested as pathological phenomena. The self-relevant relation-rules (2) are important for maintaining the stability of the whole regulation system, since their observance guarantees autonomy and identity. These rules are taken from the self-contexts into the effective regulation. There are also relation-rules (3) which follow social rules and are relatively insignificant for the self-context. When they are applied, the probability of triggering off conflicts (both intrapsychic and interactive) is low. 'Normal' patients (Gitelson, 1959) are capable of developing relation-rules that are not self-relevant but still highly differentiated. They may tempt the analyst to go along with them, since they provide emotional relief, but, in this case, there is no transference of self-relevant relation-rules.

The therapeutic relationship is generated through a series of situations, each of which is generated by setting up cognitive elements. In a real situation, a configuration comprising the patient (subject processor) and the analyst (object processor) is being set up, along with relation-rules and possibly also a motivational configuration (wish). We call these processes IN SIT REAL and IN SIT IMAG (the latter in the event of an imaginary relationship). In so far as it is cognitive, there must be feedback from the *ad hoc* experience; so the cognitive model of the relationship (the *ad hoc* model) is modified continuously.

The model postulates that the generation of the subject's behaviour-sequences (real and/or imagined) evolves over various domains or *contexts* of regulation (CXTs), which employ realization-conditions, in the form of rules and/or self-concepts, to examine the compatibility of a *wish-element* (WE) with the system—a form of cognitive 'reality-testing'. The regulation-contexts operate concurrently (multiprocessing) to modify the wish, which is represented as an interaction model. This regulatory activity is termed 'inner simulation', and produces in turn the '*ad hoc* model' which is utilized by the relation-context for the realization of a *situation-sequence* (SS). The immediate regulation of a real and/or imagined relation entails a continuous modification of this *ad hoc* model. From the point of view of a *rapprochement* between psychoanalysis and general psychology, it is worth noting that there are some clear parallels between aspects of this system and other cognitive process-models of the sort pioneered by Miller *et al.*'s (1960) 'TOTE' theory of perceptual-motor regulation.

Establishing the *ad hoc* model is the keystone for the regulation of the relationship. Both subjects participating in the interaction map out the modifications in their models continuously, so that the latter may become increasingly complex. An optimally functioning regulation is based on the content of the *ad hoc* models of both partners becoming partially alike. In particular, the relation-rules of both partners in the interaction are mapped out, and can thus be integrated, as is indicated by empirical findings such as Spence (1969) has reported in the field of language-behaviour. The emotional involvement can also be modified continuously according to the nature of IN SIT processes. Especially in cases of narcissistic disturbance, this setting-up of the *ad hoc* model is either impaired or arrested at a lower developmental level. Relation-rules must therefore be practised rigidly, since any modification would immediately jeopardize the stability of the self-system. This, of course, is a strain on interaction-competence, and can easily engender interactive conflicts (according to the extent of the emotional involvement). The model further assumes that one and the same relation can be regulated according to different principles.

Transference will occur only if the assimilatory part of the relation in the *ad hoc* model (the wish-model) can be made fully observable in the therapeutic relationship. The patient must depict the analyst in his *ad hoc* model as corresponding to a previous object in a previous relation-pattern (defined by the wish). The analytic rules are relation-rules of a particular type which facilitate, or even encourage, the generation of an imaginary relation with the analyst without the necessary consequence of the effective actualization of wishes in relation to the analyst.

A final preliminary remark: the cognitive model of Moser *et al.* (1981) includes different self-representations depending on which regulation-*context* of the regulation-system it belongs to. A self-configuration, for example, may be an integral part of the wish-model structure. There are generalized self-concepts in the self-contexts. Both forms of self-configuration pass either directly, or through transformations (which are not handled in this chapter), as real or imaginary subject-processors into the *ad hoc* model of the CXT relation where they are 'set into the situation'. Modifications to these processors are again reported back and processed for the overall regulation. The *self-context* includes *two contexts*: one with *stabilizing functions* and the other with *modifying functions*, the latter containing programs to modify the functions of other regulation contexts. There are self-reflexive functions within the monitoring functions of both self-contexts. These include emotional and cognitive search-strategies. The emotional system is a quick-reporting system for the localization of disruptions in regulation-contexts, and for the realignment of regulations. The relation-context also includes emotional functions in decentralized form within the set-up of the *ad hoc* model. Not all emotions are accessible self-reflexively, which is why the experience of emotions is so important as a therapeutic objective. It regenerates the emotional information system, and subsequently permits a contextual analysis of what has been experienced emotionally.

6.2 Interaction and Regulation-distribution

Two regulation-systems are linked in the interaction between the two process-systems, analyst and patient. Entering a therapeutic relationship arises from the wish to take advantage of the analyst's regulation-competence in order to avoid continuing to experience the ineffectiveness of attempts at restitution made when the usual regulation-processes have failed. During this process, it becomes evident that the patient is exercising a certain pattern of control over the relation-regulation in the manner of a relation-rule. The developmental levels of such regulation-links can be deduced from Mahler's developmental levels (Mahler *et al.*, 1975; Pine, 1979). In the self-context, for example, a condition of relation can develop which imposes on the object-processor the demand to participate in the regulation of the relation, or even in the total regulation of the subject-processor. There are variations of this condition of relation in the typical 'narcissistic self-object transferences' described by Kohut (1971, 1977).   form of narcissistic disturbance tries to arrange the distribution so that the regulation of the object-processor is effected exclusively by the subject-processor. All asymmetric regulation distributions lead to control struggles in the therapeutic relationship. The analyst must always ask himself what condition of distribution the patient wants to realize in his cognitive model of the therapeutic relationship. This distribution is of central importance for the stabilization of the 'self-system'. The realization of a wish may be attempted according to quite different relation rules and regulation distributions.

6.3   The Functions of the Therapeutic Relationship

The therapeutic relationship is presented below by four parallel functions of the analyst–patient relation. These functions interact. They may be weighted differently during different phases of therapy. Whatever the analyst achieves (by his 'activity' and his 'passivity') may be interpreted differently according to one of these functions.

1. *Extension of the self-reflexive and the cognitive functions of the patient in general* (affectocognitive search-processes with respect to the regulation activity, particularly the disturbances which cannot be relieved). We call this function 'elaboration of a common analytic field'.
2. Setting up and initiation of an ad hoc *model of the relationship between analyst and patient.* Acquisition of a better interaction competence with the help of the analyst. The therapeutic relationship is understood here, on the one hand, as the sponsor of the 'analytic field' and, on the other, as an 'interface' to the former and to extraanalytic reality-relationships.
3. Restructuring of the therapeutic interaction by *introducing a new regulation distribution* between analyst and patient: (i.e. development of autonomy, abandoning links in the old mother–child regulation, Blanck and Blanck (1979) 'ego-building techniques').
4. *Realignment of the regulation system by differentiating the self-reflexive functions and the modification functions* (patient's self-modification skills).

6.3.1   The Self-reflexive Functions

The analytic rules refer to the creation of favourable conditions for *affectocognitive search-processes*. These conditions are described as a 'relaxed, emotionally positive atmosphere'. Kris (1956) characterizes the features of a situation of this kind derived from the 'good analytic hour' (cp. Morgenthaler, 1978). Here a reciprocally well-adjusted emotional involvement and a well-developed, modifiable *ad hoc* model of the relation is generated. The specific analytic rules which permit the affectocognitive search-processes are incorporated into this model (but only with this objective). The affectocognitive search strategy has been relatively well investigated in psychoanalytic literature. The cognitive theories applied have naturally led to various models of this process (e.g. French, 1958; Moser, 1962; Spence, 1968; Argelander, 1979); and, although a survey of them would be beyond the scope of this chapter, much recent experimental and clinical work in this area is discussed by McReynolds in Chapter 8.

In general, the objective of these search-processes is to obtain additional information on the patient's conflicts and regulation-problems. If we ascribe the quality 'unconscious' to fantasies, conflicts, defence-processes, ideals, etc., we mean that the patient is in a state of incomplete information (Spence, 1968). The *search-processes proceed from the affects, whether experienced or not experienced, which become noticeable in interruptions* of the verbally expressed thoughts or behaviour-sequences. Affects are represented in this model as units of information which indicate either a state of disturbance in the regulation, or (as in the case of positive affects) a positive modification entailed by the settling of the disturbance or by an improvement in the regulation-process.

The analyst proceeds from these affective reactions and assists the patient further to regain the ability to experience the parts of his affective information-system which he had been incapable of experiencing. By observing affects, the analyst recognizes the state of the regulation; and, from their type, he can localize the regulation-context containing the process which is releasing the affect (cf. Sandler and Sandler, 1978). The cognitive parts of the search-process are concerned with stocking up cognitive information. Verbalization is necessary because it is the only means of linking the affectocognitive functions of analyst and patient, and of adjusting them to each other. The affectocognitive search-process terminates in reconstructions (insight). Orientation of search strategies and insight processes to the therapeutic relationship corresponds to the analysis of transference and countertransference.

The processes are *cyclic* in two respects (French, 1958; Thomae, 1981). *In the first place*, new conflicts are continually reactivated and focussed thematically in the analytic process. After processing, there is high redundancy in a conflict area, which may be retained over a considerable period (due to the soothingly high degree of certainty) and thus prevent the transference of a new conflict. If a new conflict is focussed, this again releases uncertainty and requires new processes of search and insight. *In the second place*, one and the same conflict is continually refocussed. Insight is gradual in the form of 'approach models' which the analyst is aware cannot be perfectly exact.

In our opinion, the course of the cognitive work in psychoanalysis is always *iterative*. Tentative interpretations are continually improved upon by new ones. Everything is different again from what had been thought. The patient's adoption of the iterative principle as a 'working style' raises considerable problems. Patients with a self-regulation deficit, who partially delegate regulation-competence to the analyst, are profoundly troubled if the analyst cannot provide clarity at once. The analysts themselves are not always aware of this iterative principle, otherwise what Moser (1962) calls the 'cult of correct interpretation at the correct time', with its associated self-conviction, would not be encountered so frequently. This leads to a non-autonomous acceptance of insight by the patient, a consequence of which is identification with the analyst's idealized regulation-processes; the patient then becomes an unmodified copy of his analyst.

The affectocognitive search and insight-processes set up patterns of 'activity' and 'passivity' for both analyst and patient. The analyst must remain silent to allow the search-processes the necessary time. The analyst must also remain silent if he does not have sufficient information for an interpretation. He must also remain silent so as not to forestall an interpretation by the patient himself. The degree of silence (as also a judgement as to its creativeness or defensiveness in the case of analyst or patient can be inferred only from an appreciation of the processes that are taking place. Silence in the analytic situation is not discussed further here, but it is touched upon by Cheshire and Thomae in Chapter 4 (section 4.2) and is considered more extensively by Thomae and Kaechele (1987, ch. 8) elsewhere; see also Calogeras (1967), Cremerius (1971, 1981), Thomae (1981) and Pasini (1981).

6.3.2 *Construction of a Variable* Ad Hoc *Model in the Therapeutic Relationship*

The real relationship between analyst and patient is introduced by the 'working alliance' (cp. Chapter 5, section 5.3), but the processes within this relationship have hardly been researched, because the analysis of transference/countertransference has largely been overemphasized. This relationship, like every other social relationship, must be regulated. Furthermore, it is an 'interface' with the reality of social relationships outside the analytic situation and with the analytic techniques practised within it. A whole series of skills are exercised here: skills which, on the one hand, belong to the analytic procedure in the narrow sense (cp. section 6.3.1 above), but which, on the other hand, lead to an improvement in interaction-competence.

The patient, like the analyst, gradually builds up an *ad hoc* model of the relationship; and this implies not only that his self-cognition in the therapeutic situation improves, but also that he constructs a model of the analyst. This model is used to regulate the relationship, but it is also the vehicle for adopting some of the characteristics and behaviour of the analyst. The takeover process would have to be described by a detailed model of the learning process involved: it does not help to characterize it as a (total or partial) identification with the analyst accompanied by a varying degree of internalization. Psychoanalytic theory lacks a developed learning-theory of this kind, although rudimentary attempts have been made by Bion (1962) and Schafer (1968), for example, and more sophisticated contributions have come from French (1958) and Peterfreund (1983). The patient's 'analyst' model must further be incorporated into the analyst's cognitive model of the patient, and this may diverge considerably from the analyst's own view of himself or from the picture which he thinks the patient has of him. Since the patient needs information in order to develop this model of the analyst, all occurrences in connection with the analyst are potentially important.

The effect of the abstinence-rule, which traditionally forbids any extrasessional social interaction between analyst and patient (cp. Thomae and Kaechele, 1987, ch. 7 (7.1)) should be that the 'analyst' model focusses only upon the analyst's attributes concerning his relation rules, his self-reflexive functions and their prerequisites. If the analyst has difficulty in establishing good relation-rules with the patient (possibly as a consequence of an intolerable transference), he may be tempted to apply the analytic rules *as direct relation-rules*. He is then always at an advantage because of his analytic-competence, which prevents the patient from learning how to deal with the analyst. This covers, for example, the use of tactical games which disturb the analyst, for there is no harm in the analyst falling into 'traps' if the situation is discussed and the patient can learn what can be done in such a situation.

What is meant by the *emotional involvement* of a relation has hardly been explicitly researched. From analytic experience, we know that a high degree of emotional involvement of one or both partners in a relationship requires an extremely complex *ad hoc* model. In psychological disturbances there is a disproportion between the ability to regulate relations and the desired emotional involvement, which tends to provoke interactive conflict. The therapeutic relationship of the analyst to the patient has a relatively low emotional involvement; but what does 'relatively low' imply in this context? A therapeutic relationship certainly does not have what Rosenberg (1979) calls the 'centrality' attributed to personal relationships with private partners or with members of the family. The term was introduced into social psychology as a weighting for self-attributes, but it can also be used appropriately in the comparison of degrees of emotional involvement which a person has in the various relationships within his own world of object-relations. In the present context, however, this relative lack of emotional centrality does help the analyst to construct a more complex *ad hoc* model of the patient under particularly favourable conditions.

The analyst's emotional involvement should not be restricted and fixed defensively at a certain level, since the flexibility of entering into the patient's potentialities would thus be lost. It is imperative that the patient be neither overwhelmed nor starved emotionally; patients are set a particular problem if they must lower the desired emotional involvement defensively by manipulating the IN SIT REAL processes (von Zeppelin, 1973).

6.3.3 Setting up a Differentiated Regulation-distribution

An optimally functioning *ad hoc* model of a regulation comprises models of the subject- and object-processor which are also clearly *differentiated* with respect to their share in the regulation, since it is only in this way that relation-rules can develop which enter into the characteristics and desires of both. Such rules are created through reflective abstraction (Piaget, 1977; Schneider, 1981). In the case of narcissistic disturbances, as set out by Bach (1977) in a different context with other concepts, this process is either disturbed or not fully developed in the domain of social relationships; so that the models of the partners, for example, in so far as they concern the regulation, may remain undifferentiated.

In this case, the analyst becomes a self-object, and the (partial) model which the patient sets up of the analyst does not correspond to the regulation of the analyst as he perceives it himself. Another form of disturbance is the total assimilation of the analyst into the patient's own self-regulation, when earlier developmental levels of regulation of the self-object relation are reproduced. The building up of the *ad hoc* model is impaired or difficult to modify: it is reduced to the imperative self-relevant parts. The relation-rules elaborated by the patient in the therapeutic relationship are orientated towards influencing the analyst in both forms; that is, attempting to move him to assume (completely or largely) the work of the regulation. By contrast, in neurotic disturbances which are not narcissistic, the degree of abstraction of the *ad hoc* model is usually fairly high.

We should like to point out in this connection that the problem of *transference*, which is discussed so much at present in the controversy between self-psychology and classical psychoanalysis, may be more clearly defined and reviewed against the background of our model. The classical concept of transference does not differentiate between (1) the transfer of a specific wish-structure, (2) the transfer of a special form of relation-rule, and (3) the regulation-distribution in a relationship. We differentiate these types of transference, and thus the associated types of countertransference, as follows.

(1) *Transference of a wish* implies the desire for actualization (realization) of a subject–object interaction pattern in the therapeutic relationship. A wish is a complex cognitive element with a particular affective pattern: it can be compared to a plan which determines with what self- and object-configurations, as also with what linking interaction-processes, the wish is to be actualized. For our model we used a certain type of 'frame' concept (cp. Minsky, 1975; Pfeifer and Schneider, 1977). We may note that Sandler and Sandler (1978) have described the wish in psychoanalytic terms in a very similar way; and also that Bion (1970) has proposed ideas about how to formalize various intrapsychic object-relations (using concepts from set-theory). In our terms, however, the wish can be actualized as

imaginary relation (fantasy) or as real-relation. For the implementation of a wish in a relationship there is also the impulse, in every case, to make the object (i.e. the therapist) substantialize the role assigned to him in this fantasy. The manipulation techniques, however, are not part of the wish-structure, but the content of relation-rules which the person concerned is trying to introduce to regulate a relation.

(2) A wish-element of this kind may already be linked with a particular *relation-rule* which is self-relevant. This means that the wish can be actualized only with a specific regulation-distribution. The result is an *ad hoc* model which cannot be adjusted to the specific conditions of the object. Wishes of this type can be transformed only restrictedly in inner simulation, and such a relation is very likely to become conflicted. We call these wishes *introjects*. Beyond the domain of actualizing this wish, the relation can be regulated with responsive *ad hoc* models, and the interaction does not appear disturbed.

(3) *The transference of relation-rules with a high degree of self-relevance* may occur independently of the structure of certain wishes. The development of autonomy and independence in the regulation of a person's own wishes, and in the regulation of the relationship, extends over several stages. Narcissistic disturbances demonstrate deficiencies (and compensatory strategies) of the regulation. As a consequence, they show a series of *regulation-incompetences* experienced internally if not always consciously: incompetence in the joint regulation of a relation, in the internal regulation of wishes on the way to realization, and in the ability for self-modification. This entails the absolute necessity of delegating functions in the regulation to the therapist. In a phase of increased autonomy-requirement, however, the therapist is often not even allowed to exercise the complementary self-reflexive functions. The regulation-distribution, and the control of the relation-rules, must be asserted, since they are a condition for maintaining *self-stabilization* (autonomy and identity) in a relationship. The primary importance of deficiencies in the elaboration of *ad hoc* models in the relation-regulation may have led self-psychology to accord secondary importance to conflicts set off by realization of wishes, and to place dealing with 'self-object transference' in the centre of the analytic work.

The transference of relation-rules to the analyst makes his 'role-responsivity' a condition of self-stabilization (security, well-being, etc.) within this relation. *He must assume the functions assigned to him in the regulation.* The therapist therefore feels that demands are placed on him as on a real object of the patient's early childhood. Inadequate understanding of these demands jeopardizes the working alliance.

This has nothing to do with a frustration of the wish. The crisis in the relation may break out outside the realm of an attempted wish-transference. In the mere transference of a wish, however, the self-regulation is sufficiently stable to allow the *fantasy* actualization of a desire (with the therapist as imaginary object-processor) within a concurrent *real* relationship to the therapist. The patient is then capable of experiencing his wish as a transference phenomenon, and therefore of accepting a transference interpretation.

A patient with a severe narcissistic disturbance has a constant wish to be given a bottle of milk by his (female) analyst during the session over a period of 2–3 months. He rejects any interpretations that this is the transference of a wish: it is the bottle of milk itself that he wants. In the end, the analyst gives in and fetches a bunch of fresh basil. She gives it to him, stressing how nice basil smells and telling him he could use it to cook for guests at home. The patient is completely satisfied, and does not object that he did not get a bottle of milk.

Table 1. Three forms of transference, showing differential involvement of processes and subsystems

Wish transference	WISH-ELEMENT	Subject- and object-processor; interaction process units
Introject-type transference	WISH-ELEMENT with RELATION-RULE as PROCEDURE	Subject- and object-processor; interaction process units; relation-rule as part of the wish-element
Transference of relation-rules and of the regulation-distribution (self-object transference) (3)	SELF-RELEVANT RELATION-RULES	Relation-rules for the regulation of the relation; subject–object-processor (regulation-distribution pattern)

According to the classical theory of transference, the occurrence could be explained by stating that the analyst had been manipulated to such an extent that she had helped in transforming the wish-transference from the state of the imagination to that of the reality-relationship. There is another interpretation, however. Because of a self-deficiency, the patient does not understand a transference-interpretation: he is under a compulsion to get the analyst to help him to realize his wish (auxiliary function of the regulation), since he suffers from the inability to regulate a relationship with a woman in such a way that it is not endangered by the realization of his wishes. So the analyst helps him to deal with his wish by showing him how another object can be accepted in place of the bottle of milk, and how he can satisfy the wishes of others by accepting this object (role-taking). What takes place is a *form of learning* with respect to regulation: this is what he is really striving for, and not the wish-fulfilment *per se*.

Table 1 presents a summary of the dynamic structures of these three types of transference-process. What the analyst does or does not do has a completely different significance according to these forms of transference. The analyst's silence, in the event of sufficiently developed skills of relation-regulation, can be understood as an affectocognitive search-strategy conditional on the analyst's behaviour. If the analyst becomes a 'self-object' in Kohut's (1971, 1977) terms —that is, if, for example, he must also assume the regulation of the patient (from the patient's viewpoint)—then the silence is experienced as 'being let down'—as a repetition of an unreliability experienced in childhood.

With other forms of narcissistic disturbance, in a phase of necessary distance from the analyst (i.e. repetition of separation-impulses from Mahler *et al*'s (1975) 'practising' and 'rapprochement' phase), the analyst's silence is actually desired by the patient as something which enables him to try out an interpretation of his own (and thus an 'own regulation-activity') in his own fantasies.

A further example illustrates that, for persons with a self-deficiency, dealing with the problem-complex of the relation-regulation at first has priority over the interpretation and working-through of wish-elements.

> Mr X, a drop-out and a drug-abuser, who has been attending psycho-therapy for some time, appears at four o'clock one morning, wet through, dirty and probably doped. The therapist accepts the visit and goes into the consulting room with him. In tears, Mr X recounts how he spent the night in a shelter with a group of young people, and how one of them committed suicide during a bad trip. In retrospect, he cannot understand why he did not prevent this suicide.

Mr X. is one of those patients who must continually reduce their emotional involvement by every kind of interruption, since they do not have the competence to regulate a relation with the desired emotional involvement. (As described above, this results in the experience of insufficient autonomy.) The consequence is that he escapes out of this untenable situation into fantasy, retaining only the simplest relation-rules. By keeping silent, the therapist allows him to distribute the control himself, according to his resources. The silence by no means leads to tension for the patient, because it allows him to transform into a fantasy the wish that he has introduced into the therapeutic relationship; that is, to construct a fantasied relationship which he can accept, and which he can subsequently report to the therapist. In this fantasy (we shall not go into detail), he is in a sputnik orbiting the earth. Here he is at the same time realizing his wish for warmth and security with the therapist (sputnik), his autonomy (with its negative counterpart of his loneliness) and the experience of the wish for passivity.

These patients need fulfilment of their passive wishes without having to experience dependence on an object regulating them. If they cannot withdraw from such regulation (e.g. in institutionalized environments such as prisons or hospitals), this must lead to suicide. It also explains why one must not interpret on the wish level too early. Modell (1978) describes similar patients who, in the introductory phase of their analysis, remain for over a year incapable of stabilizing an emotional relationship with the analyst and thus render mutative interpretations impossible. Subjectively, the analyst feels as if there are not two people present: the patient speaks but does not communicate; he acts as if either the analyst or himself were not present; he is afraid to share and communicate his feelings.

6.3.4 Modification Processes in Cognitive Regulation-systems

Every therapeutic process entails modifications of the regulation-processes of patient and analyst, first in relation-regulation and later in other domains of regulation (especially in the self-contexts), until there is a modification of the wish itself. How do the modifications of a cognitive model proceed in detail? For example, how is a superego rule modified, or how is a self-modification function improved? Psychoanalysis does not provide any information on this. Artificial intelligence research plays a major part in this field with the concept of self-modifying systems (cp. Sussmann, 1975; Clippinger, 1977; Moser *et al.*, 1980, 1981). If the psychic structure is understood accordingly as an interlinked network of regulation-contexts, in the form of (cognitive) programmes, then change would be defined as the improvement of a programme by the shutdown of an old programme or by the implementation of a new programme. How, then, are the self-modification functions improved, or even developed, by the therapeutic process? We shall leave this question open in the present chapter and merely outline, in the terms of our particular framework, some of the directions which the therapy-process can take; but see also Cheshire and Thomae's related discussion, in Chapter 5, of various aspects of psychotherapeutic change.

6.3.4.1 In the therapeutic relationship, the *ad hoc* model of this relationship is continually modified and extended. This leads to positive experiences of interaction-competence which are reported back to the regulation-system and especially to the self-system. Identity and self-feelings are thus strengthened. The particular conditions of the therapeutic situation (which the analyst generally guarantees) permit, within the regulation-relation, an improvement of the self-reflexive functions. These can at first proceed beyond the state of competence of the (general) self-reflexive functions of the self-contexts; and, in time, the immediate reinforcements in the therapeutic relationship enable successive modifications of the self-reflexive functions in general.

6.3.4.2 The improvement of the *ad hoc* model which has been achieved in the patient–analyst relationship can be transferred directly to another relationship, *without the self-context, and the self-modifying functions in the self-domain, having been* modified. Although this indirect transfer does show a certain improvement in interaction-competence, the patient is not yet capable of modelling an object-processor other than the analyst into his *ad hoc* model. In many cases, this transfer is associated with role-taking: the patient takes over the analyst's relation-rules which he has recognized, and this may appear as imitation of the analyst's behaviour.

6.3.4.3   In the model of psychological thinking, a transfer to another relation should occur by means of the modification of the patient's overall regulation-system. We suppose that the differentiations of the *ad hoc* model lead to an improvement in the modification-functions which the self-system has with respect to emotional feedback in other regulation-contexts (CXT reorganization). These can, in principle, have a modifying influence at any point; but how do they modify themselves? A model of self-organizing systems, such as that proposed by Varela *et al.* (1974) and Maturana (1975), is required to understand these processes.

6.3.4.4   One final comment: the analyst knows that he undergoes a process of modification himself during every analysis, and that it is very easy for him to withdraw from this modifying effect by applying rigidly many of the 'rules' of analysis. This has the effect of creating an always applicable, but not modifiable, package of relation-rules which from the start forces on the patient a certain *ad hoc* model of the relation-regulation. The consequence is that, in place of the *learning*-process, there is either conformity to the analyst or revolt.

6.4   Summary and Prospective Discussion

We have drawn attention to the fact that, although the model presented is derived from empirical experience in psychoanalytic therapy, it is seeking a new language to formulate this experience. Psychic processes are regarded from an information-processing point of view and formulated in concepts derived from artificial intelligence and cognitive science. This has made it possible to describe the invariants common to all psychotherapeutic approaches in the terms used. The *exchange* between psychotherapist and patient has had to be considered according to this model. This is important, because languages must be found that are comprehensible to therapists of more than one school (as Neudert *et al.* also insist in Chapter 10 (section 10.1)). It remains open whether a differential indication for the various methods of such schools could be worked out.

Further questions may be raised with respect to the empirical examination of the model, to the basic model by Moser *et al.* (1981), to the distinction between relation-rules and transference, and to the deduction of directives for therapeutic action.

With respect to the empirical examination of models of affectocognitive processes, it can be asserted, firstly, that the construction of such models can be purposeful only if extensive empirical experience (even if not always as 'exact' data) is already available in a certain field. There is no doubt that this is the case in psychoanalysis. Secondly, two courses are seen: the conceptual representation of individual therapeutic processes (as in this model) and also the utilization of verbal and non-verbal data from video and sound recordings. Content-analysis methods play a central role (e.g. for the examination of common factors in the speech of therapist and patient, as an indicator of the assimilation between their respective *ad hoc* models). Other means of access to the cognitive-affective processes are either not yet available or difficult to realize in the therapeutic situation (e.g. physiological variables).

The model is certainly not a neuropsychological model, in that no links are established to neurobiological hypotheses; it therefore differs in this respect from the process-model which Freud (1895) himself sketched in the famous *Project. . .* But it incorporates a regulation-theory which proceeds from Clippinger's (1977) and Schneider and Sandblad's (1979) approaches. The principle of multiple-processing is new in these regulation-theories. A series of regulation-contexts are linked together, so that the interactive processes can proceed concurrently. The classical concepts of mental organization (ego-organization, self, superego, etc.) are replaced by 'domains of regulation'. The model must be further developed (1) towards more precision according to clinical experience, and (2) towards a formal representation with the objective of computer simulation.

The model was employed to formalize the distinction between three types of 'transference': transference of a wish, transference of the introject-type, and transference of relation-rules. This raises, for the psychoanalysts, the question of the position of these processes in relation to the 'transference' and the 'working alliance'. In effect, the two concepts are in a certain sense replaced by the new one. In the case of the relation-rules, it is assumed that rules must be learned with respect to the regulation of relationships. At early levels in childhood, it is difficult to separate a wish from a relation-rule, since every wish is closely linked with a certain *form* or relation-rule. Children also learn relation-rules, however, independently of wishes, and not every interaction between adults is at the same time a wish-realization. Theories of role-taking capacity, which have been developed from Piaget (e.g. Piaget, 1976; Flavell, 1968; Feffer, 1970; Feffer and Gourevich, 1960), postulate levels in the cognition of social relationships which are necessary to the development of certain models of relationship. Narcissistic disturbances may be considered as deficits in rule-learning with respect to such relation-rules.

References

Argelander, H. (1979). *Die kognitive Organisation psychischen Geschehens*. Klett, Stuttgart.
Bach, S. (1977). On the narcissistic state of unconsciousness. *Int. J. Psychoanal.*, **58**, 209–233.
Bion, W. R. (1962). *Learning from Experience*. Tavistock, London.

Bion, W. R. (1970). *Attention and Interpretation*. Tavistock, London.

Blanck, G. and Blanck, R. (1979). *Ego psychology II*. Columbia University Press, New York.

Calogeras, R. C. (1967). Silence as a technical parameter. . . . *Int. J. Psychoanal.* **48**, 536–558.

Clippinger, J. H. (1977). *Meaning and Discourse. A Computer Model of Psychoanalytic Speech and Cognition*. Johns Hopkins, Baltimore.

Cremerius, J. (1971). Tacere: problema della technica analitica. *Psicoter. Sci. Umane*, **3**, 5–14; **4**, 12–17.

Cremerius, J. (1981). *Ueber die Schwierigkeit, Natur und Funktion von Phantasie und Abwehrmechanismen psychoanalytisch zu Erforschen und zu Definieren*. Fourth Conference of the European Psycho-Analytical Federation.

Feffer, M. H. (1970). Developmental analysis of interpersonal behaviour. *Psychol. Rev.*, **77**, 197–214.

Feffer, M. H. and Gourevich, V. (1960). Cognitive aspects of role-taking in children. *J. Personal.*, **28**, 383–396.

Flavell, J. H. (1968). *The Development of Role-taking and Communication Skills in Children*. Wiley, New York.

French, T. M. (1958). *The Integration of Behaviour: Vol. III, The Reintegrative Process in a Psychoanalytic Treatment*. University of Chicago Press, Chicago.

Freud, S. (1895). Project for a scientific psychology. *Standard Ed.*, **1**, (1966), 295–397.

Gitelson, M. (1959). Therapeutic problems in the analysis of the normal candidate. *Int. J. Psychoanal.*, **35**, 174–183.

Kohut, H. (1971). *The Analysis of the Self*. Hogarth Press, London.

Kohut, H. (1977). *The Restoration of the Self*. International Universities Press, New York.

Kris, E. (1956). On some vicissitudes of insight in psychoanalysis. *Int. J. Psychoanal.*, **37**, 445–455.

Mahler, M. S., Pine, F. and Bergman, A. (1975). *The Psychological Birth of the Human Infant: . . .* Basic Books, New York.

Maturana, H. R. (1975). The organisation of the living. *Int. J. Man–Machine Stud.*, **7**, 313–332.

Miller, G. A., Galanter, E. and Pribram, E. H. (1960). *Plans and the Structure of Behavior*. Henry Holt, New York.

Minsky, M. (1975). A framework for representing knowledge. In *The Psychology of Computer Vision* (ed. P. H. Winston), pp. 211–280. McGraw-Hill, New York.

Modell, A. H. (1978). The conceptualization of the therapeutic action of psycho-analysis. *Bull. Menninger Clin.*, **42**, 493–504.

Morgenthaler, F. (1978). *Technik. Zur Dialektik der psychoanalytischen Praxis*. Syndikat, Frankfurt.

Moser, U. (1962). Der Prozess der Einsicht im psychoanalytischen Heilverfahren. *Schweiz. Z. Psychol.*, **21**, 196–221.

Moser, U., Pfeifer, R., Schneider, W. and von Zeppelin, I. (1980). Computer simulation of dream processes. *Ber. Interdiszip. Konfliktforschung.*, **6**, (Zürich University).

Moser, U., von Zeppelin, I. and Schneider, W. (1981). *Wunsch, Selbst, Objektbeziehung: . . . Ber. Interdiszip. Konfliktforschung.*, **9**, (Zürich University).

Pasini, W. (1981). *Le silence en psychoanalyse*. Unpublished manuscript.

Peterfreund, E. (1983). *The Process of Psychoanalytic Therapy: . . .* Analytic Press, Hillsdale (NJ).

Pfeifer, R. and Schneider, W. (in collaboration with U. Moser and I. von Zeppelin) (1977). PSYPAC: a formal system . . . In *Computational Linguistics in Medicine* (eds W. Schneider and A. L. Sagrall-Hein), pp. 155–162. North-Holland, Amsterdam.

Piaget, J. (1977). *Recherches sur l'Abstraction Réfléchissante. Etudes d'Epistemologie Genétique*, nos. 34 and 35. Presses Universitaires de France, Paris.

Pine, F. (1979). On the pathology of the separation-individuation process . . . *Int. J. Psychoanal.*, **60**, 225–242.

Rosenberg, M. (1979). *Conceiving the Self*. Basic Books, New York.

Sandler, J. and Sandler, A. M. (1978). On the development of object relationships and affects. *Int. J. Psychoanal.*, **59**, 285–296.

Schafer, R. (1968). *Aspects of Internalisation*. International Universities Press, New York.

Schneider, H. (1981). *Die Theorie Piagets: ein Paradigma für die Psycho-analyse*. Huber, Bern.

Schneider, W. and Sandblad, B. (1979). A new approach to a computer based system for modelling and simulation. In *Evaluation in Medical Action* (eds A. Alperovitch *et al.*), pp. 479–495. North-Holland, Amsterdam.

Spence, D. P. (1968). The process of meaning in psychotherapy: some links with psycholinguistics and information theory. *Behav. Sci.*, **13**, 349–361.

Spence, D. P. (1969). Computer measurement of process and content in psychoanalysis. *Trans. N. Y. Acad. Sci.*, **31**, 828–841.

Sussman, G. J. (1975). *A Computer Model of Skill Acquisition*. American Elsevier, New York.

Thomae, H. (1981). *Die Aktivität des Psychoanalytikers als Determinante des therapeutischen Prozesses. Jahrb. Psychoanal.*, **6**, 1–80.

Thomae, H. and Kaechele, H. (1987). *Psychoanalytic Practice: Principles*. . . . Translation of *Lehrbuch der psychoanalytischen Therapie*, vol. I. Springer-Verlag, Berlin.

Varela, F. G., Maturana, H. R. and Uribe, R. (1974). Autopoiesis: the organisation of living systems, its characterization and a model. *Bio-Systems*, **5**, 187–196.

von Zeppelin, I. (1973). Social drop-outs and hippies: fantasy, object-relationship and aggressiveness. *Brit. J. Med. Psychol.*, **46**, 181–190.

Self, Symptoms and Psychotherapy
Edited by N. Cheshire and H. Thomae
© 1987 John Wiley & Sons Ltd.

INTRODUCTION TO PART II

Empirical Studies in the Analysis and Treatment of Self-problems

Neil Cheshire

Having discussed in *Part I* some of the main theoretical considerations that have contributed to the perpetuation or to the revival, as the case may be, of the concept of 'the Self' in various branches of psychology, we take up here in *Part II* the task of demonstrating that such ideas—abstract and elusive as they may appear at first sight (and even still at third or fourth sight)—do not need to remain in the realm of nebulous theory but can in fact be subjected to specific, systematic, empirical and even quasi-experimental investigation. In so doing, we would claim to be building some practical bridges (which may complement the conceptual bridges built in *Part I*) between cognitive, developmental and social psychology on the one hand, and psychoanalysis on the other.

What McReynolds does in Chapter 8, for example, is to show in practical detail how the theoretical thesis which was the subject of Epstein's Chapter 2 (namely that people have a very fundamental motivating need to maintain balance and coherence within their self-system) can be applied to everyday clinical problems of psychodiagnosis and therapy. His concern is with disorders that are associated not so much with the ontogenetic failure to develop a securely differentiated sense of Self in childhood (which is the focus of Cheshire *et al.* in Chapter 7), but rather with that 'backlog' of conflicting elements which accumulates within the reasonably well-established self-systems of temporarily disturbed adults. He formulates the issues broadly in terms of problem-solving and systems-description; and, in so doing, he puts into practice some features of von Zeppelin's demonstration, in Chapter 6, that the technical concepts of cybernetics and 'artificial intelligence' can be used to clarify our thinking about the processes involved in reorganizing the self-system during psychoanalytic therapy.

The exploration of such conscious reflections and conceptualizations of the Self, this time from a developmental point of view, is also the concern of Cheshire *et al.* in the first chapter of *Part II*. To this end they describe an experimental investigation into the ways in which children perceive themselves as different-iated individuals and autonomous agents in relationships with 'significant others'; and they discuss their findings, which derive largely from standardized psychometric test-procedures, in the light both of psychodynamic hypotheses about early self-differentiation and object-relationships, and also of 'personal construct' theory.

By focussing attention on self-differentiation in children, Cheshire *et al.* are following the advice given by Freud in introducing his famous case-history of Little Hans, where he indicated that the direct study of children would be an especially rich source of material relevant to psychoanalysis (1909, p. 6). The implication was that it would not only suggest new ideas and insights, but could also be expected to furnish supportive corroboration or critical refutation of those existing hypotheses about early psychic development which had hitherto been inferred retrospectively, as it were, from symptomatic behaviour, dreaming, memories, and associations observed during the course of adult psychotherapy. For, Freud himself, of course, probably did not analyse any children personally (although he did report and interpret isolated incidents of infantile play), and it was left to his famous daughter Anna Freud, and to his disciple Melanie Klein, to adapt the essential principles of psychoanalysis to the investigation and treatment of emotional disturbance, and to the understanding of normal emotional development, in young children. The theoretical differences which arose out of the methods and formulations of these two workers do not concern us at this point, except insofar as they impinge upon the central themes of this volume, which are (as spelled out in the introduction to *Part I*) the synthetic integration of different theoretical and technical approaches to dealing with self-problems in psychotherapy.

As far as their theoretical contribution to mainstream psychoanalytic thinking goes, we have already outlined (in Chapters 3 and 4) its relevance to the systematic description of the development and pathology of the self-system as conceived in Kleino-Freudian terms. And with reference to our attempted *rapprochement* between clinical-psychodynamic and experimental-academic methods of study in the psychology of the Self, it is encouraging to be able to reflect that there has been in the last decade or so a considerable 'reversal of fortune' or turning of the tables in this matter, in contrast to previous times when experimental psychologists tended to dismiss psychoanalytic theories as hopelessly vague, fatally untestable or demonstrably false. For example, not only has the open-minded psychoanalyst been given more than a little aid and comfort by recent large-scale reviews of quasi-experimental attempts to validate Freudian theory within the reigning positivistic orthodoxy (Fisher and Greenberg, 1978; Kline, 1981, 1984; Masling, 1983) but, as Cheshire and Thomae showed towards the end of Chapter 4, even a couple of Klein's most extravagant-seeming hypotheses about the mental life of infants have received remarkable corroboration from objective investigations carried out quite independently of Kleinian doctrine, and indeed sometimes apparently in blinding ignorance of its relevance.

Although we may well wish to keep some philosophical reservations about the sense in which the four-month-old baby can, in Bower's phrase, 'think he has a multiplicity of mothers' (since he or she has plainly not yet developed some of the logical operations necessary to entertain that proposition explicitly), nevertheless Bower (1977) could claim, as we saw in Chapter 4, to have produced a striking 'ostensive definition' of its pragmatic meaning. So it is against this background, or indirect and unlooked-for experimental support for some provocative tenets of Kleinian doctrine, and guided by hypotheses drawn also from Pavlovian learning theory and from cognitive personality theory, that Cheshire *et al.* explore, in Chapter 7, the psychopathology and self-perception of children with psychosomatic abdominal pain.

This particular symptom offered a challenge because, on the one hand, it presents as an example of that 'organ-speech' which Freud attributed to hypochondriacs (1914, ch. 2; 1915, ch. 7) and readily invites psychodynamic interpretation to do with anxiety about self-differentiation from the mother, insofar as it keeps the affected child dependent, protected and close to mother (and not least because it is focussed on the symbolically relevant unbilical region), while, on the other hand, it has also been explained in experimentalist terms to do with the response of a basically neurotic constitution to 'conditioned anxiety', which we have already met above (cp. Lachman, 1972). Furthermore, it provided the occasion to investigate with objective psychometric tools, as opposed to the usual clinical methods, the part played in the aetiology of this disorder both by the group-dynamics of what has been called 'the psychosomatic family' (Minuchin *et al.*, 1978) and also by the 'psychosomatic phenomenon' (Stephanos, 1979).

Cheshire *et al.* were able to show (subject to reservations about 'lie' scores on the Junior Eysenck Personality Questionnaire (JEPI)) that standardized measures of 'neuroticism', conditionability, and general social 'maturity' did not distinguish their experimental group of psychosomatic children from a comparable group whose abdominal pain was demonstrably organic, whereas psychometric procedures which tap the child's perception of himself in relation to significant others (but which are to some extent limited by 'ipsative' scoring) did indeed expose some striking differences between the two samples. These observed differences are gratifyingly apt for certain psychoanalytic theories about the early differentiation of the Self as conceived in an 'object-relations' context (e.g. Mahler, 1972; Mahler *et al.*, 1975), and they carry some fairly direct implications for the kind of psychotherapy that may be expected to benefit these particular self-problems.

The children with relatively weak ego-differentiation could perhaps be helped by being given practice in construing for 'agency' and 'individuation', by rehearsing interaction-episodes that had occurred at home or at school, and by being shown how they might think about them and negotiate them *via* the construct-system of a more differentiated and self-determining agent. This would involve filling certain gaps in (or at least further elaborating) their existing repertoire of constructs, much as Fransella (1972) did with her stammerers; and also, of course, dealing with the anxieties (the Eriksonian 'shame and doubt') attached to attempting such 'autonomy'.

But Cheshire *et al.*'s findings can also be construed as consistent with those more behaviouristic accounts of self-discovery, such as we noted in Chapter 1, which emphasize the part played by the observation of one's own behaviour in the construction of one's sense of Self (e.g. Cooley, 1922; Gergen, 1977). Indeed, some of the studies to which the writers refer, namely those of Bannister and Agnew (1977) and of Jackson and Bannister (1985), exemplify in their own method, even if implicitly and unintentionally, the very *rapprochement* between the behavioural and cognitive-psychodynamic approaches that we have been advocating.

For, although Bannister was a distinguished exponent of Kelly's humanistic (and seven 'mentalistic') Personal Construct Theory, the technique in these experiments consisted of drawing children's attention to strictly 'behavioural' phenomena: what the children had to do was to recognize after a time-lapse statements which they had previously made about themselves, and show that they could discriminate them from corresponding statements which other children had made. Bannister and Agnew were able to demonstrate, by this criterion of behavioural differentiation at least, that nine-year-olds were significantly more reliable in identifying their own self-attributes than were five-year-olds, and that even the older group still had some way to go because they were as yet only just over 50% accurate in their judgements. The older children, however, had begun to make much greater use of psychological insight (e.g. 'That's not like me'), rather than specific behavioural memory (e.g. 'I've never done that'), as a reason for making their discriminative judgements. This work has been followed up, and its implications reviewed, in a further discussion by Jackson and Bannister (1985).

Moreover, before emphasizing unduly the role of behaviour-perception in the growth of self-differentiation, we should take note of the familiar philosophical thesis that the ability to make such behavioural perceptions about Self and not-Self may itself depend upon relevant cognitive structures or logical concepts to do with the 'Self' already having been established. Thus, as Geach argues analogously in another context (1957, ch. 8), the abstractionist view that the young child acquires the idea of 'one' from perceiving (say) its own behaviour of going down the stairs 'one-by-one' is to put the cart before the horse; because the child logically cannot *perceive* its own action *as* 'going down one-by-one' *unless* it already has the *concept* of 'one' in terms of which to structure or 'construe' its experiences.

Although we do not pursue this point any further here, it is essential to bear it in mind when assessing the interaction between cognitive, psychodynamic and behavioural factors in the development of self-differentiation. We may also conclude, on the basis of the above-mentioned encounters between psychoanalysis and experimental psychology in the field of the infant's earliest relations with his world, that those developmentalists who use psychodynamic concepts in trying to understand the early growth of the self-system and its clinical aberrations, as

Cheshire *et al.* do, no longer need to feel that their experimentalist colleagues must be wearing a patronizing smile or brandishing an instant refutation. This is not to deny, of course, that silly things are still said in the name of psychodynamics as well as in the name of experimentalism, when people in either tradition neglect the observations and arguments of the other; but collaboration will produce richer understanding, more efficient therapy and more pervasive prevention than either can manage on its own.

McReynolds' contribution to this *Part* (Chapter 8) also makes quite explicit connections with central features of psychoanalytic self-theory, as they have been expounded by Cheshire and Thomae in Chapters 3 and 4: this is because the explorations by experimental psychologists of 'cognitive dissonance' and its resolution, which took impetus especially from Leon Festinger's classic study of that topic (1957, 1964), deal in effect with the same mental phenomena as are covered by the psychoanalyst's concepts of anxiety, conflict and the 'defence-mechanisms' of the ego. Thus McReynolds gives a number of vivid examples of how the sort of conflicts (or 'mental discrepancies') which people display in psychotherapy can readily be conceptualized in Festinger's terms; and he shows further how some of the common strategies for dissonance-resolution, which Festinger described superficially, correspond to basic psychodynamic defences such as rationalization and denial, Although Festinger himself did not develop this connection, and indeed seems scarcely to have noticed it, Kelly had virtually *defined* anxiety in general in terms of cognitive dissonance, by identifying it with an anticipation-thwarting mismatch between a person's available constructs and the contents of his perceptual experience (Kelly, 1963, ch. 3)

It is tempting to comment at this point that these older, and rather influential, theories of balance and dissonance (which Epstein has discussed in Chapter 2) would have been considerably enriched if they *had* drawn upon the existing wisdom of Freudian defence-mechanism theory rather than setting their face against it. Kelly, for example, in an obvious reference to the 'pleasure-principle' and its implications, specifically says that he wants to construct a theory of motivation which is *not* 'dyed with the deep tones of hedonism' (1963, p. 50). But this deliberate abstinence arguably deprived him of a viable account of emotion, and inevitably committed him to an over-intellectualized account of psychotherapy according to which the client, like a university research student under academic supervision, is embarked upon a programme of quasi-scientific exploration.

In place of such self-defeating separatism, McReynolds provides a much-needed synthesis and *rapprochement*. He specifically argues, for instance, that the psychic discrepancies and incongruities with which his 'assimilation theory' is concerned are not merely cognitive, as they seem to be in Kelly's scheme. Since they obviously have important emotional components, he prefers to call them 'affectocognitive', and, in so doing, he brings us closer to Freudian notions about the relation between intrapsychic conflict, anxiety and defence, according to which a libidinal wish which the ego cannot 'assimilate' (in McReynolds' terms) tends to precipitate anxiety and defensive repression.

Another point of contrast with that over-intellectualized view of psychotherapy, which seems to have been gaining ground under the influence of cognitive learning theories (so that we now have even 'cognitive behaviour modification'), is McReynolds' distinction between two sorts of anxiety which may underlie particular conflicts. What he calls 'primary' anxiety is indeed essentially cognitive, and as such can be expected to respond to reorganizing the patient's 'category-system' in order to facilitate the assimilation of otherwise unassimilable data. This therapeutic technique clearly has a lot in common with Kelly's various methods of revising and/or reshuffling a client's 'personal construct system'. By contrast, what McReynolds distinguishes as 'secondary' anxiety corresponds to what the Pavlovians know as 'conditioned anxiety'; and this will not be relieved by exclusively cognitive manipulations, but will need to be treated by some desensitization procedure (whether psychodynamic or behavioural) in order to produce 'extinction' of the conditioned response.

Throughout his chapter, McReynolds explicitly draws attention to these areas of common ground, works them over in some detail, and appends a fruitful discussion with some of the psychoanalytic contributors to this volume. Further contact with both social psychology on the one hand, and psychoanalysis on the other, is suggested by his characteristic procedure of assisting patients to identify an area of conflict, to formulate it in terms of specific antithetical observations, and to confront the task of deciding which way to 'jump' by way of resolution. For it reminds us at the same time both of Kurt Lewin's well-known analysis of conflicts in terms of the field of forces operating in one's subjective 'life-space' or *Umwelt*, and also of Ezriel's prescription for the ideal psychoanalytic interpretation which should be able to specify the constituent elements of a given conflict by identifying the repressed wish, the feared punishment (anxiety) and the adopted defence (Lewin, 1935, ch. 1; Ezriel, 1956/57).

For when McReynolds' patients come to formulate their conflicts in a paradigmatic 'but-statement', such as 'I want A, but I also want B which is incompatible', that is a straightforward Lewinian 'approach–approach conflict' in which the person is drawn towards both of two areas of positive 'valence' which are, however, topologically separate in his life-space, so that a behavioural 'vector' tending towards one necessarily tends away from the other. Similarly, a patient's formulation that 'I want A, but that entails B which I don't want' represents Lewin's 'approach–avoidance' model, in which one and the same area of life-space has both a positive and a negative valence, for different reasons (e.g. I like parties but I don't like *this* host's wife/husband, so *this* party is both positively and negatively 'charged'); in that conflict, a vector which tends pleasurably towards a locus of positive valence necessarily tends unpleasurably towards one of negative valence also. Fritz Heider's elaboration of Lewin's concepts into the area of conflict-resolution, and into a general theory of cognitive balance, has already been noted in the *Introduction to Part I*, with particular reference to Epstein's Chapter 2, but it is directly relevant also to McReynolds' concern with the relation between conscious strategies of dissonance-resolution and psychodynamic defence-mechanisms.

McReynolds' technique of 'encoding' into a formalized scheme his patients' references to their conflicts, as a prelude to therapeutic intervention, not only has affinities with A. Ryle's (1982) 'dilemmas', 'traps' and 'snags', but also runs closely parallel to an influential discussion by Leon Levy (1963) of the central psychodynamic concept of clinical interpretation. For Levy has argued that an essential first stage in constructing the interpretation of an action, etc. is implicitly to codify, construe or translate raw observation-statements into appropriate theoretical concepts at what he calls the 'semantic stage', before any empirical hypotheses about likely significance or causation are invoked.

On this view, McReynolds' example (in the context of 'locus of control') of someone preferring to stay under external control, rather than to exert 'internal' autonomous agency of his own, would need to be translated *semantically* into the language of 'dependency' behaviour before we can start looking to *empirical* hypotheses about what causes dependency (but cp. Cheshire, 1975, pp. 47–50). The whole question, incidentally, of moving developmentally from dependency to self-differentiation and autonomous agency is the focus of Cheshire *et al.*'s chapter in this *Part*. Both these attempts, of McReynolds and of Levy, to devise a formal scheme of objective classification for their data represent a tactic, reminiscent of Russell's 'logical calculus of propositions', which is often thought a necessary step in rigorous scientific theory-construction, and which has been taken to quasi-algebraic extremes in psychodynamics by Bion (1962).

If McReynolds concludes by insisting, in the face of the traditional psychoanalytic emphasis on *unconscious* conflict, that a great many conflicts which emerge in psychotherapy are actually quite *conscious*, and can therefore be dealt with appropriately at that level by mobilizing reasoning, decision-making and reality-perception, he stands not necessarily outside the psychodynamic tradition (and in the realm of 'cognitive therapy') but among that affiliated school of more 'active' therapists whom Freud addressed in his forward-looking paper on 'New ways for ... therapy' (1919), and whom Stekel (1938, p. 315) exemplified when he said, of the general way he dealt with a patient, 'I activate his *logos*'. McReynolds also anticipates, in so doing, the central feature of Luborsky's (1984) recent formalization of psychoanalytically based psychotherapy, which teaches that the practitioners of such 'supportive-expressive' therapy should concentrate upon what he calls 'core conflictual-relationship themes'. And this topic in turn leads us into the subject matter of the last three chapters of *Part II*.

Zitzelsberger and Kordy (Chapter 9) describe a study which is committed to bringing some manageable order and precision to the diversely expressed, and variably articulate, impressions which patients communicate when asked to reflect on the effects which psychotherapy has had upon them. The order and precision which their description seeks has to be such as will capture faithfully the variety of the phenomena reported by patients, while at the same time taking a form which enables it to be matched against the more technical formulations of the therapists themselves, both about the theoretical aims which they have in mind while carrying out their therapy and also about the methods they choose in particular cases and circumstances for achieving those ends. In the case of this study, our by-now-familiar questions about the basis of a healthy self-concept, about the nature, causes and ramifications of disturbances therein, and about techniques for rehabilitating it are addressed in the context of a group-investigation, involving some 200 subjects, and a variety of therapists and therapeutic settings.

The patients' self-descriptions, from which Zitzelsberger and Kordy draw much of their data, are structured to include quite specifically some of those fundamental sources of the self-concept to which theorists have repeatedly drawn attention (such as 'body-schema' and 'sense of efficacy'), as Cheshire and Thomae indicate in Chapter 1. Thus, at different stages of the psychotherapy follow-up, patients were required to reflect upon their experience of 'self-as-body', upon the strength of their feeling of 'self-as-agent' and also upon their sense of 'security and satisfaction', all of which have regularly been regarded as cornerstones of stable identity-definition and individuation. When it came to the therapists' contribution of identifying 'problem-areas' which needed to be worked on with individual patients, it emerged that an inadequate sense of personal 'efficacy' in specified life-situations was one of the most frequently mentioned problems.

It is noteworthy also that the analytically orientated therapists in this study met the challenge (which we associate with more behaviouristic therapies) to specify recognizable therapeutic goals and target behaviours, by setting down in advance what eventual post-therapy self-ratings would count as evidence of change, ranging from 'deterioration' through 'no change' up to 'optimal improvement'. The authors comment on the desirability of using standardized psychometric techniques, where relevant ones exist, rather than *ad hoc* rating scales, to reflect such changes during therapy (cp. the discussion of this issue by Gottman and Markman, 1978, pp. 41–47); and, in the next chapter (Chapter 10), Neudert *et al.* show how this can be done at least in the context of an intensive single-case study which does not pose the problem of capturing group trends by means of relatively 'ipsative' measures.

The latter part of *Part II*, then, focusses attention on problems that are encountered in describing the sorts of change in self-function and symptomatology which psychotherapists attempt to bring about (as discussed in *Part I*), and which their patients or clients claim to experience at least some of the time. In so doing, Chapters 9 and 10 draw together, by the diverse methods of practical clinical research, many of the threads that have been spun by the writers of the previous chapters; and, although they tackle the problem of self-change during therapy from different angles, their investigations will be seen to converge at a number of salient points. One of these differences is that Zitzelsberger and Kordy adopt to some extent a subjective or phenomenological approach, by concentrating on how different groups of patients *experience* changes in self-function, whereas Neudert *et al.* in their long-term single-case study are looking for more 'objective' variables (such as changes over time in verbal behaviour during therapy, specifiable symptom-reductions, or changes in psychometric scores) which can be monitored continuously, as it were from outside, during the course of treatment.

Thus, Neudert *et al.* take, as their principal data-base, time-samples from the *verbatim* transcript of a lengthy mainstream Freudian psychoanalysis of a woman whose self-concept problems derived, at least in part, from a specific and objective property of her body-image; namely a severe and conspicuous hirsutism. Their main objectives were first to distinguish important 'problem areas' of her self-concept (such as female identity or attitudes to achievement), in which specific conflicts can be identified in the manner of McReynolds' 'discrepancies' (Chapter 8) or A. Ryle's (1979, 1982) 'dilemmas' and 'snags'; then, to run out a number of hypotheses about what would count as evidence of beneficial changes; and finally to look and see whether the number and quality of references to those topics which she made in sample sessions, extracted at different stages throughout the treatment, would show a consistent pattern of change toward that improvement which was demonstrable socially, clinically and psychometrically 'at the end of the day', or whether perhaps they would fluctuate as a function of area-relevant interventions by the analyst.

The failure of any such clear-cut overall patterns to emerge from this pioneering time-sampling technique, which is eminently repeatable now that *verbatim* therapy-protocols are more widely available (even to the extent of having a 'text-bank' for them: Mergenthaler, 1985), must raise the question whether the patient's verbal behaviour during therapy is a sufficiently subtle reflection (even if analysed in terms of Teller and Dahl's (1981) so-called 'frames') of beneficial change in the psychic economy (cp. Kaechele *et al.*, 1973). For it may be that greater success would be achieved by using more 'projective' methods, such as derivatives of percept-genetics or of personal construct technology (cp. Kragh and Smith, 1970; A. Ryle, 1985; Ben-Tovim and Greenup, 1983; Cooper and Kline, 1986) which can tap into the dynamics underlying the organisation of interpersonal apperceptions and object-relations, as discussed above (Chapters 3 and 4) by Cheshire and Thomae.

The other main differences between Chapters 9 and 10 are those of scale and research-strategy, in that the former is concerned with common trends which are discernible in the experiences of a large number of patients, while the latter concentrates upon a microstructural examination of the course of a single patient's treatment. In this way, the pair of chapters exemplify two of the antitheses which permeate the study of self-psychology, as we saw in *Part I*: the one between subjective-phenomenological and objective-behavioural types of description, the other between two old methodological friends, the 'nomothetic' and the 'idiographic' outlooks.

But, in the case of our immediate interest in making theoretically rigorous sense of talk about changes in symptomatic self-functioning, these two chapters present typical raw material. The clinical observations of Chapter 9, which are derived from reports of what large numbers of people actually say about the changes they have experienced, bring us face-to-face with the practical need, pointed out in Chapter 1, to find ways of 'rehabilitating' self-theory in such a way that it can sensibly say such things as need to be said (cp. Harré, 1983; Shotter, 1984). For, whether we like it or not, people just do in fact *experience* certain changes during psychotherapy *as* changes in their essential identity as a person, as opposed to construing them as particular changes in the way they tend to act or in the feelings they tend to have. Post-therapy statements of the form 'Now I understand myself better', or even 'Now I have found my true self', such as Carl Rogers has been reporting for some time and which Zitzelsberger and Kordy also encountered, reflect an experiential datum of which any realistic psychological theory must be able to take account, however much that account may need to move away from the grammatically implied 'object-and-perception' paradigm of introspection against which Wittgenstein (1953) and G. Ryle (1949), among others, have warned us.

Consequently, the contributors to *Part II* are themselves naturally concerned to analyse concretely the 'cash-value' of such abstractions, and their methods of recording, classification and specification do indeed encourage both patients and therapists to be as precise and down-to-earth as possible. In so doing, they take up the experimentalist challenge about specifying targets for psychoanalysis and psychodynamic therapies, and of measuring the extent to which such goals have been attained at the end of treatment. For it had been a standard objection against traditional dynamic psychotherapies that their failure to make such provisions made it possible for the therapist in retrospect to rationalize any change that had taken place in a patient, including even the worsening of symptoms, as having been theoretically desirable: the patient who becomes disinhibited and more antisocial is said to have progressed towards being able to 'acknowledge her depression'. In fact, this sort of complaint had already been met by Malan (1976), for example, some years ago.

When these provisions are in fact made, in ways which Chapters 9 and 10 illustrate, then some of the gaps are narrowed between the so-called 'behavioural' and 'psychodynamic' methods of describing and treating self-problems, and another step is taken towards that *rapprochement* with which this book is concerned. Along these lines, Strupp presents and discusses the findings of one of the research studies at Vanderbilt University in Tennessee which appeared to show that training in specific therapeutic techniques did not add anything significant to the effectiveness of staff who gave therapeutic counselling to university students. This uncomfortable and much-publicized finding must, of course, be set in the context of Strupp's other extensive researches which paint a different picture (Strupp, 1974; Strupp and Hadley, 1979; Strupp *et al.* 1982; Strupp and Binder, 1984); and it must also be compared with the sort of evidence which Malan adduces in support of the efficacy of a quite specific psychoanalytic technique, namely transference-interpretation, in short-term dynamic psychotherapy (Malan, 1963, 1976a, 1976b).

If Malan's explorations had been prompted by Michael Balint's pioneering work on the adaptation of psychoanalytic techniques to short-term 'focal psychotherapy' (Balint *et al.*, 1972), it has now been supplemented by the like-minded studies of, for example, Sifneos (1979) and Davanloo (1980), and we can also point to Luborsky's (1984) recent demonstration of how to derive basic psychoanalytic principles of therapy from Freud's own technical writings and to focus them on the 'core . . . themes' of a patient's psychopathology, in the course of supportive-expressive psychodynamic therapy which can be done almost literally 'by the book'.

For his own part, however, Malan claims that he has shown one of the classical 'specific techniques' of psychoanalysis to be a powerful non-placebo factor in determining the success of brief dynamic psychotherapy; this is the technique of 'interpreting the transference', and linking such transference-interpretations to childhood events. The possiblity of directing systematic objective research at these phenomena within a distinctly psychoanalytic context has been taken up also by Gill and Hoffmann (1983) and by Luborsky (1984); and there is also evidence of interdisciplinary interest from the cognitivists themselves (Ben-Tovim and Greenup, 1983; A. Ryle, 1984).

However, alongside these jealous and sometimes bitter territorial disputes, more temperate souls had been trying to find ways of sorting out in practice the theory-specific or technique-specific factors from those that are held in common between a number of different practices, and of establishing which of them were therapeutically effective. One such study which has the additional interest for our purposes of paying specific attention to generalized incidental changes in *self*-feeling, as a by-product of therapy not immediately directed at that area of personality, was conducted by Gelder *et al.* (1973). They wanted to find out which of two specific behavioural treatments, 'implosion' (flooding) and 'reciprocal inhibition' (desensitization), was more effective for rather clear-cut phobias, and whether this effect was due to those 'general factors' which are probably shared by a wide range of therapeutic activities, as Cheshire and Thomae concede in Chapter 5.

They had the idea of parcelling out such general factors (including that sort of rehearsal of problems in the presence of a sympathetic listener which we have just seen Eysenck mentioning) into a kind of bogus, content-free pseudotherapy which should act as a non-specific control for the experiment. Somewhat surprisingly, if one looks at the small print of the statistics in the report, it emerges that this non-specific non-therapy was *not* significantly *inferior,* on a number of indices of therapeutic change, to the experimentally based behavioural techniques! Namely, on psychiatric, therapist and patient rating scales it was not less effective than desensitization; on some behavioural tests and on ratings of social/behavioural adjustment, it was inferior to neither; and on three of the 'self-feeling' items, it did not do worse than flooding although desensitization did (pp. 452–455).

These, however, are not the points to which Gelder *et al.* wish to draw our attention, and our purpose in introducing them is to illustrate two features of the on-going debate about the general and the specific: the fact that beneficial change may take place in areas of functioning that were not the direct focus of specific procedures; and the problem of controlling-out (for the purpose of a crucial experiment) the non-specific variables. On the former point, we notice again that Gelder *et al.* assumed, as it were intuitively, that the psychological benefits of reduction in a specific phobic anxiety would be likely to generalize to an improvement in self-feeling. In so doing, they illustrate the converse of our observation above to the effect that problems in self-feelings may arise from a variety of different specific conflicts, stresses or limitations. Furthermore, the nature of the incidental spin-off from a therapy which has had a specific focus sometimes points, not just to a generalization of improved functioning, but also to the involvement of factors which *do* play a specific part in some background theory *other* than the one from which treatment was derived.

Fransella (1972), for example, based a very specific therapy for psychogenic stuttering on Kelly's (1955) Personal Construct Theory, which is quite different from, and in some way actually hostile to, Freudian psychodynamics (as described earlier in this *Introduction*). Her method consisted in a form of cognitive-aesthetic training aimed at helping the patient to 'construe for fluency'; but some patients whose symptoms responded well to this technique described themselves, in their self-reports after treatment, as feeling agreeably less inhibited and guilty about expressing interpersonal aggression than they had been before treatment. That topic, however, had played no part in the treatment as a focus of attention (since it had no place in the assumed aetiology), although it would indeed have been central to a traditional psychodynamic account of the pathogenesis, and consequently to the treatment, of that particular disorder.

This shows that patients experience *generalized* psychological changes that go beyond the specific focus of a particular therapy (as Gelder *et al.* recognized); and we may recall that Smith *et al.* (1980) were able to demonstrate, in their much-quoted 'meta-analysis' of a great many individual outcome-studies of psychotherapy, that improvement in 'self-esteem' was greater, as an overall group-trend, than improvement in behavioural adjustment. We may take this finding to indicate again, by implication, that improvement in a relatively *generalized* aspect of psychological functioning may occur in the absence of a corresponding degree of change in symptomatic behavioural adjustments. But Fransella's study also illustrates, almost conversely, how patients may also describe readjustments in a quite *specific* area of emotional functioning which is incidental (non-specific) to that theory and practice in the light of which they have been successfully treated, but which for a different school of therapy would nevertheless be specific and characteristic.

These examples serve to show that the whole question of disentangling specific and general factors among the agents of therapeutic change, and of attributing therapeutic effects to them differentially on the basis of empirical observation, is beset with complications. For, not only may very specific techniques produce rather general effects, no doubt as a by-product of having relieved a particular symptom (e.g. improvement in general self-esteem consequent upon giving up an obsessional ritual), but they may also have rather specific effects (e.g. reduction in guilt about aggression/self-assertion, etc.) quite separate from those theoretically encompassed by the method employed. Such complexities are at least multiplied considerably in the case of psychodynamic therapies which, by their very nature, claim to deal with unconscious mental processes; and they may perhaps even make it logically impossible to distinguish such factors (specific *versus* general) from each other. And it is in any case a basic principle of psychodynamic therapy, as Strupp implies in his concluding Chapter 11, that whatever characteristics of personality or procedure (whether theoretically general or specific) the therapist in fact deploys will be apperceived by individual patients as having *specific* significance for them in their own perception and experience of themselves.

References

Balint, M., Ornstein, P. H. and Balint, E. (1972). *Focal Psychotherapy: . . .* Tavistock, London.

Bannister, D. and Agnew, J. (1977). The child's construing of self. In *Nebraska Symposium on Motivation 1976*, pp. 99–125. University of Nebraska Press, Lincoln (Nebr.) and London.

Ben-Tovim, D. I. and Greenup, J. (1983). The representation of transference through serial grids: . . . *Brit. J. Med. Psychol.*, **56**, 255–261.

Bion, W. R. (1962). *Learning from Experience*. Tavistock, London.

Bower, T. G. R. (1977). *A Primer of Infant Development*. Freeman, Oxford.

Cheshire, N. M. (1975). *The Nature of Psychodynamic Interpretation*. Wiley, London and New York.

Cooley, C. H. (1922). *Human Nature and the Social Order*, revised edition. Reprinted by Schocken, New York, 1964.

Cooper, C. and Kline, P. (1986). An evaluation of the Defence Mechanism Test. *Brit. J. Psychol.*, **77**, 19–31.

Davanloo, H. (1980). *Short-term Dynamic Psychotherapy*. Jason Aronson, New York.

Ezriel, H. (1956/57). Experimentation within the psychoanalytic session'. Reprinted in *Psychoanalytic Clinical Interpretation* (ed. L. Paul, 1963), pp. 112–142, Glencoe Free Press, New York.

Festinger, L. J. (1957). *A Theory of Cognitive Dissonance*. Stanford University Press, Stanford (Calif.).

Festinger, L. J. (1964). *Conflict, Decision and Dissonance*. Stanford University Press, Stanford (Calif.).

180 Self, Symptoms and Psychotherapy

Fisher, S. and Greenberg, R. P. (1978). *The Scientific Credibility of Freud's Theories* . . . Basic Books, New York.

Fransella, F. (1972). *Personal Change and Reconstruction.* Academic Press, London and New York.

Freud, S. (1909). Analysis of a phobia . . . *Standard Ed.,* **10**, 1–145.

Freud, S. (1914). On narcissism: . . . *Standard Ed.,* **14**, 67–102.

Freud, S. (1915). The unconscious. *Standard Ed.,* **14**, 159–215.

Freud, S. (1919). Lines of advance . . . *Standard Ed.,* **17**, 157–168.

Geach, P. T. (1957). *Mental Acts.* Routledge and Kegan Paul, London.

Gelder, M. G. *et al.* (1973). Specific and non-specific factors in behaviour therapy. *Brit. J. Psychiatry* **123**, 445–462.

Gergen, K. J. (1977). The social construction of self-knowledge. In *The Self* (ed. T. Mischel), pp. 139–169. Blackwell, Oxford.

Gill, M. M. and Hoffman, I. Z. (1983). *Analysis of Transference,* vol. 2. International Universities Press, New York.

Gottman, J. and Markman, H. J. (1978) Experimental designs in psychotherapy research. In *Handbook of Psychotherapy* . . . (eds S. L. Garfield and A. E. Bergin), pp. 23–62. Wiley, New York.

Harré, R. (1983). *Personal Being.* Blackwell, Oxford.

Jackson, S. R. and Bannister, D. (1985). Growing into self. In *Issues and Approaches in Personal Construct Theory* (ed. D. Bannister), pp. 67–82. Academic Press, London.

Kaechele, H., Schaumberg, H. C. and Thomae, H. (1973). 'Verbatimprotokolle . . .' *Psyche,* **27**, 902–927.

Kelly, G. A. (1955). *The Psychology of Personal Constructs.* Norton, New York.

Kelly, G. A. (1963). *Theory of Personality.* Norton, New York.

Kline, P. (1981). *Fact and Fantasy in Freudian theory,* second edition. Methuen, London.

Kline, P. (1984). *Psychology and Freudian Theory.* Methuen, London and New York.

Kragh, U. and Smith, G. (1970). *Percept-Genetic Analysis.* Gleerups, Lund.

Lachman, S. J. (1972). *Psychosomatic Disorders:* . . . Wiley, Chichester.

Levy, L. (1963). *Psychological Interpretation.* Holt, Rinehart and Winston, New York.

Lewin, K. (1935). *A Dynamic Theory of Personality* (translated by D. K. Adams and K. E. Zener). McGraw-Hill, New York.

Luborsky, L. (1984). *Principles of Psychoanalytic Therapy:* . . . Basic Books, New York.

Mahler, M. S. (1972). A study of the separation-individuation process. *Psychoanal Study Child,* **26**, 403–424.

Mahler, M. S., Pine, F. and Bergman, A. (1975). *The Psychological Birth of the Human Infant.* Hutchinson, London.

Malan, D. H. (1963). *A Study of Brief Psychotherapy.* Tavistock, London.

Malan, D. H. (1976a). *The Frontier of Brief Psychotherapy.* Plenum Press, New York.

Malan, D. H. (1976b). *Toward the Validation of Dynamic Psychotherapy.* Plenum, New York and London.

Masling, J. (ed.) (1983). *Empirical Studies of Psychoanalytic Theories.* Analytic Press, Hillsdale (NJ).

Mergenthaler, E. (1985). *Textbank Systems: Computer Science Applied in the Field of Psychoanalysis.* Springer-Verlag, Berlin.

Minuchin, S., Rosman, B. L. and Baker, L. (1978). *Psychosomatic Families:* Harvard University Press, Cambridge (Mass.) and London.

Ryle, A (1979). Defining goals and assessing change . . . *Brit. J. Med. Psychol.,* **52**, 223–233.

Ryle, A. (1982). *Psychotherapy: A Cognitive Interpretation* . . . Academic Press, London.

Ryle, A. (1984). How can we compare different psychotherapies? *Brit. J. Med. Psychol.,* **57**, 261–264.

Ryle, A. (1985). Cognitive theory, object-relations and the self. *Brit. J. Med. Psychol.,* **58**, 1–7.

Ryle, G. (1949). *The Concept of Mind.* Penguin, Harmondsworth.

Shotter, J. (1984). *Social Accountability and Selfhood.* Blackwell, Oxford.

Sifneos, P. E. (1979). *Short-term Dynamic Psychotherapy: Evaluation and Treatment.* Plenum Press, New York.

Smith, M. L., Glass, G. V. and Miller, T. I. (1980). *The Benefits of Psychotherapy.* Johns Hopkins University Press, Baltimore.

Stekel, W. (1938). *The Technique of Analytical Psychotherapy* (translated by E. and C. Paul, 1950). Bodley Head, London.

Stephanos, S. (1979). Das Konzept der 'pensée opératoire' . . .. In *Lehrbuch der Psychosomatischen Medizin* (ed. T. von Uexkuell), pp. 217–242, Urban and Schwarzenberg, Munich.

Strupp, H. H. (1974). *On the basic ingredients of psychotherapy. Psychother. Psychosom.,* **24**, 249–260.

Strupp, H. H. and Binder, J. L. (1984). *Psychotherapy in a New Key* . . . Basic Books, New York.

Strupp, H. H. and Hadley, S. W. (1979). Specific versus nonspecific factors in psychotherapy: A controlled study of outcome. *Arch. Gen. Psychiatry,* **36**, 1125–1136.

Strupp, H. H. *et al.* (1982). Psychodynamic therapy: theory and research. In *Short-term Psychotherapies for Depression* (ed. A. J. Rush), ch. 8. Wiley, Chichester.

Teller, V. and Dahl, H. (1981). The framework for a model of psychoanalytic inference. *Proceedings of the Seventh International Joint Conference on Artificial Intelligence,* **1**, 394–400.

Wittgenstein, L. (1953). *Philosophical Investigations* (translated by G. E. M. Anscombe). Blackwell, Oxford.

Self, Symptoms and Psychotherapy
Edited by N. Cheshire and H. Thomae
© 1987 John Wiley & Sons Ltd.

CHAPTER 7

Self-perception and Individuation in Children with Psychosomatic Pain

Neil Cheshire, Eddy Knasel and Robin Davies*

7.1   *The clinical picture and the tests*
7.2   *Dimensions of conditioning*
7.3   *Family relations*
7.4   *Self-construing, and implications for psychotherapy*

7.1   The Clinical Picture and the Tests

In the investigation whose methods and findings we discuss here, the psychological data were gathered by research psychologist Eddy Knasel from patients and their families who had been referred by their family doctors to consultant paediatrician, Robin Davies. The reason for referral was always a persistent abdominal pain of some kind. Many such pains naturally turned out to be the symptoms of familiar physical illnesses, while others occurred in the absence of any evidence of organic disorder from a battery of medical screening investigations and thus seemed to be part of the well-known but puzzling syndrome of recurrent abdominal pain in children (*RAP*), which has been reviewed comprehensively by Apley (1975) and discussed more recently, but less systematically, by O'Donnell (1985, ch. 12–17) and by Alvarez (1984). It has also been described, evocatively but unhelpfully, by Graham (1985, p. 608) as 'this mysterious condition'; and the findings from Faull's large sample of a narrow age-band of children beginning school, tantalising though they are, are not immediately relevant becasue she did not exclude organic aetiologies (Faull and Nicol, 1986; Davidson *et al.* 1986). The circumstances of our investigation made it possible to compare a sample of this anomalous psychosomatic group

---

*Robin Davies kindly made patients available to Eddy Knasel as part of the latter's doctoral programme which was supervised by the first author, who also wrote the chapter.

with a control sample of children of similar age and background who had come with 'organic' abdominal pain to see the same doctor in the same clinic. Numbers were small (40 in all), and the age-range of the children was wide (7 years to $13\frac{1}{2}$ years).

It will be evident, from what has just been said, that the use of the term 'psychosomatic' in this context is loose, to say the least; because the sample to which we have applied it was defined initially not by positive evidence of psychosomatic mechanisms in the aetiology of the presenting symptoms, but rather by the *absence* (from the results of a standard range of medical tests) of evidence of organic pathology. In view of this, it might seem appropriate to call them instead the 'non-organic' group, but for the fact that our observations turn out to have a direct bearing upon certain specific aetiological hypotheses, including what has come to be known in this particular clinical context as the 'psychosomatic phenomenon' (cp. Nemiah *et al.*, 1976; Thomae, 1981, pp. 150–166). Our immediate aim, however, in setting up the investigation had been something quite different: we wanted to examine the usefulness of certain psychological test-procedures in assessing self-perception and self-evaluation. We could say, therefore, that we set out to test some psychometric techniques, but ended up testing a psychodynamic hypothesis.

Another thing that we must explain here at the start is that our inquiry was carried out as just one part of a wider study of self-evaluation in different situations. That is why the information which we present is not as detailed as we should like, and why a number of suggestive indications which evidently need further clarification were not followed up at the time (but have, in fact, subsequently become the subject of a separate research project: cp. Tighe and Cheshire 1986). Nevertheless, some of the methods which we used in order to throw light on the psychodynamic characteristics of the two sets of pain-sufferers, and in particular on aspects of their self-perception, do seem to be sufficiently striking in themselves. We have discovered, indeed, that certain features of our psychometric data, and of our tentative theoretical formulations, have been corroborated by a quite independent research group at the University Clinic in Frankfurt (Guenther *et al.*, 1981).

We used two techniques to reflect, in a somewhat subjective and phenomenological way, the patients' family dynamics and self-concepts. Then we compared the information that these produced with the same patients' scores on another test that is supposed to be a much more 'objective', mathematically derived and generally 'scientific', tool which is designed not to reflect the dynamics, but to measure the dimensions, of personality. The first two were, respectively, the 'Family Relations Test' (*FRT*) devised by Eva Bene and James Anthony (Bene and Anthony, 1957/1978) and the self-identification form of George Kelly's well-known 'Repertory Grid Technique' (cp. Bannister and Mair, 1968, p. 51). The third was the 'Junior Eysenck Personality Inventory (*JEPI*; Eysenck, 1965).

As is well known, the *FRT* takes the form essentially of a dramatized questionnaire about family-interactions as perceived by the child. Instead of having to write or check the answers to questions that he or she reads, the child is presented with a pile of cards, each of which has a message printed on it; and these she physically 'posts', as if into a mail-box, to cardboard models representing the members of her family, including herself. The messages can be classified as expressing 'positive' or 'negative' feelings, and these may be either 'incoming' or 'outgoing'. Thus a card which reads 'I like to be with this person in the family' expresses 'outgoing positive' feeling, while one that reads 'This person in the family is always too busy to play with me' expresses a sense of 'incoming negative' affect. There are also cards expressing overprotection and overindulgence. The child may direct sentiments towards any member of the family; she may deny them by posting them to 'Mr Nobody' (as often happens with strong outgoing negative messages such as 'Sometimes I wish this person was not in my family'); or she may direct them to herself. This last possibility will be seen to have special relevance to the question of assessing the child's 'self-concept', while their appeal to Mr Nobody in the case of overprotection and overindulgence will be seen to reflect operationally the two groups' differential use of defensive 'denial' (a concept critically relevant to one of the psychodynamic hypotheses).

George Kelly's theory of 'personal constructs' (1955) is much better known; and its associated technique for assessing personality structure, by 'eliciting' from the subject a range of 'constructs' in the form of bipolar attributes in terms of which she typically organizes and conceptualizes her interpersonal experience, is much more widely used (cp. Fransella and Bannister, 1977, ch. 3). It was devised for psychodiagnostic use with adults, by contrast with the Bene–Anthony, and has only recently been applied to children. Because it combines quantitative features with the production of 'projective' and 'apperceptual' material, it has proved to be a valuable tool for assessing therapeutic change (e.g. Bannister and Fransella, 1986 ch. 7; Koch, 1983; Sheehan, 1985).

Briefly, the essence of the technique is as follows. The subject is asked to specify a number of people who have played certain emotionally significant roles in his/her life: parents, relatives, husband/wife/boyfriend/girlfriend, influential teacher, 'lost object', rejecting person, rival, etc. These are called 'elements'. In order to get a picture of the subject's system of constructs, he or she is asked to compare these 'elements' with each other in such a way that properties of her interpersonal experience which are important to her emerge spontaneously and non-directively. Thus she is asked to choose any three elements, such that two of them are alike in some respect but different from the third in that same respect: e.g. 'Father and mother were both quiet, but my husband is lively'. We have now elicited the constructs 'quiet–lively', and the subject has 'construed' her parents on that construct's 'emergent pole' and her husband on its 'implicit' pole. Further triads are selected until an appropriate range of constructs is established, and then the subject can complete the matrix (or 'grid') by going back to construe all the elements for all the constructs. The subject may also be invited to include himself/herself, as an additional element participating in the triads from which the constructs are elicited.

The extent to which some of the constructs tend to 'go together' in any particular grid can obviously be expressed numerically in various ways, but the essence of both the technique and its background theory is 'construing for similarity and difference'. We shall see later that the principle of construing for similarity in particular, when 'self' is treated as an element, turns out to be significant in our findings, and it also serves to underline quite strikingly the point that is made in a different way by the *FRT*.

7.2 Dimensions of Conditioning

By contrast with these two dynamically structured and interpersonal methods, Eysenck's *JEPI* is a conventional questionnaire whose items are designed to show where a child stands (so to speak) in the psychological space defined by the two factorially established dimensions of 'extraversion' and 'neuroticism'. It has behind it, of course, a great deal of detailed statistical and experimental work (which is not without its critics), and its scores certainly can reflect, in our experience, the emotional and temperamental state of youngsters who have frank psychiatric problems. We, therefore, employed it to find out whether our non-organic group was, in some rather general way, more disturbed, intro-verted or extraverted than the controls.

There were two main reasons for doing this. Firstly, the clinical picture of *RAP* children which is typically drawn suggests a degree of emotional disturb-ance, or at least the presence of certain rather marked temperamental traits. If, therefore, our sample were in some general way 'neurotic', 'maladjusted' or 'immature', any differences between them and our organic control group which might show up on psychometric tests could not logically be linked to their specific psychosomatic complaint, but might merely be a reflection of non-specific neuroticism, emotional maladjustment, etc. That is to say, if we are to be able to attribute the particular dispositions and apperceptions revealed by *FRT* and the Repertory Grid Test to the idiopathic psychodynamics of *RAP*, we need to have demonstrated that our *RAP* children were not just a subgroup of neurotics who happen to present with one symptom rather than another.

Secondly, the particular personality characteristics described in the clinical picture of *RAP* include features which the *JEPI* is especially designed to detect, and which are at the same time critically relevant to an alternative non-psycho-dynamic account of the development of *RAP*. These are features such as timidity, fussiness, being highly strung and showing (in 60% of cases) 'positive evidence' of emotional disturbance (Apley, 1975, pp. 43, 53), which would be expected to raise their scores on the 'N' scale; and other features such as quietness, conformity and social withdrawal which should make for low scores on 'E'. The impression which has been given recently by O'Donnell (1985, ch. 13–16), using his informal and totally unvalidated trio of 'personality types', also invites these same predictions; for he assigned a good half of his 86 subjects, on the basis of his individual clinical impression, to a category defined as 'worrier/anxious/striver/achiever/fussy/fastidious/highly-strung/tidy/ perfectionist' (p. 92). These may be compared with the traits of 'difficultness', 'irregularity' and 'withdrawal' noted by Davison *et al.* (1986, p. 541) in their aetiologically mixed sample.

Furthermore, the 'autonomic conditioning' theory of *RAP* (and of psychosomatics in general, as expounded, for example, by Lachman (1972)) assumes (1) that such children have an over-reactive autonomic nervous system (ANS) producing unusually strong somatic responses to anxiety, irritation, frustration, etc. (i.e. high 'N' by Eysenck's criteria); and (2) that these ANS responses are easily 'conditioned' to reappear in appropriate circumstances if they have been reinforced by, for example, parental attention or avoidance of stress (and an easily conditioned ANS implies low 'E' in Eysenckian terms). The idea that families do indeed collude unwittingly to provide such reinforcement of symptomatic reactions has long been familiar to psychodynamic practitioners, as in John Bowlby's recurrent case-conference question 'Who is doing what to whom?; and it has been taken up conspicuously by Minuchin *et al.* (1978, ch. 2) and briefly reviewed by Haggerty (1983).

The clinical picture, then, as drawn in the literature, leads us to expect *RAP* children to produce scores outside normal limits on measures of general stability and maturity, such as *JEPI* and the Vineland Social Maturity Scale* (Doll, 1965); while the hypothesis of autonomic conditioning appears to predict specifically high 'N' and low 'E' on *JEPI*. In fact, however, there was no significant difference between our two groups on any of the *JEPI* scales, which include a 'lie-scale' to assess test-taking reliability, and indeed all their scores were within normal limits (see Table 1).

Table 1. Comparison of *RAP* subjects and controls on Eysenck's 'E' and 'N' (after Knasel, 1982, p. 195)

JEPI	*RAP* (n = 20)		Organic (n = 20)	
	Mean	s.d.	Mean	s.d.
E	16.7	3	16.8	3.4
N	11	4.8	13.3	4.4
L	5.5	2.7	4.7	3.2

On the Vineland *SMS*, the mean 'social quotient' for the *RAP* group was somewhat *above* average rather than below (mean SQ = 108.3, s.d. = 10.1). But it must be borne in mind that scores on this questionnaire derive from an

*The elaborate revision of this Scale by Sparrow *et al.* (1981) was not available in Britain when our work started.

involved relative's statements about the child: in this case, those of the mother, who may, of course, have exaggerated her child's social competence and independence. Nevertheless, all these psychometric data, taken at face value, clearly count against both the hypotheses to do with neurotic constitution and ANS-conditioning which we have just outlined, and they allow us to assume that our *RAP* children constitute a *specifically* psychosomatic group. These test-findings are discussed in more detail by Knasel (1982, pp. 222–227).

The subsequent study reported provisionally by Tighe and Cheshire (1986) has so far confirmed much of this picture on over 30 new *RAP* patients. As a group, their mean 'E' score is well within Eysenck's norms (-0.26 sigma), so they cannot be said to be clinically 'introverted'; and, although they are half a standard deviation more 'neurotic' than the mean (because of two or three extreme scorers, and because the girls' ($N = 14$) scores were much higher than the boys' ($N = 20$) with their mean deviation at $+1.06$ as against $+0.23$ sigma), we cannot yet say whether they differ significantly from the organic controls, whose 'N' scores may also be raised somewhat by the experience of pain and hospitalization, since we have collected too few of the latter at present. Nor can this second sample of *RAP* children be regarded as 'immature' as far as their Vineland 'social quotient' goes, in view of the fact that they had a mean SQ of 97.6 (s.d. $= 11.6$).

Previous work in related fields also generates expectations about the family-structure of those who complain about pain. The trouble is that different authorities generate different expectations. Should we expect our pain-patients to be examples of Alfred Adler's 'chronic complainer', who is typically a persecuted last-born who can deal with his manifest temporary inferiority only by complaining that he never had a fair chance (Adler, 1928, ch. 8)? Or should we expect, on the contrary, that they will be like Stanley Schachter's first-born and only children who tended to be the first to give up on shock-tolerance tests as the voltage was gradually increased (Schachter, 1959)? Apley takes account of this latter expectation when he points out that the proportion of 'only' children in his stomach-pain subjects (14%) was not significantly different from that among his pain-free controls (12%) when they were investigated at school (i.e. before some had been selected out for referral to hospital). He also failed to find any other birth-rank effect (1975, p. 15), and there were no such effects to be seen in our data either. But O'Donnell, whose diagnostic criteria were less rigorous than ours, does claim to have observed a disproportionate incidence of eldest/only children (39%) in his initial sample of over 60 *RAP* patients in Southern Ireland (1985, p. 107). This percentage would indeed seem to be significant among the relatively large families typical of that country, but the author provides no statistical illumination.

But perhaps what we ought to expect is not after all an association with ordinal position in the family, but rather with number of siblings. For when Gonda (1962) compared those patients who complained much about pain after surgical operation with others who complained little or not at all after comparable treatment, he found that the complainers had significantly more brothers and sisters than the non-complainers had. It is easy to see, in a common-sense way, that a child in a large family may need to learn to shout louder or sooner for parental help when injured, or otherwise in need, than does a child with only one brother or sister, because the latter's needs are more likely to be noticed spontaneously by the parent. Be that as it may, we found no family-size effect either in our sample.

The Family Relations Test (*FRT*) allowed us to look for evidence, at least as perceived by the child, of the sort of overanxious, overcautious, overprotective parenting which is often said to produce a timid hypochondrical child (cp. Weller *et al.*, 1976) and which has been specifically associated by some theorists with the 'psychosomatic family' (Haggerty, 1983). It is also said that the relatives of pain-complainers include very many more pain-complainers than do the relatives of controls, and that pain-complaining parents tend to facilitate pain-complaint in their children by the sort of overconcern just mentioned (Apley, 1975, ch. 3).

The structure of the *FRT* is such as to be able to capture any acknowledged tendency for our non-organic sample to see themselves as objects of overprotection from either parent. For they could have 'posted' to *themselves* the cards saying such things as 'Mother worries that this or that person in the family might catch cold', or 'Father won't let this person play rough games'. But there was no particular tendency to do this: if anything, they did the opposite. We offer below an interpretation of this finding which not only renders it less paradoxical than it seems at first, but also brings it into line with the results of previous research.

Well, if none of these rather gross criteria distinguished our children with non-organic pain from the controls, was there anything that did? Yes there was: something much more subtle, but nevertheless clearly marked, and closely relevant to questions about the self-concept and its development. It was something to do with their sense of 'self-differentiation' or 'individuation', and it was conspicuous both in the analysis of the *FRT* of Bene and Anthony and in that of Kelly's Repertory Grid procedure.

7.3 Family Relations

We have seen that in this test the subject chooses cardboard models to represent people in his extended family, and then 'posts' messages to them. He also has the option of treating himself as an individual in his own right (on a par with his siblings, parents, uncles and aunts, grandparents, etc.) and consequently of posting messages to himself. In this way, when it is a question of deciding, for example, which person in the family 'always helps people when they are in trouble' or which person 'sometimes gets angry for no good reason', the child can say in effect 'That's *me*', rather than 'That's him' or 'That's her'.

The *RAP* group did this *much less often* than the organic group did. The organic group treated themselves as differentiated, participating individuals in this way about twice as much, on average, as did the psychosomatic children. The difference was significant at the 5% level. These results are shown in Table 2, where 'total involvement' means the number of cards posted to individual family-members. However, before we discuss this finding in the context of psychoanalytic theory about the development of a sense of self, we need to notice three further features of the intrafamilial dynamics reflected by the *FRT*.

Table 2.   Mean *FRT* 'total involvement' scores with principal family members (after Knasel, 1982, p. 206)

	Subjects	Controls	
Nobody	34.80	29.85	N/S
Self	4.20	8.25	*
Father	10.95	11.05	N/S
Mother	13.40	14.20	N/S
Sibling + 2	11.50	10.75	N/S
Sibling + 1	13.62	15.60	N/S
Sibling − 1	10.46	13.64	N/S
etc			

N/S = not significant.
* Significant at the 0.05 level (two-tailed test).

Firstly, although the gross quantity of 'involvement' with different family-members is much the same for the two groups, they do differ markedly in the *quality* of one of the interactions, namely that between the child and his/her next oldest sibling. This relationship is significantly more *negative*, taking both incoming and outgoing sentiments together, in the case of the *RAP* group than it is with the controls ($P < 0.001$; see Knasel (1982, p. 212) for the raw data). It may be, then, that conflict with this sibling, whom the child has at some stage displaced as the 'baby' of the family, contributes to setting the stage for a psychosomatic reaction, especially if the direct expression of resentment and hostility is inhibited by the prevailing *mores* of a text-book 'psychosomatic family'. But any such inference would be tentative and in need of replication from a larger sample (a reservation which applies, for that matter, to all our findings in this study).

Both the other observations from the *FRT* concern the dynamic of 'denial', which has of course come to occupy a central place in theorizing about psychosomatics (cp. Nemiah, 1975). There was a slight tendency, which narrowly misses significance at the 5% level (on chi-squared), for the *RAP* children to deny expressions of positive affect, by posting such messages to Mr Nobody, to a greater extent than controls did. Highly significant ($P < 0.001$), however, was the greater tendency of the *RAP* group to deny overprotection and overindulgence by mother. As can be seen from Table 3, they posted many fewer of these messages to themselves; but, instead of sending more of them to other family members, they sent them to Mr Nobody. Father and siblings, therefore, were perceived to the same degree by subjects and controls as enjoying mother's special concern; but controls acknowledged receiving it themselves much more readily than did *RAP* subjects, who were inclined to deny its existence. These last two calculations derive from reworking Knasel's data.

Table 3. Maternal overprotection (MOP)/overindulgence (MOI) (after Knasel, 1982, p. 216)

	MOP and MOI combined		
	Self	Others	Nobody
RAP	48	95	122
Controls	85	93	77

This strong tendency in the *RAP* children both to *appear* to others to be emotionally dependent, as in the typical 'clinical picture' of such children on which we have commented above, and yet at the same time to *deny* such dependency when asked to make a self-assessment, exactly reproduces a pattern noted many years ago by Witkin *et al.* (1962, ch. 12) in some of their pioneering studies of 'psychological differentiation' as assessed through tests of 'field dependency' *(FD)*. They reported that the patients who presented ulcers or asthma as psychosomatic conditions tended to be markedly *FD*, and also that the former group of patients were very much inclined to deny emotional dependency by depicting themselves in self-assessment as *less* dependent than both mixed neurotics and normal controls rated themselves, and as less dependent than their own doctors rated them (see also Witkin, 1965; Witkin and Goodenough, 1981). Consistently with this tendency to deny dependency and tension, Alvarez (1984, ch. 7) found her *RAP* subjects more inclined than controls to describe themselves as 'easy-going'.

Another study, this time of a series of successive admissions to psychiatric hospital, found that those patients who were 'talking with their bodies' as Apley put it (and thereby using what Freud (1914, ch. 2) had called 'organ speech') were poorly differentiated and resorted to denial: those patients who 'somaticised their complaints and denied their psychological problems' produced significantly higher *FD* scores than other patients did (Witkin *et al.*, 1962, p. 209). In the on-going investigation by Tighe and Cheshire (1986), this issue is being addressed specifically by two tests of 'field dependence': Witkin's own rod-and-frame technique, and a children's version of the *Embedded Figures Test* (Karp and Konstadt, 1971). So far, however, no clear trend is demonstrable; but the prediction is, plainly, that our *RAP* patients will have higher *FD* scores on these tests than their 'organic' controls do. As far as denial is concerned, it is nowadays taken for granted in general psychosomatics, as we have noted above, that it plays a critical part in the pathogenesis or maintenance of these conditions.

Our own *FRT* data, then, serve to confirm this evident association between poor self-differentiation and denial of dependency in the psychosomatic child; and this association in turn throws light on our last empirical finding, which is at first sight paradoxical, by suggesting a way of interpreting it which resolves the paradox.

7.4   Self-construing, and Implications for Psychotherapy

In the terms of 'personal construct' theory, questions about a person's self-concept turn into questions about how a person 'construes' himself/herself; and in terms of Kelly's empirical technique, we can invite the subject to take himself as an 'element', alongside the repertory of 'roles' which were described before, and to construe himself for similarity and difference as one of the elements in a standard 'triad'. That is, we can ask him to choose two other people from the range of elements to form a group with himself such that two of the 'triad' have some quality in common which is lacked by the third. This modification of the procedure is called the 'self-identification form' of the Repertory Grid Test, and has been used by personal construct theorists to map out the intrapersonal space of what they call the 'self-identification system' (Norris and Makhlouf-Norris, 1976).

Which of these alternative strategies, then, do we expect the relatively well-differentiated child to adopt? On the face of it, such a child would seem likely to say 'Those two are like that, but as for me, I am like this!': that is, in the jargon of the technique, to construe himself on the 'implicit' pole of his constructs. Conversely, we might think that the child whose self-concept is only rather vaguely or insecurely differentiated we would tend to emphasize similarities rather than difference, and to construe himself on the 'emergent' pole. But this would be to adopt a simplistic view of the relation between self-construal, individuation and identification, since the well-differentiated child will not, of course, *lack* the capacity to 'identify' and to construe himself as in some ways *like* others. On the contrary, identification with significant others *as objects* (as opposed to narcissistic fusion with them in symbiosis) is seen by much psychoanalytic theory as a necessary step towards mature differentiation; a step which is typically facilitated by the theoretically important stage of 'transitional objects' (pacifiers, Linus-blankets, favourite toys) with which all parents are familiar (Winnicott, 1971, ch. 1) and which we encountered above in Chapter 4 (4.1 and 4.3). Consequently, the healthily individuated Self will have what Stechler and Kaplan (1980, p. 89), following Erikson, have called 'aspects of *both* separateness *and* membership in a more inclusive entity'.

Conversely, it is arguable that it is the poorly differentiated child who will avoid relating himself closely with others, for fear of being taken over or swallowed up by their more strongly defined identity. This point is familiar to students of the psychodynamics of 'borderline states', but has been applied to the general context of family interactions by Bowen (1976, pp. 65–75). In the particular instance of our *RAP* children, also, we have to take into account what effect their propensity for *denial* is likely to have upon their manifest responses to the task of being asked to 'construe' themselves *vis à vis* significant others; for this propensity was evident again in their construing themselves on the supplied constructs 'nervous–confident', 'tidy–messy' and 'popular–alone', significantly *less* often as 'nervous' and 'tidy' than did the organic group ($P < 0.05$) and *no* less often as 'alone', thus flying in the face of the standard clinical impression, noted above, which describes them as highly strung, overconscientious and socially withdrawn.

At all events, there was indeed a clear distinction between our two groups with respect to their pattern of construing: the *RAP* children used the 'implicit' pole, and thus construed themselves as different from the other two people in the triad, significantly more often than did the controls (again, $P < 0.05$). Although this could conveniently be seen as a denial-motivated over-assertion of differentiation where none (or too little) is in fact felt, it also represents an avoidance by these children of the chance of perceiving themselves as qualitatively similar to, even though numerically different from, significant others. Knasel interprets this as another manifestation of their inability (or perhaps their anxious reluctance), which they had already betrayed in the *FRT*, to 'take Self as object' in the field of interpersonal perceptions and relationships. He writes (1982, pp. 230–231) that it suggests '. . . a relative inability or unwillingness for these children to construe themselves as a *person* amongst other people. . . . it is as if these children cannot or will not stand back from their own experience and self-perceptions and construct a picture of themselves which they can use in drawing comparisons between themselves and others. . . . [They] cannot or will not *de-centre* from their own experience, and hence do not have their Self *available as an object*'. His discussion continues in terms of Piagetian pre-operational perceptual egocentrism (a concept which no doubt needs to be revised in the light of the sort of research reviewed by Donaldson (1978)), and with reference to Carl Rogers's (1961) analysis of self-communication at different stages of psychotherapy; the latter being a topic which is considered in some detail in Chapters 9 and 10 of this volume.

With psychosomatic hypotheses about 'alexithymia' in mind (Sifneos, 1973; Nemiah *et al.*, 1976; Wolff, 1977), Knasel comments that the particular constructs which *RAP* children produced spontaneously do not seem, on inspection, to be any less emotionally coloured than those of controls; this is another point which Tighe and Cheshire (1986) are following up more systematically. Furthermore, if we can eventually confirm that *RAP* children do indeed significantly lack differentiated self-perception and appropriately emotionalized apperceptions of others and themselves, then, from the point of view of psychotherapy, personal construct theory would imply that we should adopt the specific practical technique of teaching them to 'construe' themselves and their actions for 'differentiation' and 'emotionality', just as Fransella (1972) cured her stammerers by teaching them to 'construe for fluency'.

With respect to self-esteem, however, *RAP* children did tend significantly (5% level) to construe themselves on the apparently *low* esteem pole of the supplied constructs 'failure–success' and 'tidy–messy'. But, as we have noted above, they were inclined to deny being 'alone' as opposed to 'popular' and it is easy enough also to see their presentation of themselves as 'messy' as a denial of that overconscientiousness which clinical description regularly attributes to them. Nevertheless, from a therapeutic point of view, the importance of cultivating and maintaining positive self-regard in all cases of somatic 'conversion-symptoms', whether they are understood in terms of the 'hysterical mechanisms' of traditional psychoanalytic theory or in the broader terms of alexithymia and the psychosomatic family, is well recognized and has been emphasized, for example, by Laughlin (1970, p. 33). It is worth noting also, from the point of view of self-esteem, that O'Donnell sees in his informally observed sample of patients a characteristic tendency towards an anxiety-laden striving for achievement, both at school and in leisure activities. So much so that he writes, 'Children with this picture are now the commonest (40%) single group I see'; and he asks, 'Is the child an ambitious striver who is failing to live up to his own self-image?' (O'Donnell, 1985, p. 101). More likely, in our view, he is a child with an *uncertain* self-image who is anxiously trying to demarcate it for himself with varied and conspicuous achievements, along the lines of 'I am what I can do' which Cheshire and Thomae refer to in Chapter 1. Maslow might call it 'self-actualization' by compulsive activity.

Be that as it may, the question with which we started was more an aetiological one, though the purpose of asking it was to provoke observations and suggestions relevant to a theory of therapy, or optimally of prevention: 'Why do *RAP* children need to 'talk with their body', and with this part of their body in particular?' In short, why do they use this particular form of what Freud (1915, ch. 7), in the context of hypochondria (which he associated with a narcissistic failure of self/object differentiation and cathexis: 1914, pp. 76–78), called 'organ-speech'? The answer that they have a generally neurotic and introverted constitution which is easily conditioned to produce ANS activity under stress did not seem consistent with the evidence of our study.

On the other hand, we did make some quite specific findings that were highly consistent with certain psychodynamic ideas, to the effect that these children still have some developmentally primitive anxieties about breaking away from involvement with mother and setting up a differentiated self-identity of their own; that these anxieties are denied, possibly because the wish to individuate is felt as both frightening and rejecting of mother (Erikson's 'autonomy vs. shame and doubt'; 1963, ch. 7); and that, since conscious verbal articulation of such conflicts, that are themselves not consciously articulated as feelings, is out of the question, there is no option but to regress to preverbal somatization of affect. And if the pervading anxiety is to do with 'cutting the cord' emotionally and ontogenetically, where else but in the epigastric and periumbilical region (as is typical for *RAP*) should such symbolic somatic expression be located?

References

Adler, A. (1928). *Understanding Human Nature* (translated by W. B. Wolfe). Allen and Unwin, London.

Alvarez, J. H. (1984). *Recurrent Abdominal Pain in Childhood: . . .* Unpublished Ph.D. Thesis, University of Wales.

Apley, J. (1975). *The Child with Abdominal Pains*, second edition. Blackwell, Oxford.

Bannister, D. and Fransella, F. (1986). *Inquiring Man*, third edition. Croom Helm, London.

Bannister, D. and Mair, J. M. M. (1968). *The Evaluation of Personal Constructs.* Academic Press, London.

Bene, E. and Anthony, J. (1957/1978). *The Family Relations Test.* NFER–Nelson, Windsor.

Bowen, M. (1976). Theory in the practice of psychotherapy. In *Family Therapy* (ed. P. Guerin), pp. 42–90. Gardner, New York.

Davison, I. S., Faull, C. and Nichol, A. R. (1986). Research Note: temperament and behaviour . . . *J. Child Psychol. Psychiat.*, **27**, 539–544.

Doll, E. A. (1965). *Vineland Social Maturity Scale.* American Guidance Service, Circle Pines (Minn.).

Donaldson, M. (1978). *Children's Minds.* Fontana, London.

Erikson, E. H. (1963). *Childhood and Society,* third edition, Penguin, Harmondsworth.

Eysenck, S. B. G. (1965). *The Junior Eysenck Personality Inventory.* NFER–Nelson, Windsor.

Faull, C. and Nicol, A. R. (1986). Abdominal pain in six-year-olds: . . . *J. Child Psychol. Psychiat.*, **27**, 251–260.

Fransella, F. (1972). *Personal Change and Reconstruction.* Academic Press, London and New York.

Fransella, F. and Bannister, D. (1977). *A Manual for Repertory Grid Techniques.* Academic Press, London.

Freud, S. (1914). On narcissism . . . *Standard Ed.,* **14**, 67–102.

Freud, S. (1915). *The unconscious. Standard Ed.,* **14**, 159–215.

Gonda, J. (1962). Some remarks on pain. *Bull. Brit. Psychol. Soc.,* **46**.

Graham, P. J. (1985). Psychosomatic Relationships. In *Child and Adolescent Psychiatry: . . .* second edition (eds M. Rutter and L. Hersov), ch. 37. Blackwell, Oxford.

Guenther, C. *et al.* (1981). Unpublished research reports. Psychology Department, University Clinic, Goethe University, Frankfurt-am-Main, FRG.

Haggerty, J. J. (1983). The psychosomatic family: an overview. *Psychosomatics,* **24**, 615–623.

Karp, S. A. and Konstadt, N. (1971). *Children's Embedded Figures Test.* NFER–Nelson, Windsor.

Kelly, G. A. (1955). *The Psychology of Personal Constructs.* Norton, New York.

Knasel, E. G. (1982). *Towards a Science of Personal Action: . . .* Ph.D. Thesis, University of Wales.

Koch, H. C. H. (1983). Changes in personal construing ... *Brit. J. Med. Psychol.*, **56**, 245–254.

Lachman, S. J. (1972). *Psychosomatic Disorders:* ... Wiley, Chichester.

Laughlin, H. P. (1970). *The Ego and Its Defences.* Appleton-Century-Crofts, New York.

Mahler, M. S., Pine, F. and Bergman, A. (1975). *The Psychological Birth of the Human Infant.* Hutchinson, London.

Minuchin, S., Rosman, B. L. and Baker, L. (1978). *Psychosomatic Families:* ... Harvard University Press, Cambridge (Mass.).

Nemiah, J. (1975). Denial revisited ... *Psychother. Psychosom.*, **26**, 140–147.

Nemiah, J. C., Freyberger, H. and Sifneos, P. E. (1976). Alexithymia: a review ... In *Modern Trends in Psychosomatic Medicine* (ed. O. W. Hill), vol. 3, pp. 430–439. Butterworths, London.

Norris, H. and Makhlouf-Norris, F. (1976). The measurement of self-identification. In *Explorations of Intrapersonal Space* (ed. P. Slater), vol. 1, pp. 79–92. Wiley, London.

O'Donnell, B. (1985). *Abdominal Pain in Children.* Blackwell, Oxford.

Rogers, C. R. (1961). *On Becoming a Person.* Constable, London.

Schachter, S. (1959). *The Psychology of Affiliation.* Tavistock, London.

Sheehan, M. (1985). A personal construct study of depression. *Brit. J. Med. Psychol.*, **58**, 119–128.

Sifneos, P. E. (1973). The prevalence of 'alexithymic' characteristics ... In *Topics of Psychosomatic Research* (H. Freyberger). Karger, Basle.

Sparrow, S. S., Balla, D. A. and Cicchetti, D. V. (1981) *Vineland Adaptive Behaviour Scales.* Distributed by NFER-Norton, Windsor.

Stechler, G. and Kaplan, S. (1980). The development of the Self ... *Psychoanal. Study Child*, **35**, 85–105.

Thomae, H. (1981). *Praxis der Psychoanalyse:* ... Suhrkamp, Frankfurt.

Tighe, M. G. and Cheshire, N. M. (1986). *RAP* children ... Unpublished research report, Psychology Department, University College, Bangor, North Wales.

Weller, L. *et al.* (1976). Birth order and risk-taking ... *Brit J. Soc. Clin. Psychol.*, **15**, 103–104.

Winnicott, D. W. (1971). *Playing and Reality.* Reissued by Penguin Books, Harmondsworth (1974).

Witkin, H. A. (1965). Psychological differentiation and forms of pathology. *J. Abnorm. Psychol.*, **70**, 317–336.

Witkin, H. A. *et al.* (1962). *Psychological Differentiation.* Wiley, New York.

Witkin, H. A. and Goodenough, D. R. (1981). *Cognitive Styles: Essence and Origins.* International Universities Press, New York.

Wolff, H. (1977). The concept of alexithymia ... *Psychother. Psychosom.*, **28**, 376–388.

Self, Symptoms and Psychotherapy
Edited by N. Cheshire and H. Thomae
© 1987 John Wiley & Sons Ltd

CHAPTER 8

Self-theory, Anxiety and Intrapsychic Conflicts

Paul McReynolds

8.1   Introduction

Theoretical interest in the psychology of the Self has increased greatly in recent years (Epstein, 1980; Horowitz, 1979; Jacobson, 1964; Kohut, 1971, 1977; Rosenberg, 1979; Wylie, 1974/1979). This renewal of attention to a basically old concept has resulted from the realization that an improved understanding of the structure and dynamics of the Self is essential for further advances in certain applications of psychotherapy, as well as for our fuller understanding of the normal personality. It may be added that the examination of the vagaries and complexities of those psychological functions that we refer to collectively as the 'Self' constitutes one of the most challenging and fascinating areas of contemporary psychology.

The present chapter is concerned with the nature and identification of conflicting perceptions in the self-structures of individuals, and with the strategies that persons employ as they endeavour to resolve these intrapsychic conflicts. The chapter begins with a brief, introductory examination of the concept of the Self, and then turns to a summary of the theoretical superstructure that will be employed in the rest of the chapter in an attempt to rationalize the nature of inner conflicts. The next topic taken up is a particular conceptualization of anxiety. This is followed by a tentative taxonomy of internal conflicts—designated as mental discrepancies—and by a survey of methods of conflict resolution. Most of the content of the chapter derives from a theoretical conceptualization that has been in the process of development over the past several decades, and which can be referred to as assimilation theory (McReynolds, 1956, 1960, 1971, 1976, in press a).

8.2   The Concept of the Self

There are two key issues that any systematic conception of the Self must deal with. The first is the question of the self-as-subject versus the self-as-object, and the second is the basis of the evaluative aspect of selfhood, usually referred to in contemporary literature as self-esteem. Both of these questions were addressed in an enlightening way by Cheshire and Thomae in Chapter 1, but a somewhat different perspective will be presented here.

With respect to the first question, the present view is that it is theoretically useful to maintain a strict distinction between the self-as-subject and the self-as-object, or—in other terms—between the self-as-*agent* and the self-as-*perceived*. The former, in ordinary language, is suggested by the pronoun 'I', and the latter is implied by the pronoun 'me'. For the former we may use the expression 'executive self', and for the latter the term 'perceived self'. Currently, most research on self-theory is concerned with the perceived self (how one defines oneself, what characteristics one ascribes to oneself, and so on), and a major aim of much psychotherapy is devoted to helping the patient to alter his or her perceived self, i.e. to come to see himself or herself differently. The executive self, on the other hand, has not only received much less attention, but is in many quarters still viewed as something mythical, even mystical, and as inherently unscientific. Nevertheless, it is the 'I' that suffers stress and anxiety, that evaluates the perceived self as adequate or inadequate, that feels guilt, and that makes decisions.

Further, the concept of the executive self, as conceptualized under other terms, such as decision-making, planning, choosing, and the like, is gradually finding a central place in psychological research. It is interesting, in this connection, to note that it was about 350 years ago that René Descartes—who, incidentally, spent a brief but crucial period near Ulm, the site of the second

Editor's Department (Vrooman, 1970)—attributed roughly what I am here terming the executive functions of the Self to the soul. Today we find metaphors like 'ego', 'executive self', 'executive programme', 'person-as-agent', and the like more apt than the metaphor of the soul; but, in either case, the significance of this evaluating, choosing, decision-making aspect of the mind can hardly be overestimated, and cannot successfully be ignored.

It is instructive to note that much of the recent thought in philosophical psychology has been moving in a direction that is supportive of my insistence that explanations of behaviour must take account of the executive self as well as of the perceived self. I am referring here to the development of sophisticated philosophical arguments to the effect that it is desirable to conceptualize the human being as an active agent, rather than solely as a reactive machine (Goldman, 1970; Hampshire, 1959; Harré and Secord, 1972; Manicas and Secord, 1983; McReynolds, in press b; Mischel, 1969; Taylor, 1964, 1970). This orientation, in its modern context, derives largely from Kant, and was implied earlier by Aristotle, Augustine, Descartes and others. It can be contrasted with the positivistic tradition, which is more consistent with an exclusive emphasis on the objective, or perceived self that characterized mainstream psychology until recently.

A more balanced view conceptualizes the executive self and the perceived self separately, and emphasizes the relations between them. The perceived self can be conceptualized as a part of the person's overall cognitive system, as a part of his or her world view, of which the perceived self is the most personal and significant part. This perceived self—which includes the notions of who one is and what one is capable of—is subject to on-going, relatively constant examination and evaluation by the executive self. The outcome of this evaluation, which in the older psychologies was often termed self-respect, has since the time of William James generally been referred to as self-esteem. Self-esteem is, of course, not merely a cognitive variable; rather, it is primarily a motivational variable, in the sense that persons constantly strive to maintain and increase their positive self-evaluation.

Why is self-esteem motivation so constant and so powerful? The late Ernest Becker (1971, p. 68) presented the metaphor of 'the inner newsreel' to illustrate how each person, in the background of his or her awareness, more or less continuously weights almost every interpersonal act in terms of whether it is crediting or debiting the value and worth of the perceived self. Basically, there are two theoretical approaches to the origin of self-esteem motivation. One view holds that such motivation is somehow fundamental in its own right. The other approach assumes that self-esteem motivation is derived from other, more basic motives. The latter approach, for example, might take the position that when an infant behaves in a manner pleasing to its mother it typically receives some kind of reinforcement from the mother, such as praise, with the result that as the infant introjects its mother it learns to view itself favourably when it behaves properly; in this perspective the developing child's motivation for self-esteem is really only a way, at a deeper level, of earning praise, and of avoiding reprimand by the mother.

Such an interpretation of the origins of self-esteem seems simplistic and incomplete. It reminds one of the discredited secondary drive theory of Clark Hull, and of Dollard and Miller's (1950) misguided attempt to explain the infant's developing attachment to the mother as merely the expression, in a disguised form, of the child's need for food. My own conjecture is that there is an autonomous development of self-esteem motivation as the inevitable result of the intellectual development of an infant to the point where it is able to conceptualize both its perceived self and its separate existence as a wishing, choosing, active being. This interpretation of the origin of self-esteem motivation does not deny the crucial importance of early socializing experiences, particularly with the mother-figure, in influencing the strength of self-esteem motivation and in determining the themes that are represented in it, but it does assert that such motivation cannot be reduced solely to more basic, underlying drives.

Research and theory on the Self has traditionally concentrated on the perceived self. Thus, a variety of theorists (e.g., Kelly, 1955; Kohut, 1971; Lecky, 1945; Mead, 1934; Rogers, 1959; Sullivan, 1953) have offered conceptions of the Self as defined by the way a person construes himself or herself. In particular, research has focussed on the theme of consistency or disparities among different elements, or aspects of the Self. In addition, extensive efforts have been made to understand how the perceived self comes into being during infancy and childhood (e.g. Allport, 1961, ch. 6; Kagan *et al.*, 1982; Kohut, 1971, 1977; Mahler *et al.*, 1975; Rosenberg, 1979) and how it changes during the life span (Allport, 1961; Feshbach and Weiner, 1982).

Research on the self-as-agent, or executive self, would seem more difficult to study, and indeed it has not been widely investigated under a 'self' rubric. Under other labels, however, research in this area is flourishing. Thus, several years ago Miller *et al.* (1960) put forth the concept of a cognitive 'Plan', which represents a kind of executive programme. Work by Rotter (1966), Levenson (1981) and others on locus of control demonstrates the importance in behaviour of whether a person (i.e. as agent) *believes* that he or she is, or is not, in control of his or her own behaviour. Further, the crucial influence of the *feeling* of personal control, which also is part of the phenomenology of the self-as-agent, has been fruitfully studied by DeCharms (1968), Perlmuter and Monty (1979), and others.

There is one aspect of personal control that I wish to comment on at slightly greater length. This is the variable of preference for control. It should not be assumed that all individuals are equally desirous of exercising control over what happens to them. Rather, the degree of preference for control turns out to be a reliable individual differences variable. Some years ago, I devised an inventory (Preference for Control Scale) to assess this variable (McReynolds,

1972). Christensen (1981) found preference for control to be positively related to somatic illness and negatively related to spontaneity. Further, his data indicated that the likelihood of unpredicted events leading to illness is increased when there is an incongruence between one's perceived degree of control and his or her preferred degree of control. More recently, Burger (1985) and associates, utilizing their Desirability of Control Scale (Burger and Cooper, 1979) in a series of investigations, have shown desire for control to be meaningfully related to achievement motivation, depression, and learned helplessness. These various findings indicate that both the extent to which one perceives oneself to be in control (in the sense of locus of control) and the degree to which one prefers to be in control are important factors in behaviour. The former is an aspect of the self-as-perceived, and the latter is an aspect of the self-as-agent.

It is evident, on the basis of the foregoing discussion, that it is possible to conduct rigorous empirical research on both aspects of the Self, i.e. on the self-as-agent and on the self-as-object. The area that most clearly brings these two aspects together is research on self-esteem (Coopersmith, 1967; Demo, 1985; Wells and Marwell, 1976) and such related concepts as effectance (R. W. White, 1959) and self-efficacy (Bandura, 1977).

Dynamic processes within the contents of the Self structure, in the sense of processes growing out of incompatibilities and disharmonies among the constituents of the Self, have traditionally been referred to by the metaphor of 'conflicts'. Such intrapsychic conflicts, which will be a major focus of this chapter, may occur between two features of the executive self (e.g. when two desires are in conflict), or between two characteristics of the perceived self (e.g. when two different ways of seeing oneself are incompatible), or between aspects of the executive self and the perceived self (e.g. when one evaluates oneself in a negative way).

To summarize this chapter to this point, I have argued that it is both realistic and useful to distinguish between an executive self and a perceived self. Further, I have maintained that empirical research on both these aspects of the phenomenal world is not only possible, but is well under way. I have speculated that the motivation for positive self-esteem cannot be reduced to more basic primary drives, but is, in large part, a fundamental human motive with its own autonomous development. And, finally, I have proposed that dynamic processes within the self structure may occur in the form of conflicts between elements of the executive self, between elements of the perceived self, or between aspects of the executive self and the perceived self.

8.3 Assimilation Theory

I now turn to the main focus of this chapter, which is the examination of certain aspects of self-dynamics, as these are manifested in psychopathology and psychotherapy. As noted earlier, my approach in this area is through the application and elaboration of assimilation theory. I will begin, therefore, with a brief overview of this theoretical model (McReynolds, 1976).

The term 'psychological assimilation'—or simply 'assimilation', as I will state it more briefly henceforth—is used here in both a metaphorical sense and a technical sense. In its metaphorical meaning, which is adopted from the word's usage in physiology, we will mean by assimilation that process whereby the contents of one's conscious experiencing enter into a harmonious and meaningful relationship with the organized representations in the person's brain of his or her previous experiencing. The fact, and the theoretical significance, of assimilation have been noted by a long line of psychologists, including Herbart, Wundt, Lecky, and Piaget. Further, the word 'assimilation' is employed in everyday language in a way not dissimilar to that intended here, as when someone says 'I haven't been able to assimilate the reality that he's gone', or 'I can't seem to fully assimilate the fact that I won the prize'.

In my own more technical development of assimilation theory, an individual's overall, organized representations of previous experiencing—of the way one perceives oneself and one's world—is conceived to include cognitive, affective and conative elements, and to comprise innumerable interrelated categories, which can be referred to in their entirety as the person's *category-system*. Though this model will not be developed in detail here, it is possible to conceptualize the process of assimilation in terms of systematic alterations in, and additions to, the category-system as a function of on-going phenomenal experiencing. The model assumes that percepts which contain *incompatibilities*, or *internal discrepancies*, cannot readily be assimilated into the category-system, and thus remain in a kind of suspension or abeyance, and tend to accumulate. This overall quantity of accumulated unassimilated material can be referred to as the 'cognitive backlog' (McReynolds, 1976), because it represents a mass of data yet to be worked through. The total quantity of unassimilated material in a given individual of course varies from time to time as a function of the person's recent experiences, his or her success in assimilating earlier material, and other factors.

The general theme of the role of some kind of cognitive inconsistency, dissonance, or incongruency in personality functioning is widespread in contemporary theorizing, and I need not review this background here. While such incompatibilities are usually assumed to be cognitive in nature, this perspective is actually unduly restrictive, since many of the mental disparities that people experience in everyday life turn out, on examination, not to be strictly cognitive, but instead take a wide variety of forms; for this reason, I have come to prefer the broader term *mental discrepancy*. The present model also differs from the more conventional cognitive consistency conceptualizations, such as those of Rogers (1959), Kelly (1955), Festinger (1957), and Heider (1958), in its central postulates that incongruent percepts are unassimilable, and tend to accumulate.

This completes our brief overview of assimilation theory. We turn next to an examination of the manner in which this process can be elaborated to explicate the nature and origins of anxiety.

8.4 Anxiety

Assimilation theory posits the existence of two separate types of anxiety, which may be thought of as *primary anxiety* and *secondary anxiety*. By *primary anxiety* I mean a condition of anxiety that arises inexorably as a function of certain cognitive processes; thus, it can also be (perhaps more meaningfully) referred to as *cognitive anxiety*. By *secondary anxiety* I will mean anxiety which occurs as a result of the adventitous pairing of neutral stimuli with a state of primary anxiety, and the re-occurrence of the neutral stimuli. In other words, secondary anxiety is *conditioned anxiety*.

Let us look in more detail at the nature of primary or cognitive anxiety. The basic variable here is conceived to be the overall quantity of accumulated unassimilated material. There appear to be three different ways in which the magnitude of the cognitive backlog can be increased, hence increasing anxiety. These are: first, the occurrences of experiences that are unassimilable—an example would be a person failing in something that is vital to his self-image; second, an input that is in principle assimilable, but which is occurring at a rate beyond the person's ability to process and assimilate the material—an example would be a man overwhelmed by a series of unexpected events at home and at work; and third, the deassimilation of previously well-assimilated material—an example would be a woman whose schemata for assimilating a wide range of interpersonal data in terms of her relationships with her husband are rendered inoperable by the death of her husband.

Cognitive anxiety, in the present conceptualization, is related to the self-concept in the following way. First, it is assumed that a large proportion of the percepts arising from a person's on-going experiencing directly involve self-orientated data, both in the sense of self-as-agent and self-as-perceived. Further, it is assumed that mental data concerning the Self are particularly likely to include discrepancies, and hence to be especially difficult to assimilate. There are a number of reasons for this conclusion, but the most prominent one is that in the case of self-orientated data there are no clear objective criteria in terms of which given interpretations can be evaluated, as there is, in contrast, with respect to perceptions of the physical environment. Hence, most instances of anxiety, in particular those of high intensity and protracted duration, will inevitably concern the Self.

However, the theory does not require that the backlog of percepts held to underlie cognitive anxiety necessarily be related to the Self, i.e. it is assumed that any percepts not assimilated contribute to anxiety. Not only is such a position theoretically parsimonious, but it is actually essential in order to explain the fact that very young infants, prior to the period in which a self-concept can be assumed to have developed, may nevertheless exhibit a form of distress that can be interpreted as anxiety.

Conditioned anxiety, as noted above, is conceived to arise through the adventitious pairing of certain neutral stimuli with instances of primary anxiety. It is manifestly obvious, however, that not all neutral stimuli occurring in such a context become stimuli for anxiety. The question of the selectivity of conditionable stimuli is one urgently requiring clarification (McReynolds, in press a), but it appears that one crucial requirement for conditioning to occur is that the level of cognitive anxiety be extremely high. Conditioned anxiety does not appear to be related in any systematic way to the self-concept, since its occurrence would depend on the nature of the stimuli that became conditioned, which might or might not concern the Self.

There is considerable supporting evidence for the interpretation of anxiety just presented, much of which has been summarized elsewhere (McReynolds, 1976). Rather than reviewing those data here, however, I wish now to examine certain implications of the assimilation model of anxiety for psychotherapy, and to summarize the current research programme of my colleagues and myself in this area.

In order to be successful, attempts to reduce primary anxiety must of necessity be directed toward the factors causing the elevated cognitive backlog. For example, if the elevation were due to certain self-related discrepancies in the person's category-system that come into play in the normal course of experiencing, then any sustained reduction in anxiety would require resolution of these discrepancies. This is one way of describing a central aim of psychotherapy. Attempts to reduce secondary, or conditioned anxiety, on the other hand, would require a quite different approach; for anxieties of this type it would be of little avail to reorganize the category system so as to remove discrepancies, since the anxiety would not be due to the existence of discrepancies. Conditioned anxiety can be relieved only by some kind of extinction procedure, such as systematic desensitization; and this will, of course, take different forms in different psychotherapeutic contexts, ranging, perhaps, from 'working through' in the psychodynamic transference-relationship to the laboratory manipulation of 'reciprocal inhibition' (Wolpé, 1958). Such procedures, however, would be wasted effort if the anxiety were cognitive in type. The question of whether the psychodynamic therapist in fact practises 'conditioned extinction' *malgré lui* is discussed further by Cheshire and Thomae in Chapter 5, and by Cheshire in the *Introduction to Part II*.

It would thus seem an important next step in the development of psychotherapy technology to develop a method for systematically determining, in given problems of particular patients, whether the core anxiety is primarily cognitive, conditioned, or both. Part of the on-going research programme of my colleagues and myself is directed to this question. Though this overall project is still in progress, several relevant studies (Baldo, 1986; Eyman, 1984; McReynolds *et al.*, 1985; White, 1981, 1982) have been completed. Before describing this research I would like to note that the general specificity paradigm that it represents, *viz.* that of selecting specific therapies for specific problems, has been strongly espoused by a number of other workers, including Bentler (1979), Bergin and Suinn (1975), Strupp and Bergin (1969), and Strupp and Binder (1984), and is touched upon also by Cheshire and Thomae in Chapter 5, and by Strupp in Chapter 11.

We began by developing, on a theoretical basis, a list of 10 criteria each for cognitive and conditioned anxiety. For example:

Cognitive anxiety	*Conditioned anxiety*
—Person can't get away from problem	—Anxiety seems tied to particular place and situation
—Sometimes anxiety seems to have no cause	—Anxiety always has a clear precipitating cause
—Person spends much time ruminating about problem as if trying to solve it	—Person doesn't think about problem unless is faced with it, then thinks about how to avoid it

Logically, the general paradigm of cognitive anxiety appears to be 'x but also y', where x and y are incongruent. The general paradigm of conditioned anxiety, on the other hand, appears to be 'A followed by B', where A is a stimulus situation and B is anxiety.

On the basis of the rational criteria, we (McReynolds *et al.*, 1985) have developed an Anxiety Type Inventory, which includes 10 items relating to each type of anxiety, and yields separate scores for cognitive and conditioned anxiety. In completing the inventory the subject first writes, or orally reports, a description of a particular anxiety problem or experience, and then answers the items with respect to that particular instance of anxiety, thus permitting the clinician to evaluate whether the anxiety is chiefly cognitive or conditioned in type. Reliability data (alpha coefficients) are in the 0.7 to 0.8 range, and obtained intercorrelations between the two scales have varied between 0.0 and 0.2. These values, in conjunction with a confirmatory factor analysis and an examination of the content of the items (examples: 'Wherever I go the anxiety is with me' [cognitive]; 'I can prevent the anxiety by avoiding certain places, things, or situations that cause it' [conditoned]), provide strong preliminary support for the hypothesis of two types of anxiety, as predicted by theory. Empirical evidence for the validity of the instrument has been provided by White (1981), who obtained significant support for her prediction that students reporting anxiety concerning vocational choice would score relatively higher on the cognitive scale, and relatively lower on the conditioned scale than students reporting test anxiety.

Research with the Anxiety Type Inventory has so far concentrated on demonstrating the existence of two types of anxiety, as predicted by assimilation theory. Other applications, however, are getting under way. Thus, Eyman (1984) and Baldo (1986) have found some preliminary evidence that the two types of anxiety lead to different kinds of coping behaviour, with cognitive anxiety tending to elicit various problem-solving manoeuvres, and conditioned tending to bring out avoidance behaviours. Baldo's research further suggests that some individuals are more likely to experience one type of anxiety than the other, and that introverts are somewhat more likely to experience conditioned anxiety than are extraverts.

8.5 Intrapsychic Conflicts

The remainder of this chapter will be devoted to an elaboration of the dynamics of cognitive anxiety, since this is the type of anxiety in which disturbances in the self-concept are most likely to be involved. In particular, I wish to examine the concept of mental discrepancy in some detail. According to the present theory it is the existence of mental discrepancies that lead to cognitive anxiety, and hence to the various neurotic defences. From this perspective the identification and working through of the peculiar mental constructions that I have termed mental discrepancies constitutes one of the major tasks of dynamic psychotherapy.

The view that cognitive conflicts, inconsistencies, or incongruences are central in psychopathology, and that such discrepancies must somehow be resolved in successful psychotherapy is, of course, an old one. Freudian theory, though it does not explicitly utilize the discrepancy theme, nevertheless has contributed greatly to this line of thought; it does this through its conception of intrapsychic conflicts and its emphasis on resolving differences between the patient's beliefs and reality. The discrepancy theme—though defined somewhat differently and more narrowly than in my approach here—is explicit in the theories of Carl Rogers and George Kelly. Victor Raimy's (1975) book, *Misunderstandings of the Self*, posits the existence in neurotic patients of invalid assumptions, as did the earlier perspective of Adler, and as does the contemporary perspective of Aaron Beck (1976). Gestalt therapy sees one of the goals of therapy to be the resolution of intrapsychic incongruities.

Despite the wide acceptance of the discrepancy theme in psychopathology there has been relatively little empirical research on it. Among the important early studies on this general theme were several conducted by investigators (Butler and Haight, 1954; Chodorkoff, 1954) in the Rogerian personological perspective. These studies indicated that the overall discrepancy between a person's perceived self and ideal self is negatively related to adjustment, and that the disparity tends to decrease during successful psychotherapy. However, this line of research did not attempt to identify and analyse the actual discrepancies that individual clients present. More recently, several innovative approaches to the assessment of individual differences in internal conflicts, patterned after the cognitive model of Heider (1958), have been put forth (Honess, 1982; Lauterbach, 1975; Slade and Sheehan, 1979).

By far the greatest amount of work related to the general discrepancy paradigm, however, has been that conducted by social psychologists under such rubrics as cognitive dissonance (Festinger, 1957), imbalance (Heider, 1958), and cognitive consistency (Abelson *et al.*, 1968). But while this work is valuable, its relevance for understanding psychopathology and psychotherapy is dubious. In particular, it is noteworthy that studies of cognitive consistency from the social-psychological perspective have focussed almost entirely on instances created artificially in the laboratory, and have paid little attention to the systematic examination of significant mental discrepancies as they occur in real life.

My own interest in developing a method for identifying and measuring existent mental discrepancies—or what, in a different context, can be termed 'incongruencies'—in given individuals dates back to the 1950s. The general approach that I first employed (McReynolds, 1958) was to ask subjects to indicate for a number of relevant personal items what their feelings (like, dislike) were and what their value judgements (good, bad) were, so that these two dimensions could be interrelated in a kind of grid. Considerable support was obtained for the hypothesis that level of anxiety is positively related to overall magnitude of personal incongruency. A later study (Byrne *et al.*, 1961), employing the same general approach, indicated that individuals having personal incongruencies in the areas of hostility and sex tend to avoid the input of percepts in those areas. In a third study (McReynolds *et al.*, 1966), utilizing a similar, but more complex methodology, meaningful relationships were found between personal areas of incongruency and dream content.

These early studies clearly indicated that it is possible to assess individual differences in mental discrepancies, and that such an orientation can yield theoretically meaningful results. Further, the methodology employed demonstrated considerable promise. However, it has the limitation that it can measure discrepancies in only a very general way, and lacks the fidelity to identify important specific conflicts in given persons.

For these reasons, my associates and I have in recent years worked toward a more idiographic method for the study of mental discrepancies, and I turn now to a review of this current research programme. We will begin with a study by Bruce Pither (1974) on personal incongruities—this is the term he used—and Gestalt therapy. Pither and another therapist conducted a three-day workshop using standard Gestalt techniques. Pither was interested in several questions, including two that are relevant here: Can individuals identify and articulate personal incongruities in themselves? And if so, would these incongruities be perceived as less problematic and worrisome after the workshop?

Following appropriate instructions Pither asked each of the 14 participants to list, on a prepared form, one or more personal incongruities at the beginning of the workshop. The median number listed was 5.3. Each incongruity was also rated, on a 10-point scale, as to its importance. Here are two examples of the personal incongruity statements that were reported. 'I want to stick to my diet' vs. 'I'll eat what I want', and 'At the rational level I believe that physical beauty is unimportant; at the gut level I feel it's everything'.

Pither found that the incongruity statements could be classified into two main groups—those taking the form of 'I want but...' and those taking the form of 'I feel but ...'. Of the 33 statements that were rated both before and after the workshop, 27 showed a decline in their problematic nature, tentatively suggesting that the therapy had been effective, at least on a temporary basis. Though essentially exploratory, Pither's study clearly indicated the practicability of conceptualizing incongruities in psychotherapy.

The next study that I wish to summarize was carried out by Alexander Peer (1975), and involved the detailed analysis of the assimilation process in five patients in long-term individual psychotherapy. The data base was the verbatim transcriptions of 68 therapy sessions.

The part of this study that I wish to report here involved the definition, identification, and analysis of four different kinds of patient statements, reflecting significant elements in the assimilation process. These elements were designated as follows:

(1) *Affectocognitive discrepancy*—here the patient spontaneously expresses a perceived or felt intrapsychic discrepancy, e.g. 'It's like wanting to be involved and not wanting to be', and 'I consider him my friend yet I don't trust him'.

(2) *Element of psychological insight*—here the patient spontaneously expresses a clear realization of an immediate experience, e.g. 'Sometimes I feel very empty'.

(3) *Movement toward integration*—here the patient spontaneously expresses—typically in a very tentative way—a possible way of clarifying or resolving a perceived discrepancy. An example is 'I can't just blame my parents; it's partly me'.

(4) *Distorted cognitive integration*—here the patient spontaneously expresses a movement toward integration of a discrepancy, but does so in a way that is unstable, typically by rejecting one side of the discrepancy. An example is: 'Our family is prone to bad marriages. I am never going to marry. I'll stay away from people'.

Peer's research was a major step forward in the understanding of the assimilation process in psychotherapy. The scoring categories that he developed, as outlined above, proved to be reasonably reliable, and to be meaningful in the analysis of what actually occurs in therapy.

The last study that I will summarize—a larger, on-going project—is still under way, so what I will present is in the nature of a progress report. My associates in this research have been Robert Jenkins, Ingrid Moore, William Crabbe, and Patricia White. This research originally grew out of the Peer study just described. In his research Peer had collected over 150 verbatim discrepancy statements from his patients. A careful examination of these showed quite clearly that they took a considerable variety of forms. We had anticipated this to some extent, in part because of Pither's results, and this is why, at that stage of development, we referred to discrepant statements as 'affectocognitive discrepancies'. I should note here that traditionally, particularly as they have been studied in personality and social psychology, inconsistencies in mental processing have been thought of as purely cognitive, as indicated by terms such as 'cognitive dissonance' and 'cognitive consistency'. However, it has long been recognized that in fact discrepancies often exist in the affective domain, so the term 'affectocognitive discrepancy' seemed very appropriate. More recent analyses, however, have shown that even this phrase is too narrow, and therefore I now prefer the less restrictive rubric 'mental discrepancy'.

The purposes of the present project are (1) to develop a taxonomic system for identifying, classifying and coding mental discrepancies, particularly as these are revealed in psychotherapy, and (2) to improve our understanding of the nature, diversity, and structure of mental discrepancies as these occur in real-life experiences. I believe that such mental discrepancies, or intrapsychic conflicts, follow an underlying logic, a grammar, and that this can be discerned through careful analysis.

I will now summarize the basic nature of the taxonomic system that we have tentatively arrived at, after many detours and tangential efforts. The system is still incomplete in a number of respects, but I feel fairly confident of its general structure. The system can be thought of as an attempt to reflect the basic structure of intrapsychic discrepancies, as these are expressed verbally by the patient or inferred by the therapist. The first step in coding a discrepant statement is to rephrase it as a 'but-statement'. This means that one side of the discrepancy is placed on the left and the other side on the right, with the disjunctive 'but' (*b*) between them. Experience indicates that all truly discrepant statements can be written as but-statements. This preliminary rephrasing may also require the elimination of certain irrelevant verbiage, and perhaps some rewording in order to point up the discrepancy. Here is an example of a mental discrepancy as originally stated by a patient, and its rephrasing into a but-statement.

Direct statement: 'I find myself doing the same thing my old man does . . . and it really bothers me'.

Rephrasing: 'I don't want to do the things my father does, *but* I do them'.

Table 1. Basic structure of taxonomic system for coding mental discrepancies
(abridged)

Elements	Syntax
A = action	*Disjunctive symbol = b*
Af = affect	*Conjunctive symbol = a*
At = attitude	*Status of categories*
B = belief	$\wedge$ = presence
C = capacity	$\vee$ = absence
D = desire	
I = intention	*Valence of categories*
M = moral	+ = positive
N = necessity	− = negative
O = outcome	
P = possibility	*Relationships among categories*
Q = quality	$\overline{x,y}$ = to be treated as unit
R = reality	m $\longrightarrow$ n = m implies or leads to n
U = understanding	m $\longrightarrow\!\!\!\!/\,$ n = m does not imply or lead to n
V = value	m $\xrightarrow{\;sh\;}$ n = m should imply or lead to n

Category descriptors

Superscripts (subjects)	*Subscripts (objects)*
s = oneself	s = oneself
o = other person	o = other person

A brief synopsis of the taxonomic code, abridged for illustrative purposes, is
presented in Table 1. The table lists, on the left, the major elements in terms of
which mental discrepancies may occur, and, on the right, the primary syntac-
tical symbols employed in coding a discrepant statement. Also presented, below,
are four examples of mental discrepancies, taken from therapy transcripts that
have been coded in our taxonomic system.

(1) 'I have to feel I am worth something, *but* I feel I am worth nothing.'

$$\overline{N^s \wedge At^s_+} \quad b \quad \overline{R^s \wedge At^s_-}$$

Literal translation: There is a feeling of necessity in the Self (N^s) for the presence
($\wedge$) of a positive attitude in the Self toward the Self (At^s_+), but the reality in the
Self (R^s) is the presence ($\wedge$) of a negative attitude in the Self toward the Self
(At^s_-).

(2) 'I want to leave him, *but* at the same time I desire not to leave him.'

$$\overline{{}_1D^s \wedge A^s_o} \quad \overline{b} \quad \overline{{}_2D^s \vee A^s_o}$$

Literal translation: There is the presence ($\wedge$) of a desire in the Self (${}_1D^s$) for a
certain action toward another person (A^s_o), but there is also desire (${}_2D^s$) for the
absence ($\vee$) of the action (A^s_o).

(3) 'I know it's wrong for me to go to these places, *but* I am not able to stay away.'

$$U^s \wedge M^s_- \xrightarrow{\text{sh}} \vee A^s \quad b \quad \vee C^s \vee A^s \longrightarrow \wedge A^s$$

Literal translation: There is an understanding in the Self (U^s) of a moral injunction (M^s_-) that should ($\xrightarrow{\text{sh}}$) lead to the absence ($\vee$) of a certain behaviour (A^s), but there is a lack ($\vee$) of capacity in the Self (C^s) to avoid the behaviour ($\vee$) which leads to the presence ($\wedge$) of the behaviour (A^s).

(4) 'I feel that I have some good qualities, like decency—I am a decent person—but in other respects, like attractiveness—well, I'm not attractive.'

$$_1B^s \wedge {}_1Q^s_+ \longrightarrow At^s_+ \quad \bar{b} \quad _2B^s \wedge {}_2Q^s_- \longrightarrow At^s_-$$

Literal translation: There is a belief in the Self ($_1B^s$) of the existence in the Self of good qualities ($_1Q^s_+$), which lead to a positive attitude toward the Self (At^s_+), but there is also a belief in the Self ($_2B^s$) of the existence of bad qualities ($_2Q^s_-$), which leaves a negative view of the Self.

These examples, though they do not portray all aspects of the coding system, will perhaps suffice to provide a general picture of the method. Each coded discrepancy, it will be noted, consists of two propositions, with the disjunctive *b* between them. By convention, when one of the propositions is dominant that half of the code is placed to the right of the disjunctive. When neither half is clearly dominant, as in examples (2) and (4), a bar is placed over the disjunctive ($\bar{b}$). Experience has indicated that almost all real-life mental discrepancies involve the Self—though there are rare exceptions—either in the sense of self-as-agent or self-as-perceived. In the examples given, numbers (1) and (3) involve conflicts between the executive self (on the left) and the perceived self; in example (2) both sides represent aspects of the executive self, and in example (4) both sides concern the perceived self.

All four examples illustrate the basic logical structure of a coded intrapsychic conflict. First, there are always two elements in conflict (one on each side of the code), in the sense that they have mutually exclusive behavioural (overt or covert) behavioural implications. In the four examples the *conflicting elements* are, in order, N and R; $_1D$ and $_2D$ (two separate desires); U and C; and $_1B$ and $_2B$. Second, there is always one element to be found on both sides of the code; this is referred to as the *discrepant element*, since its value differs on the two sides. In the first example, the discrepant element is At, which has a valence of + on one side and − on the other side; in example (2), the discrepant element is A, which has a presence sign ($\wedge$) on one side and an absence ($\vee$) sign on the other side; in example (3) the discrepant element is A ($\vee$ and $\wedge$); and in example (4) the discrepant element is At (+ and −).

It is evident from these few examples that mental discrepancies occur in a diversity of forms, both with respect to the elements in conflict and the elements that are discrepant. It is possible to draw certain parallels between the present taxonomy and earlier ones. Thus R (reality) has obvious similarities with the concept of ego functions, M (morals) with superego functions, and (values) with the ego ideal. The present taxonomy, however, offers greater fidelity and refinement than earlier taxonomies. Though several previous attempts have been made to develop fairly complex rational systems for cataloguing semantic incongruencies (Abelson and Rosenberg, 1958; Rokeach, 1973), our approach is unique in that it is based on real-life experiences rather than simply on conceptual schematizations. The proposed system appears to offer the potential for introducing greater objectivity into studies of the dynamic processes occurring during psychotherapy. Other possible topics for research include the distribution of kinds of mental conflicts in different classes of subjects and in different developmental periods.

It should be emphasized that the present taxonomic system is still in the process of evolution and development. In particular, we are working on attaining greater precision in the definitions of certain elements, in order to improve interscorer reliability (White, 1982), which currently is moderate but not high. We are utilizing several sources of data, including material from both clinical and normal subjects, but our method is not yet sufficiently refined for general clinical use. On the basis of present data, however, several conclusions seem in order. First, it is clear, as already implied, that mental discrepancies may take a variety of different forms. Thus, it is by no means true that discrepancies are primarily cognitive—in the sense of knowledge or understanding—as the literature would suggest; on the contrary, they may concern affects, attitudes, actions, capacities, and a variety of other mental concepts.

Second, it seems evident that the great majority of mental discrepancies, at least those manifested in psychotherapy, concern the Self, either in the sense of the perceived self or the executive self, as these terms were delineated earlier in this paper. I should note that it does not have to be this way—i.e. there is nothing inherent in the definition of mental discrepancy, or in the coding system, that requires that discrepancies concern the Self, and indeed one does occasionally find a discrepancy that does not. The fact that most discrepancies are self-related is not surprising, but it is nice to have supporting empirical data. Of those discrepancies that concern the Self, many, but by no means all, involve self-esteem. This is the case, for example, in the first example above. It would be interesting to plot the number and direction of self-esteem discrepancies over the course of psychotherapy, in order to determine if this index of self-esteem improves as therapy progresses, and to examine its relation to other variables.

A third observation that can be made with considerable confidence is that many discrepancies are quite complex. Some involve various contingencies and appear to be tied together with other discrepancies in intricate networks of interrelationships. It is my strong impression that the discrepancies in an individual are frequently arranged in hierarchies, such that the viability of certain discrepancies at a higher level are dependent on those at a lower, more basic level.

8.6   Assimilation strategies

Earlier in this chapter I posited that cognitive anxiety arises from the accumulation of unassimilated perceptual data, and, further, that experiences involving significant mental discrepancies are difficult to assimilate and hence contribute to the build-up of the cognitive backlog, thus increasing anxiety. It follows that reduction in anxiety and its defences can come about only through some method of resolving or circumventing the mental discrepancy barriers. In this context I turn now to a brief, speculative discussion of what can be referred to as assimilation strategies, i.e. methods that an individual may use either (1) to reduce the cognitive backlog, or (2) to prevent it from getting larger. I will describe eight different strategies which individuals sometimes employ. Some of these manoeuvres appear to be carried out in a conscious, voluntary fashion, while others take place at an unconscious, involuntary level.

8.6.1   *Selective Avoidance—Conscious*

In this strategy an individual voluntarily avoids situations that he or she believes would probably yield unassimilable inputs (e.g. a person having difficulty assimilating experiences of intimacy would tend to avoid situations in which intimate behaviour is expected).

8.6.2   *Selective Avoidance—Unconscious*

Here an individual involuntarily avoids—perhaps by raised sensory thresholds or by selective inattention—experiences providing inputs which would be difficult for that person to assimilate.

8.6.3   *Limiting Self-awareness*

In 1972 Duvall and Wicklund inaugurated a line of research on objective self-awareness which indicates that if a prospective behaviour is incongruent with one's self-concept, i.e. is incongruent with the person's conception of how he or she should behave, then that behaviour is less likely to occur when the person's awareness of Self is high than when his or her self-awareness is low.

This finding leads to the interesting hypothesis that percepts discrepant with
one's self-concept might to some extent be managed—in the sense of making
them less upsetting—by decreasing one's self-awareness during behaviours
producing the discrepant inputs. Such a decrease might, in principle at least, be
accomplished either by certain psychological or pharmacological means. This
strategy would seem to be a fruitful area for empirical research.

8.6.4   Rejecting One Side of a Discrepancy

A mental discrepancy consists of two contradictory positions embedded in the
same statement. If one of these can be denied, or in some manner separated
from the other side so that the two sides do not come into play simultaneously,
then there is no discrepancy and assimilation can proceed straightforwardly.
One often sees attempts at such denial, carried on at a conscious level, not only
in psychotherapy, but also in everyday life. A commonplace example of such a
cognitive manoeuvre would be a man justifying his not giving up smoking on
the grounds that the evidence for its harmful effects is 'only statistical'. This
strategy, when unconscious, is of course very close to, if not indeed identical
with, the psychoanalytic concept of denial. Further, I believe that the paradigm
of unconsciously rejecting one side of a discrepancy may form the basis of
many clinical instances of repression, and may provide an explanation, in part,
of the effectiveness of repression in alleviating anxiety.

8.6.5   Accentuating One Side of a Discrepancy

This strategy is logically more or less the opposite of the approach just
described. By increasing the strength of one side of a mental discrepancy the
degree of conflict between the two poles is made less intense, thus facilitating
assimilation. This manoeuvre, I believe, is more likely to be carried on at a
conscious level, and is generally less effective than denial. Workers in the
cognitive dissonance tradition have sometir es illustrated the accentuation
strategy in the resolution of post-decisional dissonance. For example, a man
planning to purchase a new automobile might find two different cars so evenly
matched in his mind as to have difficulty making a choice between them;
however, once having made a choice he might selectively seek supporting
information (from advertisements, comments by his friends, and so on) that he
had made the correct choice, thus bolstering that side of the discrepancy.

8.6.6   Rationalizations and Delusions

Rationalizations and delusions have in common the fact that both are forms of
cognitive restructuring that reduce or prevent anxiety. Further, both are
generally viewed, by the man in the street as well as by the psychodiagnostician,

as inaccurate perceptions. Finally, both—or in any event, many instances of both—can readily be conceptualized in terms of discrepancy theory. Thus a rationalization (in the sense that this term is typically used in the literature) is a way of unrealistically substituting a mild discrepancy for a more unacceptable one. For example, 'I should go to church today *but* I don't want to', i.e.

$$M^s \wedge A^s \ b \ D^s \vee A^s$$

might become 'I *want* to go to church *but* I can't because I am needed at home' (we assume, for this example, that this is an unrealistic attitude), i.e.

$$D^s \wedge A^s \ b \ M^s \vee A^s$$

There are various forms of delusions, but many, perhaps all, are reinterpretations of reality that resolve a painful discrepancy. For example, a man may have this discrepancy: 'I want people to think I'm important *but* they think I'm worthless', i.e.

$$D^s \wedge \text{At}^{o}_{\underset{s}{+}} \ b \ B^s \wedge \text{At}^{o}_{\underset{s}{-}}$$

By forming the delusional belief, however, that he is secretly being sought for advice by the United Nations, the individual can negate the view that he is unimportant, i.e. 'I want people to think I'm important *and* they do think I am important', i.e.

$$D^s \wedge \text{At}^{o}_{\underset{s}{+}} \ a \ B^s \wedge \text{At}^{o}_{\underset{s}{+}}$$

8.6.7 *Lowering One's Conceptual Standards*

Another way in which assimilation is sometimes facilitated is by a loosening of the standards for assimilation. Formally, assimilation consists of the assignment of given inputs to particular categories in the individual's overall cognitive structure. If the criteria for such assignment become excessively broad or loose, then there is a greater likelihood that an input which would normally not 'fit' now does 'fit', and hence is assimilable (McReynolds, 1960). Assimilation purchased at the cost of lowered assimilation standards would, however, lead to a general scatteredness and looseness of thought. It is evident that this method of facilitating assimilation is not voluntary, and it also seems unlikely that it is unconscious in the ordinary, defensive sense. The process appears to be characteristic of many schizophrenics, and perhaps also is sometimes drug-induced.

8.6.8   Use of Higher-order Schemata

In this method, which is often carried out at a conscious level, the fact of the discrepancy is accepted as part of a higher reality. Such higher-order schemata are often embodied in statements—some of them cultural verities—such as '*C'est la vie*', '*Das ist Schicksal*', 'That's the way it goes', 'A time to live, a time to die', 'Justice does not always triumph', and so on.

A great deal more could be said about special methods for achieving assimilation; however, these remarks will perhaps suffice to show both the complexity and the diversity of assimilative processes. We may be sure that the listing I have presented is not comprehensive, and I suspect that all of the standard defence mechanisms could be reconceptualized in assimilation theoretical terms.

8.7   Concluding Comments

This final section will briefly examine, in a frankly speculative fashion, some of the problems and clinical implications of the overall theoretical conceptualization that has been presented. In particular, I will focus on three areas: possible relations of types of mental discrepancies to diagnostic categories; problems in assessing unconscious mental discrepancies; and implications of the theory for dynamic psychotherapy.

8.7.1   Diagnostic Categories and Mental Discrepancies

An interesting question is whether or not the existence in individuals of particular types of mental discrepancies is associated with particular disorders. The basic rationale for such a possibility would be the assumption that some persons, as a function presumably of early socialization experiences, may develop certain broad but dysfunctional mental discrepancies which affect their entire life-style. Research in this area is in a very early phase, but some suggestive data are available. In cases of schizophrenia there is considerable support for the view that a central paradigm is a fear of being rejected, and, more specifically, a fear, amounting to certainty, of being rejected utterly if one fails in tasks required for acceptance. If this interpretation is valid then schizophrenics might be expected to be motivated, in a general sense and as a matter of life-style, toward the avoidance of failure, and there is considerable evidence (e.g. McReynolds and Guevara, 1967) that this is the case. Now, efforts to avoid failure, if sufficiently general, can lead only to massive withdrawal from all kinds of engagement in life, since the only way to be sure of not failing is not to participate. Such withdrawal behaviour is, of course, highly characteristic of schizophrenia, and may in turn have a variety of other symptomatic effects (McReynolds, 1960, 1968).

The underlying mental discrepancy for the behaviour I have just characterized might be phrased, in a general way, along this line: 'I wish to participate in life, but if I should do so and fail, the result would be catastrophic', with the latter proposition being dominant.

It seems possible—and I am being very speculative at this point—that the depressive, while like the schizophrenic in fearing rejection, in addition feels that he will be rejected if he does not succeed in meeting certain internalized, but unrealistic, standards. Hence withdrawal from the fray—which can prevent failure but cannot guarantee success—is not a viable option for the depressive, as it is for the person who becomes schizophrenic.

Classical psychoanalytic theory (Fenichel, 1946) has posited certain underlying conflicts, in accord with libidinal stages, for various disorders, and, though I will not attempt to do so here, I believe it would be possible, and possibly enlightening, to restate certain of these psychoanalytic propositions in terms of the present model.

In this connection, I am indebted to the first Editor for calling my attention to certain interesting interfaces between my conceptualization and that of psychoanalytic object-relations theory, as developed by Fairbairn. As Cheshire and Thomae point out in Chapter 4, Fairbairn (1952, esp. pp. 38–51) proposed a 'revised psychopathology' of the neuroses and psychoses, based on the particular object-relational conflicts which he posited to underlie them. Thus, his conception of the schizophrenic's basic mental discrepancy, when translated into the present terms, amounts to 'I want to love this object (e.g. the mother), but I fear that my love will destroy her' (by oral incorporation). The corresponding discrepancy for the depressive, transposed from Fairbairn's analysis, would be 'I love this object (e.g. the frustrating mother), but I feel guilty about destroying her by my hate'.

It is of course extremely difficult to rigorously track down the core intrapsychic conflicts in the various disorders, if indeed there are underlying patterns, but it is an important quest, and one which hopefully will be aided by the taxonomic system proposed above.

8.7.2 Unconscious Mental Discrepancies

It has been assumed, in much of the foregoing discussion, that mental discrepancies may exist at an unconscious, as well as at a conscious, level. The validity of this assumption, in a general sense, is obvious from the accumulated experiences of dynamic psychotherapists, though specific confirmation of the position, in the context of the present mental discrepancy taxonomy, remains to be obtained.

At a theoretical level, it seems evident that mental discrepancies occur in complex ways. In some cases, it appears, both sides of a discrepancy are conscious; in some instances, both sides are unconscious; and in other cases, one side is conscious and the remaining side unconscious. Further, on some occasions the manifest (conscious) content may mask an underlying unconscious mental discrepancy, by substituting a more acceptable proposition for an unacceptable one. For the following example of this process I am grateful to my psychoanalyst colleague J. Sandler. The manifest content of a man's mental discrepancy might be, 'I want to love my father, but he does not let me', with the more basic, but partially unconscious discrepancy being 'I want to love my father, but I am afraid this would be a homosexual submission to him'. Note that this transformation is an example of a rationalizing assimilation strategy, as discussed earlier.

Though empirical research has not yet been conducted on the question, it is plausible to suppose that mental discrepancies may appear in dreams, though only infrequently in undisguised form or in explicit 'but' terms. Further, I would hypothesize that dream content may sometimes reveal the particular assimilation strategies that an individual typically employs. It should not be supposed, however, that the majority of dream content reflects a person's inner conflicts. From the perspective of assimilation theory the contents of dreams are determined by two main factors: first, there would be a tendency for unassimilated material to appear in dreams; and second, there would be a tendency for the avoidance in manifest dream content of highly incongruent, i.e. anxiety-provoking, areas. These speculations are not particularly innovative, but some limited empirical data can be presented (McReynolds *et al.*, 1966). Thirty male college students kept dream diaries for three weeks, and the contents of their recalled dreams were compared with test measures of the magnitude of unassimilated material and the degree of overall incongruency in sex and hostility. The results supported the predictions to a statistically significant degree; however, most of the variance was unaccounted for, indicating that other factors, such as the influence of day residue, were primarily responsible for dream content. The study of dream content in assimilation theory terms remains a fertile field for further investigation.

The elicitation and identification of unconscious mental discrepancies remains a difficult problem. Research by White (1982) indicates that normal individuals have little difficulty in articulating inner conflicts that deeply concern them, and even in rephrasing these in 'but' terms; but of course these conflicts are by definition not unconscious. The most common method of identifying unconscious conflicts is through the insightful observations and follow-up verifications of psychotherapists. Obviously, however, additional supplementary and independent methods are highly desirable. Projective tests provide one such possibility; in particular it might be possible to develop a modified sentence completion test, along the paradigm of 'I want _____but_____' or 'My mother_____but_____,' that would suggest certain unconscious conflicts. Clearly, this is an important area for additional research.

I should add that despite the emphasis in these comments on the significance of conscious mental discrepancies, it would be a grave mistake to assume that discrepancies at the conscious level are necessarily unimportant and superficial. Not only may consciously stated discrepancies represent important real-life conflicts, but it is also the case that deeper lying discrepancies typically become conscious in the transition to being resolved.

8.7.3 Assimilation Theory and Psychotherapy

The first implication of the present model for psychotherapy is that there is a distinction between cognitive anxiety and conditioned anxiety, as elaborated earlier, and that treatment of these two types requires different therapeutic approaches. However, I will limit my present remarks to problems concerning the former of these. A major function of the therapeutic process, according to the present perspective, is to help the patient to identify and work through the crucial mental discrepancies that are blocking assimilation. Except for its terminology, this position is not particularly original; yet, such an explicit orientation may help the therapist to become more sensitive to the existence of key discrepancies. Further, the rephrasing of internal conflicts in mental discrepancy terms, by the patient, may itself be therapeutic, in the sense of helping the patient to identify and clarify certain core problems.

In some instances the working through of a mental discrepancy might take the form of the patient coming to accept it, perhaps by assigning it to a higher-order category, as described earlier. In other instances the therapeutic process might consist of helping the patient to reformulate and reconceptualize those areas of experience covered by the discrepancy, such that the discrepancy no longer exists. As already noted, many key discrepancies are unconscious, at least on one side, and can be located only with prolonged exploration. Further, it appears that mental discrepancies are often organized in hierarchical, interdependent networks, with the characteristic that a change in one discrepancy will necessarily produce changes in others. It may thus happen that a patient will try one solution after another for a given discrepancy, only to find that each solution to one discrepancy opens up a different problem.

For example, consider a woman who has the problem that 'I want to be independent and popular but I feel that if I am independent I will not be popular'.

$$\overline{D^s \wedge Q^s \wedge At^o_+}_s \quad b \quad \overline{B^s \wedge Q^s} \longrightarrow \vee A^o_{+_s}$$

The conflict here is between the desire to have both independence and popularity and the belief that they are incompatible, and the discrepant element is the presence or lack of popularity. The woman, because of her intense desire to be popular, might endeavour to resolve the discrepancy by giving up her desire to be independent, but this would only lead to frustration and subsequent intensification of the desire for independence, and this process might in turn result in a re-examination of the desire for popularity. Thus the whole problem might alternate from one unsuccessful attempted solution to another until, and unless, a more basic solution—possibly that of not seeing popularity and independence as mutually exclusive—was worked out. It may be pointed out in this connection that the natural tendency of a person, faced with a disturbing inner conflict, is to try to 'solve' it by eating his cake and having it too, i.e. by satisfying both sides of the discrepancy. Unfortunately, this is rarely possible, since if it were the conflict would probably not have attained its intensity in the first place.

I will conclude by briefly summarizing what I have tried to do in this chapter. I began by examining the concept of the Self. In this analysis I concluded that it is meaningful and important to distinguish between the perceived self and the executive self. I then summarized the basic model of assimilation theory, and applied this model to the analysis of anxiety. Two kinds of anxiety—cognitive anxiety and conditioned anxiety—were distinguished, and a detailed analysis of cognitive anxiety was undertaken. The role of mental discrepancies, in particular discrepancies involving the Self, was highlighted, and preliminary data on a method for coding mental discrepancies were presented.

References

Abelson, R., Aronson, E., McGuire, W., Newcomb, T., Rosenberg, M. and Tannenbaum, P. (eds) (1968). *Theories of Cognitive Consistency*, Rand McNally, Chicago.

Abelson, R. P. and Rosenberg, M. J. (1958). Symbolic psychologic: a model of attitudinal cognition. *Behav. Sci.* **3** 1–13.

Allport, S. (1961). *Pattern and Growth in Personality*. Holt, Rinehart and Winston, New York.

Baldo, R (1986). *A Study of Cognitive and Conditioned Anxiety as Measured by the Personal Anxiety Survey*. Unpublished doctoral dissertation, University of Nevada-Reno, Reno (Nev.).

Bandura, A. (1977). Self-efficacy: toward a unifying theory of behavioral change. *Psychol. Rev.* **84**, 191–215.

Beck, A. T. (1976). *Cognitive Therapy and the Emotional Disorders*. International Universities Press, New York.

Becker, E. (1971). *The Birth and Death of Meaning*. Free Press, New York.

Bentler, L. E. (1979). Toward specific psychological therapies for specific conditions. *J. Consult. Clin. Psychol.* **47**, 882–897.

Bergin, A. E. and Suinn, R. M. (1975). Individual psychotherapy and behavior therapy. In *Annual Review of Psychology*, vol. 26 (eds M. R. Rosenzweig and L. W. Porter), pp. 509–556. Annual Reviews, Inc., Palo Alto (Calif.).

Burger, J. M. (1985). Desire for control and achievement-related behaviors. *J. Personal. Soc. Psychol.* **48**, 1520–1533.

Burger, J. M. and Cooper, H. M. (1979). The desirability of control. *Motiv. Emotion*, **3**, 381–393.

Butler, J. M. and Haight, G. V. (1954). Changes in the relation between self-concepts and ideal concepts consequent upon client-centered counseling. In *Psychotherapy and Personality Change* (eds C. R. Rogers and R. F. Dymond), pp. 55–75: University of Chicago Press, Chicago.

Byrne, D., Terrill, J. and McReynolds, P. (1961). Incongruency as a predictor of response to humor. *J. Abnorm. Psychol.*, **62** (2), 435–438.

Chodorkoff, B. (1954). Self-perception, perceptual defense, and adjustment. *J. Abnorm. Soc. Psychol.* **49**, 508–512.

Christensen, J. (1981). Assessment of stress: environmental, intrapersonal, and outcome issues. In *Advances in Psychological Assessment*, vol. 5 (ed. P. McReynolds), pp. 62–123. Jossey-Bass, San Francisco.

Coopersmith, S. (1967). *The Antecedents of Self-esteem*. Freeman, San Francisco.

DeCharms, R. (1968). *Personal Causation*. Academic Press, New York.

Demo, D. H. (1985). The measurement of self-esteem: refining our methods. *J. Personal. Soc. Psychol.*, **48**, 1490–1502.

Dollard, J. and Miller, N. E. (1950). *Personality and Psychotherapy* McGraw-Hill, New York.

Duvall, S. and Wicklund, R. A. (1972). *A Theory of Objective Self-awareness*. Academic Press, New York.

Epstein, S. (1980). The self-concept: a review and the proposal of an integrated theory of personality. In *Personality: Basic Aspects and Current Research* (ed. E. Staub). Prentice-Hall, Englewood Cliffs (NJ).

Eyman, J. (1984). *The Relationship between Anxiety and Coping among Alcoholic and Non-alcoholic Subjects*. Unpublished doctoral dissertation, University of Nevada-Reno, Reno (Nev.)

Fairbairn, W. R. D. (1952). A revised psychopathology of the psychoses . . . In *Psychoanalytic Studies of the Personality*, pp. 28–58 Tavistock, London, (Published as *An Object-relations Theory of the Personality*, Basic Books, New York, 1954.).

Fenichel, O. (1946). *The Psychoanalytic Theory of Neurosis*. Norton, New York.

Feshbach, S. and Weiner, B. (1982). *Personality*. D. C. Heath, Lexington (Mass.).

Festinger, L. (1957). *A Theory of Cognitive Dissonance*. Row, Peterson, Evanston (Ill.).

Goldman, A. I. (1970). *A Theory of Human Action*. Prentice-Hall, Englewood Cliffs (NJ).

Hampshire, S. (1959). *Thought and Action*. Viking, New York.

Hareé, R. and Secord, P. F. (1972). *The Explanation of Social Behavior*. Blackwell, Oxford.

Heider, F. (1958). *The Psychology of Interpersonal Relations*. Wiley, New York.

Honess, T. (1982). Accounting for oneself: meanings of self-descriptions, and inconsistencies in self-descriptions. *Brit. J. Med. Psychol.*, **44**, 41–52.

Horowitz, M. J. (1979). *States of Mind: Analysis of Change in Psychotherapy*. Plenum, New York.

Jacobson, E. (1964). *The Self and the Object World*. International Universities Press, New York.

Kagan, J., Hans, S., Markowitz, A., Lopez, D. and Sigal, H. (1982). Validity of children's self-reports of psychological qualities. In *Progress in Experimental Personality Research*, vol. 11 (eds B. Mahler and W. Mahler). Academic Press, New York.

Kelly, G. (1955). *The Psychology of Personal Constructs*, vol. 1. Norton, New York.

Kohut, H. (1971). *Analysis of the Self*. International Universities Press, New York.

Kohut, H. (1977). *The Restoration of the Self*. International Universities Press, New York.

222   *Self, Symptoms and Psychotherapy*

Lauterbach, W. (1975). Assessing psychological conflict. *Brit. J. Soc. Clin. Psychol.*, **14**, 43–47.
Lecky, P. (1945). *Self-consistency: A Theory of Personality*. Island Press, New York.
Levenson, H. (1981). Differentiating among internality, powerful others and chance. In *Research with the Locus of Control Construct* (ed. H. Lefcourt). Academic Press, New York.
Mahler, M., Pine, F. and Bergman, A. (1975). *The Psychological Birth of the Human Infant*. Basic Books, New York.
Manicas, P. T. and Secord, P. F. (1983). Implications for psychology of the new philosophy of science. *Am. Psychol.*, **38**, 397–413.
McReynolds, P. (1956). A restricted conceptualization of human anxiety and motivation. *Psychol. Rep.* **2** (monogr. suppl. 6), 293–312.
McReynolds, P. (1958). Anxiety as related to incongruencies between values and feelings. *Psychol. Rec.* **8**, 57–66.
McReynolds, P. (1960). Anxiety, perception, and schizophrenia. In *The Etiology of Schizophrenia* (ed. D. Jackson), pp. 248–292. Basic Books, New York.
McReynolds, P. (1968). The motives to attain success and to avoid failure: historical note. *J. Individ. Psychol.* **24**, 157–161.
McReynolds, P. (1971). The three faces of intrinsic motivation. In *Intrinsic Motivation: A New Direction in Education* (eds H. I. Day, D. E. Berlyne and D. E. Hunt), pp. 33–45. Winston, Minneapolis (Minn.).
McReynolds, P. (1972). Individual differences in self-regulatory behavior. Paper presented at La Jolla Conference on Self-regulation, La Jolla, California, February 1972.
McReynolds, P. (1976). Assimilation and anxiety. In *New Concepts, Methods, and Applications* (eds M. Zuckerman and C. D. Spielberger), pp. 35–86. Erlbaum, Hillsdale (NJ).
McReynolds, P. (in press a). Toward a general theory of anxiety. In *Stress and Anxiety*, vol. 12, (eds C. D. Spielberger and J. Strelau). Hemisphere/McGraw-Hill International, New York.
McReynolds, P. (in press b). Motives and metaphors: a case study in scientific creativity. In *Metaphors in the History of Psychology* (ed. D. Leary).
McReynolds, P. and Guevara, C. (1967). Attitudes of schizophrenics and normals toward success and failure. *J. Abnorm. Psychol.*, **72**, 303–310.
McReynolds, P., Landes, J. and Acker, M. (1966). Dream content as a function of personality, incongruency and unsettledness. *J. Gen. Psychol.*, **74**, 313–317.
McReynolds, P., Eyman, J. and White, P. (1985). An instrument for differentiating cognitive anxiety and conditioned anxiety. Paper presented at Annual Meeting, Society for Personality Assessment, Berkeley, California, March 1985.
Mead, G. H. (1934). *Mind, Self and Society*. University of Chicago Press, Chicago.
Miller, G. A., Galanter, E. and Pribram, K. H. (1960). *Plans and the Structure of Behavior*. Henry Holt, New York.
Mischel, T. (1969). Scientific and philosophical psychology: a historical introduction. In *Human Action* (ed. T. Mischel), pp. 1–40. Academic Press, New York.
Peer, A. (1975). *A Naturalistic Study of the Assimilation Process in Psychotherapy*. Unpublished Ph.D. Dissertation, University of Nevada-Reno, Reno (Nev.).
Perlmuter, L. C. and Monty, R. A. (eds) (1979). *Choice and Perceived Control*. Erlbaum, Hillsdale (NJ).
Pither, B. (1974). *Locus of Control and Personal Incongruities in Gestalt Therapy*. Unpublished M.A. Thesis, University of Nevada-Reno, Reno (Nev.).
Raimy, R. (1975). *Misunderstandings of the Self*. Jossey-Bass, San Francisco.

Rogers, C. (1959). A theory of therapy, personality, and interpersonal relationships, as developed in the client-centered framework. In *Psychology: A study of a Science*, vol. 3 (ed. S. Koch), pp. 184–256. McGraw-Hill, New York.

Rokeach, M. (1973). *The Nature of Human Values*. Free Press, New York.

Rosenberg, M. (1979). *Conceiving the Self*. Basic Books, New York.

Rotter, J. B. (1966). Generalized expectancies for internal versus external control of reinforcement. *Psychol. Monogr.*, **80** (1) (whole No. 609).

Slade, P. D. and Sheehan, M. J. (1979). The measurement of conflict in repertory grids. *Brit. J. Psychol.*, **70**, 519–524.

Strupp, H. H. and Bergin, A. E. (1969). Some empirical and conceptual bases for coordinating research in psychotherapy. *Int. J. Psychol.*, **7**, 19–90.

Strupp, H. H. and Binder, J. L. (1984). *Psychotherapy in a New Key: A Guide to Time-limited Dynamic Psychotherapy*. Basic Books, New York.

Sullivan, H. S. (1953). *The Interpersonal Theory of Psychiatry*. Norton, New York.

Taylor, C. (1964). *The Explanation of Behavior*. Humanities Press, New York.

Taylor, C. (1970). The explanation of purposive behavior. In *Explanation in the Behavioral Sciences* (eds R. Borger and F. Cioffi) pp. 49–79. Cambridge University Press, Cambridge.

Vrooman, J. R. (1970). *René Descartes: A Biography*. New York: G. P. Putnam's Sons.

Wells, L. E. and Marwell, G. (1976). *Self-esteem: Its Conception and Measurement*. Sage, Beverly Hills (Calif.).

White, P. (1981). The differentiation of career choice anxiety and test anxiety. Unpublished paper, Department of Psychology, University of Nevada-Reno, Reno (Nev.).

White, P. (1982). *A Study of Cognitive Anxiety and Mental Conflicts*. Unpublished doctoral dissertation, University of Nevada-Reno, Reno (Nev.).

White, R. W. (1959). Motivation reconsidered: The concept of competence. *Psychol. Rev.*, **66**, 297–333.

Wylie, R. C. (1974, 1979). *The Self-Concept*. 2 vols., second edition. University of Nebraska Press, Lincoln and London.

Wolpé, J. (1958). *Psychotherapy by Reciprocal Inhibition*. Stanford University Press, Stanford (Calif.).

Self, Symptoms and Psychotherapy
Edited by N. Cheshire and H. Thomae
© 1987 John Wiley & Sons Ltd

CHAPTER 9

Patients Report on Changes in Self-concept: A Study from the Heidelberg Follow-up Project

Angelika Zitzelsberger and Hans Kordy

In this chapter we present and discuss the results of an empirical study which was carried out in the context of the Heidelberg Follow-up Project. The effects of psychoanalytically orientated psychotherapy, and of long-term psychoanalytic treatment, are dealt with and examined with reference to various criteria. These criteria are set out according to different points of view: for instance, whether they derive from the addressee or from an informant; or whether the data are 'hard' as opposed to 'soft', or are graded according to the measurement-strategy which has been applied (Kordy and Scheibler, 1984).

9.1   Who Assesses Therapy-outcomes?

It is generally agreed that the results of treatment are very complex, and that a multiplicity of criteria are necessary in order to grasp them all. The question should not be asked, therefore, whether it is the therapist or the patient who is best able to judge the result of the treatment, since they each judge the result from their own point of view, and both judgements should be heard.

The assessment of therapy-results depends upon the person who is making the estimation, and upon what his/her perspective is. In this context, Strupp and Hadley (1977) have presented a tripartite model in which society, experts (mental health professionals) *and* the patients feature as judges (cp. Strupp, 1980). Statements from patients in particular are often subject to the criticism that an outsider is more capable of judging, in the most objective way, the results of therapy. However, instead of examining the 'truth' of the possibly different estimations which are given (because of the different perspectives involved), it seems to make more sense to ask, What are the relevant values of the person who is going to have something evaluated?

When patients report on their experiences in psychotherapy, very often they will speak of changes in their 'self'; and this may turn up under various guises such as 'self-image', 'self-esteem' or 'self-confidence', etc. (Strupp *et al.*, 1969; Grawe, 1978; Luborsky *et al.*, 1980; Sloane *et al.*, 1975; Plog, 1976; Mollon and Parry, 1984). We understand that in a study by Strupp *et al.* (1964) more than half the patients (58%) reported an improvement in this area (namely a growth in self-confidence, self-reliance, self-respect and self-esteem), and that this occurred in spite of the fact that only 17% of all patients had initially been disturbed by negative self-assessments.

But it is particularly difficult to deal with patients' statements regarding self-esteem or changes therein, since individual points of reference can be different. Besides the type of person who is always in doubt about himself, we have the contrasting type who ignores everything coming from outside, as Cheshire and Thomae have noted at the end of Chapter 1. The task of defining such a global term as 'self-esteem' can be compared with that of explicating the term 'physical health', and this makes it difficult to classify corresponding statements from patients. It does not necessarily follow from this, however, that such basic goals of psychoanalysis as self-value, self-esteem and individuation, because of the vague formulation of their content, are not taken into consideration in researching and evaluating therapeutic results. On the other hand, treatment goals (or at least some conception of such goals) are brought into the therapy in an implicit or explicit way also by the therapist, and the subject of 'self' will make a prominent showing in this way (Braeutigam *et al.*, 1980; Strupp and Hadley, 1979; Reiter and Steiner, 1978).

9.2   Statements about Changes in the 'Self' from Retrospective Patient Reports

For the purpose of discussing the questionnaires which we referred to at the beginning, it is important to make clear that in these interviews all patients have made an assessment of their progress during psychotherapy and have indicated a feeling of happiness and self-esteem as a result. Furthermore, we learn about the spheres of life which the patients at the end of the therapy regard as essential, as well as about the perceived idiosyncrasies which, generally speaking, go to make up individual identity (cp. Thomae, 1980). We also hear about the patients' feelings in connection with the discovery and realization of various facets of their personalities.

In order to analyse our material, we had first to find a general system for patients' reports which would allow us to compare the complex statements regarding changes in their self-assessment in such a way that space is left for individual variety and interindividual variations to be represented. Patients' reports can mainly be represented by the three sentences in Figure 1: the first sentence (a) refers to experiences in which the patients see themselves as having different degrees of efficacy; in the second sentence (b), we can see the self-confidence of the patients in relation to these experiences; while the third sentence (c) reflects the importance of social resonances for the corresponding assessment.

The first facet (i) consists of four fields of experience in which can be ranged the aspects of personality considered to be of importance by the patients. Field 1, '*intrapsychic*', contains discoveries within the inner reality. This comprises a larger spectrum of feelings: for instance, the experience of sadness and low spirits in cases where previously it was depression; feelings of aggression, irritation, devotion and sympathy; a more differentiated observation of oneself and others; the capacity for imagination and dreaming; particular active and strong sides of one's personality; increased consciousness of problems, a deeper understanding of relationships in one's own life story.

In field 2, '*interpersonal*' experience, we see what patients consider to be of importance regarding their own competence within the social area. Here it is a question of being able to take one's own place, to hold one's own, to define oneself; the ability to regulate nearness and distance, to cope with conflicts and problems, to endure tensions. Field 3, '*work*', consists of statements on working ability and achievements, on happiness about one's own professional abilities or one's ability to study. Field 4 '*body*', comprises statements on the attitude to one's own body, to physical health or illness, and on the ability to experience one's own body, especially in sexuality.

In the second facet (ii) we take up the patients' evaluations of their experienced efficacy as individual agents (in effect, Bandura's (1982) 'self-efficacy' which we have encountered in earlier chapters), and the expression of this differs according to the various fields of experience. With regard to the intrapsychic domain, 'sufficiently effective' (alternative 1) means experience of an inner reality, a door to mental experience. For fields 2 and 4, this means taking an active part, having influence and experience, and the intention to be effective. Alternative 2 is used for patients who describe themselves as less effective in this sense. The question as to the personal valuation of these experiences concerning self-esteem is crucial (iii), since it is entirely possible, for example, to construe oneself (in Kelly's terms) as 'ineffective' rather than 'effective' but not to be distressed about it because one construes efficacy itself

Figure 1:   Schema for classification of **Self-Reports**

(i) Field of experience

(a) For my attitude towards myself, it is
important that I . . .

1   intrapsychic
2   interpersonal
3   work
4   body

(ii) Effect

1   am sufficiently feeling and lively/or
    sufficiently effective
2   do not feel and live enough, or am not
    effective enough

(iii) Evaluation

(b) Consequently, I experience in this field a self-feeling/self-assess-
ment which is:

1   rather confident and satisfied
2   rather uncertain and dissatisfied
0   not really influenced

(iv) Social resonance

(c) I experience:

1   a rather encouraging attitude from others
2   a rather rejecting attitude from others
0   no evaluation from others

. . . and this
has on my
self-esteem:

1   a rather definite influence
2   a rather encouraging influence
0   no perceptible influence

as 'unimportant' rather than 'important' (cp. Chapter 7). For presentation of the patients' statements, it is sufficient to make a rough categorization into (1) a rather confident and satisfied feeling, (2) rather unconfident and dissatisfied, and (0) no specific feeling. In connection with the related sense of efficacy, many patients bring up the question of social valuation with its consequences for self-esteem. This question is covered by the alternatives set out in facets (iv) and (v).

A concrete example of protocol-evaluation by means of this system will illustrate these points. The patient R. relates that in therapy she found a way to herself. Previously she had taken on a comic role; she was as fit as a fiddle and always active. Today she is able to allow herself feelings of sadness as well as her occasional dejections; she can relax and has become more calm and thoughtful. 'Today I laugh when I feel like it,' she says, 'not because I'm somebody's clown.' Her mother is most worried about this change and cannot recognize her, but she herself is not disturbed by it: on the contrary, 'Now I am myself, I accept myself, I feel much better'. The valuation of this protocol through all its facets reads: 1 1 1 2 1.

The results of 22 protocol evaluations are shown in Table 1. All patients consider at least two fields of experience to be of importance, and sometimes even three or four, which explains the great frequency of statements. The fields of experience 1 (intrapsychic) and experience 2 (interpersonal) play an important part in the personal experience of most of the patients: they are mentioned by 21 and by all 22 patients, respectively. Fields 3 and 4 (work and body) turn up rather seldom; they are dealt with by only seven and six patients, respectively.

Of the 22 patients who stress the 'interpersonal' field, six specifically mention their experiences in their relationship with their partner from the general valuation; and five of these regard themselves as effective enough within the general social domain, but not with regard to their relations with their partner. With the sixth patient, it is the other way round. When looking at estimated efficacy, we can see that in the 'intrapsychic' field, all 21 patients who mentioned it reported that they experienced a sense of efficacy (i.e. they have access to their inner reality and are able to experience it).

For the interpersonal field, this applies only in a limited way: although the statements claiming sufficient efficacy are clearly more frequent (71%), an important number of the efficacy-statements (28%) give a feeling of insufficient effectiveness, and they refer mainly to the above-mentioned statements in the field of partner-relationship. At this point, one could ask whether in making these observations there might be a therapeutic learning-effect which places the inner mental experience of the patient at the centre of the conversation, while social reality (with its references to action, and its possible deficiencies of behaviour) plays a lesser part but is also treated in its intrapsychic representation. The following pattern seems to us to be essential: regardless of the field

Table 1.   Frequency of statements on 'effect' and 'evaluation'

(i) Field of experience		(ii) Effect		(iii) Evaluation	
Category	Quantity	Category	Quantity	Category	Quantity
1. Intrapsychic	21	Sufficiently effective	21	Satisfied	18
				Dissatisfied	3
2. Interpersonal	22	Sufficiently effective	19 (+1)	Satisfied	17 (+1)
				Dissatisfied	2
(+ partnership)	(+6)	Insufficiently effective	3 (+5)	Satisfied	—
				Dissatisfied	3 (+5)
3. Work	7	Sufficiently effective	6	Satisfied	3
				Dissatisfied	2
				(0)	1
		Insufficiently effective	1	Satisfied	—
				Dissatisfied	1
4. Body	6	Sufficiently effective	4	Satisfied	3
				Dissatisfied	1
		Insufficiently effective	2	Satisfied	—
				Dissatisfied	2

of experience, an experience of adequate efficacy seems to be sufficient for satisfactory self-esteem (about 90%) with very few exceptions. This statement applies even more to the opposite case: in all statements of an experience of ineffectiveness, irrespective of the domain, insecure and dissatisfied self-esteem is reported.

With reference to 'social resonance', we wish finally to look at the connection which patients see between their reaction to surroundings and their self-esteem (Table 2). When looking at the statements in Table 2, we think it remarkable that, for both 'satisfactory' and 'dissatisfied' self-esteem, the experience of social resonance is not mentioned at all in half the cases. Another finding shows that positive self-esteem seems to be more stable in relation to negative social resonance; with positive self-esteem, a negative social resonance is stated in only 26% of the cases; with negative self-esteem, it is 42%. One has to stress the fact that for unsatisfactory self-esteem this negative social resonance has a clear effect, while it has almost no effect on positive self-esteem but can even have a facilitating influence.

Table 2. Frequency of statements on 'social resonance' and 'consequence'

(iii) Evaluation		(iv) Social resonance		(v) Consequences	
Category	Quantity	Category	Quantity	Category	Quantity
1. Rather confident and satisfied	41 (+1)	Positive	11	1. Effective 0.	10 1
		Negative	11	1. Effective 2. Influenced 0.	5 4 2
		None	19 (+1)	0.	19 (+1)
2. Rather uncertain and dissatisfied	14 (+5)	Positive Negative None	1 5 (+3) 8 (+2)	1. Effective 2. Influenced 0.	1 5 (+3) 8 (+2)

9.3 Therapists' Treatment Goals in Self-esteem Problems

In the Heidelberg Follow-up Project (Engel *et al.*, 1979), a modified form of *goal-attainment scaling* (Kordy and Scheibler, 1984) is used. At the beginning of each treatment, the treating therapist works out from three to five individual treatment goals (the so-called 'follow-up questions') for each patient. The basis for this is found in the complaints presented by the patient. For each chosen individual field of problems, the therapist gives five alternative results, which are ranged in a five-step scale from 'worsened' to 'optimum improvement', with alternative 2 ('unchanged') corresponding to a description of the *status quo*.

For our purpose, the following questions have to be answered:

1. How often do problems of self-esteem turn up as *declared* treatment goals?
2. What specific content do they have?
3. Which (optimum) goals are the therapists setting for this field of problems, and what is the relationship between the developments intended by the therapist and the statements of the patients?

9.3.1 Frequency of Self-esteem Problems as Treatment Goals

The data-base is the follow-up questionnaires (FQ) for $N = 207$ patients, and all these data have been checked and classified by an experienced clinician (Dipl. Psych. Buerckstuemmer, to whom we express our thanks). For 24% ($N = 50$), a self-esteem problem was diagnosed and a corresponding treatment goal was stated (Table 3). Although in this case we have a sample other than that for the retrospective reports discussed at the outset, we also take notice of

Table 3.   Frequency of treatment goals (FQ) concerning self-esteem problems

		Number of FQ	Percentage of patients with FQ as to self-esteem
A. Relative to different forms of therapy			
Individual out-patient	Psychoanalysis	25	32
	Dynamic psychotherapy	22	36
	Therapy by students	21	33
	In-patient individual psychotherapy	10	30
In-patient	Combined group– individual therapy	61	23
	Group psychotherapy	63	16
Individual psychotherapy (total)		78	33
Total patients		207	24
B. Relative to sex of patient			
Women		131	28
Men		76	17
Women, except group patients		88	32
Men, except group patients		51	24
Total patients		207	24

the observation of Strupp *et al.* (1964), to the effect that far more patients report changes in the field of self-esteem disturbances than originally started treatment for a corresponding problem. As to the questions of treatment-indication, it is interesting to observe that, among individual therapies, a self-esteem problem was stated as treatment goal for a greater number of patients than among the (partly in-patient) group-therapies (33% vs. 16%), while there is hardly any difference between the proportions for the various individual therapies offered in the clinic (for an overview of the therapeutic settings see Engel *et al.*, 1979). In this connection, we note also that the combined group/individual therapy shows a value in the middle (23%). In our data at least, there is also a slight dependence on the patient's sex (see Figures 3A/3B).

9.3.2   Contents of Follow-up Questionnaires (FQ) in the Case of Self-esteem Problems

As with the analysis of the retrospective patient reports, the necessity arises of finding a *general* system of reference in which the many *individually* formulated

'FQ' can be illustrated. What we did in practice here corresponds to the description in section 9.2, and is related to Guttman's facet-approach (Borg, 1977). Based on the formulated FQ, we have sorted these reports 'intuitively', which does not mean 'free from theory' (at least not free from implicit subjective theories), according to content-similarity. We then gave the graded collection, coded according to the abstract structure of Figure 2, as a system-reference. We shall not go further into the system as a scheme of classification, but the explanation and examples given in Figure 3 can be regarded as illustrating how it functions. The system of reference is structured in a similar way to the one for the retrospective study. Here also 'evaluation' and 'field of experience' turn up as structural components; but 'social resonance' now appears only indirectly under 'attribution', and the aspect of 'effect' is not mentioned in the FQ.

Here we shall confine ourselves to describing the observations made on the facet 'field of experience'. Just as with the patients' own reports, therapists seldom (8%) refer to the connection between self-esteem and a physical limitation in the case of patients with self-esteem problems. Moreover, the experience in relation to the feeling of being attractive or unattractive to others (field of experience 3) is not often mentioned by therapists (18%). This leads to the hypothesis that self-esteem problems are considered by therapists to be relatively independent of real external conditions and experiences. If one also takes into consideration that our patients' reports make reference only very rarely to social or occupational realities, then there is a remarkable consensus. This hypothesis does not contradict the observation that the field of 'achievement' is mentioned quite frequently: by itself in 24% of the cases, and combined with other fields of experience in a further 24%. Not once is the individual self-esteem problem described as an expression of failure in achievement, or of any other kind of failure.

All this points to the fact that therapists see these special problems of patients rather as disturbed levels of subjective evaluation, and that concrete experiences are scarcely taken into account. In terms of the 'self-esteem equation' of William James, which Cheshire and Thomae discuss in Chapter 1, the therapists are mostly concentrating their attention on the denominator (i.e. the 'pretensions'), and the same tendency is clear in their conclusions.

9.3.3 Treatment Goals in Relation to Patients' Reports

In formulating optimal treatment results for patients with problems of self-esteem, therapists express a health-ideal. The development towards such an ideal is outlined implicitly in the scale which is represented in the FQ. For the facet 'evaluation', the ideal is obvious: here it is expected that after therapy the patient will be sure of his worth and will feel well (in a sense abstracted from individual nuances of description). This is to be achieved by:

Figure 2: Schema for Classification of Treatment Goals (FQ) Concerning Self-Esteem

In my self-valuation. I feel:

E: Evaluation

1 unsure
2 inferior
3 well

with reference to

F: Fields of experience

1 non-specific or general
2 body or physical influence
3 attractiveness
4 ability/efficacy

1 with
2 without
} participation of others

A: Attribution

1 because I'm too dependent on others' judgement
2 this is because of *myself*, i.e. because I demand too much of myself
3 can't decide between 1 and 2

(a) eliminating dependency on the judgement of others in favour of a secure evaluation by the patient himself; or

(b) giving up the habit of setting oneself high standards, and thus being able to see 'realistically' the 'gap' between one's ideal and one's personal limits without detriment to self-esteem.

Figure 3.   Explanations and examples for Figure 2

(F) *Fields of experience*
    (a) fields:
    1 is chosen when the field of experience on which the evaluation is based is not specified
    3 in the sense of: being attractive, wanted; others are looking for contact, etc.
    4 in the sense of: ability as characteristic of the person; or efficacy in various areas or functions (e.g. occupation, family...)

    (b) Participation of others:
    1 for the experience mentioned, the participation of others is essential: e.g. (a) towards others, (b) for others, (c) compared with others, or in competition with others
    2 for the experience mentioned, the participation of others plays no part or a minor part

(A) *Attribution*
    Here we code for the nature of the subjective 'causes' upon which the evaluation of the experience is based. A distinction is made only between the categories:
    1 dependence on the judgement of others
    2 lack of, or disturbance in, own estimation of self-value

Examples of coding

| FQ (possible answer): | 'I am very dependent on the judgement of others with regard to my achievements, to the extent of telling lies about them.' |
| Classification: | 1 4 1 1 |

| FQ (possible answer) | 'I must achieve and do what is expected of me: then I can succeed in my own eyes and others'. But can I manage to do this?' |
| Classification: | 1 4 1 3 |

| FQ (possible answer) | 'I feel very small; I've no self-confidence; I think I am very ugly.' |
| Classification: | 2 3 2 2 |

The view of therapy which is reflected in treatment goals for patients with problems in self-esteem consequently seems to be that it should lead to a secure, independent, and global judgement of one's own worth. The global judgement is here seen as a general judgement, based on the totality of the patient's experiences. In this case, the ideal evaluation should as far as possible be independent of actual successes and failures, and of actual acknowledgement by others. This does not preclude individuals, who come close to the ideal, from being able to specify certain positive or negative experiences when 'balancing the books', or when questioned. We saw in section 9.2 above that this is what they actually do, and we may draw parallels here both with Epstein's 'cognitive balance' theory (Chapter 2) and with McReynolds' work on intrapsychic conflict-resolution (Chapter 8). In this sense, patients' reports about changes in their valuation of self-esteem coincide with the goals set by the therapists.

9.4 Concluding Remarks and Discussion

The statements about those changes within the field of 'self' (content and evaluation) which have been intended by therapists and reported upon by patients, show similarities as well as differences, and we now have a structure for mapping what happens to these differences in the course of therapy. Furthermore, in the patients' reports (as well as in the FQ) it is indicated that, in terms of psychoanalytic treatment, 'ideal' self-esteem would be *autonomous*, i.e. relatively independent of successes and failures. The Heidelberg Follow-up Project will therefore examine, for instance, how changes in self-esteem are dependent on a change in the symptomatic field, and we also have to ask how the results of patients' reports correlate with psychometric tests. Both these technical points are addressed, we notice, in a different context by Neudert *et al.* (Chapter 10) who bring detailed observations from an intensive single-case study to bear upon them.

Finally, we should like to underline the experimental character of our work, since this investigation was not supposed to be an attempt to operationalize definitively in the area of self-theories. And yet some degree of formalization is necessary to protect us from deceiving ourselves about how change takes place in self-esteem during psychotherapy. Such change is, after all, the consequence of a process influenced in particular by the reaction of the therapist to the complaints of his patient, and of his proposal to effect a change in these on the part of the patient. For the evaluation of treatment-results, the changes in structure are always likely to be measured by changes in symptoms; and yet, while acknowledging the importance of changes in symptoms and behaviour, one must not forget the global goals of psychoanalytic treatment. As Mintz *et al.* (1979) have shown, it is possible to investigate changes in dynamic formulations made in the manner of Malan (e.g. 1976, 1980), and that, when this is done, totally untrained people make the same evaluations as highly trained clinicians do.

The assumption is often made, for dubious reasons perhaps, that the assessment of an 'objective' outsider must be more accurate than that of the therapist himself, and it is certainly true that self-reports by patients often do not correlate very highly with therapists' assessments. This may be because they have different perspectives. If a patient becomes able to express sad and lonely feelings, is this an improvement or a deterioration? And what are the criteria involved? We are dealing with the question of what valuation is to be placed on a particular outcome: the value of the patient, the value of society, or the value of the mental health profession? When Freud himself was asked what the goals of therapy are, he said, as everybody knows, 'to love and to work' (*lieben und arbeiten*).

In this connection, it is not helpful, and can even be professionally clumsy, if psychoanalysts allow the instrument for measuring treatment-results to be imposed on them from outside only. It is an important task for psychoanalytic research to attempt to develop appropriate instruments which can capture the special characteristics of psychoanalytic treatment. For it is necessary to reflect that the specific values and goals of this form of treatment are often clearly different from those of other types of therapy. And yet there has been a definite reluctance on the part of many analysts to come to an explicit understanding with the patient as to the goals of the prospective treatment. The reasons for this reluctance on the part of the therapist are possibly to be found in the rigidity of psychoanalytic training; and it is certainly true that many of the more 'behavioural' types of psychotherapy make a definite point of specifying their goals, in terms of 'target behaviours', in concrete detail, and even of building them into a literal 'contract' before therapy begins (cp. Freud's discussion of the analyst's 'pact' with the patient, which Cheshire and Thomae refer to in Chapter 5). Indeed, it is another sign of the convergence between different schools of psychotherapy that psychoanalytically derived short-term dynamic psychotherapies have begun to incorporate this feature of more behaviourally orientated techniques.

Somewhat uncertain as to what may become of all this, we are inclined to invoke at this point a quotation from Goethe: 'We can do nothing but erect the wood-pile and wait for it to dry; it will catch fire in time, and we shall surprise ourselves'. What has transpired so far is that a short series of substantial progress-reports on the interim findings of our research programme has been published elsewhere (Kordy and Scheibler, 1984; Kordy *et al.*, 1983; Senf *et al.*, 1984). In the first of these, the authors report that, when the therapists were asked at the end of treatment (not yet at the follow-up stage) to assess how their patients had fared with respect to 'individual treatment goals' and the 'main individual treatment goal', as specified in advance, they replied that around 80% of the 60–70 patients involved were at least 'well improved'. This rather optimistic finding is compared by Kordy *et al.* (1983) with a range of area-specific observations made both by relatively independent clinicians and by the patients upon themselves. Such a comparison reveals that only just over half the patients declared themselves (through the medium of questionnaire responses) to be well improved in 'contentedness', and only one-fifth of them represented themselves as being well improved in 'self-image' in response to the Giessen Test. By contrast, the clinicians, who rated a good half of the 70-odd patients concerned as 'well improved' in respect of their symptoms or complaints, evidently thought that some of the patients, only one-third of whom depicted themselves as improved to that extent on a symptoms-check list, had taken too gloomy a view of their progress.

The authors illustrate how, in studying the outcomes of about 100 therapies, they have brought to bear a variety of observational methods, employed by a variety of judges (as discussed above) and focussed upon various separable *aspects* of potential improvement. Their intention in so doing is to strike a balance between the nomothetic demands of statistical analysis of group-trends and idiographic interest in trying to understand why a particular individual (with a particular problem, history or psychopathology, etc.) does well or badly in a particular type of psychotherapy. As a consequence of this strategy, it has already been possible to say something about what 'sort' of patient (psychodynamically categorized) is likely to do best in which therapeutic *milieu*: for example, it seems that patients with 'adequate ego strength' have a better chance of doing well in a group than they have in the particular combination of group-and-individual therapy which the Heidelberg system offers; whereas the patient with 'severe superego pathology' is twice as likely to be 'at risk' for doing badly, as opposed to doing well, whichever type of therapy he is assigned to.

This leads Kordy *et al.*, to the somewhat rueful conclusion that, although it is possible for significant numbers of patients to do well in respect of self-rated contentedness and clinician-rated symptomatic improvement *without* a corresponding degree of improvement in either self-image or object-relations, yet it is possible to put together a cluster of patient-characteristics which bode well for relative therapeutic success. These are: high ego strength, adequate superego, adequate drive-integration and adequate ability to express feelings; and they should be combined (perhaps surprisingly) with a medium, rather than a low, degree of general emotional disturbance. It is suggested that, by analogy with the familiar YAVIS syndrome (discussed by Cheshire and Thomae in Chapter 4, these benign characteristics could be encapsulated into a corresponding DIVA syndrome, standing for 'developed, integrated, verbal-affective'.

Against this background of empirical description and analysis derived from the Heidelberg findings, Senf *et al.* (1984) returned to the intricate theoretical questions of how to isolate and identify the complex 'indications' for this or that type of psychotherapy in the case of this or that type of patient. Not surprisingly, they appeal to the same quotation from Paul (1967) with which Neudert *et al.* begin Chapter 10, although they immediately go on to indicate that they regard it as stating a misleading 'pseudoproblem'. Clearly favouring an idiographic approach, they present even more detailed breakdowns of the findings provided by Kordy *et al.* (1983), for example, by setting out the differences in improvement at different 'assessment levels' (symptoms, individual goals, self-image, etc.) between a DIVA group and a group of 'problem patients' who had the opposite of the DIVA characteristics. Ignoring for a moment the very small numbers in some of the subsamples, this descriptive analysis makes it possible to read off predictive inferences such as that an 'alexithymic' patient (having poor ability to express feelings) is more likely to improve in self-image in group-therapy in the combined group–individual condition, whereas both the problem patient with low ego strengths and the DIVA subject with adequate drive-integration are likely to improve in 'contentedness' more reliably in the individual–group conditions.

Furthermore, they have been able to compile a short-list of what we may call 'negative indicators', hinted at above, and to quantify the likelihood of therapeutic success which attends the patient who has several of them as opposed to the fellow-patient who has no more than one of them. Specifically, if one considers the five 'risk factors'—ego-strength, ability to express feelings, integration of drives, superego pathology and drive-control—then the patient who is markedly disturbed in four or more of them is less than half as likely to do well in group therapy (in respect of symptoms, individual goals, main problem and self-image) than a patient who has severe disturbance in not more than one; and, in the case of individual psychotherapy, the differential is even wider with reference to 'individual goals' and 'contentedness' (Senf *et al.*, 1984, p. 46).

This analysis of predictive factors may be compared illuminatingly with the well-known project of Strupp, described in Chapter 11, and with the findings of Strupp and Binder (1984). For they have also been concerned to identify hopeful 'antecedent patient variables', and their list includes 'high motivation for psychotherapy, ability to form a good therapeutic relationship ... early ...., and relative absence of long-standing maladaptive patterns of relating' (p. 274). The emphasis here on the capacity for forming viable 'object-relations' is strikingly in accord with the observation of Kordy *et al.* (1983, p. 220) that when a patient entering therapy in the Heidelberg project has some 'steady personal relationship' going on, then that is a good omen for therapeutic outcome. It is important to notice that these findings do not amount to saying merely that those patients who are less disturbed will do better in psychotherapy, because, as the authors put it (p. 222), 'one result that initially surprised us is that patients with medium degrees of disturbance seem to do better than those with slight disturbances'.

If these results which have emerged so far from the Heidelberg project are not always as encouraging as we would have wished in terms of the overall efficacy of our psychotherapeutic measures, nevertheless the fact that we have been able to identify some fairly specific indicators, and to show that they are consonant with other independent research in the area, entitles us to believe

that our metaphorical wood-pile, which we introduced above with reference to
Goethe, has indeed begun to catch fire.

References

Bandura, A. (1982). Self-efficacy mechanism in human agency. *Am. Psychol*, **37**, 122–147.
Borg, I. (1977). Some basic concepts of facet theory. In *Geometric Representation of Relational Data* (ed. J. C. Lingoes), ch. 3. Mathesis Press, Ann Arbor (Mich.).
Braeutigam, W., von Rad, M. and Engel, K. (1980). Erfolgs- und Therapieforschung... *Z. Psychosomat. Med. Psychoanal.*, **26**, 101–118.
Engel, G. L. *et al.* (1979). Das Heidelberger Katamneseprojekt. *Med. Psychol.*, **5**, 124–137.
Grawe, K. (1978). Indikation in der Psychotherapie. In *Handbuch der Psychologie* vol. 8, no. 2 (ed. L. J. Pongratz), ch. 3. Hogrefe, Göttingen/Toronto/Zürich.
Kordy, H. and Scheibler, D. (1984). Individuumsorientierte Erfolgsforschung... *Z. Klin. Psychol. Psychother.*, **32**, 218–233, 309–318.
Kordy, H., von Rad, M. and Senf, W. (1983). Success and failure in psychotherapy:... *Psychother. Psychosom.*, **40**, 211–227.
Luborsky, L. *et al.* (1980). Predicting the outcome of psychotherapy. *Arch. Gen. Psychiatry*, **37**, 471–481.
Malan, D. H. (1976). *The Frontier of Brief Psychotherapy*. Plenum Press, New York.
Malan, D. H. (1980). Basic principles... of the follow-up interview. In *Short Term Dynamic Psychotherapy* (ed. H. Davanloo), ch. 19. J. Aronson, New York and London.
Mintz, J., Luborsky, L. and Christoph, P. (1979). Measuring the outcome of psychotherapy:... *J. Consult. Clin. Psychol.*, **47**, 319–334.
Mollon, P. and Parry, G. (1984). The fragile self: narcissistic disturbance and the protective function of depression. *Brit. J. Med. Psychol.*, **57**, 137–145.
Paul, G. L. (1967). Strategy of outcome research in psychotherapy. *J. Consult. Clin. Psychol.*, **31**, 109–118.
Plog, U. (1976). *Differentielle Psychotherapie* vol. 2. Huber, Stuttgart.
Reiter, L. and Steiner, E. (1978). Werte und Ziele in der Psychotherapie. *Psychol. Heute*, **11**, 65–70.
Senf, W., Kordy, H., von Rad, H. and Braeutigam, W. (1984). Indication in psychotherapy... *Psychother. Psychosom.*, **42**, 37–47.
Sloane, R. B., Staples, F. R., Cristol, A. H., Yorkston, N. J. and Whipple, K. (1975). *Psychotherapy versus Behaviour Therapy*. Harvard University Press, Cambridge (Mass).
Strupp, H. H. (1980). Problems of research: short-term psychotherapy is the wave of the future. In *Short Term Dynamic Psychotherapy* (ed. H. Davanloo), ch. 20. J. Aronson, New York and London.
Strupp, H. H. and Binder, J. L. (1984). *Psychotherapy in a New Key*. Basic Books, New York.
Strupp, H. H. and Hadley, S. W. (1977). A tripartite model of mental health...outcomes. *Am. Psychol.*, **32**, 187–196.
Strupp, H. H. and Hadley, S. W. (1979). Specific versus nonspecific factors in psychotherapy: a controlled study of outcome. *Arch. Gen. Psychiatry* **36**, 1125–1136.
Strupp, H. H., Wallach, M. S. and Wogan, M. (1964). *Psychotherapy Experience in Retrospect: Questionnaire Survey of Former Patients and their Therapists* (Psychol. Monogr. 78(11), Whole no. 588).

Strupp, H. H., Fox, R. E. and Lessler, K. (1969). *Patients View their Psychotherapy.* Johns Hopkins Press, Baltimore.
Thomae, H. (1980). Auf dem Weg zum Selbst *Psyche*, **34**, 221–245.

CHAPTER 10

Changes in Self-esteem during Psychoanalysis: A Single-case Study

Lisbeth Neudert, Hans-J. Gruenzig and Helmut Thomae

10.1 Introduction

'*What* treatment, by *whom*, is most effective for *this* individual with *that* specific problem, and under *which* set of circumstances?' (Paul, 1967, p. 111).

This oft-quoted general question in psychotherapy research marks the starting-point for the development of fruitful strategies in this area of research. We could point, for example, to the indispensable necessity of conducting process-research as an integral part of studies of therapeutic outcome. The research strategy of single-case analysis, which has become more widespread in recent years, represents an attempt to find ways of answering precisely the question formulated by Paul with which we have begun. On the one hand, it has succeeded in meeting the methodological standards of empirical work in the social sciences, while, on the other, it has had the effect of questioning those research standards themselves.

Meaningful answers, which would themselves have reliable implications for specific therapeutic strategies in particular cases, will be found only so long as the particular features of individual schools of therapy are not allowed to dictate, in an exclusive way, such individualistic research strategies that the research findings cannot even be communicated beyond the boundaries of particular schools of therapy, much less be used for comparative purposes in general. It is therefore necessary to set up a coordinated enterprise by all those psychotherapy researchers who think it worthwhile to subject therapeutic activity to the demands of rigorous empirical analysis. A necessary prerequisite for coordinating research strategies is agreement among the exponents of different therapeutic orientations about a range of central concepts which are regarded as significant for all the types of therapy involved.

These concepts would have to meet two requirements: they would need to be acceptable and communicable in a way independent of particular psycho-therapeutic theories; and they should nevertheless serve to increase the body of knowledge within particular schools. Although this second requirement may seem trivial, we want to underline it because it serves to reduce the anxiety that the particular qualities of an individual orientation may be lost sight of against such an eclectic conceptual background. Every school of therapy can, of course, reserve the right to interpret any findings in ways that are consistent with its own specific concepts and hypotheses, and in so doing to test, validate and expand its own body of knowledge (cp. Luborsky and Spence, 1978).

But certainly the realization of this aim meets with especial difficulty when it comes to investigating therapist-variables, since the intentions of the therapist and his consequent actions are to a high degree theory-directed, although this degree is frequently overestimated, as had already been shown by Glover (1955). Farrell's subsequent revival of this issue has been discussed by Cheshire (1975, ch. 4). Nevertheless, there are attempts to translate school-specific intervention-strategies into formulations independent of particular schools (Bastine, 1976). We do not hold any brief here for uncritical efforts to amalgamate different therapeutic techniques. On the contrary, it is the more radical application of therapeutic techniques which most readily allows us to assess the relative effectiveness of different methods.

The scope of the present study is confined to patient-variables, which we have investigated in the context of a single-case analysis.

10.2 Self-esteem as a Concept in Psychotherapy Research

We chose self-esteem as a concept central to psychotherapy research, as understood in the terms outlined above, and investigated how it changed during the course of a psychoanalysis. We were guided in this choice by the following considerations.

In the personality research of recent years, self-esteem and a number of related concepts have played an increasingly important part, as Cheshire and Thomae have shown in Chapter 1. On the other hand, as a clinical-psychother-apeutic concept in the framework of systematic empirical psychotherapy research, it has so far largely been neglected. Nevertheless, it is precisely this concept which can, in our opinion, most readily create meaningful links between process and outcome research, because it is a variable equally relevant to both process and outcome. If the therapy-process is understood as a gradual acquisition of certain attitudes and abilities, and if outcome is assessed in terms of the possession and availability for action of these very attitudes and abilities, then it follows that the researcher should gather information about those features of the patient that are reflections of this process of acquisition and its stability of outcome. Hence the importance of longitudinal and follow-up studies of these features, such as the group-investigation described by Zitzelsberger and Kordy in Chapter 9.

We are not suggesting, of course, that these are the only variables worth investigation. On the contrary, there are a number of fruitful *process*-variables which are relatively useless as criteria for *outcome*: the capacity for free association, for example, which is highly esteemed in psychoanalytic treatment and has consequently been investigated frequently by researchers in that area (Strupp, 1968; Bellack, 1981; Thomae and Kaechele, 1985, ch. 7); and the same may be said for the concept of transference, which is also central to psychoanalytic procedures (e.g. Graff and Luborsky, 1977; Gill, 1982; Thomae and Kaechele, 1987, ch. 2; Luborsky *et al.*, 1985). It is essential, however, to be able to define theoretically rigorous connections between these sorts of variable and those that are indicators of successful outcome, and to be able to put such connections to empirical test.

In psychoanalytic theory-construction, and also in clinical practice, self-esteem was for a long time regarded as an epiphenomenon without greater psychodynamic importance. Freud used the concept not so much as a technical term but somewhat colloquially, though in close connection with the idea of narcissism. He mentions (1914, ch. 3) three factors which constitute self-esteem: (1) 'Everything a person possesses or achieves, every remnant of the primitive feeling of omnipotence which . . . experience has confirmed'; (2) the fulfillment of the ego-ideal which represents the lost narcissism of infancy; and (3) the satisfaction of being loved in the context of a narcissistic object-choice. Self-esteem acquired theoretical and clinical importance in connection with the wider dissemination of the concept of narcissism and its revised formulation (Kohut, 1971, 1977).

But also, independently of its involvement in narcissism-theory (and consequently also in drive-theory), increasing attention was being paid within psychoanalysis to the Self and self-esteem, especially since self-psychology can be seen as a consequential development of ego-psychology (Dare and Holder, 1981; Thomae, 1980; see also Chapters 1, 3 and 4).

In client-centred psychotherapy, the concepts of self-esteem and self-acceptance, respectively, are of major importance for the underlying theory of personality and psychotherapy (Rogers, 1951, 1959). Rogers' process-model assumes that the client will increasingly be able to develop self-esteem by means of the unconditional positive regard of the therapist. Acceptance by others, however, does not lead directly to self-acceptance, but rather creates a secure atmosphere free of fear. The client can experience, re-evaluate and thus diminish incongruences between experiences and self-concept in such a climate without feeling threatened (cp. McReynolds' discussion of incongruency-resolution in Chapter 8).

The increase in self-esteem in turn makes it possible that the client integrates experiences which until now were not, or not correctly, symbolized. In Chapter 5 (section 5.4), Cheshire and Thomae have discussed how Rogers' concept of the therapist's 'regard' relates to specifically psychoanalytic hypotheses about the functioning of the transference and the 'helping alliance'; and they also indicate how some of Rogers' assumptions have been tested empirically (cp. Shlien and Zimring, 1970).

Although the term 'self-esteem' does not belong to the specific terminology of behaviour therapy, there are, nevertheless, concepts which are closely related. Elsewhere in this volume we have already encountered Bandura's concept of self-efficacy (1977) in particular: it could be understood as the consciousness of being able to effect something and to change things and one's own life, as a result of the experience of one's own abilities. Bandura himself is of the opinion that a successful therapy is characterized first by the patient's ability to become aware of his capacity to influence things going on. From this point of view Bandura's concept might be understood as the positively formulated counterpart to Seligman's 'learned helplessness' (1975).

The concept of self-confidence, and correspondingly of self-confident (assertive) behaviour, which is the basis for several types of assertiveness training within this framework (e.g. Ullrich and Ullrich de Muynck, 1978; Feldhege and Krauthan, 1979; Liberman, 1978) may be seen as another behaviourally orientated conceptualization of self-esteem. There are even empirical findings about the positive effects of behavioural assertiveness training on self-esteem as reflected in raised self-ratings (e.g. Stake and Pearlman, 1980), which means that the behavioural and experiential components of self-esteem are connected with each other to a high degree, even though this connection may be interpreted differently by different therapeutic schools. We leave aside here the concept of positive and negative self-cognition that is used especially in cognitive behaviour therapy by, for instance, Beck or Meichenbaum, because they do not take sufficient account of the evaluative aspect of self-esteem or of the affect produced by this self-evaluation.

We supplement this clinical framework by a model, derived from general psychological self-concept research, which seems appropriate for generating process-hypotheses. According to this model, a distinction has to be made between global self-esteem and a situation- or area-specific type. For instance, Korman (1970) starts from ideas of 'chronic' self-esteem (as the extent to which a person generally thinks of himself as a competent, need-satisfying individual), 'task-specific' and 'socially influenced' self-esteem. Epstein (1982) refers to different subcategories which constitute the global self-esteem: namely the evaluation of competence, likeableness, lovableness, moral self-approval, body self-image, power, and will-power. These classifications focus either on characteristics of the external situation or on different subjective qualities of emotion.

In our investigation we had data on the external situation at our disposal, but these data were altered by the subjective reaction of the patient. We therefore refrained from deciding between these two criteria of classification (namely external situation *versus* subjective quality of emotions) and started from the assumption that overall self-esteem is constituted by components of self-esteem drawn from different life-areas and/or problem-areas. This assumption is consistent with our model of therapy-process, according to which problem-areas are worked through focally one after the other (see Thomae *et al.*, 1978). Nevertheless, we deem it premature to test, in the context of this investigation, models of the 'composition' of self-esteem—at any rate in the rather simplistic form in which they are proposed for instance by Watkins (1978), who conceptualizes the overall self-esteem as the sum of self-esteem components weighted with their subjective importance. In order to develop and test sound models that may be useful in the framework of psychotherapy research, we need detailed knowledge on the interpersonal and intrapersonal contexts of the phenomenon of self-esteem in the psychotherapeutic process.

With these theoretical considerations established, we now turn to our empirical process-study.

10.3 Case-description, Hypotheses and Method

This study aims at testing process-hypotheses related to changes in self-esteem in the course of a psychoanalytic treatment.

10.3.1 Symptomatology

We describe first the patient's general life-situation and symptomatology at the start of treatment. These data together with general empirical findings about the symptomatology led to reflections about the psychodynamics of the patient and to the derivation of the process hypotheses.

The female patient is a 35-year-old teacher suffering from an abnormally strong growth of hair all over her body (idiopathic hirsutism). She has been described briefly by Cheshire and Thomae in Chapter 5, where she features as 'Miss T.' in one of their clinical *vignettes*, but we need to add here some further details relevant to the present study.

She maintains a very close relationship to her parents, with whom she spends the weekends as well as most of her vacation. This close relationship to her family is not unproblematic, however, since she feels very much under the influence of her mother and depreciated in comparison to her two brothers. Similarly, she is afraid of being compared with other women because she feels disqualified as an old spinster, and she has come to ask herself whether she is a real woman at all. These anxieties are to be seen against the following background.

She has never had heterosexual relationships, and she attributes this on the one hand to her severe hirsutism (which can be traced back to puberty) and to her extraordinarily strict Catholic education on the other. This education is seen by her as the essential reason for her strong anxieties and feelings of guilt in the realm of sexuality, not only in relation to men but also to sexual fantasies and masturbation. Together with all these problems the patient suffers from depressive feelings which surround very low self-esteem and the consequent feelings of loneliness and guilt.

In her profession as a teacher the patient feels competent enough, but is nonetheless unable to tolerate rivalries with colleagues; she has the impression that the head of the school does not take her seriously, and she complains that she cannot behave assertively towards her pupils and colleagues. When she is successful once in a while, as a result of her own interest and motivation, then she suffers from strong feelings of guilt. In her decision-making she sees herself as dependent upon approval from persons in authority.

We supplement this description of our patient with the findings of an investigation dealing with the psychology of women with idiopathic hirsutism. These findings come from an older but still most comprehensive investigation (Meyer and von Zerssen, 1960; Meyer, 1963).

The combination of genetic factors and of the consequences of stress-reaction results in an increase in the androgen level, which can lead to hirsutism if a critical level is reached. It is suggested that women with hirsutism in the absence of a clear genetic disposition, as is the case with our patient, can handle situations of stress only inadequately. This suggestion is supported by the fact that neurotic disturbances independent of the hirsutism symptomatology occur remarkably often with these women. On the basis of their empirical data, Meyer and von Zerssen suggest that the condition may be seen as a by-product of psychogenic mechanisms concerned with an (unconscious) wish to be more manly.

On this view, hirsute women are most often regarded as wishing to be a man: the authors maintain that hirsutism reactivates these widespread wishes, and that most psychologically disturbed women do have these wishes. As a consequence of the hirsutism, many women suffer from a severe difficulty in being accepted, and Meyer distinguished between a decrease in subjective acceptability (Can I love myself as I am?) and the presumed rejection by other people (Can another person love me as I am?). Accordingly, we stress these two considerations from Meyer and von Zerssen in formulating our empirical hypotheses: (1) hirsutism reactivates wishes to be a man and leads therefore to insecurity in the female identity; (2) women with hirsutism suffer from severe difficulty in being accepted.

10.3.2 Hypotheses

In investigating changes of self-esteem in the psychoanalytic process, we are especially interested in three areas. First, changes in general self-esteem, and in area-specific self-esteem as a function of the therapeutic process. Second, the impact of acceptance by important reference-people, especially the psychoanalyst, upon changes in self-esteem. Third, the identification of intrapsychic conditions which are obstacles to an increase in self-esteem (cp. Sheerer, 1949).

In explicitly formulating the hypotheses, it is assumed that these phenomena can be subject to objective assessment only insofar as they are openly verbalized by the patient. With this restriction we are formulating hypotheses about both general and area-specific changes in self-esteem.

General hypotheses

A person's self-esteem is decidedly dependent upon his feeling accepted by significant others (acceptance by others). This relationship between self-esteem and acceptance by others is of essential importance for determining the *level* of self-esteem, and also contributes to the actual genesis and maintenance of self-esteem in the first place (cp. Chapter 1 (Section 1.3)). Consequently, the patient's capacity for developing solid self-esteem in the course of therapeutic treatment depends upon his capacity for experiencing acceptance by others; and, in the realm of psychoanalytic treatment, the psychoanalyst is of course regarded as a paradigmatic 'significant other' for the patient. A successful treatment-process is therefore indicated by an increase in the experience of acceptance by others, and consequently by an increase in self-esteem.

This acceptance by others is experienced first of all in the transference-relationship. This repeated experience of being accepted in therapy enables the patient to question his hitherto unfavourable and negative self-estimation. This is regarded as a prerequisite for the patient's new experiences outside therapy, namely those to do with feeling accepted by others. This new experience of feeling accepted by others consequently enables the patient to accept himself.

This therapeutic strategy is above all aimed at reducing the discrepancy between the experienced self and the ideal-self, and therefore at self-esteem. In addition, psychotherapy must supply for the patient relief from his threatening superego; and this may be achieved by working through the feared consequences of those sexual and aggressive wishes which the patient is regarding here and now as equally dangerous as he did in his childhood.

Area-specific hypotheses
We restricted ourselves to three essential problem-areas for this patient: (1) the area of body, sexuality and female identity; (2) the area of achievement and success; (3) the area of aggressivity and assertiveness. Our formulations related to the patient's psychodynamics, and to the derivation of process hypotheses for each of the three problem-areas were as follows.

10.3.2.1   Problem-area: 'body, sexuality and female identity'

Psychodynamic considerations
The virile body hair leads to insecurities on the patient's side concerning her female identity. Real or assumed rejections decrease the patient's self-esteem, which is a further negative feedback for her attitude towards her body and her sexuality: of special importance in this respect is her anticipation of rejection by men. Therefore she is doomed to fail, both with respect to her ego-ideal, by which she is obliged to be a valuable woman with an integrated sexuality, and with respect to her superego which prohibits the fulfillment of her sexual needs.

Another most important influence in this area is the patient's relationship to her mother. Besides needing acknowledgement by men, a positively experienced female identity can only result out of the fact that mother-figures are positively perceived in their female identity, and that these present good objects of identification. In the case of this patient, it is to be expected that her insecurity with respect to her identity as a woman is connected with a negative attitude towards mother-figures.

Process-hypotheses
Since the patient's sexual needs are closely related to feelings of guilt and to castration anxiety, an elaboration and eventual realization of her sexual needs can be expected only when the themes of guilt and punishment have been worked through. An indispensable step on this way is the acceptance of her autoerotic needs.

These psychodynamics will play an important part in the transference-neurosis.

Her insecure female identity can be overcome to the extent that she is able to perceive positive elements in her 'mother-figures'.

10.3.2.2   Problem-area: 'achievement and success'

Psychodynamic considerations
The patient's low self-esteem is expressed, among other things, in her low confidence in successfully achieving something. This especially relates to her work and to the social field.

The patient's unconscious fear of envy, and of consequent aggression from others, can be traced back biographically to the relationship to her brothers, from whom she had actually experienced such consequences of achievement on her own part. With her low self-esteem, she is highly dependent upon acceptance by others. Therefore, she experiences the danger of being rejected or attacked as especially dangerous. The patient can be seen to be in the following dilemma: if she achieves too little, her self-esteem decreases; but if she achieves more than others, then she has to be afraid of their envy and aggression (cp. McReynolds' analysis of cognitive discrepancy and incongruity, in Chapter 8).

Process-hypotheses
In this problem-area it is necessary to work through her feelings of guilt about achievement; she has to become independent of valuation and appreciation from her brothers, in order to be able to be successful without constantly fearing envy and aggression; and, in addition, she has to gain the experience that she can tolerate envy and aggression if they occur.

10.3.2.3   Problem-area: 'aggressivity and assertiveness'

Psychodynamic considerations
This problem-area overlaps to some extent with the previous one. If she is not able to be assertive in an aggressive manner towards others, her self-esteem decreases. If, by contrast, she does try to be aggressive, feelings of guilt emerge out of her phantasy that her aggressivity could mutilate or (even worse) destroy others. There is a discrepancy in this problem-area too: on the one hand, she wants to be able to pursue her needs aggressively, but on the other hand feels that such dangerous aggressive tendencies are prohibited.

Process-hypotheses
These problems can be worked through directly in the transference-relationship. Experiencing acceptance by the analyst, even though she has aggressive phantasies, is a prerequisite for accepting her aggressivity herself.

10.3.3   Method

10.3.3.1   Sample. The entire treatment, which consisted of 517 sessions, was tape-recorded; a sample of 115 sessions was transcribed verbatim and stored in the Ulm Psychotherapeutic Textbank (Mergenthaler, 1983). This sample of sessions was made up of 21 separate blocks of consecutive sessions taken from different stages of treatment: namely, the first ten and the last ten sessions, plus 19 five-session blocks taken at regular intervals in between. The reason for choosing longer runs of sessions at the beginning and end of treatment was that we wanted to have a broader data-base for making comparisons between the beginning and the end of treatment.

This last consideration leads us to the choice of a suitable framework for our categories of content-analysis. Our criterion for rating the content of any part of the transcript, and for subsequently defining categories, was how it would be understood by a competent speaker of the language, bearing in mind the therapeutic context (since there is no such thing as an average meaning of words or phrases independent of context). This view of content-analysis has the effect of taking the patient's utterances seriously, in that we were paying attention to what she was trying to communicate explicitly, and not to what might be inferred about its latent or unconscious meaning. In this way, the application of this category-system, and the communication of findings deriving from it, are kept independent of the theoretical assumptions of specific schools of psychotherapy (cp. Kaechele *et al.*, 1973).

10.3.3.2   The category-system for content-analysis. In order to test the hypotheses which we had set up, we created a category-system for content-analysis. This consists of 23 categories. When defining these categories for the purpose of a coding manual (cp. Neudert and Gruenzig, 1983), we were careful to stay as close as possible to direct observation, which is an important condition for getting reliable judgements from non-experts, because it minimizes the need for inference and interpretation. The 23 content-categories, as used in the main study, together with their resultant reliability values, are listed in Table 1. Our method of defining the categories can be illustrated by the two that are concerned with self-esteem. The category of 'positive self-esteem' includes: (1) every positive or accepting utterance which the patient makes about herself (i.e. about her whole person, or about her appearance, attitudes, abilities or any other attributes); (2) every positive remark made by somebody else with which she agrees (thus taking over the positive evaluation of someone else); and (3) every utterance in which the patient contradicts a negative evaluation of her by someone else. The category of 'negative self-esteem' is correspondingly defined by utterances expressing the opposite of those just described.

Since our category-system was constructed strictly in accordance with the need to test our various hypotheses, it falls into two parts which correspond to groups of hypotheses. The first group consists of categories which we expect to play an important part with respect to changes in self-esteem during any psychoanalytic process: namely, those to do with self-esteem, acceptance by others and emotionally significant relationships. The second group consists of those that are specifically relevant to areas of change in this particular case, and to factors which may possibly impede such change.

This admittedly idealized structuring of the category-groups at least has the merit of allowing them to be applied to other investigations: in another single-case study on a corresponding theme, the categories from group 1 could be taken over more or less as they stand, while those in group 2 would be individually modified to fit the particular case. We make this suggestion because we deplore the tendency, which has also been criticized by Marsden

(1971) and Kaechele (1976), for various techniques and methods of content-analysis (which have often been devised at considerable expense of time, effort and finance) to be left on the shelf after a single application. Since the use of the same measuring instrument is a necessary condition for the valid replication of an investigation, and since it is especially obvious in the case of single-case studies that replication is necessary to generalization, we emphasize the importance of making measuring instruments that can be used again. The coding-manual mentioned above therefore contains not only basic instructions about allocating utterances to categories, but also examples and other aids to resolving doubts about category-allocation. The two categories with the lowest reliability values were picked out by both judges as being the least close to direct observation, thus underlining the point about the need to avoid inference and interpretation as much as possible. For details of how the raters were trained to use the manual reliably, see Neudert and Gruenzig (1983, p. 24).

Table 1. Reliability values derived from combined ratings according to the formula of Spearman–Brown (Lienert, 1969, pp. 119, 221).

Categories	r
1 positive self-esteem	0.81
2 negative self-esteem	0.92
3 positive acceptance by others	0.95
4 negative acceptance by others	0.76
5 positive view of motherly significant others	0.83
6 negative view of motherly significant others	0.94
7 motherly significant others (neutral view)	0.95
8 fatherly significant others	0.97
9 analyst	0.96
10 female peers	0.98
11 male peers	0.97
12 brothers	0.99
13 body	0.90
14 body hair	0.98
15 sexuality	0.97
16 real heterosexuality	0.98
17 imagined heterosexuality	0.96
18 autoeroticism	0.98
19 security concerning female identity	0.73
20 insecurity concerning female identity	0.73
21 achievement, success	0.90
22 aggressiveness, assertiveness	0.88
23 feelings of guilt, fear of punishment	0.88

Let us now illustrate how clinical hypotheses about the therapy process were converted into research predictions about category-scores. One of the clinical hypotheses runs: we do not expect the area of self-esteem to do with sexuality to improve until the connection between sexual needs on the one hand and guilt-feelings and punishment-anxieties on the other has been worked through. In terms of category-usage, a period of 'working through' amounts to a block of sessions in which raised scores on categories associated with that topic occur in combination. In this case the relevant categories for the hypothesis will be 15 to 18 and 23, and we look for a block in which relatively high scores on those categories occur in combination; we can then predict that in the part of the therapy which follows such a block, the mean score for the combination of categories 1 and 15 to 18 (i.e. self-esteem in combination with sexuality) will be higher than the corresponding value for that section of the therapy which came before the critical block. (Further details about independence of ratings between judges, and randomization of the order of session-rating, can be found in Neudert and Gruenzig (1983, p. 26).

10.3.3.3 Evaluation. In order to operationalize the notion of 'working-through', we had originally intended to look for examples of individual utterances that could be scored on both the categories relevant to the particular hypothesis; but since it turned out that there were too few of these to work with, we decided to use the sessional scores as a unit of evaluation, and computed correlation coefficients for the combinations of categories relevant to our hypotheses. The clinical hypotheses implied various predictions about the pattern of category-scores which would be observed during the course of treatment: monotonic trends, differential frequencies of occurrence of the various categories, and differences in relevant correlation values before and after a focal working-through. To test the trends we used Foster and Stuart's (1954) 'record-breaker', and a linearity test (Cochran, 1954); for the frequency of categories we used a test for change in level (Cochran, 1954); and, in the case of the correlation coefficients, we computed product-moment values and tested their significance.

Although the most powerful model for describing time-series fluctuations is ARIMA (Box and Jenkins, 1976; Revenstorf, 1979), we had to give it up in the end for two reasons. First, our data took the form of frequency-counts with many zero values, and this seemed inappropriate to the parametric algorithm of ARIMA. Second, our time-sampling is made up from a number of separate blocks and it became apparent that the five-session blocks were too short to allow us to compute both ARIMA-based time-dependencies and our process--dependent hypotheses. For a recent innovation in time-series analysis, see Tryon (1982). We are grateful to Helmut Wild and colleagues at the Department of Mathematics V in the University of Ulm for statistical advice on this point and others.

10.4   Results and Discussion

10.4.1   Results of Process Study

The two central hypotheses about changes in overall self-esteem could be confirmed. That is to say, positive self-esteem increased during the course of treatment ($P < 0.01$), but the trend did not set in right at the start of treatment but only after wide fluctuations over the first 100 sessions; negative self-esteem, on the other hand, shows a continuous decrease from the beginning of treatment ($P < 0.01$). However, the hypotheses to do with changes in acceptance by others were not confirmed, because there were no systematic trends. Nor were the hypotheses to do with the relative incidence of different categories before and after focal working-through confirmed. But with regard to hypotheses about differences between correlations among categories, there are indeed two confirmatory results: self-esteem in connection with imagined heterosexuality improved according to expectations ($P < 0.05$); and negative self-esteem in connection with autoeroticism decreased as predicted ($P < 0.05$).

10.4.2   Comparison between the Beginning and the End of Therapy

In addition to our investigation of the continuous treatment process, we present a comparison between initial and terminal stages of the treatment; and we establish a connection between research on the treatment process and that on treatment outcome. We are referring here to the same variables as we used in the process study, and are supplementing them by the use of typical standardized personality questionnaires.

   As a sample for this comparison of initial and terminal treatment periods, we used the first ten treatment sessions and the last ten treatment sessions which were evaluated by means of the same content-analysis system. For statistical purposes, we are assuming the independence of these two samples. This assumption seems plausible since an objective period of five years has passed in the course of treatment, during which the essential problems of the patient have decidedly changed.

10.4.2.1   For each of the content-analytic categories, a test was done on the differences between the means of the two samples. Those eight variables whose significance value is $P = 0.10$ or less were included in a MANOVA (discriminant analysis). As was expected, the two samples were sharply discriminated by these variables ($F = 20.8$; d.f. $= 41.15$; $P < 0.01$), although only four of these variables contributed substantially to the discriminant function because of high intercorrelations (Table 2). These four variables are the categories 'positive self-esteem' (1), 'negative self-esteem' (2), 'fatherly significant others' (8) and 'analyst' (9).

Table 2.   The eight statistically significant categories for the first ten and the last ten
treatment sessions: means, *t*-values, and probabilities (*P*) for *t*.

Category		First ten	Last ten	*t*	*P* (two-tailed)
1	positive self-esteem	2.4	5.8	−2.67	0.02
2	negative self-esteem	20.4	7.7	7.07	0.00
6	negative view of motherly 'significant others'	2.0	0.6	2.41	0.03
8	fatherly 'significant others'	8.5	2.6	2.08	0.06
9	analyst	5.6	14.5	−3.77	0.00
11	male peers	7.4	15.2	−2.80	0.01
12	brothers	9.2	2.3	3.22	0.00
14	body hair	1.1	0.0	1.72	0.10

Let us briefly summarize this outcome. The level of the patient's self-esteem
at the end of treatment is considerably higher than at the beginning. She talks
less often about father-figures, more often in contrast about the analyst and
about peer men. Her brothers have lost their importance to a considerable
extent at the end of treatment, as also has her negative experience of mother-
figures. She does not mention her body hair any more, and is more secure in
the realm of the autoerotic as well as in that of her female identity. Compared
with her state at the beginning of therapy, the patient is presenting herself as a
woman who has succeeded in her psychic separation from parents and siblings,
and who is able to establish relationships to people who are of significance for
her reality-life and for the further development of her life-circumstances.

10.4.2.2   A comparison of the factorial structures of the content-categories, as
between the two samples, might indicate how far a cognitive restructuring
within the different problem-areas had occurred in the course of treatment. To
this end, a descriptive principal-component analysis was computed for both
samples. A differentiation of the two samples produces the following picture, if
only those factorial loadings higher than 0.60 are considered. Table 3 shows the
factorial structure for the first ten sessions, and Table 4 shows that of the last
ten.

A quantitative algorithmic comparison of the factorial structures (Gebhardt,
1967a,b) yields a similarity-value of $R = 0.53$. According to Gebhardt, a
high similarity is indicated by *R*-values of more than 0.90; so an *R*-value as low
as ours points towards considerable differences between the two factorial
structures, and thereby to fundamental psychological changes in the course of
treatment. Especially striking are the structural changes that have occurred in

the problem-area which is represented by the initial factor II: the co-occurrence of the categories 'sexuality', 'real heterosexuality' and 'feelings of guilt' on one factor has disappeared in the terminal period of treatment, and sexuality is now related to body and negative self-esteem (terminal factor II), while 'real heterosexuality' is explicitly mentioned without being related to acceptance by others or achievement/success (terminal factor I).

Table 3. Factorial structure of the content-categories for the *first* ten sessions (only factor-loadings higher than 0.60 are considered).

	Factor-loading
Factor I:	
'positive self-esteem'	0.79
'positive view of motherly significant others'	0.73
'achievement, success'	0.70
'body'	-0.76
'analyst'	-0.78
Factor II:	
'real heterosexuality'	0.76
'feelings of guilt, fear of punishment'	0.76
'sexuality'	0.93
Factor III:	
'fatherly significant others'	0.82
'motherly significant others (neutral view)'	0.77
'female peers'	-0.61
Factor IV:	
'negative self-esteem'	0.82

From a psychodynamic point of view, it is highly interesting to find that positive self-esteem in the initial factor I is connected with the positive view of mother-figures as well as with achievement and success, and that this relationship has completely dissolved at the end of treatment. Instead, positive self-esteem now stands in opposition to body and sexuality. This last finding is somewhat surprising, and can lead to the inference that the patient cannot accept her bodily hairiness and her sexuality. It could be understood as indicating that the treatment was not successful in this respect, and was perhaps terminated too early. Another possible interpretation might be that the patient has given up denying that the pleasurable experience of her body and of her sexuality is in reality restricted, and that she is still complaining about her fate in having a hairy body; but that she is able at the same time (as indicated by other data) to enter into healthy and satisfying relationships despite this restriction.

10.4.2.3 Up to now we used verbal data immanent in therapy, since they are based on the verbatim transcripts. In contrast to this, we now introduce some findings resulting from data assessed by *psychological tests* applied outside the therapeutic situation proper. As outcome measures we used the *Freiburg Personality Inventory* (FPI; Fahrenberg *et al.*, 1978) and the Giessen Test (Beckmann and Richter, 1972). These inventories were presented to the patient at the start of treatment, at the end of treatment, as well as two years after the treatment had ended. At this last, follow-up point of investigation the patient was given in addition the questionnaire on experience and behaviour (Zielke and Kopf-Mehnert, 1978). Table 5 shows the questionnaire scores in a standardized form (the stanine scores have a mean of 5 and a standard deviation of about 2).

Table 4.   Factorial structure of the content-categories for the *last* ten sessions (only factor-loadings higher than 0.60 are considered).

	Factor-loading
Factor I:	
'analyst'	0.79
'fatherly significant others'	0.75
'real heterosexuality'	0.67
'motherly significant others (neutral view)'	0.62
'negative acceptance by others'	−0.63
'positive acceptance by others'	−0.77
'achievement, success'	−0.81
Factor II:	
'positive self-esteem'	0.78
'brothers'	−0.65
'negative self-esteem'	−0.69
'sexuality'	−0.76
'body'	−0.77
Factor III:	
'male peers'	0.71
'imagined heterosexuality'	0.66
'feelings of guilt, fear of punishment'	0.63
'brothers'	0.60
Factor IV.	
'positive view of motherly significant others'	0.84
'aggressiveness, assertiveness'	0.75

Table 5. Stanine scores on personality questionnaires at three points of investigation (see text for values of mean and s.d.).

Psychological test data	Start of treatment	End of treatment	Follow-up
FPI			
1 psychosomatic irritation	5	3	5
2 aggressivity	6	8	5
3 depressivity	7	3	1
4 excitability	7	5	5
5 sociability	5	7	7
6 calmness	1	5	3
7 striving for dominance	2	4	4
8 restraint	8	4	5
9 openness	7	6	5
E extraversion	3	7	4
N neuroticism	9	4	4
M masculinity	2	7	7
Giessen Test			
1 sociability	4	4	5
2 dominance	4	2	3
3 control	5	4	4
4 depression	7	5	5
5 accessibility	4	3	3
6 social skill	3	3	4

Several scales in the FPI which had deviant scores at the beginning of treatment show values within normal limits at the end of treatment. These are scale 6, 'calmness' (at the start of treatment the patient showed herself extraordinarily irritated and hesitant); scale 7, 'striving for dominance' (the patient was at first highly compliant); scale 8, 'restraint'; and the 'neuroticism' scale (according to which the patient presented herself as quite neurotic). At the end of treatment, in addition to this, the patient presented herself with only minor psychosomatic irritations (scale 1), as spontaneously aggressive (scale 2), as less depressive, i.e. as content and self-assertive (scale 3), as sociable (scale 5), as extravert (scale E) and as masculine (scale M). At the point of the follow-up investigation after two years, a nearly identical profile emerged, with only 'contentedness' and 'self-assertion' having definitely increased. According to an analysis of correlation and of similarity, then, there is no correspondence between the profiles at the start and the end of treatment.

10.4.2.4. The following results were found in the Giessen Test. The correlation between the two profiles (at the start and at the end of treatment) is remarkably high ($r = 0.92$), *but the level* of the profile had changed. The corresponding coefficient of similarity (Cattell *et al.*, 1966), which reflects the absolute level of the scores in each profile, is consequently much lower ($r_p = 0.35$) and is statistically significant at the 10% level. Profile comparison yields the striking finding that the high value in the depressivity scale at the start of treatment has decreased to a 'normal' value, and that the 'normal' dominance at the start of treatment has clearly increased. In summary, it can be said that the personality structure remained the same, although a change in level emerged insofar as the patient presents herself at the end of the treatment as more dominant, less obsessive, less depressive, and as more in touch with unconscious contents and mechanisms. The follow-up profile is almost identical to the one at the end of treatment.

In addition to this, the questionnaire on changes in experience and behaviour was presented at the follow-up stage of the investigation. This questionnaire consists of 42 items which ask directly about changes. In working through this questionnaire, the patient is asked to evaluate the changes between the start of treatment and the present day. This questionnaire yields one total score; there are no subscales. The patient's total of 245 out of 250 possible points corresponds to striking positive change ($P < 0.001$). 'Positive change' means an increase in self-assertiveness, in contentedness, and in social abilities; and a decrease in anxiety and agitation.

10.4.3 Discussion of the Results

These very favourable results from personality testing, which include a two-year follow-up as we have seen, combined with other observations such as social and behavioural changes in everyday life, and the clinical judgement of the treating analyst, give us good reason to believe that this was in fact a rather successful analytical treatment.

10.4.3.1 Category-analysis. From the point of view of category-analysis, however, we need to ask why the very considerable psychological changes which must have taken place in the patient did not show up more conspicuously in our chosen process-measurements. In accordance with this favourable therapeutic outcome, the observed therapy process is characterized by increasingly positive and decreasingly negative self-esteem, as is evident from the difference between category ratings for the first ten sessions and those for the last ten. This observation is all the more meaningful in this kind of treatment, because the final phase of an analysis tends to be an unstable one for the patient's emotional functioning. Here then are some important psychological changes which the content-analysis technique was able to capture successfully; and the validity of these changes is confirmed, as we have seen, by the independent results of three different personality tests.

Why then did our method not also produce significant patterns of data relevant to the hypotheses about self-esteem as a consequence of acceptance by others, and about area-specific self-esteem? Clearly this can be either because the method was unable to reflect changes which in fact were there, or because the changes were not there and our theories about change in psychotherapy were wrong.

10.4.3.2 Methodological issues. In order to maximize objectivity and reliability, we deliberately confined ourselves to what the layman or the sceptical-psychologist would regard as explicit evidence for the categories, and thereby we no doubt deprived ourselves of a good deal of potentially significant material. This point is especially important for any investigation which touches on the thorny question of the relation between language and latent meaning, and especially for one where language is used as a vehicle of psychotherapeutic change (cp. Forrester, 1980). Ultimately this amounts to a question about the validity of our measuring-instrument.

It is against this background that we have to assess the fact that some of the categories which were regarded by the therapist as especially pertinent to the problems of the patient are in fact called into play rather seldom. For example, the categories concerning security and insecurity with respect to female identity were checked in only 10 and 17 sessions, respectively, out of the total sample of 115 sessions; and even in these sessions, their frequency was very low. Thus the data-base for some of the categories was too narrow to be likely to support any of the hypotheses in which they were involved.

We started with the assumption that psychodynamically relevant interaction between particular themes would be reflected in single utterances having to be scored on more than one theme-related category (so that the single utterance calls up, as it were, more than one scoring-category), but it turned out that this in fact happened very infrequently, and we were compelled to substitute the indirect within-session correlation which we have described above (section 10.3.3.3). Although clinical experience speaks well for the expectation that themes which emerge in a given session do belong together in a psychologically significant way, nevertheless this enforced revision of our procedure may have affected the testing of our hypotheses.

10.4.3.3 Theoretical considerations. Our conception of overall self-esteem as being composed of a number of area-specific elements, which had the advantage of lending itself readily to objective testing, was always perhaps somewhat simplistic, and only one of various possibilities. Another of these possibilities, which is more consistent with our results, is that area-specific and general self-esteem are in fact a good deal more independent than we had supposed. Our results on the topic of overall self-esteem may reflect something more akin to Bandura's conception of 'self-efficacy' (discussed in section 10.2 above) which consists in a fundamental sense of being able to bring about changes in one's life, but which is entirely consistent with having problems in specific areas of self-esteem and consequently bringing them into therapy. It may well be this essential independence which has been captured in our observation that ratings of area-specific esteem fluctuate much more widely over the sessions (perhaps because they are relatively situation-specific and cognitively monitored), whereas overall self-esteem (which may reflect a more fundamental emotional property) stays relatively constant over time.

Furthermore, it is perhaps to be expected that during the course of therapy the patient's problems with overall self-esteem will be analysed out into more specific areas, which then become individually the focus of attention at different times and with different degrees of attendant anxiety or other emotion. Since, also, a main function of psychotherapy, at least from the patient's point of view, is to deal with difficulties and malfunctions in various areas, it is not surprising that what she actually talks about (and what is therefore recorded in the categories) does not show either an increase in general positive self-evaluation or a decrease in its negative counterpart.

Our study also set out to clarify how favourable changes in self-esteem might be brought about in therapy, and for this purpose we paid attention both to its presumed infantile origins and also to here-and-now experiences of being accepted by others. Accordingly, we assumed that the analyst would function as a catalyst for both these sorts of feeling, by serving as a projection-screen in the transference and by exemplifying acceptance by others in the reality-situation. We were unable, however, to draw any conclusions on this point from the category-scores, since there were too few references to acceptance-by-others (in only 15 out of 115 sessions) to allow us to compute their correlation with references to the analyst, as would have been necessary to serve as the evidence relevant to our hypotheses. Two suggestions may be made about why this was so.

The analyst's acceptance of the patient would have been communicated largely, and even exclusively perhaps, by non-verbal means, which the patient would have acknowledged and responded to, not by explicit verbalization, but by (for example) being able to relax and produce more material which she felt able to release in the atmosphere of acceptance. It will be evident from this that we were conceptualizing the therapist's acceptance as a quite specific factor in the treatment of patients suffering from disturbances in self-esteem, and not simply as part of a generally facilitating background. This whole theoretical issue has been discussed in some detail by Cheshire and Thomae in Chapter 5.

The second possibility is that the patient had internalized rejecting objects from the past so effectively that she was unable to perceive any acceptance in some contexts of her present situation even when it was there. This impression is given by many passages of the verbatim transcript, including one where she indicates that it is self-evident to her that every man will experience her hairiness as repulsive, without her ever having taken the risk of encountering this judgement in reality. From this point of view it might be expected that such obstructive internalizations gradually become to be recognized for what they are, in the course of therapy, and are eventually tested out in reality against the perceived judgements of currently significant others: in which case, an increase in the categories to do with acceptance by others is to be expected. But this result would be observed only if the testing-out were explicitly reported in therapy, as opposed to being alluded to or symbolized in the latent content of various utterances, or taking the form of an improvement in interpersonal perceptions and social skills. To clarify these questions further it would be important to establish whether the therapist did in fact give non-verbal indications of acceptance, etc. which were simply not recognized as such by the patient, or whether such cues were unclear, inconsistent or infrequent.

A second general purpose of our study, apart from that of trying to monitor changes in self-esteem, was to use the category-data to test a model of the therapeutic process according to which it is seen as a succession of focal workings-through of particular psychodynamic themes. To this end we formulated a number of hypotheses about changes in three problem-areas which might be apparent after relevant focal working-through had taken place. But these hypotheses, which were couched in terms of differences between mean values of category usage and changes in correlation values, were supported by the data in only two instances.

Our findings, therefore, do not in themselves support such a model; but we are aware that our method of identifying a therapeutic focus (section 10.3.3), although appropriate enough in itself, may have been invalidated by the fact that our sampling left out 80% of the total data. As far as the process-model itself goes, even changes that do set in after certain themes have been worked through focally cannot be expected to do so at once, let alone to be revealed immediately in overt verbal behaviour. In any case, we suppose that focal working-through may be only a necessary, and not a sufficient, condition for lasting psychological change. It may simply lay the foundations for revised patterns of information-processing and cognitive structuring, which in their turn are the basis for acquiring alternative ways of behaving. In which case, to base calculations on data from sessions immediately after a therapeutic focus is to fail to give such complex processes time to develop.

These are all points to be borne in mind for future studies of the complex processes which contribute to beneficial change, such as was observed in this case, over the course of interpretive dynamic psychotherapy.

References

Bandura, A. (1977). Self-efficacy: toward a unifying theory of behavioral change. *Psychol. Rev.*, **84**, 191–215.

Bastine, R. (1976). Ansätze sur Formulierung von Interventionsstrategien in der Psychotherapie. In *Klientenzentrierte Psychotherapie Heute* (eds P. Jankowski *et al.*). Hogrefe, Goettingen.

Beckmann, D. and Richter, H. E. (1972). *Giessen-Test:* . . . Huber, Stuttgart.

Bellack, L. (1981). Psychoanalysis as therapy. . . In *Changing Concepts in Psychoanalysis* (ed. S. Klebanov), pp. 3–10. Gardner Press, New York.

Box, G. E. P. and Jenkins, G. M. (1976). *Time-Series Analysis: Forecasting and Control*, revised edition. Holden-Day Inc., San Francisco (Calif.).

Cattell, R. B., Coulter, M. A. and Tsujioka, B. (1966). The taxonometric recognition of types and functional emergents. In *Handbook of Multivariate Experimental Psychology* (ed. R. B. Cattell). Rand McNally, Chicago.

Cheshire, N. M. (1975). *The Nature of Psychodynamic Interpretation*. Wiley, Chichester.

Cochran, W. G. (1954). Some methods for strengthening common chi-squared tests. *Biometrics*, **10**, 417–451.

Dare, C. and Holder, A. (1981). Developmental aspects of the interaction between narcissism, self-esteem and object relations. *Int. J. Psychoanal.*, **62**, 323–337.

Epstein, S. (1982). The ecological study of emotions in humans. In *Advances in the Study of Communication and Affect*, vol. 5 (eds P. Pliner *et al.*). Plenum, New York.

Fahrenberg, J., Selg, H. and Hampel, R. (1978). *Das Freiburger Persönlichkeitsinventar (FPI) Manual*, third edition. Hogrefe, Goettingen.

Feldhege, F. J. and Krauthan, G. (1979). *Verhaltenstrainingsprogramm zum Aufbau sozialer Kompetenz*. Springer-Verlag, Berlin.

Forrester, J. (1980). *Language and the Origins of Psychoanalysis*. Columbia. University Press, New York; Macmillan, London.

Foster, F. G. and Stuart, A. (1954). Distribution-free tests in time-series. . . *J. Roy. Statist. Soc. (B)*, **16**, 1–22.

Freud, S. (1914). On narcissism, an introduction. *Standard Ed*; **14**, 67–102.

Gebhardt, F. (1967a). *Ueber die Aehnlichkeit von Faktormatrizen. Psychol. Beitr.*, **10**, 591–599.

Gebhardt, F. (1967b). *FAST. Vergleich von Faktorstrukturen*. Deutsches Rechenzentrum, Darmstadt.

Gill, M. M. (1982). *Analysis of Transference. Vol. I: Theory and Technique*. International Universities Press, New York.

Glover, E. (1955). *The Technique of Psychoanalysis*. International Universities Press, New York.

Graff, H. and Luborsky, L. (1977). Long-term trends in transference and resistance:. . . *J. Am. Psychoanal. Assoc.*, **25**, 471–490.

Kaechele, H., Schaumburg, C. and Thomae, H. (1973). *Verbatimprotokolle.* . . *Psyche*, **10**, 902–927.

Kaechele, H. (1976). *Maschinelle Inhaltsanalyse in der psychoanalytischen Prozessforschung*. Qualifying thesis, Faculty of Clinical Medicine, University of Ulm.

Kohut, H. (1971). *The Analysis of the Self*. International Universities Press, New York.

Kohut, H. (1977). *The Restoration of the Self*. International Universities Press, New York.

Korman, A. K. (1970). Toward an hypothesis of work behavior. *J. Appl. Psychol.*, **54**, 31–41.

Liberman, R. P. (1978). *Personal Effectiveness*. Research Press, Champaign, (Ill.).

Lienert, G. A. (1969). *Testaufbau und Testanalyse*, third edition. Beltz, Weinheim.

Luborsky, L. *et al.* (1985). A verification of Freud's grandest clinical hypothesis: . . . *Clin. Psychol. Rev.*, **5**, 231–246.

Luborsky, L. and Spence, D. P. (1978). Quantitative research on psychoanalytic therapy. In *Handbook of Psychotherapy and Behaviour Change*, second edition (eds S. L. Garfield and A. E. Bergin). Wiley, New York.

Marsden, G. (1971). Content-analysis studies of psychotherapy: 1954 through 1968. In *Handbook of Psychotherapy and Behavior Change*, first edition (eds A. E. Bergin and S. L. Garfield). Wiley, New York.

Mergenthaler, E. (1983). Text Base Management-Systems. *Angew. Inform.*, **6**, 262–267.

Meyer, A. E. (1963). Zur Endokrinologie und Psychologie intersexueller Frauen:. . . *Beiträge zur Sexualforschung. Organ der Deutschen Gesellschaft für Sexualforschung.* Enke, Stuttgart.

Meyer, A. E. and von Zerssen, D. (1960). *Psychologische Untersuchungen an Frauen mit. . . Hirsutismus. Psychosom. Res.*, **4**, 206–235.

Neudert, L. and Gruenzig, H.-J. (1983). Beurteilungsmanual für Selbstgefühlveränderung. Unpub. manuscript, Psychotherapy Dept., Univ. of Ulm.

Paul, G. L. (1967). Strategy of outcome research in psychotherapy. *J. Consult. Clin. Psychol.*, **31**, 109–118.

Revenstorf, D. (1979). *Zeitreihenanalyse für klinische Daten:. . .* Beltz, Weinheim.

Rogers, C. R. (1951). *Client-centered Therapy.* Houghton Mifflin, Boston, (Mass.).

Rogers, C. R. (1959). A theory of therapy:. . . In *Psychology: A Study of a Science*, vol. III (ed. S. Koch). McGraw-Hill, New York.

Seligman, M. E. P. (1975). *Helplessness.* Freeman, San Francisco.

Sheerer, E. T. (1949). An analysis of the relationship between acceptance of. . . Self and acceptance of. . .others. . . *J. Consult. Clin. Psychol.*, **13**, 169–175.

Shlien, J. M. and Zimring, F. M. (1970). Research directives and methods in client-centered therapy. In *New Directions in Client-centered Therapy* (eds J. T. Hart and T. M. Tomlinson), pp. 33–57, Houghton Mifflin, Boston, (Mass.).

Stake, J. E. and Pearlman, J. (1980). Assertiveness training as an intervention technique. . . *J. Couns. Psychol.*, **27**, 276–281.

Strupp, H. H. (1968). Psychoanalytic therapy of the individual. In *Modern Psychoanalysis*: . . . (ed. J. Marmon). Basic Books, New York.

Thomae, H. (1980). *Auf dem Weg zum Selbst. Psyche*, **34**, 221–245.

Thomae, H. and Kaechele, H. (1985). *Lehrbuch der Psychoanalytischen Therapie*, vol. 1. English (1987): *Psychoanalytic Practice*: vol. 1, *Principles.* Springer-Verlag, Berlin and Heidelberg.

Thomae, H., Kaechele, H. and Gruenzig, H. J. (1978). *Ueber einige Probleme. . . der psychoanalytischen Prozessforschung.* Paper presented at DPV conference, Ulm.

Tryon, W. W. (1982). A simplified time-series analysis. . . *J. Appl. Behav. Anal.*, **15**, 423–429.

Ullrich, R. and Ullrich de Muynck, R. (eds) (1978). *Soziale Kompetenz:. . .* Pfeiffer, Munich.

Watkins, D. (1978). The development and evaluation of self-esteem measuring instruments. *J. Pers. Assess.*, **42**, 171–182.

Zielke, M. and Kopf-Mehnert, C. (1978). *Veränderungsfragebogen des Erlebens und Verhaltens.* Beltz Test GmbH, Weinheim.

Self, Symptoms and Psychotherapy
Edited by N. Cheshire and H. Thomae
© 1987 John Wiley & Sons Ltd

CHAPTER 11

The Future for Time-limited Dynamic Psychotherapy

Hans H. Strupp

11.1   The Question of Efficacy

There is really only one basic question that has interested me over the last 25 years, and that is the question of how therapeutic change comes about. How does it happen that lasting changes in personality and behaviour may result from one person sitting with another, or lying on a couch in another's presence, over a period of time? Intrapsychic change is what psychotherapy is ultimately all about: that is the basic scientific issue. Freud made the statement in one of his later papers (perhaps it was a somewhat cavalier statement) that the nature of the therapeutic action in psychoanalysis was really well understood, and that there was not much new to be learned (cp. Freud 1940, ch. 6). It may well be doubted whether this is at all true. For it seems, on the contrary, that we are just on the threshold of learning a great deal more about the nature of therapeutic action, and that much more remains to be learned.

By way of introduction, let me say something about psychotherapy research in the sense that I and many of my colleagues practise it. This area of activity is about 40 years old at most, and as a science it is very much in its infancy. We are also aware that psychotherapy and psychotherapy research are nowadays politically very sensitive. In the United States today psychotherapy has assumed an importance which it did not have before. Before, the questions were 'merely' scientific: clearly there was interest in finding out whether therapy works, or what works with whom. But today the situation is different, in that it is Government authorities which are asking, and asking with great insistence, 'Is psychotherapy safe, and is it effective? Is it effective much like a drug?'. In fact, the drug model, involving talk of 'clinical trials', is very popular these days. The questions of effectiveness (efficacy) and safety are very much in the picture, and there is one major reason for this. In the old days, if Bill Smith or Susie Q. went to see an analyst or a therapist, no one really cared whether the patient benefited unless there was gross evidence of malpractice. But today the question is very different. In the United States, society and the Government have become involved and, indeed, they have a right to ask about the return for a particular investment of psychotherapeutic time and effort. Consequently, practical issues often determine the lines of investigation followed in psychotherapy research.

It is noteworthy that the question of effectiveness continues to be asked despite the fact that hundreds of studies have been carried out. Admittedly, many of these studies are not very good: many are old (that is, 'old' in the last 30 years), not well-controlled, involving a variety of patients, poorly trained therapists and diverse disorders. Nonetheless the evidence is pretty clear. Various reviewers who have dealt with the literature have substantially come to the same conclusion. In the work of Smith *et al.* (1980), the use of a technique known as a 'meta-analysis' allowed them to compare hundreds of studies, and to bring them under a common denominator. What were the major conclusions?

(1) 'After everything is said and done, psychotherapy is beneficial, consistently so and in many different ways. Its benefits are on a par with other expensive and ambitious interventions, such as schooling and medicine. The benefits of psychotherapy are not permanent, but then little is.'
(2) 'Different types of psychotherapy, verbal or behavioural, psychodynamic, client-centred, systematic desensitization, do not produce different types or degrees of benefit.'
(3) 'Differences in how psychotherapy is conducted, whether in groups or individually, by experienced or novice therapists, for long or short periods of time, etc., make very little difference in how beneficial it is.'

These conclusions highlight the importance of common, non-specific, and interpersonal factors in all forms of psychotherapy. However, we must be careful not to deduce, as a number of people have done, that careful training, clinical understanding and expertise, technical skills, and the like can be dispensed with; and the relationship between these so-called 'general' and 'specific' factors in psychotherapy is the subject of Cheshire and Thomae's

Chapter 5. For one thing, individual observations cannot prove a null hypothesis (such as that there is no difference in therapeutic effectivenss to be found between 'naive' and clinically sophisticated practitioners) but can only, in principle, refute it. For another, it is hard to think of a single adequate study in which the therapist's technical skills have been put to a crucial test. To be sure, there is a general tendency for many patients to improve with some kind of attention. That, however, does not prove that experienced psychotherapists are no 'better' than laymen, nor that professional training counts for naught. Many medical patients, too, improve, with or without professional care; but nobody proposes on the basis of such evidence that we should therefore abolish medical schools. Simplistic thinking, unfortunately, continues to pervade our field.

11.2 The First Vanderbilt Programme

Let me concentrate on the programme of research my group at Vanderbilt University has been pursuing for a good many years, and, in so doing, trace its development and indicate the direction in which we are moving.

The primary aim of the Vanderbilt Psychotherapy Project was to investigate the relative contributions to outcome, in time-limited psychotherapy, of the therapist's technical skills as opposed to the qualities inherent in any good human relationship. It was reasoned that highly experienced professional psychotherapists might be expected to contribute to the therapeutic relationship an optimal combination of technical and relationship factors, whereas counsellors untrained in psychotherapy (but selected for their untutored ability to form understanding, warm, and empathic relationships) would achieve their impact primarily through relationship factors. Accordingly, it was hypothesized that, if professional skills are uniquely effective, they should have a demonstrable influence on therapeutic outcome over and above that deriving primarily from relationship factors. Thus, highly experienced professional therapists might effect greater therapeutic change than lay counsellors.

In broad outline, the design called for each of five highly experienced psychotherapists (T) to treat in individual psychotherapy at least three patients drawn from a relatively homogeneous population. Treatment, for practical reasons, had to be limited in frequency and duration (twice a week up to 25 hours). A comparable group of patients was treated by college professors (AT, for 'alternative therapists') under similar conditions. A third group of patients was assigned to a delayed, minimal-treatment control group (MC). Finally, a silent control group (SC) consisted of college students who did not seek psychotherapy, but who were characterized by difficulties similar to those of the treated patients.

11.2.1 Subjects and Methods

A common failing in psychotherapy research has been the use of widely heterogeneous patient samples. Thus, to progress further in this area, it appeared important to identify a specific stable, genuine, and replicable psychiatric entity. In exploratory work by Strupp and Bloxom (1975), the '2-7-0 syndrome' had been identified as such an entity. Specifically, it was shown that male college freshmen who manifested elevations on scales 2 (depression) and 7 (psychasthenia) of the *Minnesota Multiphasic Personality Inventory* (MMPI) were more likely than a comparable normal sample to seek psychotherapeutic help during their college years, as well as after graduation (scale 0, 'social introversion', was added later). Five years following graduation (which tended to be delayed), these individuals were less likely to be settled in a career, less likely to be married, and were earning lower incomes. These findings did not apply to females, which was a major reason for dealing exclusively with males in this study.

In terms of more traditional nosology, the 2-7-0 syndrome refers to individuals with rigid defences and obsessional character traits (not excluding borderline personalities), as well as with neurotic exacerbations of these traits. Intrapsychically, these individuals suffer from a sense of loneliness, isolation, depression and anxiety. Behaviourally, they are non-spontaneous, tend to withdraw from social situations, are passive and non-assertive, troubled by awkwardness and ineptness in interpersonal relations, and unable to relate warmly and pleasurably to peers, particularly members of the opposite sex.

Thus, in the present investigation, major screening criteria included T-scores > 60 on the three *MMPI* scales mentioned above. In addition, we stipulated that candidates should be male, single, between the ages of 17 and 24 years, and college undergraduates. Excessively severe emotional disturbance, suicide risk, and other factors that might contraindicate assignment to an AT or the MC group were criteria for exclusion.

It should be emphasized that only about a third of the patients suffered from a 'pure' 2-7-0 syndrome by usual criteria, and significant elevations on other clinical scales were common. While it would have been desirable to confine the study strictly to this syndrome, such a criterion would presuppose the existence of a much larger pool of potential patients than was available to us. Despite concerted efforts to recruit a truly homogeneous patient population, we were only partially successful. While patients represented reasonably pure phenotypes, their personality structures (as emerged from subsequent study of assessment and therapy interviews) differed considerably.

During the pilot phase ($N = 5$) and at the beginning of the main study, patients were recruited from applicants to the Interuniversity Psychological and Counseling Center. However, since this referral source proved inadequate, it became necessary to search for alternative approaches. To this end, letters announcing the availability of therapy for certain kinds of problems were sent to random samples of the male student body at Vanderbilt University. Respondents, all of whom had to meet the screening criteria mentioned above, made up the majority of the students participating in the project. Great care was taken to dispel possible misapprehensions that candidates were 'volunteering for an experiment'. While the departure from the original recruitment procedure was unfortunate, subsequent comparisons provided satisfactory evidence that all patients met our selection criteria as well as reasonable criteria of true clinical disturbance.

Post hoc comparisons of the two intake groups disclosed that Counseling Center patients' scores on the depression and psychasthenia scales of the *MMPI* were significantly higher, but there were no statistically significant differences on the social introversion scale. Likewise, no significant differences were found on the ratings made by independent clinicians following the standard intake interview. Finally, we determined that, while a somewhat disproportionate number of Counseling Center patients had been assigned to Ts, there was no systematic relationship between referral source and therapy outcomes on a variety of measures.

Individuals meeting the above stipulations were scheduled for an in-depth interview with an independent clinician (not the treatment therapist). These interviews, which were recorded on videotape, followed the format of the psychiatric status schedule of Spitzer *et al.* (1968) with certain modifications designed for our particular out-patient population. Consent for recording was obtained from all patients. At the close of each interview, which lasted one-and-a-half to two hours, three individualized therapeutic goals or target complaints were defined jointly by the patient and clinician. Following the interview, patients were assigned either to treatment by a professional therapist ($N = 16$) or an alternative therapist ($N = 15$), or to a delayed, minimal-treatment (control) group ($N = 14$). Assignment was intended to be random, but certain compromises were dictated by clinical realities, such as availability of therapists. The 'silent' control group ($N = 19$), mentioned above (SC), consisted of '2-7-0' individuals in the general college population, who had been identified by testing large groups of undergraduate students. These individuals did not present themselves to us as patients, and were merely retested at intervals corresponding to the periods for the therapy and waiting list patients. The control groups were designed to test the stability of the 2-7-0 syndrome over time, and to serve as a baseline for assessing treatment effects.

11.2.2 Selection of Therapists and Assessment Clinicians

The five professional therapists (T) participating in the study were selected on the basis of their reputation in the professional and academic community for clinical expertise. Their average length of experience was 23 years. Three were analytically orientated psychiatrists; two were experientially orientated psychologists. Alternative therapists (AT) were college professors selected on the basis of their reputation for warmth, trustworthiness, and interest in students.

Personal interviews were held to assess the ATs' ability and willingness to work productively within the project guidelines. None of the ATs had any formal training or experience in therapy; however, they were comparable to the Ts in age, academic status, and length of professional experience. The group comprised professors of English, history, mathematics, and philosophy. While the Ts recruited originally remained with the project to its conclusion, a certain amount of turnover occurred among the ATs. Independent clinicians (C) were recruited from among practising psychotherapists in the academic community and/or in private practice. We began the study with two clinicians and ended having used four (replacements were necessitated by departures from the area). Professional therapists were reimbursed at the prevailing local hourly rate for psychotherapy; ATs and Cs were reimbursed at a somewhat lower hourly rate. To maximize homogeneity, all Ts, ATs, and Cs were male.

All therapists exhibited considerable interest in the goals of the project, which had been described to them in general terms. Their cooperation with the stipulated procedures was a major factor in the successful implementation of the study. We found no evidence that they viewed the project as a 'contest'.

11.2.3   Treatment Procedures

At the conclusion of the initial assessment interview, all patients other than those assigned to the MC group were given a description of procedural details (duration of counselling, frequency of sessions, etc). They were then given their therapist's name and telephone number and instructed to contact him as soon as possible (therapists had been alerted to expect the patient's call). No specific information concerning the therapist's professional or lay counsellor status was given to the patients. Rather, they were simply told they would be seeing a person who was interested and experienced in helping people with problems similar to those the patient was experiencing. (Of course, patients immediately became aware of their therapist's professional status, since initial contacts were always made through the therapist's office or academic department. In only one case did an alternative therapist's professional status necessitate reassignment, when it was discovered that the AT was one of the patient's instructors.)

To provide reasonable initial uniformity, and to permit videotaping of the third therapy session, the first three sessions were held in the project's therapy room. Thereafter, they met in the therapist's office. Therapists and patients were requested to meet, as far as possible, twice weekly, up to a maximum of 25 hours. (In one case, due to the patient's physical problems, which required surgery and involved added emotional distress, the therapist requested a few additional sessions.) The mean number of sessions for T and AT groups was 17 and 18, respectively.

No constraints were placed on the therapeutic process proper: that is, both Ts and ATs were encouraged to use whatever verbal techniques they deemed most helpful. They were also at liberty to refuse to see particular patients referred to them, a prerogative exercised only once by a professional therapist who considered a patient unsuitable because he was a psychopathic character. Therapists were requested to audiorecord all therapy sessions and to prepare a written record of significant events during therapy. One of the later sessions, the 17th whenever feasible, was also recorded on videotape.

Members of the research team maintained surveillance of the session recordings of Ts and ATs alike. In addition, the project coordinator kept in close touch with the therapists concerning their reactions to the patients and progress in therapy. Detailed notes of all such contacts were made part of each patient's record. At termination, and again several months later, clinical assessments of each patient were conducted.

Patients were assigned to the MC group when all counsellors were carrying a full load and consequently no treatment openings were available. These patients were informed of the circumstances prior to their initial interview, at which time they were offered the option of waiting a maximum of three months for therapy in the project or returning to the University Counseling Center for immediate treatment. All patients agreed to the waiting period and to an immediate assessment interview. The assessment interviews for MC patients were identical in all respects to the interviews with immediate treatment patients, including the formulation of individual target complaints. At the close of the interview, MC patients were told they would be contacted as soon as an opening became available, probably in two to three months' time. In the meantime, they were to feel free to contact any of three members of the project staff, including the interviewing clinician (names and telephone numbers were supplied). Further, the patients were told they would be contacted periodically by the project coordinator. Notes of these calls were included in the patients' records. Following the waiting period, MC patients were scheduled for a somewhat abbreviated clinical assessment, which was in fact a 'termination' interview for the purpose of our research. Minimal-treatment control patients were often reluctant to return for termination assessments; furthermore, although therapy was offered to all these individuals at the end of the waiting period, only four chose to accept it. Our experience supported the common observations that assignment to a waiting list, even if mitigated by occasional contacts, is in fact a very real 'treatment' (often experienced as rejection), the effects of which must be acknowledged and assessed.

A detailed description of the study will be found in Strupp and Hadley (1979).

11.2.4 Results

The chief statistical analyses that were initially undertaken centred around comparisons of the major treatment and control groups. As it turned out, patients who received treatment fared better than individuals in the control groups; however, it appeared that the differences between the two treated groups were non-significant statistically. In other words, the findings indicated that professional therapists, on the average, were no more effective than college professors. In terms of the initial hypothesis, this suggested that non-specific factors were contributing more to the outcomes than the professional therapists' technical expertise. We therefore interpreted our results thus:

> 'Our findings clearly invite speculations concerning use of untrained counselors as therapeutic agents. While it became apparent that, under the specific conditions of our investigation, a specially selected group of college professors could function quite effectively in the therapeutic role, it should be underscored that both professors and patients had been carefully selected and that college professors performed their therapeutic work under the supervision of professional staff who were available for consultation and guidance in case of emergency. Even so, some professors experienced difficulty in discharging their assignment; (for example, they seemed to run out of relevant material to discuss, they were unable to work toward specific goals and very few would have been willing or able to treat patients over more extended periods of time. Professional therapists, by virtue of their training and clinical experience, are clearly much better equipped to deal with the vagaries and vicissitudes encountered in the interactions with most patients. However, it does seem fair to conclude that, given a carefully specified and protected context, mature and competent individuals, even in the absence of professional training, can engage appropriate patients in an interpersonal relationship whose outcome is therapeutic.'
>
> (Strupp and Hadley, 1979, p. 1136)

In spite of our careful qualifications which we have elaborated elsewhere (Strupp and Binder, 1984, pp. 272–280), many people quickly jumped to rather sweeping conclusions, as mentioned above, but there were additional pieces of evidence that pointed in a different direction, as follows.

11.2.4.1   Second thoughts
More recent statistical analyses of the data have raised questions about the appropriateness of the statistical model we initially used, but there is space to review only a few of them here.

1. Because of the great (uncontrolled) variability within each group, the standard analysis of variance technique may have created an unwarranted bias favouring non-significance.

2. This problem may have been compounded by the use of so-called residual gain scores, a technique that seeks to adjust statistically for differences in the patients' initial status.
3. A number of more refined analyses undertaken subsequently pointed to rather impressive differences between the changes of T patients in comparison with AT patients. Specifically, it became clear that patients who had impressive ego-resources, and were able to enter into a collaborative relationship with the therapist, showed much greater improvement if they were treated by a professional therapist. We elaborate on this finding later.

Following the initial group comparisons, a number of studies were undertaken that paid close attention to the *process* of psychotherapy, as opposed to simple pre/post group comparisons. The study by Gomez-Schwartz (1978) is relevant here, as are a number of comparisons between so-called high and low changers treated by the same therapist (Strupp, 1980a–c). The latter comparisons were intended to shed light on the question of why some patients—recall that they were drawn from a relatively homogeneous sample—showed impressive improvements whereas others did not. If a high and a low changer were treated by the same therapist, we might get important insights by examining the on-going interactions between patient and therapist over the course of therapy. The results of these analyses, here briefly summarized, pointed in some rather specific directions.

11.2.4.2 *Patient selection*

Patients with substantial personality resources, high levels of motivation for therapy, relatively circumscribed problems, and the capacity to work productively within a traditional therapeutic framework are likely to show the greatest and the most rapid improvement. From the therapist's standpoint, these persons generally constitute the most desirable and rewarding patients. When viewed from the broader perspective of the needs of society and the future development of psychotherapy, however, these are the least problematic cases. (It is apparent, nevertheless, that even with this population the full potential of sharply focussed treatment techniques has not yet been realized.)

By contrast, patients falling short of optimal suitability for short-term approaches (according to the criteria mentioned above) represent by far the largest segment of the patient population. Paradoxically, while these individuals are in the greatest need of professional services, they are also the ones who have been most neglected by mental health professionals (Rabkin, 1977). This judgement applies with particular force to short-term dynamic psychotherapy which has traditionally focussed on the selection and treatment of the most promising candidates (Butcher and Koss, 1978). It is noteworthy, in this regard, that the extensive contemporary literature dealing with borderline conditions and narcissistic personality disorders is almost entirely devoted to long-term intensive therapy (e.g. Giovacchini, 1979; Kernberg, 1970; Kohut, 1971).

Conclusion 1   In order for psychotherapy to meet more adequately the needs of patients as well as society, it is essential to focus attention upon patients who have typically been rejected as suitable candidates for short-term psychotherapy and to explore systematically the extent to which such patients can be treated more effectively by a well-defined, time-limited approach.

Conclusion 2   Psychiatric assessments must be sharpened to include (a) evaluations of the patient's character structure; (b) determinations of the patient's suitability for time-limited psychotherapy in terms of the criteria that have been identified as important prognostic indicators; and (c) reformulation of patients' presenting complaints in terms of central issues or themes which lend themselves to focussed therapeutic interventions. In order to effect more specific treatment planning, these determinations must become an integral part of the assessment process. Through this step, a closer link will be forged between diagnosis and treatment, thereby improving both.

11.2.4.3   Therapeutic operations

As shown by our analyses of patient–therapist interactions, therapists tended to use a broad-gauged approach aimed at helping patients to achieve insight into certain aspects of their current difficulties. Except for the fact that the treatment was time-limited, psychodynamically trained therapists typically followed the analytic model of long-term intensive psychotherapy. Accordingly, they adopted a passive-expectant stance, left the initiative for introducing topics to the patient, and largely confined their activity to clarifications and interpretations of conflictual patterns. Therapists tended to provide relatively little warmth and support, did not focus on the specific problems identified at the beginning of treatment (including scant references to the 'target complaints' which had been formulated in the assessment interviews), rarely acquainted patients with the nature of the therapeutic process, and infrequently confronted patients' negative personal reactions. In sum, the therapists' approach tended to be relatively invariant and patients were expected, without significant efforts on the therapists' part, to feel comfortable with and respond favourably to the requirements of this therapeutic framework. (It should be noted that, with relatively few exceptions, this approach reflects the model followed in most training centres for psychologists and psychiatrists, despite the fact that the majority of patients are unable to take optimal advantage of this regimen.) Furthermore, as shown by our research results, the absence of a good 'fit' between pertinent patient characteristics and the therapist's framework frequently leads to an *impasse* early in treatment, such as poor therapeutic alliance, premature termination, and/or poor outcome.

Of particular significance to the course and outcome of treatment were therapists' negative personal reactions to patients whose resistance took the form of anger, hostility, negativism, and pervasive mistrust. In view of these findings, we believe that systematic efforts must be made to help therapists deal with this problem.

Conclusion 3 In order to realize the full potential of short-term dynamic psychotherapy, therapists should receive specialized training, with particular emphasis on the following elements:

(a) Techniques should be optimally geared to the achievement of reasonably specific therapeutic objectives identified early in the course of treatment.

(b) The therapeutic situation should be designed to meet the unique needs of the individual patient, as opposed to the tacit assumption that the patient conform to the therapist's notions of an 'ideal' therapeutic framework. Techniques should be applied flexibly, sensitively, and in ways maximally meaningful to the patient.

(c) Steps should be taken to foster a good therapeutic relationship (working alliance) from the beginning of therapy, thus enhancing the patient's active participation and creating a sense of collaboration and partnership.

(d) Negative transference reactions should be actively confronted at the earliest possible time.

(e) Concerted efforts should be made to help therapists deal with negative personal reactions which are characteristically engendered by patients manifesting hostility, anger, negativism, rigidity, and similar resistances.

(f) While time-limited psychotherapy poses particular challenges to all therapists (especially demands for greater activity and directiveness), they should resist the temptation to persuade the patient to accept a particular 'solution', impose their values, and in other respects diminish patients' strivings for freedom and autonomy.

(g) Rather than viewing psychotherapy predominantly as a set of 'technical operations' applied in a vacuum, therapists must be sensitive to the importance of the *human* elements in all therapeutic encounters. In other words, unless the therapist takes an interest in the patient *as a person* and succeeds in communicating his interest and commitment, psychotherapy becomes a caricature of a good human relationship (the ultimate negative effect!).

(h) Closely related to the foregoing, therapists should keep in mind that all good therapeutic experiences lead to increments in patients' self-acceptance and self-respect; consequently, continual care must be taken to promote such experiences and to guard against interventions that might have opposite effects.

11.3 New Directions in Research: Vanderbilt II

In the light of the Vanderbilt I study, whose results we have just described, we are now in a position to take a number of additional steps. Specifically, we are interested in exploring whether we can design a 'treatment package' of time-limited dynamic psychotherapy which takes advantage of all we have learned from the Vanderbilt I study as well as the accumulating clinical and research knowledge in this area. Secondly, we would like to study whether groups of reasonably experienced therapists can be trained in the application of this therapeutic approach, and to observe the changes in therapists' behaviour that occur as a result of this training. Thirdly, we want to study systematically whether the new treatment approach results in better therapeutic outcomes, such as fewer drop-outs or more lasting amelioration of the patient's condition. Finally, we are embarked on an exploration to determine whether the new approach can be used with more 'difficult' patients (that is, individuals with personality disorders of long standing, less than ideal motivation for therapy, and the like). In other words, we wish to define more stringently the radius of applicability for time-limited dynamic psychotherapy.

11.3.1 The Pilot Study

To begin with, we engaged in pilot work to determine the feasibility of a major study which we planned to undertake in subsequent years. So far, we have expended considerable effort in defining a suitable patient population. As in the earlier study, we concentrate on persons (this time a broader range of adults rather than college students) who have marked elevations on the Depression, Psychasthenia and Social Introversion scales of the *MMPI* and who meet the criteria of 'personality disorder', as defined in the *Diagnostic and Statistical Manual of the American Psychiatric Association* (DSM–III). These patients fall into the categories of Avoidant Personality Disorder, Compulsive Personality Disorder, Dependent Personality Disorder, or Passive–Aggressive Personality Disorder. Next, we have recruited a small group ($N = 4$) of young therapists (psychiatrists and psychologists), each of whom has treated a patient meeting the foregoing criteria for 25 hours of individual psychotherapy, in twice-a-week meetings. In these treatments, the therapists follow a therapy-as-usual approach: that is, they employ whatever techniques they consider optimal, based on their training and experience. As in the past, these therapies are being closely monitored (via audio and video recordings) and the patients are carefully assessed before and after by an independent clinician. In addition, they complete a battery of tests, rating scales, and other assessment instruments.

The next phase of the work, currently in progress, is a training programme for these therapists, conducted by Dr Jeffry Binder and myself. This programme is based on and follows closely a treatment manual which we have been developing over the last years. This manual and the associated training programme represent an integrated approach to time-limited dynamic psychotherapy, called TLDP for short. An outline of this approach is presented below. Upon completion of the training, the same therapists will treat a second cohort of patients who meet the same criteria. We shall then determine the extent to which the training has produced changes in their techniques.

11.3.2 A Manual for Time-limited Dynamic Psychotherapy

Time-limited dynamic psychotherapy (TLDP), as described in this manual (cp. Strupp and Binder, 1984), is an integrated approach to individual psychotherapy, aimed at the achievement of circumscribed objectives in 25–30 sessions. It is intended for patients whose difficulties in living manifest themselves through anxiety, depression, and conflicts in interpersonal relations (e.g. lack of intimacy, inhibitions, social withdrawal). Current difficulties should be of long standing and the product of chronic maladaptations. Accordingly, TLDP's major goal is not the amelioration of presenting symptoms (although improvements in the patient's feeling-state are obviously expected), but rather a more lasting modification of the patient's character-structure. To benefit from TLDP, patients must be capable of forming a collaborative relationship with the therapist.

11.3.2.1 Objectives of the manual
TLDP is not presented as a unique approach or as a finished product; rather it forms part of a programme of research designed to explore the extent to which this form of psychotherapy can produce therapeutic changes in patients who are often considered unsuitable for time-limited psychotherapy. A second objective is to study systematically whether a training programme based on this manual can significantly modify and improve the therapeutic practices of reasonably experienced psychotherapists, namely psychiatrists or clinical psychologists with several years of postdoctoral experience. No form of psychotherapy can be learned from a manual, but a manual can provide the basis for a systematic training programme. The present manual has been prepared with this purpose in mind. It is designed to provide a succinct overview of the approach, thereby to assist therapists in training to gain a clear picture of basic ideas, principles, and techniques. The steps are illustrated by clinical examples. The present version of the manual has aided in, and in turn benefited from, the training programme for the first group of therapists. It will be modified in light of accumulating clinical and research evidence.

11.3.2.2 Principles of TLDP
TLDP views the patient's presenting difficulties as the product of disturbances in human relationships with significant others, both past and present. The outcomes of unfortunate experiences in living are reflected in the symptoms, conflicts, and malfunctions of which the patient currently complains and which cause him to seek professional help. Central to these problems are deficiencies

in self-esteem, inability to form satisfying interpersonal relations that gratify the person's needs for intimacy, and interferences with autonomous functioning as an adult.

Earlier difficulties with significant others have given rise to patterns of interpersonal relatedness that originally served a self-protective function but are now anachronistic, self-defeating, and maladaptive. Since they are basic aspects of the patient's personality-structure and interpersonal repertoire, they tend to come into play whenever the patient forms a relationship with a significant person, including the therapist. These enactments are the source of the patient's current difficulties, but they also provide unique opportunities for significant corrections. TLDP seeks to identify these patterns as they emerge in the context of the patient–therapist relationship, and through this process to produce therapeutic changes in the patient's cognitions and feelings, and in the quality of his interpersonal relations. Thus, TLDP serves as a vehicle for interpersonal learning within a specialized human context.

Once a collaborative relationship has been established, the therapeutic process encompasses the following major ingredients; (1) identification of a central issue, dynamic focus, or theme pervading the patient's current interpersonal difficulties; and (2) systematic attention to and pursuit of this central issue throughout therapy, with the goal of helping the patient work out more adaptive solutions. Time-limitations and issues pertaining to termination are clearly kept in mind and addressed in therapy.

Major emphasis is placed on the contemporary transactions between patient and therapist, and the patient's increased understanding and appreciation of their role and function in terms of his current life. The therapeutic relationship thus comes to serve as a laboratory for studying *in vivo* the patient's difficulties in living, as well as a means for correcting them.

The therapist's principal tools are empathic listening, understanding of the psychodynamics of the patient's current difficulties in terms of his life history, and clarification of their self-defeating character. A key issue here is the patient's resistance to change and the stratagems he unwittingly uses to defeat the therapeutic effort. Consistent focus rests on the patient's manner of construing and relating to the therapist both as a significant person in the present as well as a personification from the past. Similarly, by attending closely to the patient's enactments, the therapist gains important clues from his emotional reactions in the on-going process. In other words, the patient–therapist relationship is conceived of as a dyadic system in which the behaviour of both participants is continually scrutinized. The overriding goal of TLDP is to mediate a constructive experience in living resulting in increased well-being through strengthening of the patient's adaptive resources.

11.3.2.3 Background

The conceptions embodied in TLDP derive from a wide variety of sources. Of greatest significance, clearly, are basic psychoanalytic principles pertaining to transference, countertransference, resistance, and the growing understanding of the ego's defensive functions. Woven into the approach are also the changing conceptions of transference, ideas from Harry Stack Sullivan's theory of interpersonal relations, object-relations theory (cp. Chapters 3 and 4) and the teachings of systems theorists (cp. Chapter 6).

The forward-looking ideas of Alexander and French (1946) with reference to limiting the duration of psychoanalytic therapy have greatly influenced our thinking, as have the contemporary writings of specialists in time-limited dynamic psychotherapy. Prominent among the latter are Malan (1976, 1979), Sifneos (1972, 1979), Davanloo (1978, 1980), and Mann (1973); and invaluable experience has been gained from the observations and results of the Vanderbilt Psychotherapy Project described in part above.

TLDP also forms part of the contemporary trend in psychoanalytic theory to free clinical observations and therapeutic operations from the influence of metapsychology, whose relevance for therapeutic work has increasingly been questioned (cp. Holt, 1981). TLDP attempts to stay close to clinical and observational data, avoiding as far as possible higher level inferences and complex theoretical constructions. We have striven for an approach that is sensible, practical, communicable, and teachable.

11.3.2.4 Organization of manual
The manual is organized as follows.

Part I provides an introduction to TLDP, including objectives, basic assumptions and working concepts, the therapeutic process, the therapist's role and function, technical problems, and therapist's qualifications. Each topic is elaborated in subsequent sections.

Part II: following delineation of TLDP's theoretical framework and *modus operandi*, a brief statement of the theory guiding the therapist's operations is given. The purpose here is not to present a complete exposition of psychodynamics or personality development—the therapist's familiarity with prominent theories and basic psychodynamic concepts is assumed—but rather to help the reader develop a systematic and coordinated approach for viewing phenomena that are regularly observed in the patient–therapist interaction. More importantly, such understanding should guide the therapist's approach to therapeutic work, provide clear guidelines for the therapist's stance *vis-à-vis* the patient, and structure the nature of all therapeutic interventions.

Part III addresses problems of patient selection, assessment of suitability, and the identification of a central issue or dynamic focus.

Part IV extends the discussion to early interviews, and describes the structure of the patient–therapist interaction in TLDP. Further details are given concerning the working arrangements between patient and therapist, with special reference to the formation of a therapeutic alliance.

Part V contains an exposition of the therapeutic process, amplified by clinical examples. *Part VI* deals with major issues of technique, including the central role and function of resistances. The importance of the patient's negative reactions and the therapist's reciprocal responses will be highlighted throughout. *Part VII* addresses critical problems pertaining to termination and appropriate ways of dealing with them. The final section, *Part VIII*, provides a summary.

11.3.2.5   Significant features

A major emphasis of the manual is upon integration of theoretical and technical aspects of the therapist's work. To this end, all aspects of theory that have no apparent action-consequences are avoided. Secondly, all phenomena are systematically viewed within an interpersonal framework. Accordingly, terms like 'symptoms', 'resistance', 'transference', 'interpretations', etc. are not seen as referring to discrete classes of phenomena; instead, their meaning is defined in terms of the operations occurring between patients and therapists and their adaptive significance for the patient. Thus, the transactions occurring in the two-person system of patient and therapist and their reactions to each other are assigned central importance. In this process, the impediments to therapeutic progress are systematically addressed. Among the critical implications of this approach are the abandonment of concepts like disease, syndrome, and treatment. Rather, patient and therapist are seen as engaged in interpersonal transactions designed to produce beneficial changes in the patient.

TLDP highlights the importance of identifying reasonably specific goals. The therapist's efforts are systematically geared toward their approximation, and techniques function in the service of these goals. Thus, TLDP attempts to forge a clear link between a problem ('diagnosis'), therapeutic objectives, technique, and outcome. Specifically, on this point, we have developed techniques for identifying a 'dynamic focus', construed as having four main components, and for tracking it over the course of therapy (Strupp and Binder, 1984, ch. 5).

TLDP is not presented as a uniquely effective approach to psychotherapy. Rather, it is based on the recognition, supported by the bulk of the accumulating research evidence, that no form of psychotherapy is presently entitled to such claims. Major variables determining the outcomes of psychotherapy are not found in the techniques as this term is commonly understood, but instead are a function of the quality of the interactions between patient and therapist. The quality, in turn, is determined to a large extent by the patient's ability and willingness to enter into a productive therapeutic relationship with a therapist. The latter must have the necessary human understanding and technical skills to implement an experience for the patient whose outcome can be described as therapeutic. Such outcomes can be achieved in a number of ways, none of them perhaps intrinsically superior to another. What is claimed for the present approach is its rational, reasonable, and non-coercive character. It is expected that patients with fairly adequate adaptive resources who suffer from marked psychological disturbances of long standing and who can enter into a productive working relationship with an appropriately qualified therapist are likely to show significant therapeutic gains.

The approach presented in this manual is not restricted to time-limited forms of psychotherapy; indeed, it is proposed as a general model for more prolonged forms as well. One of its defining characteristics is the stress on specifiable objectives which the therapist is continually encouraged to keep in mind. These objectives are necessarily circumscribed in TLDP but may be extended, as necessary. It is our expectation that the general approach will prove comprehensible, teachable, and congenial to practising therapists. Above all, we are committed to the goal of making psychotherapy more realistic by laying the groundwork for systematic investigations designed to define more stringently the limits of what therapy can accomplish with particular persons and specified investments of therapeutic time and effort. The time has come to abandon the unrealistic view that psychotherapy can be all things to all people, nor should it be expected to change lifelong patterns of maladaptation in a few sessions. However, much work remains to be done to explore its potentialities and limits.

References

Alexander, F. and French, T. M. (1946). *Psychoanalytic Therapy*. Ronald Press, New York.

Butcher, J. N. and Koss, M. P. (1978). Research on brief and crisis-oriented psychotherapies. In *Handbook of Psychotherapy and Behavior Change: An Empirical Analysis* (eds S. L. Garfield and A. E. Bergin). Wiley, New York.

Davanloo, H. (1978). *Basic Principles and Techniques in Short-term Dynamic Psychotherapy*. Spectrum Books, New York.

Davanloo, H. (1980). *Short-term Dynamic Psychotherapy*. Jason Aronson, New York.

Freud, S. (1940). *An outline of psychoanalysis. Standard Ed.*, **23**, 141–207.

Giovacchini, P. (1979). *Treatment of Primitive Mental States* Jason Aronson, New York.

Gomez-Schwartz, B. (1978). Effective ingredients in psychotherapy: prediction of outcome from process variables. *J. Consult. Clin. Psychol.*, **46**, 1023–1035.

Holt, R. (1981). The death and transfiguration of metapsychology. *Int. Rev. Psychoanal.*, **8**, 129–143.

Kernberg, O. F. (1970). Factors in the psychoanalytic treatment of narcissistic personalities. *J. Am. Psychoanal. Assoc.*, **18**, 51–85.

Kohut, H. (1971). *The Analysis of the Self*. International Universities Press, New York.

Malan, D. H. (1976). *The Frontier of Brief Psychotherapy*. Plenum Press, New York.

Malan, D. H. (1979). *Individual Psychotherapy and the Science of Psychodynamics*. Butterworth, London.

Mann, J. (1973). *Time-limited Psychotherapy*. Harvard University Press, Cambridge (Mass.).

Rabkin, J. G. (1977). Therapists' attitudes toward mental illness and health. In *Effective Psychotherapy: A Handbook of Research* (eds A. S. Gurman and A. R. Razin). Pergamon Press, New York.

Sifneos, P. E. (1972). *Short-term Psychotherapy and Emotional Crisis.* Harvard University Press, Cambridge (Mass.).

Sifneos, P. E. (1979). *Short-term Dynamic Psychotherapy: Evaluation and treatment.* Plenum Press, New York.

Smith, M. L., Glass, G. V. and Miller, T. I. (1980). *The Benefits of Psychotherapy.* Johns Hopkins University Press, Baltimore.

Spitzer, R. L., Endicott, J. and Cohen, G. M. (1968). *Psychiatric Status Schedule.* New York State Department of Mental Hygiene, New York.

Strupp, H. H. (1980a). Success and failure in time-limited psychotherapy: a systematic comparison of two cases (comparison 1). *Arch. Gen. Psychiatry*, **37**, 595–603.

Strupp, H. H. (1980b). Success and failure in time-limited psychotherapy: a systematic comparison of two cases (comparison 2). *Arch. Gen. Psychiatry*, **37**, 708–716.

Strupp, H. H. (1980c). Success and failure in time-limited psychotherapy: further evidence (comparison 4), *Arch. Gen. Psychiatry,* **37**, 947–954.

Strupp, H. H. and Binder, J. L. (1984). *Psychotherapy in a New Key: . . .* Basic Books, New York.

Strupp, H. H. and Bloxom, A. L. (1975). An approach to the problem of defining a patient population in psychotherapy research. *J. Consult. Clin. Psychol.*, **22**, 231–374.

Strupp, H. H. and Hadley, S. W. (1979). Specific versus nonspecific factors in psychotherapy: a controlled study of outcome. *Arch. Gen. Psychiatry*, **36**, 1125–1136.

Strupp, H. H., Hadley, S. W. and Gomez-Schwarz, B. (1977). *Psychotherapy for Better or Worse: . . .* New York.

Index